My Father's House

My Father's House

MATTHEW CARR

HAMISH HAMILTON · LONDON

HAMISH HAMILTON LTD

Published by the Penguin Group
Penguin Books Ltd, 27 Wrights Lane, London w8 5tz, England
Penguin Books USA Inc., 375 Hudson Street, New York, New York 10014, USA
Penguin Books Australia Ltd, Ringwood, Victoria, Australia
Penguin Books Canada Ltd, 10 Alcorn Avenue, Toronto, Ontario, Canada m4v 3b2
Penguin Books (NZ) Ltd, 182–190 Wairau Road, Auckland 10, New Zealand

Penguin Books Ltd, Registered Offices: Harmondsworth, Middlesex, England

First published 1998
10 9 8 7 6 5 4 3 2 1

Copyright © Matthew Carr, 1998

The moral right of the author has been asserted

The lines from T. S. Eliot's *Four Quartets* and from Derek Walcott's *Collected Poems* and *Pantomine* are reproduced by permission of Faber & Faber Ltd. The quotation from Mervyn Morris is taken from his collection *The Pond* (New Beacon Books Ltd, 1973). The quotations from Martin Carter are taken from *Poems of Succession* (New Beacon Books Ltd, 1977).

The lines from Bob Dylan's 'It's all over now, baby blue' are reproduced by permission of Sony Music Publishing. The lines from 'The Pilgrim' by Kris Kristofferson are reproduced by permission of EMI Music Publishing Ltd.

Set in 11.25/12.75pt Monotype Fournier
Typeset by Rowland Phototypesetting Ltd, Bury St Edmunds, Suffolk
Printed in England by Clays Ltd, St Ives plc

A CIP catalogue record for this book is available from the British Library

ISBN 0-241-13748-9

For Lara

Acknowledgements

I could not have written this book without the help of the many people who contributed to it in different ways. I would like to express my thanks to all the friends, former colleagues and students, political comrades and even enemies of my father in Guyana, who generously gave me their time and provided me with crucial insights and information about his life.

I wish to express a special thanks to my father's widow Marjorie Cambridge Carr, for giving me her help and co-operation against her own instincts, and also to her daughter Vanessa.

Dr Cheddi Jagan died less than a year after my visit to Guyana. I would like to pay tribute to a good man, one of those rare politicians, as George Orwell wrote of Mahatma Gandhi, who 'left a clean smell behind him'.

Other people outside Guyana have also contributed in various ways to the making of this book. Derek Walcott, Mervyn Morris and Martin Carter kindly allowed me to publish excerpts from their work.

I would like to thank Andaiye, Kathleen Drayton, Flora Smith, Tony Scull, Louis James, Jean and David d'Costa, Ivor Oxaal, and Roy Welbourn at the Cambridge University Library. Charles Drazin's skilful editing greatly improved the text without intruding on it.

I also owe a special debt of gratitude to Julian Hayle, without whom this book might never have been written at all.

Love and thanks to my girlfriend Jane, for being part of my life, and for her invaluable comments and criticisms at different stages of the book.

Finally I would also like to express my love and appreciation to my mother, for her unswerving commitment to all of us through difficult times, and for her help and co-operation during my exploration of a period in her life that she, more than anyone else in this story, had good reason to forget.

I saw history through the sea-washed eyes
of our choleric, ginger-haired headmaster,
beak like an inflamed hawk's,
a lonely Englishman who loved parades,
sailing, and Conrad's prose.
When the war came the mouths began to bleed,
the white wounds put out tongues.

Nostalgia! Hymns of battles not our own,
on which our fathers looked with the black, iron mouths
of cannon, sea-agape,
to the bugle-coloured light crying from the west,
those dates we piped of redoubt and repulse,
while in our wrists the kettle drums pulsed on
to Khartoum, Lucknow, Cawnpore, Balaclava.
'How strange,' said Bill (Carr),
'to find the flag of my regiment,'
where on the razorblack ridge
the flag of the Inniskillings every sunset
is hung to bleed for an hour.
A history of ennui, defence, disease . . .

'Another Life', DEREK WALCOTT

O long is the march of men and long is the life
And wide is the span

MARTIN CARTER

Chapter One

On a grey March morning in 1996, I flew from London to Barbados, on a plane filled mostly with package tourists fleeing the last dregs of the English winter for the sun-kissed beaches and swaying palms of the Caribbean. It was not a holiday for me and I knew that none of them, if any, would be going to where I was going. Four years after the first clean elections in nearly three decades had supposedly brought the country back into the ranks of civilized democratic nations, the Co-operative Republic of Guyana was not likely to figure very highly on anyone's list of holiday destinations. For a start few people even knew where it was. When I had told people beforehand where I was going, the typical reaction would be a blank look, followed by the inevitable question: 'Guyana, where is that exactly?' Or else the listener would think I had said Ghana. 'No,' I would reply. '*Guyana*, in South America. Next to Venezuela. It's part of the West Indies.' If this still elicited more confusion than illumination, I would say another word to jog their memory. 'Jonestown.' This would usually produce a nod of recognition. 'Right, where all those people killed themselves.' 'Well, it wasn't exactly suicide,' I would reply, 'but mass murder too . . .' And that was about it. Guyana as a country would immediately fade into the background, subsumed into the memory of the Reverend Jim Jones's tropical apocalypse.

Even French Guiana was better known, thanks to Papillon, Devil's Island and Steve McQueen. Guyana, it seemed, had somehow fallen through the net. Perhaps the fact of being an English-speaking former colony on the South American mainland that was part of the West Indies made it even more difficult for people to locate the country mentally. The nearest comparison was Belize, the former British Honduras. But Belize was now an integral part of Central America, while Guyana's political and cultural orientation was entirely West Indian, separated as it was from its South American neighbours by a vast wilderness of jungle and savannah.

A country whose main claim to international fame was its dubious association with the largest mass suicide in modern history was never likely to attract the average package tourist, but there were other more prosaic reasons for Guyana's lack of popularity. The country had no beaches. It gave out on to the gloomy, desolate Atlantic rather than the sexier Caribbean. A large part of it consisted of uninhabitable jungle. These details simply did not fit most Europeans' conception of the Caribbean. And so Guyana remained, in most people's minds, a blank space with a question mark hanging over it, a West Indian enclave of South America and an extension of South America into the West Indies, vaguely linked to one of the more spectacular eruptions of late-twentieth-century irrationality. This was the country where my father had spent the last twenty-five years of his chaotic, turbulent life, right up to his death in 1992.

My own previous contact with Guyana had been brief and unforgettable, for all the wrong reasons. My family moved there in September 1966, the same year that the former sugar colony finally achieved independence. We had spent the previous six years living in Jamaica, where my father taught English at the University of the West Indies (UWI) in Mona and my mother worked as a lawyer. My father was a well-known figure both on and off the Mona campus. As well as his academic work, he acted in university drama productions, appeared on TV and radio discussion programmes, and was a vocal critic of the right-wing government of Alexander Bustamante.

In his own home, however, he was a violent alcoholic, who regularly beat up his wife and was prone to wild, destructive rages, when he would yell and curse and smash the house up in a kind of frenzy. Our six years in Jamaica were dominated by these scenes, and an atmosphere of instability and impending collapse as my parents' marriage unravelled. In 1966, my father's outspoken criticism of the government and the university establishment obliged him to leave Jamaica, and a fresh start seemed to offer itself, when he found a new job at the recently created University of Guyana (UG). I was ten years old and I knew nothing about Guyana, but I think there must have been an unspoken hope from everyone that in a new country things might be different between my parents.

The country itself was certainly different. I remember that we arrived at night, at a tiny airport like a wartime landing strip cut out of the jungle, where we were driven to our new home by Harry Drayton, a colleague of my father's from the university. Even then there was a sense of isolation and remoteness about Guyana, in relation to the rest of the West Indies, as though the society had only recently been hacked out of the surrounding wilderness and swamp. On arriving at our new house in Georgetown, I stepped out of the car and immediately sank up to my waist in one of the open sewer ditches which line the streets of the capital, and I had to be hosed down to get rid of the stinking grey slime. That was my first taste of the country where my parents had come to build a new life. Nine months later my mother and four children were back on a plane to England, after two weeks of my father's alcohol-fuelled violence and insanity had finally destroyed my parents' marriage.

In the beginning things did seem to go better. We settled into new schools, which we liked. Our new house was not far from the Botanical Gardens, and there was plenty of overgrown wasteground and swampy marshland to play in and explore. We bought two parrots and my father called them Mod and Rocker. My mother was not working and spent most of her time at home, while my father threw himself into his new life with his usual energy, making new friends and involving himself in university drama productions and other extra-curricular activities, in addition to his demanding evening teaching schedule. But after a brief lull, the familiar patterns began. He soon started to drink even more heavily than before, and seemed to be drunk more often than he was sober.

Once again the late-night fights began, and our neighbours soon became as familiar with his shouted tirades as their predecessors in Jamaica had been. Once again my mother began to wear dark glasses to hide her black eyes in the daytime, while my father was either out of the house or brooding in his study downstairs. The familiar atmosphere of gloom and tension descended on our household, punctuated by his explosive rages and drunken raving, most of it incomprehensible to my brothers, my sister and myself. These scenes had been bad enough in Jamaica, but they now began to reach a new level of intensity and destructiveness which made them impossible to contain, so that friends and colleagues of my father's, the university authorities and even the British High Commission in Georgetown found themselves sucked into the mayhem he was generating around him.

The end came suddenly the following May. It was preceded by an unusual period of calm between my parents. One Sunday my father suddenly insisted that my mother attend a lecture that he was giving at the university. Without her presence, he said, he would not be able to give the lecture. His sudden need for her moral support seemed rather incongruous, given the way things had been going between them. Even then he was openly carrying on a relationship with a student called Sandra Williams. Nevertheless my mother duly went, hopeful to the last. The lecture was a success, and she returned home without him later that evening, expecting him to come back soon afterwards.

Instead he spent most of the night drinking, and ended up at the house that Sandra Williams shared with two friends. In the early hours of the morning he finally came home, in an advanced state of inebriation, whereupon he handed my mother a cheque for £100 and told her that we could go back to England and that he no longer needed us. Exhausted and defeated, with all hope of saving the marriage finally gone, my mother agreed to go in principle, but she told him that £100 would not be enough to support us. It was agreed that more money would be found, and that we would leave at the end of the summer, so that we could return to England and begin school in the new academic year. Instead his behaviour now became so dangerously out of control that the original timetable for our exodus had to be hurriedly revised. Two weeks after that Sunday lecture we were out of the country, on a BOAC jet headed for England.

My own memories of those last two weeks in Guyana are hazy and fragmented, like pictures from a worn, black-and-white film with the soundtrack missing that I have been showing to myself ever since. Some of the clips seem to be missing, so that the exact order of events seems disjointed and confused, but the sense of disintegration, fear and incomprehension at the adult madness that was going on around me still remains. Across the years my father still dominates the frame, a swaying colossus, waving his arms theatrically like a drowning man, pouring forth a stream of words and insults that I cannot hear. He seems lost in some place where no one can reach him, his face a mask of anger, hatred and self-pity, surrounded by bemused adults who are trying in vain to reason with him.

In one of the clearest sequences I am woken up by my mother

sometime in the middle of the night, and we flee the brightly lit house together with my brothers and sister, while he rampages from room to room, cursing and shouting at the night and throwing things around. These nocturnal flights were a regular feature of those two weeks. We often had to stay at other people's houses, and I remember being driven around Georgetown at night by a succession of different friends. During one of these enforced absences my father somehow ended up keeping my sister in the house with him. My mother was afraid that something would happen to her, and I went back to the house with her and some friends to get her. Here another incomprehensible sequence has remained lodged in my memory. We are in the sitting room of our old house and my father is raving and sobbing and stroking a wooden nude sculpture and playing, 'We are sick, we are sick, we are sick sick sick . . .' from *West Side Story*. As usual he pays no attention to me or anyone else. This was a feature of those two weeks. Although I was often present even during his most extreme performances, I always had an overwhelming feeling of being a spectator, watching an inexplicable drama that was being enacted in front of my eyes.

Throughout all this he never showed any sign that he was even aware of the effect that his lunacy might have had on his children, but even then, I sensed that his simulation of madness was in some way a rejection of all of us, and that whatever was happening to him was much more important than how I felt. The emotional fallout of those few weeks would last for years afterwards, a mixture of fear, horror, sadness and rage, together with a peculiar fascination, a sense that I was watching something historic and momentous, the collapse of a dynasty, the epic fall of a tragic hero, or the last scene in a horror film, when the mad genius gleefully rages as his castle collapses around him. What I was watching, although I didn't know it then, was the collapse of my childhood and the end of my family, and the confirmation of all the fears that I had carried around inside me throughout most of our years in the Caribbean.

It was only later that I would realize that my father was in effect saying goodbye to us, using his own special codes and signals. Music was an important part of the deranged psychodrama that he was acting out, and the other keynote song was Dylan's 'It's All Over Now, Baby Blue'. In those last two weeks he played it again and again, in what seems to have been both a soundtrack to the end of the relationship

with my mother and a poetic definition of the roles that he had allotted
to the two of them:

You must leave now, take what you need, you think will last.
But whatever you wish to keep, you better grab it fast.
Yonder stands your orphan with his gun,
Crying like a fire in the sun.
Look out the saints are comin' through
And it's all over now, baby blue.

At some point during the mayhem even the two parrots Mod and
Rocker lost their patience with this madness and abandoned the house
without anybody realizing when they had gone. Most of my father's
anger was directed towards his wife, but the raw, destructive emotional
energy that he splattered in all directions was as disturbing and
inexplicable to the adults who witnessed it as it was to his own family.
Faced with this rather unusual behaviour from their new English
lecturer, the university authorities sent two psychiatrists round to the
house to observe him, an Irishman called Frank Farilee and a Chinese
Guyanese called Mr Chin. I have a clear memory of the two of them
climbing the stairs to the house and watching with a kind of solemn
curiosity as my father paraded up and down before them in the
living-room, making an extraordinary fuss over my sister, alternately
cooing and stroking her and then ranting and raving and waving his
arms about, in a kind of parody of insanity.

On the basis of that single visit, they produced a report, diagnosing
him as a psychopath, without the ability to feel guilt or empathy with
other people. They also concluded that he showed a tendency to
physical violence that was likely to find other outlets once his wife
had left for England. By now my father was no longer living at home,
but he continued to appear at the house and was publicly threatening
to 'kill that fucking bitch'. The university authorities took the threat
to my mother seriously. They decided that her physical safety could
not be guaranteed without posting a permanent bodyguard outside
the house and began to make emergency arrangements to get us out
of the country as soon as possible.

All attempts by my father's friends to get him to moderate his
behaviour failed. During one scene, a colleague of his tried to get him
to calm down by reminding him of his children. This had no effect.
My brothers and I, he declared, were merely 'extensions of her

personality', and therefore nothing to do with him. The only one of us he seemed to find difficult to let go of was my sister Anna, but he did not seem to want her to stay with him either.

At the time none of us knew that the separation was intended to be permanent. To make it easier, my parents had decided to tell us that we were going to be apart only for a few months and that my father would be joining us in England the following year. On the last day before leaving Georgetown, we were taken to see him to say goodbye. My mother had been afraid for our safety and was reluctant to let us go, but a friend of hers told her, 'If you don't let the children see him, you'll lose them.'

As a result we were taken to see him, but here the sequence in my memory gives out completely and I can remember only what I was told. It seems that the visit was supposed to be short, but my father suddenly took us walking around the swampy area near our house for most of the afternoon without telling anybody where we were going. We were gone so long that my mother became seriously anxious that something had happened, but we eventually reappeared, unscathed and rather bewildered. Exactly what he said to us during those few hours none of us can remember, and only Anna has a hazy recollection of my father haranguing us all with his views 'on life'. Probably we would not have understood what he was talking about at the time, but I have often felt that the secret of what happened to us remains buried on that lost afternoon, when my father wandered round the swampy wasteground of Georgetown pouring out his views 'on life' to a hapless, uncomprehending audience of his own children.

The last time we saw him he stood on the little balcony of the house where he was staying and calmly waved us goodbye as we were driven away to the airport. Harry Drayton was there that day and he afterwards told my mother that he had never seen anyone just give up everything he loved so calmly. We flew out of the country with the help of the British High Commission, whose involvement in the wreck of the Carr family is documented in the following letter, from the consul H. M. S. Reid to the university vice-chancellor, Alan Earp:

> Dear Alan,
>
> This is just to confirm the message which I passed on to you on the telephone this afternoon about Mrs Carr.
>
> We have had a telegram from London saying that the BOAC

staff have been alerted to meet Mrs Carr and the children on arrival and to assist them by coach to Victoria Air Terminal. Mrs B of the Women's Corona Society will meet them there and take them to Liverpool Street Station.

You might care to give this letter as it stands to Mrs Carr to take with her to show to BOAC and Mrs B to identify herself.

My mother had not had much opportunity to meet many people in Guyana, but some of her female friends came to say goodbye to us. There were, inevitably, a lot of tears, and even laughter, when my mother, in a touch of gallows humour, went off to buy some duty-free rum to take back to England as a souvenir. At this point she still did not know where she was going to take us on arrival in England. She was determined not to go back to her family in Cambridge if she could possibly help it, and Harry Drayton had written to a friend of his asking him to meet us at the airport and take us to London. Instead there was only Mrs B of the Women's Corona Society waiting at the airport to welcome us back from the tropics, looking and sounding not unlike the Queen Mother as she commiserated with my mother on 'the difficulties of living amongst the blacks, my dear'.

'The blacks' had not been the problem, but my mother did not go into the details of her marriage with Mrs B. Instead she waited at the airport, until it became clear that no one else was coming. Reluctantly she took us back to Cambridge that day, and we moved temporarily into my grandparents' pub on the Arbury estate, while she began to look for work and a place to live. A few days later she took us to a playground and fell into an exhausted sleep on a park bench. It was the end of May. There were hippies on television with Paisley shirts and sunflowers in their hair and the pop charts were full of songs about peace and love and good vibrations. The summer of love was already blooming and the mother country enclosed us in its damp, unsympathetic bosom. In two weeks of inexplicable madness my father had finally expelled his wife and children from his life.

It was another twenty years before I saw him again. At first we kept up a sporadic correspondence, which finally stopped sometime in the early 70s. The letters that he wrote me could not have been more different from the scenes that had preceded our departure. The few that remain are chatty, affectionate and paternal, filled with friendly comments and praise on the poems I sent him, on d'Oliveira and apartheid and the cricket crisis, on Che Guevara and the Cuban Revolution. Nevertheless it is impossible for me to read them without irony, such as this piece of advice, written in October 1967:

> *Are you still a James Bond fan, or have you found another hero? It's a good thing to have heroes, but wouldn't it be better to have one who is less violent? A punch on the nose doesn't really solve anything, and to be brave will often mean to be quiet. I have twice broken up fights in Georgetown – an unwise activity – but then it is a dreadful thing watching two men fly at each other and a real fight is never as simple or as precise as it usually seems in the cinema. I think the film* A Man for All Seasons *is probably too old for you, but there you might have a hero.*

At that time I was regularly visiting a child psychiatrist in Cambridge as a result of my frequent violent outbreaks of temper. These rages bore a remarkable similarity to my father's, as far as my limited physical strength allowed, but they were destructive enough for my mother to seek expert help. One day I was taken to an office with french windows looking out on to a garden, where a serious, rather distant man in square-rimmed glasses asked me to put a series of square pegs in round holes, or perhaps it was the other way round. After a few of these visits he declared me to be mentally maladjusted and recommended that I be sent to a special school.

My mother was reluctant to do this and wrote to the Jesuit school that I had attended in Guyana, asking the headmaster, Father Hopkinson, for advice. Father Hopkinson replied that I was not maladjusted at all and that my behaviour was a direct result of what had happened in Guyana. He recommended that I go to a Jesuit school in the north of England, with close connections to Guyana. My father opposed this proposal, which would have meant that he would have had to contribute to the fees, but I was eventually sent there anyway with the help of a special needs grant from Cambridge City Council. I loathed the place and told my father so. In my first term he wrote me:

> *I do hope you are settling in all right. You will be bound to feel a bit homesick at first, but you should get to like it very much. I was at two boarding schools, as you might know, and the second one I finally enjoyed very much. All schools have their fair share of thugs*

and bullies, as you put it. Try to be patient with them, don't let them get you down, and above all never become one yourself. There isn't a great deal to say about life here just now. The rainy season is about to begin and it is very hot and close. I envy you the climate in England, especially in the part of the world you live in just now. I was born not too far away and I often miss it very much . . . I have been doing a bit of acting. I played the bad King Claudius in Shakespeare's Hamlet *a few months ago. I don't know if you know the play but Claudius is a bit like the man I played in* Othello. *He manages to fool everybody but finally gets killed in the end. I think I took you to see the play when we were last in Cambridge. I seem to have a flair for playing bad guys . . .*

The letters to his other children are all written in the same loving, paternal tone. In none of them is there any reference to what happened in Guyana or the reason for our being back in England in the first place. Then, in 1972, he wrote a short letter to Bruce, who was then twelve, which seemed to offer a kind of explanation:

> *'Give a thought once in a while to this little soldier of fortune of the twentieth century. A kiss to Celia, to Roberto, Juan Martin and Pototin, to Beatriz, to everybody. An abrazo for you from your obstinate and prodigal father. Ernesto.'*
>
> *Matthew will explain it. It's the last letter written by Che Guevara before he left Cuba and it comes in* Reminiscences of the Cuban Revolutionary War. *Try and understand, our son. Mummy understands, Anna can understand, Matthew is there already. As for Christian, well, let me do a piece of the work for him.*
>
> *With love (which you must give to all),*
> *Daddy*

What did this cryptic message from 'Daddy' mean? No one knew. The reference to me was in connection with a history project that I was doing at school on the Cuban Revolution. Like many people of my age from that era, I was fascinated by the romantic image of Che, the Christ-like martyr of the Revolution, and I had written to my father asking him for advice on books to read about Cuba. In one of his replies he wrote:

> *I would like to think that you admired Che as I do but that is your business because I am not finally entitled to tell you what you should*

think and feel any more. It is open to question if I ever was. You
must discriminate, however, you must make some kind of choice,
and don't get silly about revolutions. Revolutions mean people dying
as well as the possibility of change, and shooting people is not a
joking matter nor the business of neurotics. Many neurotics claim
to be revolutionaries, many are just plain silly. I don't think either
Che Guevara or Castro were − I take them seriously. But this
is all something you must decide for yourself. Especially as you grow
older.

While I was pleased to think that he took my youthful infatuation
with revolt seriously, even then I still found it difficult to see my father
as a 'little soldier of fortune of the twentieth century'. As far as I
knew, he was an English lecturer in a sleepy ex-colony where nothing
as glamorous or as exciting as the Cuban Revolution was ever likely
to happen, and the idea that his delirium in Guyana had some kind of
political significance seemed ludicrous, even to a politically ill-informed
adolescent. I knew little about the political situation in Guyana, beyond
the fact that it was ruled by a corrupt president called Forbes Burnham,
whose ruling party, the People's National Congress, the P N C, regularly won elections through massive vote-rigging. In the early 70s I
saw a *World in Action* documentary examining Burnham's fraudulent
use of 'overseas voters', most of whom were either dead or under-aged,
to help him win elections.

This phantom constituency of children and dead voters from abroad
was only one strategy employed by the regime to keep itself in
power, and my father's occasional letters contained increasingly grim
references to the political situation in the country. Around the same
period he told my mother that he had now joined the opposition
People's Progressive Party, the P P P, and his letters to her began to
hint at dark conspiracies that were being hatched against him, which
he claimed were preventing him from leaving the country and coming
to see us:

> *... I can come to England in the sense that nobody can physically*
> *prevent me. But it wouldn't be a good idea. THEY are hustling*
> *the radicals out ... THEY bank on my leaving, which more or*
> *less solves their problem. My books etc. would be incarcerated here*
> *and I don't think I would be much use in England. It would take*
> *two years to readjust. It seems that I belong where I am.*

In May 1972, in reply to a letter from my mother asking him to come to Cambridge for the summer to see us, he replied in even more dramatic terms:

> I don't think your Cambridge suggestion would work . . . I surely wouldn't be able to afford it and finally the V C has strongly hinted that if I were to leave the country the Government would debar me at the airport and put me back on the plane. That wouldn't help anybody. These bastards are that ruthless – you have to check carefully when you lock up the car after work in case some party thugs are hanging about – niggers hunt in packs . . .

And again:

> . . . A colleague of mine . . . is initiating a campaign against me through his cousin . . . what a nasty, dirty, nigger-ridden Byzantine place. The gentleman is a flagrant and vicious racist who has been scurrilously hunting for me a long time.

It was difficult to know what to make of this from England. Given my father's tendency to self-dramatization, there was always a suspicion that he was exaggerating his own importance in order to cast himself in the role of persecuted victim. After we stopped writing to each other, the little bits of news about him that filtered back from Guyana became entirely second-hand, which made it even more difficult to imagine what he was really involved in. There was no final angry exchange of letters between us, but rather a growing sense of indignation and disillusionment on my part as the realization set in that he really had thrown us out, and that he had no intention of coming back. Although in the beginning I had warmed to his letters and felt flattered by them, I gradually began to see them as false and hypocritical, with their affectionate salutations of 'My dear boy' and 'My dear son' and the inevitable closure, 'Peace, love and justice'. It was as though he were playing a role on paper that he had been unwilling to play in real life.

By the mid-70s the disenchantment was complete. I had ceased to regard him as a father at all in any meaningful sense of the word and the memory of my life with him had become a kind of morbid psychological undercurrent, that was always in danger of dragging me downwards if I thought about it too much. The best thing to do with my childhood, it seemed, was to forget it and move on. Yet no matter how many times I made the conscious decision to put the past behind me, I was never able to detach myself from it entirely. Even as the concrete details faded, the emotional memory of that period lingered on, in the form of dark moods and depressions that often seemed to have no relation to what was taking place around me, so that I was constantly looking back over my shoulder and wondering what had really taken place during those years.

I also wondered, from time to time, what had become of my father himself. My evolving mental picture of him was entirely based on the contradictory rumours and bits of information that drifted back from Guyana, through his occasional letters to my mother and the odd visit from mutual friends. I knew that he had split up with Sandra Williams and that he had subsequently remarried after my parents' divorce in 1974. The news that his new wife was a woman with two children from a previous marriage seemed to confirm that we would never be part of his life again, and it was around the same time that his letters to my mother virtually stopped. I heard that he was desperately trying to get out of Guyana, that he was heavily involved in Guyanese politics, that he was drinking so much that his students were picking him out of the gutter, that he was living a life of wine, women and song, that he was sick and dying, and that he had reconverted to the Catholic Church.

The only member of my family to see him after we left was my sister Anna, whose troubled life during the 70s was also a direct consequence of what had happened in the West Indies. Unlike the rest of us, she continued to carry an idealized picture of her lost father with her into adulthood, and in 1978 she finally went to see him in Guyana. Perhaps not surprisingly, 'Daddy' failed to live up to her romantic expectations, and the visit had such a salutary effect on her that for the first time she began to steer her life out of its downhill, self-destructive trajectory. She brought back a picture of a sentimental old drunk, who played Cat Stevens' 'Father and Son' to her ad infinitum, who shouted at his wife, and whose political activity consisted of talking about socialism on his patio with the leader of the opposition, Cheddi Jagan.

Everything suggested a man in steep decline, a man worthy of pity rather than anger, whose apparent physical and mental disintegration seemed to be matched by the dizzying collapse of the country that he had chosen to live in. For most of the 70s, Guyana received virtually no media attention at all, but the occasional news that did get back to Europe described a process of catastrophic economic and social decline. As early as 1972 my father had written to my mother:

> Why do I wish to stay here? Everybody asks me that. I've been bashed on the head and robbed. I've been beaten up twice because I committed the sin of being born white. Net damage — two cracked ribs and impaired vision in the right eye. I've had a drunken policeman threaten to kill me for the same reason — he had a gun in his pocket. And I had a month in hospital with suspected cirrhosis. If I drink with any amplitude I am told I will be lucky if I live to be fifty. I sometimes wonder if it matters. Certainly I handled all of you damned badly and I have got my comeuppance. Knowing this, however, does not make it any easier to take . . .

By 1977 things had not improved:

> . . . I don't know what appears about us in the English papers. But if you were here now, you wouldn't make it. The lies, the shortages, the beating, the bullying, the arrests, the queues, the blackouts, the water failures. Our daughter's first adult glimpse of Guyana was a man being beaten up at the airport for spitting at Burnham's portrait. Next year, you see, I have to get out. At forty-seven I've had enough of it. I want to be able to do my own work. You cannot be neutral in this country and years of combat are wearing me down. After all, even Karl Marx had to take refuge in exile.

In 1978 Guyana exploded into the international headlines for the first and only time in its history when the murder of US Congressman Leo Ryan by members of a religious sect called the People's Temple was followed by the horrendous slaughter at Jonestown. The largest mass suicide since the ancient siege of Masada was a genuine media event, and scores of journalists descended on Guyana, bringing back pictures of bloated bodies and vats of poisoned Kool-Aid. With its white madness in the tropics, its charismatic leader of an authoritarian Utopian sect leading his followers to destruction – above all, its hundreds of corpses – the Jonestown slaughter was an international media event. For a week or two the world's press feasted on Jim Jones's gory harvest, before Guyana slipped back into its characteristic obscurity once again. By then the revelations of the close connection between Jim Jones's followers and the Burnham regime had provided the first real indication to the outside world that something seriously weird was going on in Guyana, but the brief flurry of international attention failed to result in any significant pressure being brought to bear on the regime.

There was other, less spectacular evidence that Guyana was not the stable Caribbean democracy it had once appeared to be. In 1979 a Jesuit priest, Father Bernard Darke, was bayoneted to death during an anti-government demonstration calling for the release of the historian and academic Dr Walter Rodney and others from prison. Father Darke was my former mathematics teacher in Guyana, and his killers were members of a religious sect called the House of Israel, whose members believed in a coming race war and acted as a strong-arm group, bordering on death squad, for the government.

Rodney was released but was himself blown up the following year by a booby-trapped radio in Georgetown, given to him by a member of the Guyanese Defence Force. That same year I was living in Amsterdam, where I went to see a film called *The Terror and the Time*. The film dealt with the British military intervention in Guyana in 1953, using poems from the Guyanese national poet Martin Carter, and a rather portentous narrative heavily laced with Fanon-esque anti-colonialist jargon, which laboriously traced the impact of British colonialism on Guyanese society. The combination did not work for me, but afterwards I met two members of the collective responsible for it, a Guyanese woman called Gloria Lowe and her American partner Ray. In the course of the conversation I mentioned that I had lived in Guyana, and when I mentioned my name, Gloria looked at me incredulously. 'You're not Bill Carr's son?'

I admitted that I was, intrigued and also a little embarrassed by her tone of admiration.

'He's the only white man in Guyana who's done anything against Burnham!' she told me, in a voice that indicated that I should feel proud of the fact. Pride was not an emotion I was accustomed to feeling in connection with my father, and I felt uncomfortable bathing in his reflected glory, given the way things had gone between us, and the fact that I had had no contact with him for years. It was the first time I had spoken to anyone who knew anything about his life in Guyana since we left, and my curiosity was aroused by the fact that she seemed to see him as a kind of hero, something I had stopped doing a long time ago. I expressed surprise at his commitment to

Guyana, since he had only recently told Anna he wanted to get out of the country.

'Ah,' she laughed knowingly, 'he must have been going through one of his burnt-out periods.'

For the first time I began to wonder whether my father's comparisons to Che Guevara were not as far-fetched as I had originally thought. What had he done to arouse such admiration and respect? What were his 'burnt-out periods'? And what else did they know about him? I took their address and promised to get in touch with them again, but somehow I never got round to it. At that time there seemed little point in getting involved with people who knew him in Guyana and I had no desire to bring him any closer to my life than he was already. Soon afterwards I left the city, and my father and his adopted country faded back into the past once again.

By the early 1980s, my sister was the only member of my family who still kept up any contact with him. Sometime around 1983, a farcical episode occurred when an emissary from the Diocese of Southwark approached my mother, apparently on instructions from my father, and asked her to sign papers annulling the marriage, on the grounds of 'mutual immaturity at the time the marriage was contracted'. The reason given for this unusual request was that he wanted to be able to receive all the sacraments without the stain of divorce, but since an annulment would automatically have made us all bastards, my mother was less than sympathetic to these exalted religious sentiments, and refused to co-operate.

Needless to say, the annulment was not carried out, but the bizarre episode provided further confirmation that we had become as irrelevant to his present life as he was to ours. By this time none of us expected to see him alive again, not even my sister, and then, suddenly, against all expectations, when he had ceased to be more than an occasional topic of conversation, he came back.

Chapter Two

A long time ago, in the early 70s, a friend in Cambridge had come up to me in the street and told me that my father was waiting for me back at the house. In a single moment all the previous antipathy I felt towards him had melted away, replaced by spontaneous enthusiasm and excitement. Without hesitation, I had run back home. It was one of those moments in which the ambivalence of my feelings towards my father revealed itself. On the surface I felt only anger and bitterness towards him, and yet there was still a part of me that looked up to him and resented anybody else's attempts to take his place. I was the keeper of the vacant throne, waiting for the king to return from exile, and now it seemed that the moment had come, and I ran as fast as I could back to the house, only to find to my great disappointment a friend of my parents from the West Indies waiting in the living-room instead. The friend was Jerry Owens, a former English colleague of my father's from UWI, and for the rest of the evening I regarded him with disinterest and even resentment for not being the real thing.

On that occasion my friend had got the message wrong, but there was no mistake about my father's appearance now. It was September 1987, and I had just returned to London after a summer working in the Gaza Strip, when my sister gave me the extraordinary news that he was in London with his wife Marjorie and that he wanted to see us all. She had spoken to him herself and she now gave me his number and left the matter in my hands. Despite the fact that there was no possibility of a disappointment this time, I did not run to see him, nor was I in any hurry even to call him. I was thirty-two years old, and I had got so used to living without him for so long that I was not even sure I wanted to see him again. The throne had become cobwebbed. It had stood neglected for so long in the recesses of my memory that I no longer felt any need to dust it off. As far as I was concerned the fact that he was my father no longer referred to anything but a remote biological connection and a failed relationship that could never be put right. And yet my curiosity was aroused, and perhaps something else as well. What could he possibly want after all these years? What was I going to talk to him about? Should I even see him at all? My mother was away on holiday, and after some hesitation I rang up the number my sister had given me and an unfamiliar West Indian accent sounded on the other end of the phone. It was my father. We had a brief, polite chat, like two distant relatives after a long absence who no longer know what to say to each other, and I arranged to meet him.

That same week I went round to the house where he was staying in South London. I knocked on the door and a moment later he appeared on the doorstep. Despite everything I had heard about his physical disintegration I was stunned at the sight of the ghastly apparition that appeared in the doorway. There is a photograph of my father taken in Jamaica which I had often looked at when I wanted to remind myself or show anyone else what he looked like. The picture is a close-up, almost like a police mugshot, of a powerful, bull-necked man in an open-necked white shirt, staring at the camera with an expression of cold hostility. Despite the aggressive, confrontational expression, it is a handsome, even a striking face, the face of a boxer rather than an English lecturer. Over the years this picture had become my only mental image of the father I remembered, the raging bull, who had beaten up my mother and destroyed rooms, whose powerful physical presence had loomed over me throughout my childhood and inspired a poem I had once written that began:

> When I was in my father's house
> his heavy hand
> covered up the sun

Now, twenty years after he had expelled us from Guyana, a tiny old man with grey hair, a beard and glasses stared myopically at me and ushered me awkwardly into the house. I was appalled and saddened at his physical deterioration. He was moving extremely slowly, with short little baby steps. He also seemed to be having difficulty breathing, and there was a large, pointed swelling around his belly button, which I later found out was due to a swollen liver. At the time, what struck me most about him were his feet. They were absurdly small. I could not associate these feet with the image in the mugshot, nor with anything else that I could remember about him. How could a man with such tiny feet have been capable of wreaking such havoc? I wondered. It was as if he had withered away. I saw him then as a spent volcano, all ash and grey lava, and I thought of Rimbaud's line, 'women nurse those invalids, home from the hot countries'.

I remember feeling a sense of unreality and wonder as we went into the living-room. I didn't know whose house it was, but I guessed that the inhabitants had been previously prepared for this historic reunion, since we seemed to be the only ones there. A few minutes later a young black woman came into the sitting-room to see if we wanted anything. She looked as nervous as I was and rapidly left, leaving my father and me alone in the room with the curtains drawn.

Exactly what we talked about that night I cannot remember, but I recall that the conversation was rather stilted and impersonal, concerned only with the external details of each other's lives. I told him a few of the things I had done during the last twenty years and asked him questions about Guyana and his own life. He said that he had come back to England for medical treatment which could not be carried out in Guyana, and that he was going to be here for three months. We talked a little bit about Guyanese politics, and he told me that he had actually watched Father Darke being killed in front of my old school. That was the only time he referred to anything connected with our mutual past in Guyana. He described life in Georgetown, the continual blackouts, the robberies and crime, which had converted his neighbourhood into a no-go area after dark. He said that life in Guyana had become unbearable and that he hated it. He also talked about England, and his plans to visit his surviving relatives in Yorkshire, and spoke about his old public school in Dulwich, and his Cambridge University days.

In this conversation, and all the other conversations I had with him during that visit, his vision of England seemed to be entirely rooted in his own youth, a Hovis-loaf advert world of cricket pitches and rugby posts, redbrick northern towns, green remembered hills, and cloistered Cambridge colleges, all steeped in a rosy nostalgic glow. He seemed totally absorbed in that past, and whenever he talked about it his face softened and he seemed to stare into the distance as if he were straining to recapture every detail. This romantic, almost Housman-like vision of England seemed particularly ironic, since I had always understood that it was his contempt and revulsion for

English society that had induced him to leave the country in the first place, and he himself had often used his inability to fit into English society as an excuse for not coming back to see us.

Now he finally had come back, but in the interim years his vision of England seemed to have undergone a curious metamorphosis. The change was ironic, since at that time I felt the same disgust and frustration at English society that he had once felt himself and frequently reiterated during my childhood. Shortly after our return to England he had made some contemptuous reference to a society of 'Guardian-reading liberals' in one of his letters to my mother. Now I myself was on the point of abandoning Thatcherite England and I talked angrily about the Wapping strike, the defeat of the miners and the destruction of the welfare state, but he did not seem interested in contemporary English society at all. Only the England of his own youth seemed to matter to him, all of it bathed in the same rosy sunset glow.

A long time ago I had fantasized about being face to face with my father again and how I would confront him about the past and demand an explanation from him and show him that I had survived it all, but that night, it seemed to me that he was the one who had been destroyed, and that we had all survived much better than he had. This realization did not make me feel triumphant, and the idea of confronting a man in his condition seemed pointless and cruel. That night I did not feel any anger towards him at all. Had he brought up the past I would have talked about it, but I was unwilling to broach the subject myself. It all seemed so long ago, and from the way he talked about us I wasn't sure that he could even remember what had happened after so many years. Certainly he did not seem remotely contrite or even aware that anything unusual had happened. It was as if the last two decades had passed like an alcoholic lost weekend, eradicating anything painful or unpleasant, leaving nothing but the sentimental memories of a ruined old man, who had finally returned like an old, lined elephant in search of his own past.

At some point in the evening I remember that he asked me how old I thought he was. I felt that I was being tested in some way, but I couldn't remember when he was born, so I took a guess and said sixty-five. A look of disappointment, even despair, appeared on his face.

'Christ man,' he said, 'I don't look that old, do I? I'm fifty-six.'

I didn't say anything, but the realization that he was as young as that only brought home to me further how much he had deteriorated. The conversation soon faltered and we went out to the pub for a drink, accompanied by his wife Marjorie. On the way we often had to slow down as he took his little baby steps, and his rasping, wheezing breath became even more noticeable.

My immediate impression of Marjorie was one of a long-suffering wife, who was very attentive to my father's needs and concerned about his health. She was a quiet-spoken Afro-Guyanese woman with glasses and short black hair who kept herself in the background, but none the less I felt that she was more sensitive to the possible impact of my father's unexpected visit on us than he was himself. She seemed anxious for us all to get on, but I was impressed by her tact and discretion. At the same time I also remember being surprised and even slightly irritated by the way she constantly referred to him as 'your father', as though she thought that I had forgotten who he was. I did not need the repetition and the words had a slightly absurd ring. For years I had grown used to regarding him as a part of my remote past, and I still could not fully accept the idea that the ghastly apparition who had suddenly stepped into my present really was the father I remembered.

The reaction from the rest of my family was mixed. My mother had just returned from one of her far-flung holidays abroad and she saw no point in a reunion with him, although they did have a perfectly amicable conversation on the telephone, while I was visiting him at the house of one of his friends. My sister Anna had no problem seeing him and invited him down to Cambridge. Christian, my youngest brother, had only been a toddler when we left Guyana, and couldn't even remember what he looked like, so that when he went to visit him in hospital in London, he had to ask the nurse to take him to his father's bed. Almost the first thing he asked him was: 'Why did you hit my mother?' Undoubtedly taken aback, my father replied that he had only hit her 'now and then, as husbands do'. My other brother Bruce also questioned him briefly about his violence, only to meet with equally vague and evasive replies. No one brought up the subject of his rejection of *us*, nor did he show any inclination to bring up the subject himself. This was not a collective decision on our part, since each of us dealt with his visit in our own way, but it seemed clear to me that for us to have brought it up would have been to admit that we had once been hurt by him. That was something that no one was prepared to do, and my father, for his own reasons, clearly did not want to talk about it either.

From my own point of view there seemed little point in confronting him about the past, especially as he was not going to be in England very much longer. I saw him three more times, each time with other people around. The strangest visit was when he came to Cambridge with Marjorie, and my sister and I went with them to his old college at Pembroke, together with my niece and brother-in-law. Throughout his re-encounter with this crucial part of his life he seemed more absorbed in himself and his own past than ever, as we escorted him round the town, while he told Marjorie stories about Cambridge and pointed out landmarks and places that he remembered. These places were associated only with him, and he did not visit or talk about any of the places in Cambridge where he had lived with his first wife and family. As we were walking around Pembroke, he snapped at Marjorie and called her stupid because of some question she had asked him. For the first time since his return I felt a flicker of anger towards him for talking to his second wife like that in public, after all those years, when it was obvious that he would hardly have been able to walk down the street without her.

Later that afternoon, he called me 'a big dummy', when I drove too fast round a corner and skewed the car across the road in the countryside. The jibe was obviously intended to be affectionate, in a heavy-handed way, but it seemed clumsy and inappropriate and suggested a familiarity that as far as I was concerned he had no right to. At the same time it was also a reminder that the child in me had not disappeared completely, and that the old resentment was still there, somewhere below the surface. I gritted my teeth and said nothing, wondering what I was doing dutifully playing the escort to this cantankerous egomaniac, who had treated his first wife like a punching-bag, abandoned his children without apparently a second thought when he had had no use for them, lied and wheedled his way out of all the agreements he had ever made to help us, and still showed no sign of even recognizing that he had done anything wrong.

Throughout the whole visit I had the same sensation that I had had all those years ago, that we, his children, were not people to him at all, but merely stage props, bit actors playing secondary, supporting roles in a private drama that he was acting out – the great man home from the tropics in search of his roots. We were adults now, no longer powerless, with our own lives and personalities and experiences. Yet my father did not seem interested to know very much about us, or perhaps he simply did not know how to communicate with the children he had kicked out of his life nearly three decades before. All the time I was watching him, looking for some sign that he had changed, that he had some insight into what he had done, but there was nothing, only this narrow, blinkered immersion in his own adulterated memories. It seemed an absurd coda to a domestic tragedy, but there was no alternative but to continue with it, not for us, but for him, and I consoled myself with the thought that soon he would be out of our lives once more.

That afternoon we drove him to Little Gidding – on a grey winter's day, 'Daddy' and his new wife, two of his children and a grandchild on an unlikely family outing across the drab Huntingdonshire countryside, past the cruise missile base at Molesworth, where I had been at a demonstration the previous year. He had been very insistent that we take him to the chapel at Little Gidding. It seemed to be part of a pilgrimage that he wanted to make, that might have been literary, religious, or both. Whatever the reason, the obscure village had clearly assumed some kind of symbolic importance for him during his years in Guyana, just as it had done for the author of the *Four Quartets*.

Shortly before leaving for the West Indies all those years ago, he had visited Little Gidding with my mother, and now he was back, like Eliot's 'broken king', nearing the end of his journey on earth, perhaps seeking to close the famous circle that the poet had described:

> *We shall not cease from exploration*
> *And the end of all our exploring*
> *Will be to arrive where we started*
> *And know the place for the first time.*

I remember that we visited the little chapel in which Charles I had prayed after the Battle of Naseby, where the saintly Nicholas Ferrar had founded his small Catholic community which had been disbanded by Cromwell's soldiers in 1647. The little chapel had been burned and subsequently rebuilt a long time ago, and we stood there in silence, our breath throwing out little clouds of steam, while my father shuffled around by the altar, illuminated by the weak light filtering through the stained-glass, a sick alcoholic 'suspended in time, between pole and tropic', smiling enigmatically as he communed with the spirits of his native land:

> . . . *for history is a pattern*
> *Of timeless moments. So, while the light fails*
> *On a winter's afternoon, in a secluded chapel*
> *History is now and England.*

I only saw my father once more after that, when I invited him and Marjorie for lunch at the squat where I was living. Once again it was a friendly but strangely formal occasion, and the same distance remained, which neither of us was able or willing to cross. I was planning to move to Spain and I didn't expect to see either of them again. I remember feeling afterwards a sense of dissatisfaction and missed opportunity that nothing important had been said, together with a mild irritation at his total lack of interest in my life. My father had been to Yorkshire by himself, and was full of the great time he had had there, talking to his uncle and his few surviving relatives, drinking beer in pubs.

I remember that he went to the toilet just as we were about to leave to take him back to the station. Marjorie and I walked down the road and waited for him by the railway bridge. He seemed to take a long time, and a few minutes later, he came shuffling down the road with his little baby steps, his shirt untucked, wheezing and cursing to himself. We shook hands and said goodbye and I watched him disappear across the railway bridge towards the tube station. That was the last time I saw him alive.

Caspar the Friendly Ghost had only just come to an end, when I caught my first glimpse of the Caribbean in twenty-nine years, at the little airport at Tobago. As the aeroplane touched down for a brief stop-over I could see the clear, transparent ocean only a few hundred yards away, behind a row of banana trees. I stood on the stairway, blinking in the heat and the dazzling sunlight, as a handful of tourists disembarked and others got on board for the return flight to London. They looked suntanned and relaxed, the men in shorts, the women in loose cotton dresses and sarongs, one or two of them with their hair still wet as if they had just come straight from the beach. Some of the passengers also came out to take a breath of fresh air. They were already in holiday mood, chatty and relaxed enough to talk to strangers in the way that the English can sometimes manage to be when they are out of their own country.

Even that brief glimpse of the ocean and the banana trees was enough to bring memories of my childhood in Jamaica welling up to the surface once again: the powdery white sand of Negril Beach, the water clear as glass, the giant slide at Montego Bay, some sixty foot high, which you had to swim out to to climb, the speedboat trip to Lime Key where my back had got so badly sunburned that I was covered in blisters, the wooden house by the sea where we sometimes spent Christmas and my father had once read us *A Christmas Carol* on Christmas Eve, his superb reading voice evoking a lost world of foggy London streets and cramped offices and red-faced men in waistcoats and top hats as we sat round the table entranced, with the sound of the ocean washing up on the beach outside, almost regretting the fact that in Jamaica there were no chimneys for Santa Claus to descend and the weather was too hot for reindeer and red fur suits.

We lived in Jamaica before the advent of mass tourism and package tours, when the Caribbean fantasy was still largely available to middle-class tourists only. My father's job at the university had granted us permanent access to an exotic world that few English kids our age could even have dreamt about. The weather was the same throughout the year, except for the short period of the rainy season, and we never wore jackets or even sweaters. We spent our weekends at the beaches at Negril or Montego Bay, or the university swimming pool at College Common, and sometimes my father took us to a movie at a drive-in or one of the indoor cinemas around Kingston. We drove to well-known spots around the island, with evocative names like Morgan's Harbour, Discovery Bay and Port Royal, or into the mountains outside Kingston, up narrow dirt roads with hair-raisingly steep drops, splashing through shallow streams as we descended.

In our last years in Jamaica we lived in an old rectory at Stony Hill, just outside Kingston, a beautiful wooden house built on stilts, standing on a hill, with a long rectangular sitting-room overlooking some two acres of wild, overgrown countryside beneath our garden. There Bruce and I played Wild West and jungle warfare games with fierce intensity and commitment, defending the house against hordes of invisible enemies or making expeditions into the undergrowth, like Jeff Chandler in *Merrill's Marauders*. A favourite game was pretending to be Tarzan and his son Korak, which we used to act out with loincloths and wooden knives, till one day an entire wasp's nest fell on my back, and the two of us waged a war of extermination against every wasp within a hundred yards of the house, climbing trees and hunting them down and squirting them with every available weapon, including my mother's hairspray.

There was something about the Caribbean that lent itself perfectly to the fantasy games in which we spent most of our time. In that bright, luminous landscape, the imagination easily ran riot, and we populated it with hummingbirds and mongooses, pirates and buried treasure and wrecked ships, and ruined plantations haunted by witches and the ghosts of mad creole plantation owners, like the famous witch of Rose Hall who was supposed to ride around the countryside with her long black hair and scarlet dress and riding crop. In the relative isolation of Stony Hill especially, what was imagined often seemed more vivid and immediate than what was real, and certainly more preferable. It was easy to believe in 'duppies', the Jamaican word for zombies, that roamed after nightfall, and Donny, our gardener's son, took pleasure in pretending to be one, chasing us round the yard and making ghost sounds, to our great delight. Sports came a poor second to this intense fantasy life. Most of the time we hardly bothered with them at all, preferring instead to borrow my mother's cardigans and pretend to be the Hardy Boys or spend the afternoons trekking through the overgrown vegetation around Stony Hill fighting the Japanese or pretending to be the Lone Ranger and Tonto.

Our grip on reality was always extremely weak. We lived in a world of stories and myths, in which characters from Jamaican folklore like Anansy the Trickster Spider co-existed with our own invented animal heroes like Monk the Mongoose. Once my brother and I beat up my sister, and decided to run away to sea to escape punishment. That same afternoon we wrapped a few clothes and possessions into a bundle and tied them to a stick, the way Jim Hawkins would have done, and fled across the undergrowth. We had only just scaled the steep embankment at the end of the wasteground and emerged on the main road with the vague idea of hitching a lift to Kingston Harbour, when we were picked up by some friends of my parents and brought back with our bundles. Another time we broke into the costume room of the university drama department. It was like discovering Aladdin's cave. There was a costume for every fantasy, and we tried on various combinations. Finally we walked home dressed as conquistadores, with our oversized armour, pikes and sabres, which my mother immediately ordered us to take back. Towards the end of our stay in Jamaica, builders began to work on the countryside around our house in Stony Hill, and dug up what seemed to be a mass grave of cattle. My brother and I leapt into it and danced gleefully around, putting the bones in our shorts, smearing ourselves with dirt and shouting with excitement like a pair of deranged extras from *Lord of the Flies*.

From the outside we lived a privileged and comfortable life, the white children of an English university lecturer and his lawyer wife, playing cowboys and indians in a little cocoon untouched by politics or race. We arrived in 1960, on the cusp of independence, when the former slave islands that made up the 'dustbin of the Empire' were finally being discarded, as the pre-war Moyne report had recommended, along with most of Britain's imperial possessions elsewhere. British cultural and political influence in the West Indies was still strong, but already the United States was becoming the dominant power in the region and actively seeking to contain the radical nationalist currents unleashed by the Cuban Revolution. In Jamaica the political scene was dominated by Norman Manley and Alexander Bustamante, the two leaders who had first risen to power during the labour unrest of the 1930s and now led opposing parties, on the left and right respectively.

It was another Jamaica, of low crime rates and relative political stability, before the use of hired gunmen by both political parties turned the Kingston ghettoes into a bloody battleground in the 1970s, when the attempts of Michael Manley – Norman Manley's son – to steer Jamaica down a non-aligned 'Third Path' finally foundered in the face of local and foreign opposition. Despite the achievement of national independence in 1962, the light-skinned Anglophile middle class continued to dominate the upper levels of Jamaican society, and the cultural upheaval associated with reggae and the Rastafarian movement was still a phenomenon of the future. To the Jamaican middle class, Rastafarians were no more than a dangerous, isolated sect of ganja-smoking wild men living up in the hills, like some latter-day version of the old Maroon communities formed by runaway slaves. Even Haile Selassie's brief visit to Jamaica in the early 60s went more or less unnoticed, and the Ethiopian dictator must have been as non-plussed and disappointed by the dreadlocked disciples who came to meet him at the airport, as they were at the sight of this frail little man, who was supposed to be the Lion of Judah.

The smooth and orderly transition to self-government, in Jamaica, as elsewhere in the English-speaking Caribbean, was deceptive. Beneath the apparently tranquil surface a volatile mixture of nationalist pride, Third World liberationism and racial resentment was already beginning to reshape the politics of the region in the post-colonial era. Not much of this, if anything, filtered through to the four white children of liberal, left-wing parents. We lived in a succession of nice houses provided by the university. Like all expatriates and most middle-class Jamaicans, we had maids and gardeners and we went to Catholic schools, where we wore our neat little uniforms of blue short-sleeved shirts and trousers and were given a half-day when the Queen came to visit, turning out with hundreds of other schoolkids from around the island to line the streets and cheer and wave Union Jacks. We quickly picked up Jamaican accents, and learned folk songs like 'Carry me akee, go Linstead market, not a quatee go sell', and ran round the playground with the other kids gleefully singing, 'Bustamantee bust his pantee,' because it sounded funny. The houses we lived in were filled with books and an eclectic collection of records that included early Dylan and the Beatles, Purcell's *Dido and Aeneas*, the satirical calypso of 'The Mighty Sparrow', *Swingin' Safari* by Herb Alpert and his Tijuana Brass, and the melancholy songs of William Byrd.

There was nothing extraordinary about this lifestyle by English standards, but it would certainly have seemed luxurious to the thousands of West Indians who had been emigrating to England since the early fifties, or pouring in from the countryside to fill the Kingston slums. But if we were privileged, we were not aware of it, nor did we know anything about the complex relationship between colour and social class and degrees of whiteness that had dominated Caribbean political and social life since the days of slavery. Like most children we did not think about class or colour at all, and formed relationships with anyone on equal terms, regardless of their background.

Only once, when I was about seven or eight years old, was I ever made to feel conscious that my own whiteness elevated me above others. I was playing a game with bubblegum cards with some black street kids outside my school, while I waited for my parents to come and pick me up. They were typical poor Jamaican street kids, barefoot, in dirty, ragged khaki shorts, but it seemed as natural to play with them as anyone else. Suddenly Miss Irons, a formidable black Jamaican teacher, came charging out of the school and angrily dragged me away from them as if she feared contamination, telling me that I was never to play with such people again. I was led away, furious and humiliated, to the classroom, where for the rest of the afternoon I had to sit in class watching my new-found friends playing outside and wondering what I was supposed to have done wrong. That was the only time I ever sensed that there was something artificial or different about our position in the West Indies, that there were certain barriers that whiteness conferred which I was not supposed to cross and which were connected to a wider world that I was hardly even aware of.

Inside the family cocoon, however, life was not nearly as comfortable and secure as it might have appeared from the outside, as the relationship between my parents continued its long-drawn-out breakdown. Once, during one of the worst periods in Jamaica, my mother fell into such a state of depression and despair that she pretended to be dead, ignoring our frantic attempts to wake her up. There were many occasions when she was driven to such despair, but I could never remember exactly when this had happened. It might have been after the night my father beat her from one end of the house to the other, and finished up flailing punches at her in the shower. Eventually she had managed to run outside and shout at the silent campus for someone to come and save her, but no one did although everyone must have heard. Or it could have been the time when we were living in the little concrete house at Mona, cut off from the world with all the windows boarded up, waiting for Hurricane Flora. My father was living apart from us, leaving my mother to cope with four children, including a new-born baby, my youngest brother Christian. The hurricane did not hit Jamaica directly, but for three days we were sealed up in the house, while a fierce storm raged outside, lashing at the boarded-up windows and flooding the streets so that the cars outside were almost covered with water when we finally re-emerged.

The image of my mother pretending to be dead in front of her own children had always been symbolic to me of the atmosphere of unhappiness and despair that was the other side of our life in Jamaica. Another memory that has stayed with me was the aftermath of a car crash that we witnessed after coming back from a day out on the beach. I remember it was late afternoon, already getting dark, and we were driving back from the beach along Washington Boulevard, when we saw an overturned sports car lying by the side of the road. There was blood everywhere and the ambulancemen were carrying a covered body on a stretcher into the ambulance. Later we heard that a couple had been driving at 80 miles an hour when a tyre had burst and the vehicle had flipped over. It was my first contact with death. I was horrified and disturbed by the sight of it. But my father just grunted, 'Bleeding like a stuck pig,' an image that only made me feel worse, so that I became hysterical and kept turning round to look at the retreating horror until he lost patience and started shouting at me to shut up.

The way I remembered my childhood in the Caribbean had always oscillated between two extremes, between my mother's misery and my father's explosive rages, between the fantasy landscape that we lived in outside the house and the claustrophobic, pressure-cooker atmosphere inside it, between long sunny days that rarely lived up to their initial promise and even longer nights lying awake sweating with an irrational fear of the dark, as alarmed by the silence of the house when my father was away from us as I was by the noise when he came back and the fights began.

Often I would lie awake listening to him shouting into the night, working himself up into a pitch of rage that would temporarily subside and then climb back up again until exhaustion overcame him. Many times these rages would end with him throwing plates and glasses, overturning the furniture, punching the walls, throwing ketchup, or even carrying out some mad, drunken act of self-mutilation, as if he were trying to bleed the poison out of himself, like the time in Mona when he had slashed his hand open with a piece of broken glass and had to be taken to hospital. The house at Mona was covered with marks where he had thrown things or punched the walls or bent back the bars on the windows. When we left, the landlord went around counting them one by one, without saying a word, in a deliberate ritual of humiliation.

None of us had the remotest idea what made my father act the way he did. We were all afraid of him, yet not so much that we always did what he said. We often talked back and refused to obey his orders, despite the usually violent reaction. We were all angry with him for what he was doing to my mother, but there was nothing we could do to stop it. Once Bruce actually attacked my father during one of these scenes, even though he barely came up to his waist, and got a black eye for his pains. Another time both of us attacked him and got thrown on to the lawn in front of one of my father's friends. But the worst scenes usually took place at night, after we had gone to bed, when there was nothing to do but lie awake and listen and wait for the tirades to die down and hope that they did not end in violence.

Usually we did not appear, but lay awake and in silence in our rooms. The next day, it would always be there, the same atmosphere of sadness and desolation, my mother picking up the pieces, literally and metaphorically, organizing breakfast, planning some expedition, getting us off to school, while we waited for my father to emerge from the bedroom and see what kind of mood he was in, all the time wishing that my mother could stop being unhappy and my father could stop being violent and we could all be normal like other people seemed to be. In fact things were rarely 'normal' for long, and it was the conspicuous abnormality of my family situation, not my Englishness, that made me conscious of being separate from other children.

In these circumstances I was so bound up with what my parents were feeling that it was difficult to know where my own emotions began and ended. I learned to read their moods and silences, to anticipate disaster, although it was impossible to make safe predictions, since my father's rages could blow up out of nowhere, especially when he was drunk. And when my parents did seem to get on, when my father read to us or told us stories, I would feel both elated and fearful that these periods would not last.

As I grew older, the realization of my mother's unhappiness made me guilty but also resentful, since it was impossible for me to be happy myself. At times I felt I had no existence apart from my parents, except in the fantasy games and stories I invented. I was terrified of my father's rages and at the same time fascinated by their power and energy, which seemed at times to be a legitimate way of dealing with the suffocating weight of the world.

Jean d'Costa was a young Jamaican postgraduate who got her first job teaching English with my father at U W I in 1962 and subsequently became a close friend of both my parents. Now living in the States, she sent me this description of her first encounter with the Carr family, when the then head of Department Jerry Owens took her to meet us, at our house in College Common:

We got there in the early evening. It was a typical College Common house, everyone on the veranda. Most prominent was a small boy of about five or six, playing with a toy plane and a toy ship. He did not look up or react to the grownups at any time. He was bent on sinking that ship with that plane as often as possible. Slender, pale, with very fair hair like his father's, he made all the right noises for the attacking plane and the blasts aboard the ship. I was fascinated. I watched him all evening: he became the frontispiece for that evening, while Jerry explained the departmental situation (in which I was not much interested). Something about this boy's intensity and about the way he ignored us made me pay attention to him, and then to his parents. I sensed that his mood was connected to his parents, although I had no idea what it all might mean.

You were and are my chief memory of that night — and one other matter.

Your mother came out to greet us. I saw a young woman, dark-haired, not as pale as the little boy, with a harried look about her. She was dressed in a sort of absent-minded way. She greeted me pleasantly but all of her attention was on her husband. All of the time.

Bill sat on the edge of the veranda just across from you, and balanced his glass on the extreme edge. It was a normal-sized tumbler full of a water-coloured fluid, no ice. He talked in a lively way to me and Jerry; I can't remember anything said by any of us, save that Bill was vivid, cutting and witty, a good match for Jerry's dry sardonic humour. Bill was also rather dishevelled, his hair standing up, his face a bit sweaty, his smile electric, his gestures sudden and sharp.

All of a sudden, your mother stared at the glass beside your father and said: 'What's that? You're doing it again?' She darted over as he grabbed at the glass. I can't remember which of them got it first — she was fast. 'You've got straight gin in there! That's not water!' she cried.

The next bits are blurred. I can't recall who did or said what, but she did get the glass and toss the contents on to the grass outside. Jerry and I were totally 'not there' as the scene took place. Then Bill went off to get a beer, or something like that, Kathleen slowed down and resumed conversation with me and Jerry, and you went on bombing the ship.

The thought ran through my mind: 'This is what they mean by "the white man's grave".' An ominous something ran through the three of you which my own spirit felt. This is not a later, calculated memory, for I asked Jerry about all of you on the way home that night.

My mother's close attention to my father that evening may have been due to the fact that he had already developed an obvious attraction to the new English teacher, and later sent what Jean herself called 'a fan letter', although nothing came of it. Nevertheless the situation she described was nothing unusual. Whatever we did, wherever we went as a family, there was nearly always a sense of tension and latent conflict. My father often gave the impression that he did not want to be with his family at all, and even when he was in a good mood there was always the possibility that he would suddenly explode, usually in public, that my mother or one of us would say something wrong, that he would lose his temper with a driver and get out of the car and start cursing them at the top of his voice in the local street slang, you *raasclaat* this, you *bloodclaat* that.

All this was extremely embarrassing, and very different to the way other people's fathers seemed to behave. At home he was often sullen and unapproachable, especially when he was drunk, a brooding, volcanic presence that set everybody else on edge. In those moods anything could provoke him, even when people were around. One afternoon, in Stony Hill, my parents were having friends to lunch and I had an argument with my brother and was sent to my room. Whatever we had argued about, I thought the expulsion was unfair. My room led off directly from the dining-room and I wrote 'Bruce is a dirty snake' on a piece of paper and silently pushed it under the door. This act of defiance caused laughter amongst the guests, but a moment later I heard the sound of footsteps coming across the wooden floor. Then suddenly the locked door flew open and my father charged into the room, swearing and lashing out with his fists.

This drastic disproportion between the offence and the response is one of the things I remember most about my father's dealings with us. He was never methodical enough to be called a strict parent, but he had no ability to control himself and could not tolerate the slightest contradiction or defiance of his wishes. Often, when we refused to eat our food, he simply emptied the bowl or plate over our heads. Bruce has only two clear memories of those years. One of them is an absurd, almost comical image of Christian looking around him in bemusement as a toddler, with a plate of runner beans pouring down his face. The other is of being hit by my father for being sick in bed during the night. On another occasion, I tried to get off school by rubbing hot pepper on my face to make it look like I had the flu. But the pepper burned so much that I was bawling with pain. My father dragged me outside to a sink and repeatedly forced my head under water till I finally chose to stop crying as the alternative to drowning.

These memories were all that was left of my father — fragmentary, sketchy incidents wedged like splinters in the mind, which I did not understand then and which nobody had been able to explain to me subsequently. The fact that most of these memories were little more than wordless images made them seem only more inexplicable. Over the years my mother had told me many stories about my father. Only two weeks before coming to the Caribbean, in a freezing Andalucian village near Granada, I had 'interviewed' her on tape in an attempt to put her memories into some kind of order. At night we had sat in front of a wood fire, drinking red wine, trawling through what she remembered, comparing my memories with hers.

Most of the stories I already knew, but there were details I had either forgotten or had never been told: how my father was obsessed with her blue eyes and would punch them regularly because he said she was 'committing adultery' with them; how the night before Christian's birth he had come back drunk and shouted that she was a 'fucking obscene cow' who would give birth to something 'as disgusting as yourself'. This tirade had gone on for about three hours before my father left, and could be heard across the campus. Once again there had been no intervention from anyone, not even the following day when the doctors were so worried by the state he had left my mother in that they were afraid the birth might have to be induced.

These stories raised as many questions as they answered. What caused such extraordinary cruelty? Why did no one try to stop him? Why had my parents stayed together for so long? And what made him finally throw us out? All these questions were flitting through my mind as the plane took off again for Barbados. In a way I had been asking them on and off for some time, but they had acquired a new urgency now that I had finally come back to the Caribbean. My attitude towards the past had gone through many metamorphoses over the years, from the early desire to put that blighted childhood and its emotions behind me to a gradual realization, as I grew older, that a part of my life had almost disappeared without my ever having understood what had really happened.

Now, nearly three decades later, the need to retrieve and understand the past had become something of an obsession. The more conscious I was of the blank spaces in my memory, the more I wondered what they contained, and the more inexplicable my few remaining memories seemed to be. I had always been vaguely aware that what I and my family remembered was only one perspective on my father, which was not universally shared. As the rejected eldest son, I had constructed an image of him that was mostly negative – the liar, the bully, the drunk who had rejected his own children. Yet I also knew that many of his relatives in Yorkshire had had great difficulty in accepting my mother's version of events in the West Indies, and some of them had refused to believe it at all. My cousin Pat remembered him from her own youth as humorous, an idealist, always reading books and full of advice on which books to read. My uncle on my mother's side also remembered him warmly, and I knew that there were friends of his from Jamaica who had hardly a bad word to say about him, even people who had known how he treated his own family. On the one or two occasions I had met Jerry Owens after he had returned to England he had spoken about his old colleague with fondness and amusement, and not even to have considered the possibility that his own family might regard him differently.

All this was puzzling, to say the least. What were the mysterious qualities that had enabled his friends and relatives to overlook or skip over certain aspects of his behaviour and personality whenever they remembered him, so that Jerry Owens could describe him to my mother as 'a charming man' as if there were nothing more to be said? As one of my father's closest friends and a bar-room companion, he would have been perfectly aware of what he was like at home, he would have seen my mother walking round in dark glasses, but somehow none of this seemed to figure in his final assessment. I resented such uncritical appreciation, which seemed to ignore or discount what had happened to what my father's own family had suffered, yet at the same time it was obvious that my image of the drunken bully in the mugshot photo was incomplete. What accounted for this extraordinary discrepancy between the way we remembered my father and the general esteem he clearly received from other people? Why had his own family apparently been singled out for such special treatment? These questions were impossible to answer without returning to the place where those distant events had occurred. So now, four years after his death, I had finally come back to the Caribbean to see how other people saw him, to compare my memories with theirs in order to reconstruct what I could of the man who had disappeared from our lives all those years ago.

I had brought with me the few letters of my father's to my family that still remained, a collection of articles that he had written in Cambridge University and Caribbean journals during the 50s and 60s and a handful of his poems. Besides my own and other people's memories, these documents were the only clues I had as – amidst the same atmosphere of confusion and ambiguity that had surrounded our mysterious expulsion from the Caribbean in 1967 – I tried to retrace my father's steps backwards from the point where they had ended in Guyana.

Had it not been for the mysterious circumstances of my father's death, I would probably not have come back to the Caribbean at all. Even after he returned to Guyana in 1987, I had a niggling suspicion that there was some hidden motive behind his sentimental journey that had not been explained, a fear that perhaps the whole thing was a kind of reconnaissance mission for a more permanent return, which would eventually drag some member of my family into having to look after him. As time passed, it now seemed that this suspicion had been unfounded. I presumed instead that he had satisfied his need to re-establish contact with his own past, and I did not expect to see him alive again.

A few months after he returned to Guyana, however, he wrote asking me if I could send a book on Derek Walcott and some pipe tobacco to the 'old man'. The request annoyed me. As far as I was concerned, my father had been treated much better in England than he deserved, but he was not, and never would be, 'the old man'. He had no right to ask me for anything. I wrote him an irritated letter saying that he could not expect me to do anything for him without some kind of real accounting for the past. The letter was not hostile and was not intended to be a final communication. It was the first time since his reappearance that I had referred directly to the father/son relationship that had once bound us together. The response was not positive. Soon afterwards, a short, unfriendly letter arrived from Guyana, about a paragraph long, which stated among other things that 'it is beneath my dignity to account for my past actions'.

That, it seemed, was that. Thus ended our briefly renewed correspondence. I had no intention of writing to him again. Such a man, I thought, was not worth bothering about. He wrote letters to all of us at the same time, but I was the only member of my family whom he asked for anything. A letter to my younger brother, in which he described himself as '*un homme vieux et audace*', was a little more forthcoming on the subject of the past, though not particularly enlightening:

> *That I struck your mother I do not deny. That I was in the habit of regularly beating her up I do not remember. Perhaps my memory is working conveniently for itself. Perhaps that is a role for memory that we all find hard to understand. I don't think I want to say much more about this. At least not now. Whatever I might say could have a variety of interpretations clustering around it. As a lawyer you know that. As a critic of literature – which means language alive – I know it too. You can discuss this with your mother and with all of the others. I am saying to them what I am saying to you. Compare and discuss it if you all should wish.*

He even wrote to my mother a short, rambling letter – written in an even more haphazard, wobbly script – in which he disclaimed responsibility for the attempt to annul their marriage. This letter also seemed to offer a kind of explanation of the past:

> *All I ever said was that something seemed to have drained out of our marriage and I blamed you for nothing. All responsibility I assumed myself. Many people have been cruel to me. I think I was never crueller to anyone than I was to you. Only to you. I have no glamour of myself. But I would like a kind of reawakening with you. Ships that pass in the night well-lit. Sailing ships guided by current and weather. Not by know-it-all engines. Our children are your major creation.*
> *Thank you, Bill*

Who had been cruel to him? What kind of reawakening was he looking for? The murky alcoholic currents of my father's mind seemed to conceal as much as they revealed. But the mixture of self-pity and self-glorification was echoed in the introduction to a series of poems written to all four of us:

> *Your silly, ageing father*
> *Writes you now*
> *Long unheard of. Doubtless not regarded.*
> *That's my style,*
> *Cavalier idiot, that I am.*

This 'doubtless not regarded' was irritating enough, with its suggestion that *we* had rejected *him*, but it was followed by a sequence of four poetic epistles, one for each of his four children, containing personalized philosophical advice. The poems seemed to me hollow, sentimental and totally inappropriate. There was so little connection between the poem and the person each one was intended for that it was as if my father had forgotten what we were really like and had conjured up a vague approximation based on his own past memories. The poems ended with another joint message:

> *All four must know that strength is hard.*
> *I falter. So will you.*
> *Yet to your mother give her courtesy.*
> *Not mine. Yours.*
> *Stand up that you may be seen*
> *And brace:*
> *Before the hands of the living God.*

It was difficult to read those poems and letters without feeling that my father's famous intellect had finally dissolved in the alcohol he had been drinking for so many years. Despite what he had said to my mother about having 'no glamour of myself', he seemed to be doing exactly that, using us all as little mirrors in which to reflect the fading glory of '*un homme vieux et audace*'. Why had he sent these poems? Was it intended as some kind of gesture of reconciliation or a belated expression of parental concern? His last will and testament? Did he really believe that a handful of poems with our names attached could provide some kind of philosophical validation for everything that had happened? Once again, the poems left me with the overwhelming impression of a man who was playing a role in some private drama, in which his long-lost children were less important than the drama itself.

All this was sad but harmless, as long as he was over there, and after the brief flurry of poems and letters the contact between my father and his family resumed its usual silence. But then, four years later, in the summer of 1991, a letter was sent to my cousin Pat and her husband, Keith, with the following astounding message:

> *I have submitted my retirement from UG after twenty-five years here. My intention is to come back to England mid to end July this year. I shall be what is known as a Professor Emeritus and still looking for work. I cannot just sit around doing nothing and have applied for work at the universities of York and Leeds. It's my part of the world even after thirty-one years out here. I'm waiting to hear but then universities are slow at this time and I felt it time to tell my important people in England what I have in mind . . . Marjorie will be with me or will soon join me . . . Kathleen will likely blench when she hears of this. Mais ne me fâche pas. I would not wish to put y'all to any inconvenience but if you should hear anything about houses, or if there is anything you might wish to advise me on, then please tell me, bearing in mind that my two stepchildren (twenty and seventeen) will subsequently join me. At the moment I cannot be more explicit – save briefly on literary matters.*

This was followed by a brief comparison between Patrick White and Henry James. The letter also said that he had written announcing his intentions to his aunt and uncle in Yorkshire, and to his 'important people in England' – a list from which my name and those of my two brothers were absent. The fact that he had had no contact with most of these 'important people' in nearly thirty years did not seem to have diminished his new-found affection for them, and the contemptuous reference to my mother suggested that he was far more aware of the past than he had seemed to be. Another letter also arrived in the early summer to Taryn, my thirteen-year-old niece:

> *My very dearest Taryn,*
> *Such a bore this typing. Especially when you are not a typist. And I should apologize. I do. I should also apologize for taking a while to reply, but I had to sort a few things out. I have now retired*

from the university and should return to England by the end of July.
For good. After all I have spent 25 years plus 6 years at the University
of the West Indies away from England. It is long enough . . . We
are all of us well enough, although local news is depressing. But
from me there should not be any wheezing or choking like last time.
Coming home in July. Gives me time to acclimatize. As soon as I
hear from Leeds etc. I will let you know . . .

These letters sent a tremor of alarm throughout my family. At the
time they were written, my cousin Pat's husband had recently died of
cancer. Her father had also died not long before and she was in no
state to look after my father – a possibility that seemed extremely
likely given the vague, unspecified plans outlined in his letter and his
own phone calls to her. As for his definition of himself as a 'Professor
Emeritus' – he might just as realistically have described himself as a
member of the House of Lords. The idea that someone in his physical
condition could find a job at an English university, when Humanities
departments were being cut back all over the country, was a pathetic
self-delusion, which further revealed how cut off he was from the
realities of contemporary England. The 'venerable old man' persona
from the poems had gone. This, it seemed, was the old Bill Carr,
blinkered, manipulative and utterly unconcerned with anybody's feelings but his own.

As disgusted as I was by the letters, they were, strictly speaking,
none of my business. Like everyone else I thought the plan to return
to England was disastrous, from his point of view and ours, but the
country did not belong to us, and he had not said explicitly that he
intended to stay with anyone in his family.

By the end of the summer he had still not come back, and it was
beginning to seem as if the whole episode had been a false alarm, but
the family melodrama now entered the realm of total derangement,
when he wrote to Taryn again, giving a date and time for the arrival
of his flight at Heathrow in October, and asking my sister to meet
him at the airport. There was no attempt to inquire whether this would
be convenient, nor any explanation of where he intended to go after
his arrival. The only news was that he would not be accompanied by
his wife and stepchildren until the following year, and he would not
be bringing anything with him except a suitcase full of books. It was,
in effect, a *fait accompli*.

The letter was accompanied by a photograph of my father sitting on a patio. He was bearded and wore a stern expression as he held up a copy of a book by Henry James like a flag of convenience. I knew that James had always been one of the most important authors in my father's life, and the photograph was perhaps intended as another of his mysterious signals, a clue to the role he was currently playing. Was it the last act in the drama of his life – the European man of letters, steeped in the classics, finally turning his back on the sordid political struggles in the tropics, to take his rightful place amid the universities and cathedrals of the old continent? Had his mind finally keeled off into complete insanity? And why on earth had he announced his return to his thirteen-year-old grandchild, whom he barely knew, instead of writing directly to my sister? Around the same time he called my cousin Pat and confirmed that he would be coming to England in a couple of months. She tried gently to dissuade him, pointing out that the prospects of work were not good, but he was determined to come back regardless of the consequences.

Once again the familiar guessing game began, but this time with more urgency than usual. The news that he was coming back not to Leeds but to Cambridge was greeted with horror. Anna, who was five months pregnant and suffering from clinical depression, was no more able to cope with him than my cousin would have been. Suddenly the awful prospect loomed that my father might end up staying at my mother's house, or at least that she would have to pay for his keep somewhere.

The idea that my mother would end up supporting my father's fantasy life infuriated me, but it was equally depressing to contemplate the alternative prospect of this sick, old man living a lonely, miserable life in a country that he no longer understood, purely on the basis of a sentimental vision of an England that no longer existed, if it ever had in the first place. Why did he want to leave Guyana at all? And why was his wife allowing him to behave in such a crazed and utterly selfish manner? Why had she not written to my sister herself to explain what was going on? The more I thought about his return, the more outraged and depressed I felt about it. The prospect became an obsession. In my worst imaginings I pictured him either sitting before the fireplace at my mother's house, chatting amiably with a drink in his hand while his former wife and children waited on him year after year; or living in a bedsitter in front of a gasfire somewhere, lonely, sick and isolated. Both fantasies seemed equally appalling. I was desperate to stop him coming, but he had no phone number in Guyana, he had now left the university and there was only a month or so before he was due to arrive.

And so I took the only available course of action. I wrote him a furious letter, telling him exactly what I thought of his decision and telling him not to come. The letter was intended to bring him to his senses before it was too late, and there was nothing remotely conciliatory about it. At the same time I sent a slightly more toned-down letter to his wife, pleading with her to stop him coming. Anna also wrote to them both as well, and we waited to see the result, without really believing that it would have any effect.

The date of my father's arrival came and went, without his making an appearance. There were no more phone calls from Guyana, nor was there any reply to the letters. It seemed that the strategy had worked, and we all assumed that the crisis was now over. Then, about five months later, in February 1992, a telegram was sent to Anna, which announced simply, 'Your dad's dead.'

Chapter Three

'A winter holiday in Barbados — most people only dream about doing this!' said the excited passenger behind me to his female companion, as the plane finally disgorged its exhausted cargo, at the neat, modern airport. A group of smiling schoolgirls in green uniforms chanted, 'Welcome to Barbados, we hope you will enjoy your stay,' as the line of passengers flowed sluggishly through the gates. The airport functioned with smooth efficiency, rapidly processing the hundreds of winter tourists so that ten minutes later I was in a taxi on my way to the nearby town of Worthing, along a brand-new modern highway. The countryside was mostly flat, dotted with little bungalows with verandas, some of them more like shacks, and all of them painted in bright Caribbean colours, pink, yellow and green. Here and there I could see small fields of sugar cane, goats grazing, a modern sports ground, a cricket game in progress next to a factory. As we drove past the neat wooden houses and small cultivated fields, I felt a nostalgia for the Caribbean that I had never expected to feel again, longing for what might have been if my parents' marriage had been different and we had stayed in the West Indies after all.

Everything from the quality of the light to the black faces all around me and the sight of the sea in the distance brought the memory of my childhood rushing back with an almost physical intensity. I had never really felt at home in England, and the nostalgia for the Caribbean grew stronger when I arrived at the pretty little guesthouse in Worthing where I had reserved a room.

Immediately in front of it stood a few blackened timbers, all that was left of another guesthouse that had burned down the previous month.

'Hope no one was hurt,' I said to the taxi-driver.

'Naah,' he drawled, unsympathetically, 'it needed refurbishin'.'

I laughed. All around there were palm trees and banana leaves and florid tropical vegetation, cacti and bougainvillaea tumbling over white wooden fences. I could hear the liquid whooping and trilling of exotic birds and the roaring sea less than a hundred yards away. After booking into my room I walked to the beach and there it was, the same incomparable white sand that I remembered from Jamaica, soft as talcum powder, the same heavy, sweet smell, the slow breaking of the waves against the reef a few hundred yards offshore. I went to a seaside bar filled with tourists and ordered a Banks beer to celebrate. It was Happy Hour, and all around me people were drinking cocktails and beers and pina coladas. The combination of jet lag and the strangeness of being back in the Caribbean after so many years made the whole experience seem dream-like and unreal, as though I'd somehow wandered into an advertising hoarding for Canadian Club or Martini, full of bright young things with perfect tans and immaculate white teeth.

Perhaps, I wondered, it wasn't really the Caribbean itself I felt nostalgic for, but that intensity of feeling and imaginative closeness to the world that had characterized my childhood, which had simply coincided with the place. Perhaps my father had felt the same about England and had wanted to turn the clock back, to jump over the missing years in some Jungian act of reconciliation with his own past, to go back to the point where everything had begun and his life was still ahead of him. Whatever his intentions had been, I had no doubt that my letter had stopped him, and now, here I was, coming in the opposite direction, stepping back into my own past, and his, for reasons I still did not entirely understand.

The news of my father's death had not in itself reawakened any desire to return to the Caribbean, and I might not have come back at all had the story not taken another strange twist. Anna wrote to his widow more than once asking for details about the funeral and how he had died, but received no reply. It was nearly two years before a friend visited Guyana and came back with the astonishing news that 'Bill Carr died of a broken heart because his kids didn't love him'.

This was too much. It seemed so unfair, so illogical, so contrary to the entire history of our relationship with my father, that I could not understand how anybody could even bring themselves to repeat it seriously. But someone in Guyana had obviously spread that rumour. Who was it? And why had they done it? Given my father's endless capacity for self-delusion, I would not have been surprised if he had wanted to play the role of King Lear, rejected by his children and forced out on to the Guyanese heath, but that someone else could have believed it – that was too much.

The rumour was obviously based on the letters my sister and I had sent telling him not to come to England. But my father's death was a death foretold at least two decades before. What had love got to do with it? How could he have managed to convince people that he had been rejected by us when we had lived most of our lives feeling rejected by him? And what explained his widow's curt telegram and subsequent refusal to reply to any of Anna's inquiries concerning our father's death? Was it to do with money? Were his new family afraid that we wanted to get our hands on his inheritance? Or was the silence an act of spite and revenge for having written the letters, which my father himself had imposed on his second family before he died? Perhaps the three letters my sister had written had simply got lost in the post?

There seemed to be no way of finding out without going to Guyana. Nor was it only a question of clearing up the murky circumstances of his death. Now that I had embarked on this quest, I wanted to try and answer all the other questions about my father that I had been carrying around for years. I wanted to find out what other people had thought of him and whether there was anything positive to be extracted from his life. And perhaps there was another reason why the rumour about his death had disturbed me, why it had continued to itch away at the back of my mind even though I could dismiss it objectively. *Suppose it was true?* Suppose he really had loved us? Suppose I had completely misread the purpose of his visit? Suppose I had never really understood him at all?

There were a lot of questions to answer, and, as I sat there drinking beer among the suntanned holidaymakers, I wasn't much looking forward to asking them. Once again I wondered whether the whole journey was not just a masochistic enterprise likely to create more problems than it solved and whether I would not have been better off at home with my girlfriend and my four-month-old baby than chasing my father's ghost across the Caribbean.

That night I made my first contact with my past in Guyana, when I took a taxi to Bridgetown to meet Kathleen Drayton. Appropriately enough, she had been the very last person to see us in Guyana. She had been among the group of women who had come to say goodbye at the airport and had actually come on to the plane with some farewell gifts for us, including an Amerindian spear which had later found its way into my youngest brother's nose during a fight with Bruce. A Trinidadian educationalist, she had worked in Guyana from the early 60s till the mid-70s. Her husband Harry was a Marxist economist, a close friend of my father's, and one of the academics who had helped to establish the University of Guyana in 1963. He had met us at the airport on our first night in Guyana, and the two of them had subsequently become closely involved in the gothic melodrama at the Carr household.

I hadn't seen either of them since then. I knew of Kathleen as 'a formidable woman', a Marxist and a feminist, and one of the few people in the West Indies who had actually challenged my father about his behaviour to his wife and kids. I had a vague memory of us taking refuge at their house on at least one occasion, and I knew that they had often tried to act as mediators between my parents. I knew also that the Draytons had been involved in the battle with the university authorities to stop my father being sacked after we left. The evidence to support my father's dismissal was none other than the report produced by the two psychiatrists who had visited our house shortly before our departure. As a result of its findings, the university authorities had asked my mother to stay for longer to act as a witness against her husband, with the aim of getting him sacked from the university, but she had refused. My father's defenders claimed that the university's use of the psychiatric report was spurious and that the real motive for his attempted dismissal was political – part of a campaign by the Burnham regime and the board of governors to root out political opposition within the university. In the event, the university lost its case, even though the Draytons themselves were later hustled out of Guyana as the PNC began to clamp down on dissidents.

This close involvement in the events of 1967 made Kathleen an important person to talk to. She was, in effect, the first non-family material witness I had spoken to since then, and perhaps the only one I was likely to find. Most of the people who had known us in Guyana had either died or emigrated years before, and I had no idea whether there was anyone left in the country at all from that period. I had felt anxious about this before coming, since I didn't know what kind of reception I was going to get in Guyana and I sensed that I might need some kind of objective confirmation of what I and my family remembered. Nor was it only for other people's benefit. I was also aware of the gaps in my own memory, and the ease with which family history can turn to mythology, with the imagination filling in the missing details to the point when one ends up actually re-inventing the past, and I wanted to test what I remembered against someone else's memories.

The taxi had trouble finding the address, but we finally pulled into a large, flat-roofed house built on the side of a hill overlooking Bridgetown. I recognized Kathleen immediately, even after so many years. She was a vigorous seventy, light-skinned, and limping slightly from an injured leg, with an initial impression of severity which soon disappeared as she greeted me warmly and asked me about my family. She was retired, but still active, writing freelance and lecturing in Barbados. Like virtually everyone in the West Indies I had tried to contact in the last few weeks, she was separated, and she told me that Harry was now working at the University of Texas. She lived alone in that large, modern house filled with books and carvings and photographs of her grown-up children. It was strange to see someone from that period after so many years, and I suppose she must have been equally surprised to see the ten-year-old boy whose family she had helped to rescue from a distant domestic disaster standing before her as an adult.

We sat there in that long rectangular sitting-room, with the music of a steel band drifting up from an open-air concert downtown, and she talked with her precise, careful speech about the early days of the University of Guyana, the lack of resources, funding and organization, and the first principal's predilection for unproofed white rum, which had made him fall off the plane on arriving in the country. My father had gone to Guyana to help establish the English department at the university and Kathleen had worked with him on a special committee to devise an English syllabus for Guyanese secondary schools. 'He was a charming and bright and very entertaining man, very good with words, liked to talk, and carried on long conversations till all hours of the night. What I remember is his colouring – reddish hair and blue eyes, and a striking sort of presence when he spoke to you. He was very dramatic. He held forth with his body as well as with words when he was making a point. He was not as big as you are, he must have been about five foot six at the most, and stocky, not very big, but a big voice, which certainly boomed through a room, or through a classroom, or a theatre when he performed.'

This big voice was something that I myself remembered, in somewhat different circumstances, but so far the portrait was generally favourable. For the first time, I realized, I was being presented with a portrait of my father from someone outside my family, whose intelligence and integrity were immediately obvious. Kathleen had known him at the same time I had known him as a child. She had seen him, as I had done, at his worst, yet she had clearly appreciated other aspects of his personality that enabled her now to recall him as something more than the bullying drunk I remembered. She talked about his passion, his humour and intelligence with a warm smile that was almost totally absent whenever anyone from his own family remembered him.

This favourable image was briefly disconcerting, but I quickly got used to it. What else was I expecting? Wasn't the gulf between my father's public and private personae one of the many contradictions about his life in the West Indies that I had come to resolve? That gulf had been wide enough while he was alive and it seemed logical that it should continue after his death. It was equally obvious that no understanding, of either my father or what had happened to us, would be possible unless I was prepared to make the imaginative leap and try to see him as other people had done. So I sat and listened, as more positive images emerged from Kathleen's recollections, most of which coincided with what other people had told me about him; my father the actor, the charismatic teacher, the passionate and brilliant literary critic, the idealistic socialist and fighter against oppression.

The portrait became less positive as it went on, and the smile frequently gave way to a frown. She also remembered him as a chronic alcoholic, burying bottles of rum in his back garden in Georgetown, or getting hospital cleaning staff to smuggle a bottle into his ward during one of his frequent hospitalizations for alcoholic poisoning. The image of my father burying rum bottles in his garden reminded me of the consul in *Under the Volcano*. The comparison seemed even more appropriate when Kathleen told me that in the early 70s he used to go to rum shops and pick political arguments with Burnham supporters. Usually he would get badly beaten up, and on one occasion even having a cigarette stubbed out in his face.

This was something I had not heard about before. In his letters my father had often casually referred to the physical attacks he had suffered as a result of his political activities, but this was the first time I realized that these occurred not in the political arena but in bars where the mere presence of a white man would have been enough to antagonize the clientele, let alone a loud-mouthed English professor drunkenly denouncing the Comrade Leader with a string of creole expletives. It reminded me once again of Malcolm Lowry's novel, of the last scene, when the delirious consul walks into a bar filled with Mexican fascists, the last rung on his descent into the earthly hell, and deliberately picks a fight to get himself killed in a suicidal act of self-immolation which is simultaneously a political gesture, providing Lowry's doomed alter-ego with a last glimpse of the possibility of human solidarity that has come too late to save him.

Kathleen also talked about what she called the 'black scenes' of our last two weeks in Guyana. She remembered getting calls from my mother in the middle of the night, and that she or Harry had come round to rescue us and take us back to their house while my father was raging. During one of these 'black scenes', she had come by late at night to find my mother and the four of us hiding behind the low wall in front of the house, while my father stood on the little veranda hurling plates at us and screaming abuse at the top of his voice. I had forgotten this episode completely, and the image of my father throwing plates at us cowering outside in the darkness seemed particularly nightmarish. It also confirmed my impression that his behaviour was so over-the-top, so unashamedly public, that no one who knew him could have been unaware of it. How, I asked her, had people in Guyana reacted to such incidents?

'People were shocked and nobody quite knew how to deal with it,' she said. 'You couldn't reason with your father. If you tried to reason with him about behaving in this fashion, out would come a spate of words that would drown you, because that was one of his gifts and abilities, this ability with words and with speech, and he would present a rationale, which was not reasonable really, a lot of the time, quoting from this or that writer.'

'What kind of rationale could he use for forcing his wife and kids to hide out in a ditch like that while he was throwing plates at them?'

She paused and looked thoughtful. 'I don't know if he actually tried to defend the behaviour, or if he just glossed it over. He never made any sense whatever about his relationship. He loved the children dearly, and I remember saying to him, "How can you love your children if you behave like this? How can you love them if you send them away?" And he was silent, he was' — again she paused — 'I sometimes wonder if he didn't have a streak of insanity.'

This possibility had often crossed my mind too, and everything that Kathleen was telling me seemed to confirm it. She remembered clearly the famous Sunday lecture that my father had insisted my mother attend, she had been there herself. She recalled that there had been 'a great closeness between him and your mother' in the week preceding the lecture, and that the lecture had been very well received. Afterwards, my father and some of his male friends had gone off drinking. The first sign she had that something was wrong was when my mother called at 10 o'clock that night asking if she knew where Bill was. She called around and eventually, in the early hours of the morning, found that he had been to visit the house where Sandra Williams lived with a couple of friends. Here he had done some more drinking. This much I already knew, but I listened to the tale with close attention now, wondering if, after twenty-nine years, I was finally going to find out what had been going through my father's mind that night.

'The very next day he came to visit us,' Kathleen went on, 'and said he'd told your mother that you all had to go home, it was finished and they had to leave, and there was absolutely no reason given for this.' She shook her head wonderingly. 'It was the most extraordinary thing. I cannot – I could not – understand how one action could follow the other.'

I asked if anyone had asked the reason.

'I asked him.'

'And what did he say?'

'He just could not give a reason. And then he just began to drink and drink, and I remember that we had serious concerns about your physical safety and we got your father out the house into my house, so I had this madness in my house, a man who paced up and down, who was drinking all the time, who did not sleep – this was the thing about him, he did not sleep, he just drank and talked, was not eating, and it was extremely exhausting.'

I told her my memory of him stroking a statue and playing *West Side Story*.

'I remember a scene when he was doing just that!' she exclaimed. 'I think there was something arranged for him to speak to your mother, and one or two of us to be there, to be a kind of mediating force to prevent any violence, and I remember something being acted out, when he was stroking his body. I can't remember the details because I tend to shut all this out of my mind, because it was too painful and uncomfortable and quite terrible at the time. I remember feeling quite devastated by all of this.'

I had also felt devastated by it, but my own attitude towards the past was different from Kathleen's. I could not be selective about what I chose to remember, and certain events – what Orwell once called 'unpleasant facts' – had a habit of reasserting themselves, as if to say: Account for me.

I remembered my father's cryptic message to my brother, 'It may be that my memory is working conveniently for itself. Perhaps that is a role for memory we find hard to understand.'

Had he also tried to shut these 'painful and uncomfortable' details from his mind in his twilight years? Had he ever remembered them at all? As I listened to Kathleen's account of those last two weeks in Guyana, I wondered if his motives were not as obscure to himself as they were to everyone else. We talked about his drinking, and the self-destructive streak that fuelled it. Once he had told her how he disliked his parents, how he felt that they had never given him any affection. He recalled his miserable Yorkshire upbringing, and living with an aunt who didn't care about him, 'who sort of suffered his presence'. Perhaps it was this experience of being unloved, Kathleen suggested, that caused the rage that characterized not only his personal relationships but also his intellectual pursuits. It was a plausible theory that I had heard before, but seemed almost too obvious. This bleak picture of a loveless Yorkshire childhood also conflicted with the romantic, idealized view of the North that my father had expressed during his visit in 1987.

'You have to make allowances for your father's dramatic memory,' said Kathleen, 'and his ability to dramatize everything that happened in his life. Maybe he romanticized it as well, but this facility with words – it created situations, it created things that may not always have existed, but he created them for himself – and for other people.'

This, I thought, was an important insight into my father's character. Kathleen seemed to be saying what I had often suspected – that he was a fantasist, who was able to invent his own past by telling stories that he – and other people – seemed to have believed. This was different from lying, although he had done his fair share of that too. Certainly it fitted the way I remembered him. Everything suggested a man who was in the process of continually re-inventing himself, trying out new roles and then discarding them. But why? And what accounted for the streak of masochism and self-destruction that lay behind this role-playing and his relentless pursuit of alcoholic oblivion that had dominated his life in the West Indies?

'I don't know if his coming to the Caribbean was a good thing,' said Kathleen, 'because alcohol is cheap and easily available, and the culture is one where people sit around and drink, and I think that helped the destructiveness. If you have any tendency to be addicted to anything, the Caribbean is not a good place. I don't know if your father's great promise and talents ever got reflected. I don't know what he wrote, because if you drink a lot then you don't really have time to do the research and do the writing, but I would have thought he had several articles and books in him.'

I told her about the articles he had written for the Cambridge magazines and the *Caribbean Quarterly*, and the various unrealized book projects that he used to mention in his letters. I also told her about the poems he had sent us and my low opinion of them. She nodded as if she were not surprised. The last time she had seen him, she said, had been in the late 70s and even then she thought his memory and sharpness had gone. He had come to Barbados with Marjorie, who had been in a state of 'great tension and exhaustion' from her attempts to control his drinking. She dismissed the talk of my father dying from a broken heart as nonsense, but she also saw it as the possible consequence of his playing the role of an 'inverted Lear'.

The conversation turned to the political situation in Guyana after we left. She said that my father's decision to join Cheddi Jagan's P P P had been a courageous and unusual step. Burnham would certainly have been aware of it, but she doubted whether he had ever really regarded my father as a serious enough threat to try to expel him, or worse. This interpretation of my father's political activity suggested that he was less important than he had portrayed himself in his letters. It was another contradiction to resolve, but I was exhausted and jetlagged and it was getting late. Finally I took a taxi back to Worthing at around 11 o'clock.

Saturday night was in full flow, the bars packed with tourists and locals, blaring soca and American rock music, but I was not in the mood for entertainment and I went straight back to the guesthouse, still turning the conversation over in my mind. I was surprised at how reassured I was by the fact that Kathleen's memories of what had happened in Guyana so closely matched my own – as though it were proof that the whole thing had not been some kind of freakish nightmare that my family had collectively dreamed up. The image of my father standing on the veranda throwing plates was something that none of us, not even my mother, had remembered. What accounted for such barking lunacy? The description of his fights in rum shop bars had revealed a new, unexpected dimension to my father's life in Guyana after we had left. That night I looked through his letters again. In one he apologized to me for not writing because of a broken hand. In a letter to my mother, dated July 1972, he wrote:

> *Nothing has changed here very much. A large PNC man whopped me over the face with a tyre lever. Six stitches in the forehead and one broken nose. Situation normal.*

There was also the following, written in February the following year:

> *I have suffered too and I have to live (sic) with the knowledge of what I have done and try not to do it again. Where the offence is let the great axe fall. It has — right on my fucking head.*

Previously I had considered the routine references at that time to illnesses and mysterious fights and beatings whose origin was never explained as a kind of strategy in the divorce proceedings to make my mother feel sorry for him, or an excuse for the letters and birthday presents that never came or else arrived months late. But I now saw these letters in a different light. Was it guilt about what he had done that had driven my father into this oblique masochistic pilgrimage? Had he been deliberately punishing himself and then reporting it back to us to let us know that he was paying the price, using a form of punishment that he had chosen himself? Or was there some other reason for his guilt that I was not aware of? As always, the more I found out, the more the questions seemed to multiply. I turned out the light, but the image of my father throwing plates and shouting inaudibly like a man underwater was still engraved on my mind, as if it were saying: Account for me. Other images overlapped — the consul's lonely death in *Under the Volcano*, glimpsing the possibility of a better kind of life before his bullet-ridden body is thrown into a ravine; my father staggering home from the ghetto with his face covered with blood; the broken old man reflected in the open doorway of the house in Brixton. Finally I fell asleep, with the sound of distant music echoing above the roar of the sea.

The next morning I flew to Guyana.

Chapter Four

All family history is a mixture of facts and legend, memory and gossip, and what I knew about my father's early life before he came to the Caribbean was no exception. He was born William Ian Carr in 1931, the son of a Harrogate solicitor's clerk and a sometime secretary. My grandparents' marriage was not a success. The couple separated when my father was five years old, whereupon his mother promptly sent him to the first of three boarding schools, where he was educated until he was eighteen.

For the rest of his life he rarely saw his father. His mother, Josephine, took little interest in him and, when he came home for the holidays, she virtually handed him over to the care of her two sisters, Annie and Edie. To his Yorkshire relatives he was always known as Ian, and I have always associated that name with a more innocent phase of his life. All his Yorkshire relatives had, and still have, nothing but good memories of 'Ian'. My cousin Pat, an adolescent girl in my father's teenage years, remembers him as charming and intellectual, with strongly held views on politics and literature. Aunts Annie and Edie are both dead now, but they were so devoted to the little boy they helped to raise that one of them refused to speak to my mother when we came back from the West Indies, accusing her of being the 'scarlet woman' who had corrupted 'Little Ian'. I met these two rather dotty old women some time in the 70s not long before they died, and they seemed to belong more to the nineteenth century than the twentieth. By this time they had finally managed to bring themselves to recognize my mother's existence, but their perception of her ex-husband was still firmly rooted in the days when Little Ian used to run around in short pants and they would give him a half-crown for his weekly pocket money.

The aunts' fond memories are virtually all that remain of my father's early childhood. But there is also a more disturbing story that he once came across a corpse of a tramp while playing in a park, although no one seems to know what effect that had on him.

The break-up of his parents' marriage ushered in a long, lonely period of his life that was to have a decisive influence on his future behaviour and personality. On the outbreak of World War II Josephine sent her son to a convent boarding school on the Welsh border, while she went to work in London as a secretary. The ostensible reason for sending him away once again was the possibility that Harrogate might be bombed by the Germans, but more likely she just wanted him off her hands. Whatever the reason, the school was so brutal that his mother's sister, a headmistress at a Scottish girls' school, felt obliged to rescue him herself after two years and install him at Heriots in Edinburgh.

Josephine meanwhile was enjoying 'a good war' on the home front as far as men were concerned, so that even when her son won a scholarship to Dulwich and in 1945 came to London, she took little interest in him. But my father's memories of Dulwich were among the happiest of his childhood. The school was at that time run by a Christian Socialist headmaster called C. H. Gilkes, whom my father always remembered fondly. He was poorer than many of the other boys, and once complained to my mother of the shame he felt when his uniform was sent back from the school laundry with a note saying that it could not be patched up any more. The school was one of the places he visited in 1987, and he reminisced about his time there with great warmth and nostalgia.

It was in the liberal atmosphere of Dulwich that his political and literary interests first began to make themselves evident. In 1950 he stood as a communist candidate in a mock-election at the school to coincide with the General Election. He also wrote articles on literature and politics for the school magazine *The Alleynian*. These articles – on Lawrence, Eliot and communism – reveal a serious, earnest mind, concerned with literature and its moral dimensions and already involved in the political and aesthetic debates of the time. Even at this stage in his life, there is a sense of a man already consumed by the stories he was reading, for whom literature offered both an alternative world and a means of enlarging the one he already lived in. A key influence on his thinking was D. H. Lawrence, whose maxim 'One must speak for life and growth, amid all this mass of destruction and disintegration' he quoted with approval in an article celebrating the writer's hatred of the 'machine-consciousness which inexorably ground out every vital human impulse'. More than any other writer, Lawrence's vision of life coincided with my father's in those years. He would later describe his first encounter as a kind of revelation:

> *I remember when I first read one of D. H. Lawrence's novels. I was sixteen at the time and sitting alone in a railway compartment. I had very seriously the sense that I was the object of Lawrence's intention in the writing of* Sons and Lovers. *My response to the book was hopeful, ardent and confused. But I seemed to understand that life would never present quite the same surface again.*

His ideas on literature, morality and society were also influenced by F. R. Leavis, the spiky, iconoclastic professor of English at Cambridge, and a great admirer of Lawrence. Leavis's moralistic conception of literature still dominated the English tripos, when in 1950 my father won a scholarship to Cambridge to study English; he chose Cambridge specifically because Leavis was teaching there.

Before going to university he went into the army to do his two years' national service, which he then voluntarily extended by two more years, ostensibly in order to 'deepen his knowledge of the working class'. Until then he had had little contact with the English working classes at all, and was painfully conscious of the gap between his bookish socialism and the outside world. But the army transformed 'Little Ian' into the more proletarian 'Bill', and it was in the army too that his rebelliousness and dislike of authority first manifested itself.

The subject of my father's army days fascinated me as a child, especially the last period of his national service, when he was sent to Malaya during the communist insurgency. I was too young then to appreciate the irony of his first introduction to the colonies as a humble squaddie defending the interests of British rubber companies, but I was impressed by the stories he told. Even though he wasn't involved in any fighting, he spoke about weapons with great assurance. One of his favourite stories, and mine, was how he was discharged for punching a high-ranking officer in Malaya.

My mother remembers the same episode in a somewhat less glorious light. According to her, my father was a member of a mortar squad, whose members were all working class. He was apparently so self-conscious about his public school background and so anxious to be considered one of the boys, that when his squad was sent off on a mission into the jungle without him he refused to accept his exclusion and walked off into the jungle to follow them, only to find himself thrown in the back of a truck and brought back to base, accused of disobeying orders. Whatever the exact circumstances, some fight or altercation with a senior officer must have occurred, because he was stripped of his sergeant's stripes and thrown out of the army before his period of service had expired, although his status as a future Cambridge man saved him from a court-martial or dishonourable discharge.

His experience of national service, his first-hand contact with the working class, and his minor role in one of Britain's last colonial wars consolidated his drift to the left. On arriving at Cambridge in 1953, he quickly became involved in student left-wing intellectual circles and was briefly a member of the Communist Party, although his political activity was restricted to mostly student debates and writing articles for left-wing university publications.

Apart from politics my father's main interest at Cambridge, and his reason for being there in the first place, was literature. Although he did not go to F. R. Leavis's college, he remained one of his disciples, and often attended his lectures. He also developed what was to become a lifelong admiration for Matthew Arnold, whose work became the subject of his Ph.D. thesis. He also wrote book and film reviews for university literary magazines, as well as a handful of short stories. One of these was based on his experiences in Malaya and was published in an anthology of Oxford and Cambridge writing. A London publishing company was so impressed that they wrote asking to see any novels he might write in the future, an offer that he never took up.

It was at Cambridge that my father met Kathleen Curtin, my mother. Before coming to university he had lived most of his life in mostly male institutions, and he had never had a regular girlfriend. Whether he had any sexual experiences in the army is not known, although there were rumours among his Yorkshire relatives about a relationship in Malaya, and there were fears that he might come home 'with a brown girl on his arm', a prospect, my cousin remembers, that would have caused 'mayhem' in Harrogate.

In general, his closest friends had all been men and the pattern of male camaraderie begun at boarding school seems initially to have continued after he went up to university. At that time there were few female students at Cambridge and those who were there seem to have been regarded with some condescension by my father and his intellectual friends. None of this is particularly surprising in view of the covert misogyny that informs so much of the dominant literature of the fifties, alongside the anti-establishment posturing of the 'angry young men'. Even though my father dismisses John Osborne as 'not as good as we thought he was' in one of his university articles, his own behaviour at Cambridge later earned him the reputation among his friends as 'the original angry young man', and I have often thought that his life in the West Indies might have made a logical sequel to *Look Back in Anger*.

Certainly his first meeting with my mother was vintage Jimmy Porter. At the time she met my father, she was twenty-one years old and was training to become a solicitor. Unlike my father, she came from a working-class background and had no connection with the university. Before moving to Cambridge, she had spent a bleak childhood on a farm near the city, and on one of the disused R A F bases that the government had converted into temporary housing after the war. She was shy and insecure, a former convent girl from a repressive and emotionally barren family background, which she has often described as a bleaker version of *Cold Comfort Farm*.

Yet her youth before she met my father has often seemed to me an innocent, carefree period, especially in comparison with what came later. She liked cricket and often went to the Fenners ground by herself to collect the autographs of touring teams. She was fond of dancing, and used to go up to the 100 Club in London to dance to New Orleans jazz, especially Sidney Bechet. She once hitch-hiked to France, an unusual thing to do for someone of her background. A youthful photograph shows her smiling with a rucksack on her back, surrounded by male friends, 'hopeful, ardent and confused', like my father – a young woman on the brink of her life, who had still not found out who she really was or what she wanted. At that time she was very much under her family's influence, and to a large extent her decision to go into the law was the result of parental pressure. But she also showed signs of independence and a desire for a different kind of life to the one that was opening up before her.

It was this desire for 'something different' that initially attracted her to my father. The way she describes it, she was invited round for tea at Pembroke one afternoon by a male student friend of hers. When they got to his room, my father appeared and suggested that they have tea in his room instead, since it was bigger and more comfortable.

Other people came in and they began talking and making tea and crumpets. That day my mother was not looking her best. She had just had a front tooth removed, so that there was a gap between her teeth. She was covered in ghostly white makeup and wearing a rather sexless Hepworth's suit that her parents had her buy. She was sitting in front of the fireplace when suddenly my father began insulting and abusing her. Everyone was surprised since they had never met before, but, as usual, no one took him to task and for the rest of the afternoon he stood glowering in the corner, hardly taking part in the conversation except to insult her.

A few days later my mother learned that my father had been making a scene in his college, walking up and down outside his room shouting that she was a 'fucking whore'. When my father's friends asked him why he was behaving in this unusual manner, he told them that he had fallen in love with her. Shortly afterwards one of them asked her to come back to Pembroke, 'as a favour to Bill'. My mother agreed, more out of curiosity than anything else. They went to the cinema, and afterwards he read to her from Swift, in a voice that 'really made him come alive'.

Thus began my parents' courtship. Despite its rather unpromising beginning, it is not difficult to understand what the attraction must have been for my mother. My father was good-looking, intelligent and fiery. He was also, in her words, 'weird', and the dramatic effect she seemed to have on him must have been flattering. But what accounted for my father's strange exhibition of aggression/attraction? Did he really fall passionately in love at first glance with the shy young woman making crumpets in front of the fire? Or was he merely acting out the role of the tortured angry young man? On the surface he and my mother were quite different, although neither of them could have known how different at the time. Temperamentally he was explosive, declamatory and rather self-consciously rough-hewn. My mother by contrast was quiet, more subdued and far less sure of her ideas. Both, in their different ways, were unformed and incomplete, starved of affection in their respective childhoods, and humiliated in their Catholic schools. Whereas my mother had inherited from her own arid childhood a deep-seated insecurity and lack of confidence, my father had carried with him a furious anger that had not even begun to reach its peak when they met and had yet to be subjected to the trials of an adult relationship.

It was not, as it turned out, a healthy combination. My father once told my mother that there was something in her that he could bring out. In a way he was right, but it was not the way he intended or that anyone could have wished. From the early days in the relationship there were tensions between them. My father's views on the conflicts in their relationship are not known, but my mother remembers that he was often jealous and competitive towards her, and that he would exclude her from his intellectual conversations with his male friends.

One area where these conflicts seem to have surfaced, was the dance floor. In those days my father did not know how to dance properly, and my mother did. Once they went to a local jazz dance, and my father threw a pint glass of beer on the floor and stormed out of the hall when he saw her dancing with someone else. Another time they went to a May ball together and he accidentally stood on her dress and tore it on the dance floor. Afterwards they quarrelled, and came back alone in a punt. My mother sat miserably in her torn dress like a disappointed Cinderella, while my father gloomily manoeuvred the boat.

Years later, in Jamaica, they did learn to dance together, so well that at one party at Stony Hill the guests said that they were the best couple there. Once my mother was dancing round the bedroom by herself, in a rare carefree moment, when my father gave her the brooding angry look that usually preceded an explosion. Expecting the worst, she asked what was the matter, and he said quietly, 'I just saw a spark in you of something that I've snuffed out.'

The year after their first meeting my parents got married at St Gregory's Church in Wandsworth. The wedding took place in May – the same month that my father eventually broke up the marriage in Guyana – and the day is still preserved in an album of black-and-white photographs. The whole idea of the wedding photograph, with the beaming bride and bridegroom, the proud parents, the supporting cast of relatives and close friends, is to commemorate and preserve for posterity the beginning of a lifetime's mutual bliss, and to provide a historical family artefact to be produced and fondly remembered on family occasions as the years pass, and children and grandchildren spring up. In the aftermath of any failed marriage, these photographs often take on an entirely new significance, in which everything – the white dress, the suits, the face-splitting smiles, the bridesmaids with their bouquets

– becomes a bitter reminder of the gulf between the illusion the participants are so intent on creating and the subsequent reality.

Looking at my parents' photographs, it is difficult to avoid the feeling that neither of them – even in the moment of trying to create the illusion – entirely believed in it themselves. Nor, on the evidence of the photographs, were they the only ones. In one the photographer seems to have inadvertently achieved a most un-wedding-like effect, precisely at the most solemn moment of the ceremony. At the moment the ring was put on my mother's hand she can be seen staring at it doubtfully with a fearful, mesmerized expression, as though she were staring at a striking snake. My father looks equally disturbed by the whole process. But the strangest aspect of the photograph is the people kneeling down behind the bride and groom. One guest has his head buried in his hands, the best man has his head bowed, resting on his left hand. All of them, even the little bridesmaid, look equally solemn and miserable. It looks more like a funeral than a wedding.

The other photographs are more standard. In one my mother and father are holding hands and smiling at the camera. She looks vulnerable, pretty and extremely dubious about the proceedings, dressed up like a sacrificial offering in a lace dress that reaches just below her knees, with white gloves and a veil, and holding a small bunch of flowers. My father is more relaxed, smiling amiably in a rather cheap-looking 50s suit with a carnation in his lapel. His tie is crooked, his hair cut extremely short and combed back with a parting on the right and a slight cowslick, his right arm held rigidly by his side. In another picture, my parents are standing by the bridal car, an old-fashioned black limo. My father, still smiling amiably, is holding my mother's arm, while she frowns back at the camera with an almost accusing expression.

There are also photographs of my parents with other family members. As is often the case at weddings, the battery of smiles conceal a host of tensions, conflicts and internal conspiracies, all wilfully suppressed for the occasion in order to help preserve the illusion. At the time they were married, my mother was already four months pregnant with me. The pregnancy took my parents by surprise, and neither of them were sure that they wanted to go through with it.

One person who definitely did not want to go through with it was my father's mother. Josephine had not been keen on my mother from the start. Having placed her only child on the back burner for most of his life, she now hoped that his entry to Cambridge would convert him into a 'gentleman' and open the door for her to a new elevated social world of dons and Cambridge professors; she regarded my mother as a step down. No stranger to unwanted pregnancies herself, she recommended that she have an abortion, which was then illegal. This option was considered, since neither of my parents felt sure enough about their relationship, but my maternal grandfather intervened and threatened to tell the police if they went through with it.

In the face of this family pressure, my parents overcame their mutual doubts about each other and decided to make a go of it – especially my father, who was much more eager to get married than my mother was. Perhaps it was my grandfather's role in the decision that explains why he looks so happy and pleased with himself in all the photographs. Josephine, on the other hand, was able to manage only a rather sour, tight-lipped approximation of a smile at the marriage that she had been unable to prevent, but which she had still tried to control with characteristic hypocrisy, insisting that my mother wear a pink dress, since, she reminded her, a white one was not appropriate.

Whatever doubts and reservations the participants may have had, it is doubtful that anyone that day, least of all my parents themselves, could have imagined the brutal breakdown of the marriage twelve years later in a remote former British colony on the other side of the world. After the wedding they continued to live in Cambridge, in a house in Jordans Yard, where they were known to their friends as B & K, after Bulganin and Khrushchev. My father finished his degree and began to prepare his Ph.D. thesis on Matthew Arnold, while my mother took her law finals and had two more children. They had an active social life, mostly connected with the university. My father's generation at Cambridge included many famous names of the future – Simon Gray, Jonathan Gaithorne-Hardy, Margaret Drabble, Ted Hughes and Sylvia Plath – some of whom they knew or came into contact with at student parties, where my father tended to drink too much and often became abusive to my mother or to other people. But despite this predilection for alcohol, the riotous disorder of his life in the West Indies was not yet in evidence. My parents lived quietly at Cambridge, and their social activity consisted mainly of long intellectual debates in friends' houses.

At that time they had no plans to work abroad. My father continued to write articles and the occasional short story, including one called 'A Golden Opportunity', which was based on his relationship with my mother. He also wrote some ninety pages of a novel, which he subsequently tore up in a rage, thus beginning a pattern of unfinished book projects that was to last throughout his life. Besides these sporadic incursions into fiction, he had also developed a clear vocation as a teacher. Like most research students he gave supervisions to undergraduates, who included the unlikely figure of John Selwyn Gummer and a former Dulwich schoolmate called Tony Scull, who sent me this sketch of his former friend and supervisor.

> *I recall a slight, pale chap, not very tall, casually dressed with open-neck shirt, fairly quiet in demeanour and with a slightly sardonic, amused expression . . . If I'd been asked to sum up my memory of Bill, I would have described him as a rational, slightly puritanical guy with a sense of duty and of morality both personal and public – someone who would have regarded wife-beating and habitual drunkenness as infantile and anti-social.*

Even though university posts in English were few and far between, my father might well have continued to work in England had he not failed to get his Ph.D. The exact reason why his thesis was not accepted is unknown, although he would later say that Leavis was sick the day that he presented it, thus leaving him without a sympathetic ear among the examiners. All my mother can remember is that the thesis was considered too critical and opinionated by the examiners, and that my father had earlier refused to modify it even though he had been warned by his tutor that it would be unlikely to be accepted as it was. His failure to get his Ph.D. made him extremely bitter and was a decisive reason for his deciding to leave England. In an article he wrote at the time, entitled 'On Being a Research Student', he described his four years of research as a sterile period of intellectual servitude and wasted effort:

> *I wonder if I shall ever enter the Library without a feeling of guilty depression, without a sense of having been let in simply because I'd come, and without feeling a charlatan of grotesque magnitude. The very books should have clapped themselves to and trapped my fingers. I'm sure I shall never drink scorched coffee without a tremor, or forget the Library's cheese, always on the extreme verge of sour middle*

age, or forget the silent corps of shelves straddling my ignorance . . .
In trying to understand what was the matter I have first to look at
myself. I never had any confidence in myself or my work, and I had
almost always the feeling of acrid frustration. My life seemed to
glide off on its own while I grappled with my wretched apparatus of
notes, quotations and simulacrum of a filing system. I was, of course,
perhaps not cut out for it: then how sorry I have to feel for those who
are.

Much of the article is a sarcastic condemnation of the university system
itself, with its insistence on academic research rather than a vocation
to teach as a prerequisite to a university chair. The tone alternates
between bitterness and pride:

Where my academic life is concerned, most of my best memories are
connected with supervisions. There have been moments that one does
not forget; the effort to find oneself, the effort to help someone else
discover what he really feels, the sense that one has perhaps helped
to put something into a life that would be the worse without it. They
may seem like small matters to those with larger ambitions, but in
a subject like English, and at our age in particular, they are about
as much as one has a right to hope for.

Whether he really felt as indifferent to the Ph.D. as the article
suggests, his chances of finding a job teaching at an English university
were extremely limited without one, and he began to look overseas.
After sixteen rejections, he was offered a job at the University of
Singapore and another at the University of the West Indies in Jamaica.
My parents did consider the possibility of returning to my father's
stamping ground in the Far East, but the offer of a full lectureship
tilted the balance in favour of Jamaica. Even then there was a hitch:
my father had to be vetted as a result of his brief membership of the
Communist Party.

Shortly before they left, my mother remembers a friend saying,
'Ah, the West Indies – that's where everyone runs off with everyone
else's wives.' Things were not going well between my parents at the
time, but the remark offended my father's puritanical instincts, and he
snapped back that nothing like that was going to happen to *him*. After
some delay while my father was being cleared of being a communist
agitator by the Jamaican authorities, we finally flew to the West Indies

in the summer of 1960. Tony Scull never saw my father again after his departure for the Caribbean. The only news he ever received of him came in a letter from a mutual friend who visited my father in Jamaica in the mid-60s:

> *Bill Carr was asking about you but I was unable to give him any up-to-date news. May I say in confidence that the reason you will not have heard from him is that he has been having rather an unsettled time domestically and has been very much tied up in his own affairs . . .*

Chapter Five

The view of Guyana from the air was an awesome sight. As the twin-propeller plane rounded Trinidad and approached the coast, I could see little tufts of clouds reflected like islands beneath the emerald surface of the ocean down below. Nearing the South American mainland, the ocean blended into the familiar beige strip where the mud and effluvia from Guyana's great rivers pour out into the Atlantic and form a muddy slick the length of the coast. Running parallel to the coastline, a single straight road connects the sparse little settlements and clusters of white houses belonging to the villages and plantations.

Immediately behind this single highway, the land is cut into neat rectangular strips, before giving way to yellow scrubland and the dark green of the rainforest that constitutes much of the country's land surface. As the plane descended, I could see rivers and canals, patches of marshland adjoining the jungle, and occasional clearings in the rainforest cluttered with felled trees and tree trunks. Suddenly the mighty Essequibo river came into view directly below, a huge expanse of brown muddy water winding its way out of the interior, before forking out in two narrower channels round a cluster of islands as it neared the sea.

Virtually the entire population of Guyana is concentrated into this narrow coastal strip, some forty miles in length. Behind it lie some 83,000 square miles of dense rainforest and bleak open savannah, much of it uninhabitable and unpenetrated by anyone except mining and logging companies. It is this tiny strip of swampy land, dissected by rivers, wedged in between the sea and the jungle, that constitutes the real heart of Guyana. The land was originally drained in the seventeenth century by Dutch settlers, who brought with them the engineering methods and techniques and patient application learned during their own country's long struggle with the sea. Today, three centuries later, Guyana's existence still depends on the constant maintenance of the sea wall and the drainage system whose foundations they built. Without it, the solid ground on which these towns and villages and plantations had been built would swiftly turn to mush, leaving nothing but porous, uninhabitable swampland and a few roads jutting out into the jungle, connecting abandoned towns.

The myth of the flood, of civilizations vanishing beneath the sea, has entered the realm of material possibility for many countries in recent years, but for Guyana it has always been a constant threat, requiring a prodigious investment of manpower and money to keep it at bay. At the height of the Burnham era, when hundreds of Guyanese were fleeing the country into exile every week, and the population was reduced by some 40 per cent, the bizarre possibility loomed that there would be more Guyanese living outside the country than there were inside it, and that there would be no one left to maintain the sea defences. Burnham himself seems to have regarded this outcome with equanimity. 'We will survive,' he once coolly told a *New York Times* reporter, 'and even if we all perish, since we are only about one million people, we wouldn't create a public nuisance.'

Now, as the plane approached the airport that I had last seen on that desolate afternoon in May 1967, I felt a flash of paranoia at the thought of what awaited me down below, in that strange, inconceivable country that had come close to erasing itself from the map. I got off the plane and walked with the handful of passengers across the tarmac to the little airport terminal, a newish concrete building with a brightly painted mural proclaiming *Welcome to Guyana*. Apart from the terminal, the airport looked pretty much as I remembered it, with the same narrow landing strip surrounded by jungle and the same sense of primitive isolation.

It could not have been more different from the laidback, tourist-driven prosperity of Barbados, with its modern roads and international airport brimming over with tourists. Guyana seemed empty, almost deserted: there were hardly any visitors either leaving or arriving. The contrast was even more dramatic on leaving the airport. Georgetown was some twenty miles away, and the only way to get there was in a dilapidated taxi that looked as though it was shortly due for the scrapheap. The single road leading to the capital was in disastrous condition, pock-marked with huge potholes and worn away at the edges by rain and floodwater. As the rickety old vehicle bumped its way along the atrocious surface, the driver talked about cricket, analysing the recent West Indies defeat in the World Cup semi-final as though recounting a national tragedy. From time to time he fiddled desperately with his radio in an attempt to pick up the World Cup final, but the stricken machine continued to emit a relentless hail of static on all stations.

Soon we came alongside the Demerara, another of Guyana's many wide rivers, its muddy, choppy waters lapping up only a few yards from the road. The occasional wooden steamboat chugged by and a group of East Indian families were getting into canoes by a little jetty for what looked like a Sunday outing. In the rainy season, the driver said, the floodwaters from the Demerara made the road impassable in places, effectively cutting off the capital from the airport. There were, he said, plans to widen the road, and even to build a new hydro-electric plant to put an end to the constant blackouts that continued to plague the capital.

From the physical evidence of decay and economic stagnation, it seemed unlikely that either of these projects would be realized in a hurry. All along the road there were heaps of rusted, corroding industrial machinery, wrecked cars and piles of refuse which had been disgorged by the river or simply dumped by the roadside. *AIDS. It could be your last laugh*, warned a curious roadside sign promoting the use of condoms. Everywhere I saw the same white wooden shacks and houses that I remembered, built on stilts in the Guyanese style, all of them looking equally shabby and rundown. Everything testified to the same drab poverty and neglect – from the mean wooden houses that lined the road, to the sad-looking shops, the cheap clothes of the mostly black population, and the occasional roadside market stalls with their meagre offerings of fruit and vegetables.

There were certainly more glamorous and prestigious locations for an academic to have chosen to spend more than half his working life. As I thought of those distant symposiums on 'Socialism and Literature' over which my father had presided at the Cambridge University Socialist Club, the intellectual debates over tea and crumpets in his Pembroke rooms, and the articles he had written about bringing literature to the widest possible audience, I could not help feeling a kind of admiration for him, for having come here, to this impoverished ex-colony, which the legacy of the sugar planters and three decades of Burnhamite corruption and mismanagement had brought to the brink of total collapse, in order to 'spread sweetness and light' and 'learn and propagate the best that is thought and known in the world', as his mentor Matthew Arnold had called on critics and intellectuals to do. Here at least, it seemed, there was something in him to be proud of, and in spite of our mutual past, I was.

Even though I had read about Guyana's catastrophic decline in books and newspaper articles, it was another thing to see the physical evidence of stagnation and involution with my own eyes. Nothing, it seemed, had changed in my twenty-nine-year absence, except for the worse. Nothing new seemed to have been built, except for the occasional mosque. Alongside the Hindu temples and Anglican churches, the presence of Islam testified to the eclectic civilization conjured out of the South American jungle by colonialism, an unlikely melting pot of faiths and races, made up from the descendants of Indian indentured labourers, African slaves, Portuguese and Chinese traders and indigenous Amerindians from the interior.

The taxi-driver was Afro-Guyanese, with a single African name on his ID tag which suggested that he had probably changed it himself, like many Guyanese and West Indians of his generation, in a rejection of the name he inherited from slavery. He was as knowledgeable and articulate about Guyanese politics as he was about cricket, and I asked him what he thought of the Indian president Cheddi Jagan. Cheddi, he said, was 'doing something for the small man'. It was not as much as Burnham, who had done a lot for the 'small man', but it was certainly more than Burnham's PNC successor Desmond Hoyt, who had done nothing at all for the 'small man'.

Such behaviour didn't seem very different from that of Burnham himself, who had become one of the richest black men in the world during his years in power. 'Making the small man a big man' was one of the many pseudo-socialist slogans and catchphrases invented by Burnham to placate the population while he and others eagerly enriched themselves. The taxi-driver had taken the rhetoric at face value even though he could not think of a single material benefit that the Comrade Leader had brought to the 'small man' and admitted that he had wrecked the country. Was this an example of racial loyalty to the leader who had made a public virtue out of 'standing up to the white man', no matter what his own regime did to the country, or was it a polite reluctance to speak badly of the dead? Perhaps, I wondered, the taxi-driver simply accepted what Burnham said and rejected what he did without seeing any contradiction between the word and the deed.

We were still debating Burnham's legacy as we approached central Georgetown. After all the articles I had read about the anarchic crime rates in the capital and the 'choke and rob' gangs roaming the streets that made it dangerous to walk around even in the daytime, I was surprised at how calm and sedate the city seemed as we drove into the administrative heart of the old colonial town. It was Sunday afternoon, and the streets were mostly deserted. We drove past the High Court, a long, rectangular wooden building with a sloping red roof. On the lawn in front stood a statue of Queen Victoria, her nose partly eaten away. In recent years, the driver said, the rain often poured in through the roof and drenched the magistrates, a predicament he thought extremely amusing.

The city centre was more or less how I remembered it, but I had forgotten how beautiful Georgetown was, with its colonial architecture, its white picket fences and wooden buildings topped with red tin roofs. The streets were flanked by a network of canals, storm drains and grass verges, with coconut palms and wild green vegetation sprouting up everywhere out of the prevailing whiteness. I saw the Anglican cathedral, a huge blue and white fantasy of a building, studded with dozens of windows and Arab-style wooden pillars and topped by an elegant spire that made it one of the highest wooden buildings in the world. I also recognized the familiar clocktower above Stabroek Market, patterned with ornate red woodwork, where my mother used to shop for fruit and vegetables, and would sometimes come across Burnham himself, still in the incipient stages of his megalomania, riding out amongst his subjects on a great white horse.

Apart from a few stallholders clustered round the entrance, there was no sign of any activity from within. Georgetown had sunken in its afternoon sleep; there were only a few cars and bicycles on the streets, and isolated groups of people talking quietly in the shade of wooden awnings. Finally we arrived at the Tower Hotel, a plain concrete building on Main Street, with an open-air swimming pool at the back, where various Guyanese families and their children were having a Sunday afternoon swim. By the pool was a bar, decorated pseudo-jungle style, with a raffia roof and dozens of giant pot plants. A steel band was plunking out the melody of 'Those Were the Days' to a single table of foreigners who appeared to be the only guests.

Apart from the local families round the pool, the hotel was empty and deserted, like Guyana itself. It was pleasant and comfortable enough, however, and I went downstairs to have a beer and decide what to do next. As I listened to the children laughing and splashing in the water, I felt suddenly tense and nervous. Until then I had been merely following the steps of the journey, letting myself be carried from one form of transport to another, without any real idea of what was going to happen when I arrived.

Now the journey was over, and I was in my father's territory. Apart from an interview that I had managed to arrange with Cheddi Jagan, I had only a handful of names and addresses of people in Guyana, and I had no idea how many of them were even in the country. I had planned to wait till the following morning before beginning the search, but the more I thought about the possibilities that awaited me outside in the city the less I felt like sitting around the hotel trying to imagine what was going to happen. So I decided to begin that day in what seemed the logical place: my father's old house in Campbellville.

Everything I had heard about Georgetown suggested that it was unwise to walk the streets or even take a taxi at night; and a notice in the hotel lobby advising guests not to go out on the street after six o'clock seemed to confirm the capital's sinister reputation. It was late afternoon by the time I left the hotel, and the sun had already disappeared below the horizon, but I was resolved to get to Campbellville somehow, so I asked a taxi-driver to take me to there. The streets didn't look particularly threatening, as we drove along Brickdam and up Sheriff Avenue, where I had once been knocked off my bike on my way to school. The coolness and the fading light had brought more people out of their houses, and the city looked surprisingly sedate and peaceful, with no obvious signs of predatory street life or advanced social disintegration.

I was not looking forward to this visit, which was why I was determined to get it over with as soon as possible. Two months before I had written to my father's widow, telling her that I was coming to Guyana, but this latest letter had met with the same silence that greeted my sister's previous attempts to find out more about my father's death. I was not sure if Marjorie was even in the city, but I knew that she had got the letter, since I had called the school where she used to work only a few days before and they had confirmed that they had passed it on to her. It was difficult not to interpret her refusal to reply, and the curt, tight-lipped telegram that had announced my father's death in the first place, as an expression of hostility and anger, but the lack of direct contact with any member of my father's new family made it impossible to be absolutely certain.

In my letter, I suggested three possible reasons for why she had not replied to my sister's letters: she was angry about the original letters in which my sister and I had asked my father not to come to England; or she was afraid we were after whatever money he might have left; or finally she had never got any of the letters my sister had sent in the first place. Of the three possibilities I knew that the first was the most likely. I could not believe she had not received any of my sister's letters. I also doubted whether my father had had much money to leave, and there was no reason in any case to think that we wanted any of it. And so I had reiterated to her the circumstances in which my original letters to her and my father had been written, as an explanation, rather than an apology, since I didn't see that I had anything to apologize for.

Now, as we left Sheriff Avenue and came into Stone Avenue, where my father had lived, I wished I could have spoken to some member of his family by phone in order to get an idea of the reception I could expect. There was a certain irony, I thought, in the fact that it was my father's lack of a telephone that had provoked the flurry of angry letters in the first place. Had we been able to talk to him or Marjorie, it might have been possible to explain the situation and make him listen to reason. Standing in Stone Avenue, however, it was not difficult to understand why his house was not on the phone. The road looked as though it had been bombed. Wild vegetation had sprouted carelessly over the crumbling edges and enormous potholes that forced the taxi to crawl slowly along. Not surprisingly, there were no other vehicles, and the street was quite lively, with children playing and groups of adults standing around talking outside their darkened houses.

The address I had been given turned out to be a small run-down wooden house divided into rooms and flats. No one there had heard of a white man called Bill Carr who had taught at the university. From the curious stares that my presence was attracting, I doubted whether there had been a white man in the neighbourhood for some time. The taxi-driver asked around, and it turned out that there was some confusion between the lot numbers and the house numbers. As we drove on up Stone Avenue, negotiating the potholes at the same snail's pace, the houses began to improve in quality and size. By now I was beginning to wonder if the address I had been given actually existed, when a neighbour finally directed us to a two-storey concrete house on the corner. Compared with the rest of the neighbourhood, it was a big, comfortable-looking house; there was a large garden and a patio at the back, with a row of shelves with bottles and flowers on them. Immediately I recognized the patio from the Henry James picture and I knew that I had found my father's house at last.

The moment of truth had arrived. A little girl was standing by the metal gate and I asked her if Marjorie Carr lived there. She nodded and went inside. A moment later I heard voices from inside the house, and my uneasiness increased when no one came out. Finally Marjorie appeared in the doorway, looking grim and distinctly unwelcoming. 'Hello, Matthew,' she said quietly in a tired, resigned voice. I asked if we could talk. She nodded and led me through the garden, deliberately avoiding the house. There were some people in the patio, her brother Dudley, a family friend called Compton Abrams, who my sister had met on her visit to Guyana, and her daughter Vanessa. The collective tension and unease were obvious, and I barely had time to shake their hands before the three of them hurriedly evacuated the area, like a flock of scattering pigeons, leaving Marjorie and me alone in the patio.

The afternoon was already settling down, and the sunlight was slowly draining away. I could see the burned-out, gutted skeleton of a building silhouetted against the sky alongside the house and I could hear the sound of a TV-set from inside. What followed was one of the worst conversations of my life. Marjorie was sitting upright, her back to the open sitting-room, her hands folded on her lap, watching me with the same grim, hostile expression, as I began to explain why I had come to Guyana. I had hardly opened my mouth when she suddenly burst out, 'You killed your father with that letter!'

I gaped in horror. I had anticipated some hostility, but the ferocity of this outburst took me completely by surprise. Whatever else I had expected, it was not to find myself being accused of the Oedipal murder of my father by his widow within a few hours of arriving in the country. I tried to deny the charge, but it was difficult to get a word in edgeways as the soft-spoken, gentle woman I remembered from 1987 now sat bolt upright, her hands on her lap, and transformed herself into my father's avenging widow. Her face was a mask of fury as she vented four years of pent-up indignation and outrage. At times her voice would rise to a pitch of anger and then she would suddenly become sorrowful and tender as she sung my father's praises and described how happy they had been in the few months before he died, how they had both retired at the same time the previous summer, how they had spent all their time together, watching T V, reading and talking and 'laughing like children'.

In the middle of this idyll my letter had arrived, and my father had withdrawn from the world into his bedroom. He had become apathetic and depressed. He had lost his will to live. Some five months after receiving the letter, he had been taken into hospital for medical treatment, as he had been many times before, but this time he had recovered. The reason why was obvious – the evil letter from his spiteful son. 'You killed the man I loved!' she shouted, ramming the point home. 'You're headstrong, just like him! If it hadn't been for you, he would be sitting here right where you are now!'

The explanation for the brutally curt telegram announcing our father's death and the silence that had followed it was now glaringly obvious. Marjorie, and perhaps the rest of his second family, perhaps all his friends in Guyana, thought that I had killed him. Nor had she received any letter from my sister – the charge was levelled at me alone.

As I sat there in the gathering darkness, in the patio where my father used to sit, gloomily listening to his widow repeating the accusation over and over again, like a mantra, I felt as if I had walked into a neatly sprung trap. 'So what am I supposed to do?' I replied sarcastically after the charge was repeated yet again. 'Kill myself?'

'No! Don't do that!' Marjorie looked suddenly alarmed, as if she was worried that she might have gone too far.

In fact I had no intention of doing anything of the kind, but it was difficult to know how Marjorie expected me to respond to the accusations she was throwing at me. Did she want me to feel guilty for the rest of my life? To fall at her feet and beg forgiveness for having expressed anger at my father for the first time in my adult life? The whole situation seemed surreal and grotesque. After everything he had done to us, my father was now being portrayed as the innocent victim of his heartless children and I was his executioner.

After my initial shock, I in turn began to feel angry as the barrage continued, but engaging in a shouting match seemed futile and counter-productive. There were things I wanted to find out, concrete details and facts that I wanted to extract from the flood of words, and I knew I was not going to find out anything if I lost my temper and ended up storming out of the house. But it was difficult to remain calm as the accusations continued.

'When are you going to grow up and stop hating your father?' Marjorie cried. I told her I did not hate him. And this was true. There had been many times in my life when I had been furious with my father, but I did not hate him. If she appreciated the difference, she was not prepared to say so, and I sat there and waited for her outburst to subside, occasionally interjecting questions and denials and trying to put my case. It was now completely dark, but Marjorie did not move to turn on the light. The two of us sat in the gloom, with our faces obscured and the gutted house alongside like some desolate symbol of ruin and disaster. I could hear voices somewhere from the street behind and the sound of birds and crickets settling down for the night, but the house itself was absolutely silent.

I remember thinking that the conversation was my father's revenge for the letter I had written, as if the emotional mayhem that he had generated throughout his life was somehow continuing beyond the grave. At the same time I believed that the accusation that I had killed him was ridiculous. I told Marjorie that I was not sorry for writing the letter if it had stopped him from coming, and that he had only himself to blame if it had such a devastating effect. But Marjorie dismissed my explanations. She refused to accept that my father was in any way responsible for what happened and continued to heap the most extraordinary praise upon him. In the last months of his life their house, and the patio in particular, had been 'the H Q', where people were always coming to visit. 'He was like the old lion in the folk tale,' she said tenderly, 'who is too old to hunt, and draws all the other animals into his cave, but in a nice way. Your father was a good man, a kind man, a gentle man! He was a poet and a visionary who felt guilty for the whole British Empire! And you . . .'

Her voice trailed off in disgust. Compared with such greatness and nobility of spirit, it was clear, my sense of injustice about the way my father had treated his family was too insignificant to mention, a sign of immaturity and stunted emotional growth. Other fathers in Guyana had done worse things than my father, she said, but their families had not rejected them. Why was I such a child that I couldn't forgive him? I told her that I might have forgiven him had he ever expressed any regret or apologized for what he had done.

'Then why didn't you talk to him when he came to England?' she sighed, sounding suddenly tired. 'What did you talk about all the time you were alone together?'

This was a fair point and I tried to answer it. I told her about my ambivalent feelings when he had come to England, how I had found it difficult to put myself in the role of his son again, especially when he himself had shown no awareness of what had happened in the past.

'Of course he knew what happened,' she snapped back. 'He just wasn't the kind of man who knew how to apologize for it. Your father was a man who didn't know how to say sorry, but he loved you all! He loved your mother! I knew all the details of your births and lives. He talked about you all the time.'

This was the second time in twenty-four hours that someone had told me how much my father loved us, and I still did not believe it. Why was she telling me this? Did she expect me to walk away with a warm glowing feeling after all these years? I said that the idea that he had loved my mother or his children was absurd and that his own actions had disproved it many times over. What about the poems he had sent us? she asked. Didn't they prove that he loved us? As far as I was concerned, they did nothing of the kind. I told her that he was the one who had thrown us out and had had nothing to do with us for years. Just because he might have cried into his rum about his lost children now and then, that did not mean he loved them.

'He wasn't just crying into his rum!' Marjorie insisted with melo-dramatic intensity. 'He loved you! He loved you all!'

This outpouring of visceral emotion was clearly not going to be staunched by any arguments I could put forward. It was also obvious that on one level at least I had got things badly wrong. As well as the angry letter I had sent to my father, I had also sent a letter to Marjorie. In it I had suggested that she was as crazy as he was for letting him come back to England, and I asked her whether she was deliberately trying to foist him off on his old family as a way of getting him off her hands.

She was, not surprisingly, furious about that letter too and said that she had been deeply hurt at the suggestion that she had wanted to get rid of my father. 'How could you *think* that I would want to get rid of him!' she exploded. 'That man gave me so much *joy!*' Her anger aroused once again, she now added the charge of racism to the accusations against me. The first reference to this was in connection with her sister, Joan, who apparently, had said that I had written the letter only because of her colour. At first Marjorie claimed not to agree with her, but finally she shouted: 'Why *did* you write that letter? Was it because I am *black*?'

'For God's sake, Marjorie, don't start that,' I snapped bad-temperedly. I had no intention of going down that route. I told her that race had nothing to do with it, and that if I had misunderstood her part in my father's attempted return to England then I was sorry.

I meant this apology and I repeated it more than once in the course of the conversation, but it didn't mollify her. Even though I felt that her anger was partially justified, at least as far as my letter to her was concerned, I also felt that she was overdoing it. Why had neither she nor my father replied immediately if they were so upset by what I had written? Instead she had held on to her anger for four years, and it might have been longer had I not come back to Guyana to provide her with an outlet for it. From time to time there were lulls in her intensity as the conversation wore on. At one point she told me to my surprise that there was not a word in my letter to my father that she had not agreed with. Only the tone had upset her, she said, and the fact that I clearly didn't like him. What kind of tone did she expect and what was I supposed to like about him?

'When he was dying he told me he could see a golden bridge across the sky,' she said. 'I couldn't see anything, but I told him, "Yes, I see it." He said, "It's a lovely bridge, a beautiful bridge." Do you think he would have said something like that if he wasn't a nice man?'

Many years ago, when I was a child in Jamaica, my parents had given me *The Chronicles of Robin Hood* in one of their many attempts to wean me off James Bond. I had cried at the ending, when the dying Robin fires his last arrow through a window and asks to be buried where it lands. For some reason, I thought of that scene now, as I pictured my sick father hallucinating a golden bridge as he lay dying upstairs in his bedroom. Yet this deathbed vision did not cancel out his earlier behaviour. It was her experience, not mine.

In order to give an idea of the ferocity of my father's behaviour, I told her about the university's fear in 1967 that my mother's life was in danger, and I mentioned the Earps, the Canadian vice-chancellor and his wife, who had helped us. 'The Earps!' she replied contemptuously. 'They were responsible for the British Empire!'

I knew that Alan Earp had not been popular with the Guyanese, who disliked having a white vice-chancellor 'imposed' by the colonial power. But I also knew that he and his wife had helped us, where many people had not, and that a child of theirs had died of gastro-enteritis in Guyana. So I was surprised by such vehement hostility towards a man who seemed a well-meaning, politically moderate university administrator.

The subject did not seem worth pursuing, and the sterile exchange of accusations and denials, of arguments and counterarguments, continued. Eventually her anger subsided, but the atmosphere remained charged with animosity and tension. From time to time her daughter, Vanessa, came out on to the patio and tried to play a mediating role. She was a thoughtful, soft-spoken woman in her early twenties. Unlike her mother, she was prepared to try and understand my point of view. She also seemed able to recognize something of what I described in her late stepfather, so much so that Marjorie accused her of taking my part.

'But Bill could be miserable, you know,' Vanessa reminded her mother.

'And I'm miserable too,' sighed Marjorie gloomily.

I wasn't feeling that great myself, as I asked them if they could suggest other people I might talk to and wrote down a list of names. Finally I asked if someone could call me a taxi, and Marjorie called for the little girl who had been at the gate earlier and sent her to a neighbour's house to get me one. Afterwards the three of us carried on talking. Vanessa told me that the house next door had burned down the night before, and the fire had very nearly spread to their house. Unlike her mother, Vanessa seemed entirely free of anger or hostility, as she asked me about my brothers and my sister, whom she had known as a child during her visit to Guyana. Marjorie remained distant and morose, but had mellowed enough to agree to show me where my father was buried later on in the week. When the taxi arrived we said goodbye coldly, without shaking hands, and I drove out into the night with a feeling of relief that the meeting was over.

On my way back to the hotel I stared out at the dimly lit, deserted streets and wondered once again what the hell I had let myself in for by coming back to Guyana. During the four hours I had been at the house I had had no consciousness of time passing at all. The entire conversation, with its peculiar subject matter and its charged emotional intensity, was somehow removed from the everyday world. I felt physically drained, but my mind was buzzing as I tried to assimilate what had been said. Even though I did not believe that I had 'killed' my father, I was disturbed and depressed by his drastic reaction to my letter. Intellectually I refused to accept the mantle of the villainous, vengeful son that Marjorie was so intent on making me carry, yet no matter how much I told myself that I had nothing to reproach myself for, it was impossible to ignore the nagging inner voice that now said, 'You did it, you killed him' over and over again. Was this what I had come back to Guyana for, to walk away with this Freudian Ur-crime hanging over me for the rest of my life?

There was also another idea that had been germinating in my mind ever since Marjorie had told me about my father's guilt for the British Empire: had his rejection of us been based on the fact that we were white? At first sight the possibility seemed too weird, but then there was not much about my father that was not weird. Back at the hotel I sat in the deserted bar and had a few rum-and-Cokes to calm my agitated nerves. Later I retreated to my room, still sifting through the conversation and looking obsessively through my father's letters for some clue to his real motivation, as if I had missed something. Within a few hours the whole settled version of the past that I had accumulated over the years had been cast in doubt and nothing seemed fixed or certain any more. I could not get to sleep and I lay on the bed listening to the thunderous roar of the air-conditioning and zapping through TV stations in a futile attempt to distract myself. The channels contained nothing but violent American films and ghostly Indian movies with a barely audible soundtrack and I soon gave up the effort and turned out the light.

No sooner had I got into bed than I heard the sound of paper being pushed under the door. By now I was so jumpy that the paranoid fantasy crossed my mind that it might be a clandestine message or a death threat, but it turned out to be a local newspaper called *The Starbroek News*. On the front page was a photograph of the gutted house I had seen earlier. According to the paper it had belonged to a local East Indian businessman, and it was the third fire in and around the capital in a week. Pushed under the door with *The Starbroek News* was also a copy of the *Catholic Standard*. My attention was immediately drawn by the following headline:

LUNATIC LOCKED INSIDE
CASTELLANI HOUSE

A man believed to be of unsound mind was locked inside Castellani House from the evening of Thursday 7 last until Friday morning.

When he was discovered he had caused a noticeable amount of havoc in the National Gallery.

It is believed the man was able to evade detection by the curator by hiding himself in a cupboard.

Another article described how the dead body of a woman had been left in the vicinity of the Bank of Guyana on Wednesday morning, despite 'an impassioned appeal on the "Good Morning, Guyana" radio programme' for the authorities to collect it. The appeal had not been answered for some time and the body had thus presented 'a most depressing sight to people on their way to work and other passers-by, including young children'. In a similar incident, the report continued, a man had been left to die by the roadside, with an equally indifferent response from the authorities, who had displayed 'as in almost every case where corpses are left to rot depending on their location a total lack of awareness of their obligation bordering on outright insensitivity'.

This indifference, the paper claimed, was one more symptom of the disintegration of Guyanese society. Other symptoms included the fact that fire victims were frequently robbed by the very people who had come to help them get their possessions out of the building. And the 'macho style drivers' who parked their vehicles 'plumb on a No Parking part of the road or in front of someone's entrance'. Such phenomena testified to the fact that the Guyanese were becoming 'cold and brutal' and too busy making millions, sometimes dishonestly, to waste time over the adversities of even their friends.

Another article entitled 'Lord, Protect Me through this Night' also addressed the theme of social breakdown. It described how many Guyanese had left the land of their birth because they were unable to sleep at night from the fear of being robbed in their homes. To cope with the problem of national insomnia, the writer called for a bigger and better trained police force and the introduction of neighbourhood watch schemes, so that the 'confidence of citizens will be restored and hopefully their peace of mind will usher in sleep with its potential of good dreams and a happy awakening the next day'. In the meantime, and even after these measures were introduced, the writer recommended the same nightly prayer to his readers that he usually used himself: 'Lord, protect me through this night . . .'

Lunatics in the cupboard, corpses in the street, buildings bursting into flames, the dangers of magic and divination, the death penalty and the resurrection of Christ – all of these subjects received the same deadpan treatment. It was a heady mixture, on top of the day's extraordinary revelations. Somehow I doubted whether prayer would get rid of my insomnia and bring about that 'potential of good dreams and a happy awakening the next day', and so I took a sleeping pill instead, bringing my first twelve hours in Guyana to a welcome conclusion.

Chapter Six

The next day there was no happy awakening. I woke up from my drugged sleep and for the first time since I was a child found myself actually crying because of my father. I did not even know why I was crying, but the wave of emotion, now that it had begun, was impossible to contain. If only I had not written the letter, if only he had not tried to come back ... The chain of imagined alternatives stretched back over three decades to the original disaster and beyond, to the ruined, overgrown house of my childhood, where he and I had once lived together as father and son, bound together for life, or so it had once seemed. Now overnight the gap of time, the whole process of growing up and forgetting that separated me from those lost years had closed, and old emotions that I did not even know existed came welling up.

I did not feel like going out at all, but the day had to begin sooner or later. Finally I went down to breakfast, still in a daze. The waitress sleepily took my order and shuffled off towards the kitchen. After a fried breakfast and two nerve-jangling cups of muddy Guyanese coffee, I felt better. I spent the morning calling people around Georgetown and making appointments, before going off to visit the house where we used to live in Canje Street, Campbellville. In 1966 the area around Canje Street had been a quiet, middle-class residential district, with a high concentration of foreigners, university lecturers and local businessmen. Now, as we drove into the tiny little street, I felt relieved and excited to see it, as if the mere fact that the street existed was further proof that the things I remembered had actually happened.

Apart from the TV aerials, the occasional satellite dish and the crumbling road, not much had changed since we lived there. Our house was smaller than I remembered, but people and places always seem smaller to an adult than they do to a child. In the missing years since I had last been in Guyana, the physical details had retained the same scale in my memory, now everything seemed reduced, as though I were a giant looking down at a doll's house that I had once inhabited.

In every other respect the house coincided exactly with the image that I had carried in my head. There was the narrow drainage trench that I had stepped into on my first night in Guyana, and the breezeblock wall, a little blackened with mould, where we had taken refuge that night in 1967 from my father's plate-throwing. There was the little strip of lawn, where one of our cats had once mistaken a small black snake for a piece of string and fought a vicious battle before the snake finally crawled away.

Like most of the houses in the area, it was built from bricks, not wood, with a gently sloping roof to run off the rain. It was supported on wide concrete pillars, with a wooden stairwell outside leading up to the small veranda where our two parrots had lived. There was only one room on the ground floor, which my father had once used for his study. At the back of the house, I could see the raised concrete sewer tank that my brother and I had converted into an all-purpose fantasy vehicle with the help of one of the wooden packing crates that my parents had brought from Jamaica.

During the day we had spent much of our time playing war games on that raised platform, spinning out endless heroic fantasies of war and violence as we changed it into a submarine, a PT boat, a James Bond Aston Martin, a Sherman tank. As I stood by the gate, I had a vivid mental picture of the two of us standing in our ludicrous wooden cockpit firing our plastic machine-guns, entirely immersed in the world of our own imagination on top of a pile of sealed-in sewage. I had always thought of these aggressive war games as a kind of comic-book reflection of what was going on inside the house, but now I wondered whether they had not also been something else – a way of exerting control over a world that was slipping away from us, enabling us to cling on to the vestiges of childhood, the world of play and the imagination, even as everything around us crumbled.

One incident above all came to symbolize the way things had fallen apart in Guyana. It happened during the only Christmas we spent in the country. My father had made some potent rum punch, which he immediately began to drink. In the morning the neighbours came round for a Christmas drink, and he continued drinking after they had gone, becoming steadily more brooding and morose. By the time we sat down to eat our Christmas dinner in the late afternoon, the Christmas spirit was conspicuous by its absence. My father was not speaking to anyone and the tension was so great that no one dared to speak to him. He was sitting at the end of the table, glaring at us with glazed eyes, like a resentful, trapped beast, when I decided to try and break the ice.

'Drunk again?' I inquired cheerfully.

My father's response to my attempted witticism was dramatic even by his own standards. 'You bastard!' he exploded, lurching unsteadily to his feet. Without another word he whipped the tablecloth away, sending plates and dishes flying. I stared in horror at the mess of cranberry sauce, turkey and potatoes and Christmas crackers that lay scattered across the floor, while he lumbered out on to the veranda. The scene was so unbelievable, the disaster so total, that it was a moment before anyone could even react to it. Some of us, if not all of us, must have cried, as my mother bent down and began to clear up the mess, but all I remember is a sense of shock and disbelief at what my father had done, and an overwhelming feeling of guilt for having caused it. After a few minutes I went outside to say I was sorry and to try to put things right.

I remember that he was crying as I made my apology, holding a drink in one hand and a cigarette in the other. He seemed sober and even subdued, as if this latest act of gratuitous destruction had purged him of the anger that had been building up inside him all day. What was he so angry about? I had no idea, but I sensed that it was to do with us. He did not say sorry himself. He never did, but I do remember that he put his arm on my shoulder in a conciliatory gesture as I stood looking up at him, wanting everything to be all right and at the same time dimly perceiving that it never would be, and that in some way he was already lost to us.

Strangely enough I felt not anger towards him but sympathy, even though he had just wrecked our Christmas. It may be that he wanted me to feel exactly that, and he was crying more out of self-pity than because of any regret about what he had done, but as we stood there together, watching the sun going down over Georgetown, there was an intimacy and closeness between us, and I felt that everything that was happening was part of some grim, inexorable tragedy I was still too young to understand, and that none of us would ever be happy again.

I remember nothing about the rest of the day. I suppose we must have resumed our Christmas dinner somehow, although it would have been a rather funereal celebration. Years later the image of my father

crying on the veranda remained perfectly preserved in my memory –
the other side of the thuggish face in the mugshot photograph. Now
as I stood by the gate, wondering at the strange chain of circumstances
that had brought me back there after so many years, I found myself
superimposing that remembered image on to the real veranda. I wished
I could recall what the two of us had said to each other, but as always
there were no words to go with the picture, just the two silent figures,
father and son, frozen as they had always been in the same little corner
of my memory.

I wanted to go inside the house, but it looked unoccupied. So I went
next door to the little pink bungalow that had once belonged to the
Delphs, our former neighbours, the same ones who had been invited
for a drink that Christmas morning. Mr Delph, a retired Guyanese,
had lived there with his adult children, Malcolm and Shirley. I
remembered Mr Delph as a gentle, quiet-spoken old man, who had
taken the Carr children into his house during some of my father's
worst scenes, and played Scrabble with us in the little patio in his front
garden. I knew that he had died shortly after we had left Guyana, and
that his son Malcolm had moved to New York some years before, but
that morning I had been amazed to find Shirley Delph's name in the
telephone book under the same address. I tentatively called out to her
through the barred windows now, and a moment later a round-faced,
light-skinned woman appeared at the window, with her hair in curlers.
   'Shirley? Shirley Delph?' I asked.
   'Yes?' She looked at me curiously.
   'I'm Matthew Carr. My family used to live next door to you.'
   An amazed smile now appeared on her face. 'Oh my God!' she
exclaimed.
   I was grateful for that smile, after the reception I had had the
previous night, and we shook hands warmly as she rushed out into
the garden and ushered me into the house. We sat down in the
sitting-room next to the fan, where a Catherine Cookson novel lay
face down on the coffee table. The room where we had once sought
sanctuary from my father's rages was small and immaculately tidy,
with a little bookshelf, a Georgia O'Keefe poster on the wall and
numerous strategically placed ornaments everywhere. I had only the
vaguest memory of Shirley herself, but she remembered us very well.
She was a cheerful, gregarious little woman in her sixties, an odd

mixture of sophistication and housewifely simplicity as she padded around in her slippers and turquoise slacks and with her hair in rollers. She was retired now and lived alone. She spent her time reading novels and *Hello!* magazine and watching videos of old musicals and plays, particularly anything with Laurence Olivier, whose voice she loved. She looked as astonished to see me as I was to see her. She showed me photographs of her brother Malcolm and his children, and the two of us exchanged notes on three decades of family history.

I was hugely relieved to find her there. After the rapturous description of my father's virtues the previous night, I was glad to find a material witness to what had happened to us inside Guyana itself. More than ever I felt in need of some kind of external confirmation of what had happened. We had not been sitting down long when she suddenly asked me if I had ever read my father's book. I was surprised by this, since I hadn't known that he had actually written a book. Yes, she assured me, with great conviction, he certainly had, and she and a friend of hers had actually typed it. 'I've got a copy of it here,' she said, going over to the bookshelf.

'What was the book called?' I asked, still doubtful.

Now it was her turn to look surprised. '*Teach Yourself Magic!*' she said, as if she couldn't believe I hadn't heard of it. 'I know I've got a copy of it here.'

My brain began to tremble as I tried to assimilate this information. My father, the disciple of Leavis and Matthew Arnold, had written a book called *Teach Yourself Magic?*! I rapidly consulted my memory of him for any references to magic or the paranormal, as Shirley went on about the book, explaining how it contained all the customs and magic spells from the different countries he had visited in his travels. As far as I knew, he had not been on any travels, but Shirley insisted that he had. 'He gave me a talisman,' she said, rifling through a box. 'Here it is.' She handed me a round card with various occult symbols etched into it, and a Latin phrase. 'It means, "This will always protect you,"' she explained. I was still gaping at it, as she resumed the search for the book, before she finally gave up and said she would look for it later.

This new image of my father as some kind of magus dispensing charms and talismans was so alien to anything I knew about him, that I wasn't sure I wanted a copy. But the combination of her absolute conviction and the fact that she remembered my father and us so well in other respects made me think it had to be true. I was still struggling to get used to the idea, when she looked suddenly apologetic and held up her hand to her mouth.

'No wait! I'm confused! It wasn't your father. It was the Nunns!'

I laughed, more out of relief than anything else. The Nunns were an English family we had known in Guyana, who had lived in our house after us. Mr Nunn had also taught English at the university, but he could not have been more different from mine. I remembered him as a bearded, quiet Englishman who went around in khaki shorts and kept a wild boar called Horace as a pet, which used to skid along the shiny wooden floorboards in his house and crash its tusks into the living-room wall. The Nunns' son Anthony had been a friend of mine, and Shirley said that they had lived in the house for a few years after we left. Since then there had been various tenants, but there was no one living there now except for a Portuguese family, who were renting my father's former study.

Apart from this aberration Shirley's memories of her former neighbours were extremely vivid. She recalled the fights and quarrels, and the regular spectacle of my father tottering back home at night from the university bar, the nocturnal flights from the house, and the sight of my mother wearing dark glasses during the day. She even remembered the famous Christmas punch. 'He once invited us over Christmastime to have a drink,' she said, shaking her head, 'and he prepared such a drink that I have never felt myself to be so completely blotto, if you want to call it that – that's a fact. Everything was spinning, everybody was in that state – the drink was so potent.'

I told her what had happened afterwards and she was not surprised. My mother, she said, had been going through 'thralldom'. I had never heard this evocative word before, but it seemed appropriate to what she described. 'Many a time you used to hear things breaking, and what used to strike me in particular was that on many occasions she was black and blue! Her eyes – she always had black and blue, where he had obviously struck her. I know that your mother had a hard time. I suppose we all know, but nobody interferes. We might whisper, "Oh gosh, Mr Carr come home again drunk," but nobody would interfere. People were afraid for his children.'

Were there ever fears that my father might kill anyone?

'He *was* violent!' she declared emphatically. 'There are no two ways about it. He was violent when he was drunk. Yes, I used to feel that something like that might happen one day, that he might do something drastic.'

Her explanation for my father's violent behaviour was perfectly straightforward – his alcoholism. When he was not drunk, she remembered, he had been perfectly pleasant. The trouble was he had been drunk most of the time. Shirley was philosophical about alcoholics in general and seemed to regard them almost as a natural phenomenon. In her opinion there were two kinds of drunks, good drunks and bad drunks, and my father definitely belonged to the second category. An example of the first category could be seen outside the house, in the shape of her black gardener Joseph, who was walking up and down swaying unsteadily and mumbling and laughing to himself. 'Now Joseph doesn't get violent when he's drunk,' she said, 'but I don't let him into the house when he's like this because I don't like drunks. I fight shy of them.'

Throughout the conversation Joseph continued to lurch up and down outside, giggling and talking to himself, as various beggars came up to the gate and called out for money and a trickle of weary, ragged-looking Afro-Guyanese with machetes offered to cut the grass, although it had already been cut. This procession of hopelessness was obviously a daily occurrence in the neighbourhood and Shirley seemed to know most of the petitioners by sight. 'I don't help him because I know he can work,' she said after sending one of the beggars away. 'He's just blame lazy.'

Before I left she offered me some black cake and ginger beer. The ginger beer was delicious and I told her I hadn't eaten black cake since 1967.

'That's why I offered it to you,' she said with a smile. 'You know we couldn't make it under Burnham. He wouldn't import flour because he said it was colonial. He told us we could only use plantain flour, but you can't do anything with that – it makes everything hard. If you wanted real bread you had to buy it abroad. People used to come back from Trinidad and Barbados with suitcases full of loaves of bread.'

Shirley smiled wearily, as if the absurdity of this housewifely anecdote spoke for itself. If she had not been impressed by the Comrade Leader's anti-colonial rhetoric, she seemed no more enamoured of the PPP either. She remembered growing up in colonial Guyana as a period of efficiency, when roads were built when they needed to be and finished quickly. Nowadays, she said nothing was being built or done properly even under Cheddi. Everything was 'patching'. The roads were being patched. The worn-out electricity generators were being patched, while the people at the Guyana Electric Company were stealing public money. 'I don't know how they do it, but they are,' she said almost admiringly. Meanwhile the blackouts continued, and fires were being caused by the sudden flood of electricity when the power was being turned back on. There were shortages of water, everyday goods were still scarce, and, despite Cheddi's personal integrity, most politicians were still corrupt. She described all this with cheerful resignation. Unlike the thousands of Guyanese who had left the country, including her brother, she had never thought of leaving herself. Whatever had happened to Guyana, she said, it was still her country and she couldn't live anywhere else.

I asked her about the Mendonzas, the Portuguese family who had lived on the block behind us. The Mendonzas had been the only family in the neighbourhood to possess a television, a singularly futile asset, since there was no television antenna in Guyana at the time and it was impossible to pick up any stations from abroad. Nevertheless the status-conscious family would regularly turn on their TV and sit in front of it religiously, blaring static out on to the street, to show their neighbours that they were able to afford one. Their fifteen-year-old son Roger had been relentlessly hostile to us. Once he and his friends had chased me on bicycles all over the neighbourhood. On that occasion I managed to evade them, but in the end he caught up with me and gave me my first ever black eye during a fight outside our house. I now learned that Mr Mendonza had been involved in some criminal activity and had been murdered inside his own house, and Roger had accidentally drowned in a river in the interior a few years later.

After I said goodbye to Shirley, I walked up to the little canal at the end of the street where some of the local kids used to fish for eels and had once chased me, trying to put one round my neck. The canal was smaller and shallower than it had been then. Some cows were grazing alongside it, and a derelict female beggar was drinking lethargically from the unhealthy-looking water. I went round the corner to where the Mendonzas had lived, and thought about the tragic fate that had overtaken the unpleasant *nouveau riche* family with their absurd, non-functioning status symbol. The neighbourhood was certainly plugged into the international airwaves now, with satellite dishes and

TV aerials sprouting up everywhere. Behind where the Mendonzas had lived there used to be a wasteground adjoining the Botanical Gardens. My brother and I had often played there, and my father had taken us there on that last walk around Georgetown to expound his views 'on life'. But the area had been drained and reclaimed, and now there was a businessman's organization called the Lions Club where the lake had been. Once my brother and I had made a kind of raft out of a large floating log and paddled around in the murky water, in imitation of the raft used by Huckleberry Finn, while my sister stood watching from the bank.

A short distance behind the Lions Club I could see the row of trees and the little river where we had once gone fishing with a safety-pin attached to a piece of string. We used to cross a waterpipe to get into the Botanical Gardens for our jungle adventure games. This rather unimpressive little river, hardly more than a stream, had once been a crucial prop in our overheated fantasy life, a kind of imaginative bridge connecting us to the vast, mysterious world of the Guyanese interior, with its snakes and jaguars and rivers teeming with piranha fish. The 'script' for many of these jungle games was often provided by the film *Swiss Family Robinson*. Together with the Von Trapps from the *Sound of Music*, the tale of the heroic, utterly normal family shipwrecked on a tropical island and living in a treehouse in the jungle with their animals was a kind of idealized version of everything that my family should have been, and patently was not. The sight of Julie Andrews and Christopher Plummer escaping across the Austrian mountains with their happy blonde brood had once impressed me so much that I had gone to see the film some seven times, cycling off by myself to the Georgetown cinema, before coming back to the *Götterdämmerung* at Canje Street with the tunes to 'Edelweiss' and 'I am sixteen' going round in my head.

I looked over the transformed landscape now and I thought of my brother and me sloshing about in the swampy wasteland and that distant rum-sodden Christmas when even the neighbours had been swept along by my father's relentless pursuit of alcoholic oblivion, a pursuit that had eventually transformed him from the dangerous, frightening drunk who Shirley Delph remembered 'coming down the road' all those years ago to vent his rage on his wife and kids, into the broken wreck who had come back to England in 1987.

*

There is no doubt that our coming to the Caribbean had a decisive impact on my father's personality, and the impact was most obvious in terms of his drinking. At Cambridge he had certainly revealed a tendency to drink heavily, and the connection between alcohol and his violent, aggressive streak was already apparent. At that time his drinking was usually confined to parties, and these social occasions often seemed to provoke quarrels between my parents, although my father's aggression still seems to have been verbal rather than physical. One Christmas Eve my mother remembers that he put his hands round her throat and made as if to strangle her during a quarrel about his mother, but such incidents seem to have been the exception, and were nothing in comparison with the two-fisted assaults that would later be unleashed in the West Indies.

It was in Jamaica that my father first acquired the taste for rum that would eventually destroy him. At first he drank mostly at parties and social events – as in Cambridge he seemed to need to drink in order to perform socially – but this pattern of social drinking quickly evolved into something more serious and intense. Rum was an altogether more powerful and seductive brew than the beers and whiskies he had been used to in England. It was cheap and plentiful and so deeply woven into the fabric of Caribbean life that my father was utterly unable or unwilling to resist it. On the contrary, he embraced both the rum and the veranda lifestyle that went with it with the single-minded determination of a religious convert. He soon became a regular fixture at the university bar at College Common, where he occupied the strategic position of treasurer, and he began to drink around the house during the day. He also began to tour the Kingston rum shops, mostly in the company of his best friend John Maxwell, the editor of the People's National Party journal *Public Opinion*.

To some extent this headlong plunge into alcoholism was part of a long-established tradition in the Caribbean – the white man removed from the family constraints and social codes of his native country who succumbs to the siren call of 'ardent spirits', but my father's intense drinking was only one element in the extraordinary transformation that took place in him after coming to the Caribbean. Even physically he began to change. He put on weight and became more solid and well-built. He also began to discover women, or rather, women began to discover him. Fifteen months after arriving in Jamaica the puritanical research student who had expressed such horror at the Caribbean's reputation for extra-marital sexual activity was having his own extra-marital fling, with an English gynaecologist's wife, who acted with him in a university production of *Twelfth Night*. This was around the time when Richard Burton and Elizabeth Taylor were having their highly public romance on the set of *Cleopatra*: when my mother called my father a 'cut-price Richard Burton' he took it as a compliment.

My father subsequently moved out of the house to have his affair, leaving my mother looking after three children with measles. Six weeks later he came back, telling my mother that he really loved her after all. The gynaecologist's wife had announced that Bill Carr was a psychopath and so were his children, and had left the island to go back to her husband.

This tendency to 'fall in love' with his leading ladies was part of a pattern that was to continue throughout our seven years in the West Indies. He never made the slightest attempt to conceal these affairs, either from his family or anyone else. On one occasion my mother took the three of us to the College Common pool, where we found him sitting with a Jamaican actress with whom he had spent the previous night. 'Why's Dad with her and not us?' we asked my mother. She did not reply, but she was so angry at the humiliation that she later smashed the windscreen of his car, an act of defiance that seemed only to amuse him.

The apparent inability even to consider what effect his behaviour might have had on his children, let alone on his wife, was typical of my father in those years. He seemed to be living out some Hemingwayan masculine fantasy – the hard-drinking, skirt-chasing, two-fisted, anti-establishment rebel. It was a fantasy in which his wife and children became an increasing burden and irrelevance. His behaviour was not out of keeping with the prevailing standards of masculinity in the Caribbean, but the fantasy seems to have been equally attractive to other people as well. To some of his more strait-laced English colleagues he was a larger than life 'character', an intimidating yet charismatic figure, who was always the centre of attention wherever he went, and who lived his life with a dramatic intensity and disregard for social convention that few of them would have dared to emulate themselves.

He was, said Louis James, a former English colleague at the university, 'a bridge to a more popular world', whose willingness to get involved in Caribbean rum-shop culture provided entry to areas of Jamaican society that were normally closed to white people. James remembered him as a man of 'manic, enormous energy' and 'enormous warmth and humour' who 'lived constantly on his nerves'. He was also hugely popular with his students, both as a result of his flamboyant, theatrical teaching style and his leftish politics.

Perhaps it is not surprising that the adulation and attention he received seems to have gone to his head. He was only twenty-nine years old when he arrived in Jamaica, and within a very short space of time he had been transformed from an unknown research student at Cambridge into a well-known public figure on the island, a subject of gossip and scandal, who drove around in a flash car and was involved in everything that was going on. He was a regular fixture on the Jamaican literary and cultural scene as a critic, teacher and actor; he appeared on local TV and radio discussion programmes, like *Brains Trust*, on which he expounded his views on a range of topics from politics and literature to marriage and family life, and for the first time he began to act on stage in university drama productions of Shakespeare and contemporary playwrights like Edward Albee. He was also writing: his political articles in *Public Opinion* eventually aroused the attention of the prime minister, Bustamente himself, who reportedly dismissed requests to deport him with the contemptuous comment: 'The little Englishman – let him write.'

For the first few years in Jamaica my mother did not work. She got involved in various activities to keep herself busy, such as a brief involvement with the Howard League for penal reform, but most of the time she was at home, a campus wife, looking after the children. My father clearly wanted her to play a supportive, background role, occasionally accompanying him to parties, but generally keeping well out of the limelight and allowing him to dazzle. He resented anything that detracted from his own glory and although he felt free to have affairs, this did not prevent him from being extremely jealous of her. Whether or not she felt envious of the life he was leading, she certainly felt neglected and unhappy. Always quieter and more subdued than my father, she often found it difficult to make herself heard even when they were not at loggerheads, and there must have been times when she felt completely drowned out by him. Whereas in England the conflicts between them had been mostly latent, in Jamaica they soon took on a new intensity and regularity.

One obvious reason for the breakdown of my parents' relationship is that they got married too soon and discovered too late that they were not compatible, by which time they already had three children. In a different culture and country the differences between them became more glaringly apparent, and theirs was certainly not the only English marriage on the campus to run aground in Jamaica during those years, although few came apart so loudly or so violently. But marital incompatibility was not a sufficient explanation in itself for my father's violence. Whether his extraordinary personal transformation was provoked by his arrival in the West Indies, or whether it merely coincided with it, he clearly discovered areas of his personality that he had not been aware of before, or that he had previously suppressed. Having married and started a family before he was emotionally ready, he must have realized that there was no room for his wife and children in the new life that he now wanted to lead, but he was unable to accept the consequences that his changed priorities made inevitable. The whole pattern of his behaviour throughout our seven years in the Caribbean suggests a man who was continually trying to break away from his family, yet lacked the courage to do it. At the same time he did not allow my mother to break away either, bullying or begging her not to go whenever she threatened to do so.

The ingredient that finally enabled him to make the break was alcohol. From the beginning alcohol was an important facilitating agent in the glamorous, exciting life that was now unfolding before him. It gave him the confidence and sense of omnipotence to become the person that he wanted to be. The socially awkward, puritanical research student quickly became a Falstaffian 'veranda lion', the life and soul of the party, who dazzled and amused his friends with his flow of words, his jokes and literary references and quotations. To his students he was 'mad but brilliant', while close friends like Jean d'Costa remembered him in a letter to me as a figure of gaiety and laughter, a man so hopelessly impractical that during one of my parents' separations he ate the same food as our sheepdog Blunder when she and her future husband David went to visit him in Stony Hill:

> It was a mess. Bill's idea of haute cuisine was to cook everything together in one big pot for him and Blunder: a head of cabbage, a big chunk of king fish, some potatoes, a carrot or two, and a gallon of water. David and I paid a visit when this meal was being served

to Bill and Blunder, and he took our comments on his housekeeping in amiable part. On another occasion David and I were giving a party and Bill arrived early with John Maxwell. They had been touring the bars of downtown Kingston for some days, it seemed from their smell. I sent them home to wash. They returned hours later, clean and sheepish.

Underscoring this bohemianism, his old puritanical streak continued to manifest itself in odd and sometimes disturbing ways. On one occasion Jean d'Costa was furious with him when in the Senior Common Room he loudly accused my sister Anna, who was then only four years old, of 'trying to catch men' because she was sitting with her legs apart:

I nearly killed him for that. He seemed not to understand me. His eyes were unseeing, I was not there. Then he became genial and joking again. Anna, almost in tears, frightened, was trying to disappear but didn't know why her father wanted her to. But very soon his charm returned and he was her father again, wasn't he?

Jean remembered another revealing incident when a particularly heavy period obliged her to take the day off and she went to my father to hand him some teaching materials:

He was very concerned. 'What's wrong with you?' 'I feel ill.' 'What's wrong?' 'I feel awful.' 'What's WRONG?' 'Bill, I've got a godawful period and I'm going home.' Bright-red face and much choking from Mr Carr, but no more questions. A week later, one of the part-timers told me with hoots of laughter that he had wanted my help with a particular exercise, but Bill wouldn't tell him where I was, or let him phone me. The fellow persisted . . . Bill got most incensed and said: 'She's in her flat but people like YOU can't go over there for she's having her period.' I relate this story because it has so much of the curious innocence and 'gene' of those days, both now gone for good.

The problem was that the 'innocence', which made him attractive to his friends, became something quite different when he was at home with his own family. And if rum helped him to play the role of Falstaff in his public life, it also brought a darker side of his personality to the surface, which had previously lain mostly dormant and which had nothing much to do with fun or gaiety. Drunkenness always made his violence more likely, removing the psychological and moral restraints that might have kept his worst instincts in check and enabling him to give free rein to his ferocious anger. He was certainly intelligent enough to recognize this, and yet he did nothing to stop himself, and seemed to leap headlong into the new self that he was creating regardless of the consequences.

'My memories of Bill are inextricably bound by liquor, veranda dialogues, and laughter,' wrote David d'Costa. 'I sensed then and I see now a dark vein running through those bright times, and I believe your father recognized it keenly — and embraced it. He knew very well that he was embarked on a complicated self-destruction and he was fascinated and appalled by it.'

Within a short time of arriving in Jamaica his rages grew more frequent and intense. The verbal 'sniping' that had characterized my parents' relationship in England began to enter new, uncharted areas of physical violence. Both my parents inherited from their different childhoods a sense that unhappiness was their natural fate, and both of them felt trapped by the ill-fated marriage they had ended up in. Once the punches had started flying, it seemed, there was no way to contain them, and each new act of violence paved the way for the next. But the actual physical attacks on my mother were only one part of the extraordinary marathon ranting sessions that used to go on in my parents' bedroom at night, in which he would yell a stream of vicious taunts and insults at her for hours on end. During one of these sessions he locked her in the bedroom and refused to let her out while he railed at her for nearly twelve hours. I could not understand much of what was being said, but the venomous intensity of my father's verbal outpourings was terrifying and painful to listen to. The same gift of language that so charmed and mesmerized the outside world became, during these rages, a kind of blunt instrument for inflicting grievous psychological harm.

Much of the time my mother did not, indeed could not, speak at all, as my father raved on into the night, at the same hysterical pitch, drowning her out and shouting her down whenever she tried to respond. Why, in these circumstances, did she stay with him as long as she did? The inner dynamics of any failed relationship are often difficult to fully unravel afterwards, even for the participants themselves, and it may be that she herself does not really know the answer. There is no doubt that to some extent she felt trapped by the situation in which she found herself in Jamaica, where work opportunities for foreign white women were few and far between. After three years she found a job with a local firm of solicitors, and by the time we left the island she had begun to build up a successful practice. It was, remembers Jean d'Costa, an important and much-needed change in her life:

> *The transformation of your mother from unhappy housewife into successful solicitor was one of the marvels of life. She was very good at her job, and soon had the satisfaction of earning and, more importantly, of having people depend on her and thank her for her work. Her work made her less bitter and less inclined to hurl accusations at Bill or, as she did on one mad occasion, get herself let into his office so she could search his desk. At the time, I asked her if she wanted to be murdered so Bill could hang?*

While my mother's changed work situation gave her a positive new role in Jamaica, she still lacked the confidence to break free of the relationship and strike out on her own. Despite her professional success, it was by no means certain that she would have been able to create a life for herself with four children on the island, and she was also desperately anxious to avoid going back to England and having to fall back on her family. At that time the stigma that accompanied a failed marriage was far greater than it is today, especially for women, and especially in the circles my mother came from. Indeed her fears would eventually be borne out by the general shock and disapproval that she encountered when she did return, both from her own and my father's family. She also possessed a stubbornness and a determination not to give up, which made her stick with the marriage much longer than she should have done in the hope that things would get better. Last but not least, there were her own children, for whom a bad marriage with my father was better than having no father at all. During their first separation Anna's teachers reported that she was drawing pictures of bloodstained knives at school, and the rest of us were no happier about losing our father than she was.

There was also my father's characteristic ability to make her feel sorry for him. He consistently refused to let her end the relationship, and she lacked the emotional strength to break away without being pushed. When once she did return to England for a break, he sent a letter pleading with her to come back to him for good. He had been through various women, he wrote, but had now come full circle and realized that it was her he loved all the time. On another occasion after smashing up the house he said he was sorry and she gave him a picture as a gesture of forgiveness. Perhaps this cycle of violence and reconciliation also gave a tragic glamour and intensity to the relationship, a sense that it was unique and special, which blinded both my parents to the fact that it was, and had always been, unsalvageable.

The marriage did have various false endings – once my father lived away from home for eighteen months – but each time it somehow managed to resurrect itself. After each reconciliation, however, my father reverted to the same pattern and the violent fights would begin again. All this was public knowledge, yet few people ever confronted or criticized him for his behaviour towards his wife and children. Whatever his friends and colleagues may have thought about his behaviour in private, few dared to say anything to him about it to his face. Even during the worse scenes, there were no anonymous phone calls to the police, not even to complain about the noise. One reason for this non-intervention was clearly the universal reluctance to interfere in domestic violence that Shirley Delph had mentioned. The concept of the family as a private, sacrosanct space, which outsiders can never fully understand and therefore have no right to interfere with, has allowed many men to do exactly what they like within the confines of their own home, and 1960s Caribbean society was no exception.

There is also the fact that my parents were foreigners in another country, where the kind of direct family or personal pressures that might have forced my father to control himself were not present. In a new country, without the familiar weight of his own society pressing down on him, he was able to give in to his own worst instincts in a way that he might not have been able to do had he stayed in Cambridge. Many people were simply too intimidated to risk incurring my father's wrath. When my mother held her own party and invited various mutual friends, some felt it necessary to seek my father's permission before accepting their invitations. One former colleague admitted to me that he had known what was going on but that he had felt too scared to criticize. Some of my father's friends may have shared his belief that how he treated his wife was just something 'that husbands do'. Certainly some regarded his behaviour at home as an unfortunate but necessary consequence of his flawed greatness, a case of 'each man kills the thing he loves'.

Whatever the reasons for the prevailing non-intervention, its consequences were not exactly positive as far as my mother and the rest of us were concerned. What help she did receive tended to be low key, behind the scenes, and after the event. Without the intervention or even disapproval of the outside world, my father's violence grew progressively worse until some people in Guyana became seriously concerned that he might kill his wife. My father himself hinted at this possibility when in one of his letters to my mother he wrote that as bad as their separation had been, 'something far worse might have happened' had they stayed together. It is easy in retrospect to be judgemental about the tolerance that his behaviour seems to have received, and there is certainly no evidence to suggest that people nowadays are any more able to recognize the dangerous spiral to which domestic violence can lead than they were then, let alone act upon it. The point where a private relationship becomes a public responsibility remains a dangerously grey area in many societies, and wife-beating is still an issue that many people prefer to ignore or excuse. There is nothing particularly Caribbean about *that*. Nevertheless it is impossible to avoid the conclusion that this tacit social acceptance of the unacceptable was not helpful to anybody, not least to my father himself, since it merely allowed him to sink deeper into his own dark side, until finally it engulfed him and us in the mayhem that took place at 49K Canje Street.

I visited the house once more a few days later. This time I was let in by the owner Dr Joseph, who lived down the road and turned out to have been one of the many Georgetown doctors who had treated my father over the years. It was a cloudy, overcast morning and, just as we were climbing the stairs, the rain began to pour down, one of those intense tropical downpours that I remembered as a child, when the storm drains would overflow on to the street and the ground floor of the house would be ankle-deep in water, and the thirteen stray cats and kittens that lived there would take refuge in their home under the back stairs.

'It's raining now, but warm, lucid and pleasant rain, a kind of paradisiacal rain – one of the few paradisiacal things we have here,' my father once wrote to my sister. I remembered those tropical rainstorms differently, as something sad, desolate and oppressive, when it was impossible to go out and play and the house seemed even more claustrophobic than usual. I felt a similar sense of desolation now at the thought of the six of us cooped up in that house all those years ago, cut off from the outside world by that same dense curtain of rain, waiting for the next explosion as our father drank himself into a stupor.

The house was even tinier inside than it looked from the outside. It was really no more than a flat, with three bedrooms and a large L-shaped sitting-room, divided by thin wooden walls that stopped short of the ceiling to allow ventilation. In the corner of the sitting-room was a little table facing the kitchen counter, in exactly the same place as the table had been that dismal Christmas. Dr Joseph left me alone in the house and I walked around, the noise of my feet echoing noisily on the wooden floor. Here my father had performed his berserk gestalt for the two psychiatrists and Christian had stuck a metal ruler into the roof of his mouth and had to be taken to hospital with a bleeding palate. The last tenants had moved out some time ago, but a few possessions and pieces of furniture had been left behind, including a little bookcase full of books. In one corner of the sitting-room a little jokeshop tombstone on a coffee table bore the inscription:

Ma loved pa.
Pa loved wimmin.
Ma caught pa with
Two in swimmin –
HERE LIES PA.

Next to the little sofa there was a pile of old 78s: 'When My Dream Boat Comes Home', 'I Almost Lost My Mind', 'The Great Pretender'. None of them were ours. The titles seemed curiously appropriate, but I had always associated that house with different music – doomy early Dylan songs like 'A Hard Rain's A-Gonna Fall', 'The Ballad of Hattie Carrol', the Joan Baez version of 'Farewell, Angelina' and the Beatles' 'Help!'. One night I had been left alone to babysit while my parents went out, one of the few occasions in Guyana when my father took my mother anywhere. While they were out, the record-player got broken somehow. I was too scared to tell my father and so I whispered it to my mother instead when they got home. She told me to go to bed and said that she would take responsibility for it. Shortly afterwards he tried to put on a record and her false confession triggered another violent explosion, while I lay in bed seething with anger at my father and with guilt at having put my mother in the firing line once again.

Virtually everything I remembered about that house was connected to some manifestation of my father's rage. Looking out the back window, I saw the stairwell where I had crawled backwards into the house in agony one afternoon after badly spraining my ankle while playing football next door. The ankle was so painful that I could not walk or even touch the floor with it, but my father lay on the bed and ignored my mother's requests for help.

'What a mean man,' she said disgustedly, walking away. Immediately he cursed and leapt off the bed and half dragged, half frogmarched me down to the car and drove me to the hospital. There he continued to swear at me and my mother in front of the nurses. When one of them asked why we didn't use a wheelchair, he said: 'She's too fucking stupid to think of that.'

As I walked around the house, taking snapshots of the empty rooms, like a tourist of my own past, the underlying meaning behind these dimly remembered explosions seemed as elusive as ever. I had hoped that being there again might bring some new memory or incident to the surface that would shed some light on what had happened, but the empty house had no secrets to reveal. There was the bedroom which I had shared with Bruce, where I had spent many hot, sweaty nights lying awake, being eaten alive by mosquitoes in spite of the window netting. A portrait of Christ with a glowing sacred heart now stared out from the wall where my bunkbed had stood, a symbol of forgiveness and compassion. Next-door was my parents' small bedroom, the main battleground during those nine months, where so many of my father's scenes had begun and ended. The walls were so thin that it was impossible to imagine that anything could have been said or done there without everyone else knowing about it, and yet it was amazing how little I actually remembered.

Nowadays people use cameras and camcorders obsessively to record the most significant and the most ordinary moments in family history, freezing them in an unbroken reel of domestic happiness that can later be played back as a reminder that they really happened. We film and take pictures of everything, holidays, birthday parties, Christmas dinners, our children growing up, as if we are already looking back at the present from the point of view of the future and anxious to provide some external evidence someday of our own uniqueness and individuality, our physical existence even, and that of the people close to us. It is as if we know that memory is a fallible instrument ultimately doomed to wear out and disappear along with the rest of the human body, and that something more is necessary to prove that we were ever here at all.

There were very few pictures taken of my family in Jamaica, only a few worn individual snapshots. Anna sitting on a tree, me playing on the beach with an unidentified woman; a romantic shot of my mother and my father sitting together, holding hands and smiling at the camera, looking surprisingly happy. There are no pictures of the whole family nor are there any photographs of my father with any of his children, either individually or as a group. This, in itself, perhaps reveals more about the underlying emotional atmosphere in Jamaica than all the other photographs put together. My mother says that it was not the custom in those days to take photographs of everything. This may be true, but the absence of *any* photograph of the family together suggests to me that my parents did not see themselves ever looking back nostalgically on our days in the West Indies. And the fact that my father does not figure in any of the pictures of the children seems equally symbolic. Were there never any moments in which he wanted to be recorded for posterity with any of his children? Had there not been a single day when we had all been happy together?

As I stood watching the rain hissing down on the little lawn, the same rain, the same lawn, the same house, from all those years ago, I thought of my father and the inexplicable madness that had taken place within those walls and I felt both closer to the past and at the same time as far from understanding it as I had ever been. Not a single photograph of us had been taken during those nine months in Guyana. My parents had no camera and the events that took place were not something that they would have wanted to record for posterity. Everything about that house was connected in my mind with destruction, severance, rupture, and yet the only evidence of what had happened there consisted of the worn-out memories of my family, a few people scattered around the world, and our old next-door neighbour Shirley Delph. Objectively, there was nothing to prove that my father had ever been connected to us at all.

The rain was coming down even harder now, and while I waited for it to subside I looked through the bookshelf for something to read. I picked up an old copy of Shakespeare's complete works and, opening it at random, found these lines from *Richard III*:

> *Why wither not the leaves, the sap being gone?*
> *If you will live, lament; if die, be brief,*
> *That our swift-winged souls may catch the king's*
> *Or like obedient subjects, follow him*
> *To his new kingdom of perpetual rest.*

In the summer of 1966 my family went back to Cambridge for a holiday before coming to Guyana, and my father took me to see Olivier's *Richard III* at the Arts Cinema, in one of his many failed attempts to get me to appreciate Shakespeare. Although my interest was mildly aroused by the evil King Richard, I was bored as usual by the speeches and my attention only pricked up during the murders and the fight scenes. The reaction would certainly have irritated him. Now, as I sat there listening to the monotonous drumming on the roof, I thought how much I would have liked to talk to him about our shared past together, without anger or emotion. I imagined his ghost appearing in that empty house, and how we would have a drink together, and I would ask him why it had all happened.

In my fantasy there would be no recriminations and I would not insult him or curse him out or demand an apology. Instead I would just sit quietly and listen to his explanation of what he thought had happened when we had lived in that house together. Perhaps, like Iago, he might have said, 'Demand me nothing. What you know, you know. From this time forth I will never speak word.' Or perhaps he would tell me everything that he had not said when he was alive, and afterwards fade away again, like Hamlet's father, and there would finally be a kind of peace between us. But there was no peace, no ghost, just the same raw memories that still made no sense and the paradisiacal rain beating down, beating down, just as it had done all those years ago, on the roof of an empty house where nobody lived any longer.

Chapter Seven

The University of Guyana campus at Turkeyen is situated just outside Georgetown, a short taxi or minibus ride from the city centre along the coastal road towards New Amsterdam, past the sea wall on one side and acres of fenced-off parkland on the other. The taxi-driver relished the rare opportunity to show off his skills on a decent road and drove unnervingly fast, like most of the other vehicles, paying scant regard to the warning sign near the turn-off to Turkeyen, with its all-too-believable message: *Persons died here! Don't be the next!*

The campus consisted of a number of nondescript, functional wooden buildings separated from the main entrance by a wide playing field. Despite the anonymous, box-like architecture and the irritating background hum of an electric generator, it had a pleasant, slightly bucolic feel, with its trees and open stretches of grass, where goats and cows were lazily grazing, in open defiance of the *No Animals on Campus* sign. Here and there classes and seminars could be seen in session through the open windows, and groups of students were strolling along the open corridors connecting the buildings or playing cricket on the grass.

Apart from his national service, and a few odd jobs as a postman and a bus conductor in Cambridge, my father spent his entire adult life studying or teaching English literature at different universities. Whatever contradictions and unexplained episodes marked other areas of his life, there is an unerring integrity and coherence in his work as a teacher and his commitment to his students. In an article published in the 1985 Turkeyen Arts faculty journal, he defined his attitude towards his teaching in a typically abrasive response to a PNC technocrat who accused the university's Humanities faculty of disseminating 'irrelevant knowledge':

> *What exactly is 'irrelevant knowledge'? Literature in whatever language? History? Sociology? The freak phrasing of a party-serving*

economist about sums it up. It should be clear to the mind of any
educated and intelligent man that science and technology have the
deepest relevance to an underdeveloped society. All of us at the
university know this and are therefore not in dispute about it.
A university also encourages a liberal habit of mind by virtue of the
breadth of knowledge and imagination that it tries to expose its
students to. Inevitably this must help to mould a critical intelligence
and the natural habit of curiosity. 'Criticism' does not mean Nosey
Parkerism . . . What it all means is that ANY university can be
defined as a natural inquirer into the quality of the society it dwells
in. It may question the society's culture, its economic competence,
the quality of its government. It must do this not by the assumption
of a superficial right but as an act of duty. A university anywhere
that is the total and amiable friend of Government is no longer a
university. It has become simply a versatile whore.

For someone with my father's politics and passionate commitment
to higher education, the University of Guyana was a natural place to
gravitate towards in the Caribbean of the mid-60s. The establishment
of a national university separate from the University of the West
Indies was an initiative taken by Cheddi Jagan himself during his
second, aborted presidency in 1963, at a time when his government
was already reeling from the impact of domestic and international
conspiracies. From the beginning the university had a strongly nationalist, left-wing orientation which reflected the political atmosphere in
Guyana itself, an orientation that was very different from the University
of the West Indies, as my father later remembered it:

I joined the staff of UCWI in 1960 and found myself (as a young
man) startled by its Anglophile sense of itself. Inevitably one found
oneself involved. UCWI made West Indian noises but its basic
sensibility was Anglophile. I wrote many political articles and brought
myself to the verge of deportation. Summoned to the office of the
vice-chancellor – in his black suit and executing himself with his
bow-tie; the kind of English gentleman I could never be. He was in
fact a Jamaican. I felt I had had enough. Where else could I go and
remain in the West Indies? Clearly the University of Guyana.

There is more than a touch of self-congratulation in this paragraph,
from the concealed moral imperative in that impersonal 'inevitably

one found oneself involved' to the suggestion that my father was more
in tune with West Indian sensibilities, was in fact *more truly Jamaican*
than the Anglicized Jamaican vice-chancellor himself. Nevertheless
the radical aura surrounding the new university was an obvious
attraction to the expatriate rebel, while the task of building up an
English department virtually from scratch provided him with a unique
professional challenge within his chosen field. When we lived in
Guyana the embryonic university did not even have its own premises,
and the teaching consisted of evening classes at the Georgetown
secondary school which Cheddi Jagan himself had once attended as a
boy. Years later, my father nostalgically evoked the early pioneering
spirit of what the university's opponents derisively called 'Cheddi's
Marxist night school':

> *In those days we were installed in Queen's College. It was difficult*
> *but I shall never forget Queen's and I feel a genuine gratitude to*
> *that school. Going upstairs to take your class, stairs and rooms*
> *smelling of boys, stale buns, spilt sweet drinks, and assorted vermin.*
> *And your students (big men and women packed into schoolboys'*
> *benches and desks), the night teaching (up to 10.25), the inevitable*
> *meetings held during the day ... Perhaps I have grown old and*
> *sentimental, maybe, indeed, nostalgic, but we had a kind of pioneer*
> *gaiety then. The uses of adversity were highly beneficial.*

The 'uses of adversity' is a favourite expression of my father's,
which often crops up in his articles and letters, and its use in this
context had a certain unintended historical irony when I thought of
him getting himself drunk after class, then staggering back from this
bracing atmosphere of selfless educational commitment and 'pioneer
gaiety' to wreak havoc at his home in Canje Street. I had no doubt
that the idealism he described was genuine, but it was a side of his
life in Guyana that we had never seen, just as few of his colleagues
from Queen's College had ever seen what happened when the crusading
professor went home to his family.

After we left Guyana he continued to teach at Queen's College
until 1969, when the Turkeyen campus was officially opened, and he
remained there till his retirement, becoming eventually head of the
English department and dean of the Arts faculty. His commitment to
the university was greatly appreciated by many Guyanese, including
uneducated people who had never been anywhere near the university

campus, but for whom the existence of a national university was none the less something to be proud of. My father shared this pride in the institution that had absorbed so much of his time and creative energy:

> I have worked at UG for eighteen years, mainly with a strong feeling of affection and concern — for the subject I teach, for my students and for an Institute that I feel (the longer I stay) is validating itself in terms of the immediate context of the Guyanese community . . . My propositions are simple. UG is small but known. I am proud of it and of my colleagues, whose morale has held, whose work and honesty still maintains a free institution that you can walk into without shame, an institution that has the liking of the humblest members of this community, an institution that ensures that in any place where talk about progress, freedom and social change are meaningfully talked about UG people will be there — students and staff.

The Arts faculty building had the same box-like structure as the rest of the campus, its architectural monotony partly relieved by a colourful forest mural on the ground floor. It felt strange to be in the place where my father had spent most of his working life, and hear myself being introduced as 'Bill Carr's son' to a succession of his former colleagues, all of whom greeted me with warmth and friendliness. Any remaining fears that I would not find enough people in Guyana who knew him were quickly dispelled as I was shepherded from one office to another by Joy, the faculty secretary. Just about everyone in the faculty knew my father, and all of them were happy to talk to his son about him. No one seemed to think it unusual that one of his English children should come all this way to visit the faculty after his death.

I was taken briefly to my father's old office, where a seminar was in progress, and as I glanced in at the little room I tried to imagine Professor Carr sitting behind that same desk, the stern, committed teacher with a passionate concern for literature and its moral implications, whose spirit was enshrined in the Henry James photograph that he had sent to us. Years ago, in my early teens, when he and I were still writing to each other, I had got it into my head that he was a 'professor' when he had not yet become one. I was just beginning to read 'literature' and was sending him copies of my first poems. I had been impressed by the thought of him as a professor, with its suggestion of great learning and intellectual achievement, but then he corrected me in a scrawled postscript to one of his letters. By the time he really had become a professor, we had stopped writing to each other and I no longer took any pride in his achievements, academic or otherwise. I had never seen him lecture, either in Jamaica or Guyana, and then would not have understood what he was talking about, so that the entire teaching side of his life was an aspect of his public persona that I knew of only through my mother. From her descriptions, I had imagined him as a brilliant and charismatic speaker, whose lectures were like theatrical performances: students would be seduced as much by his verbal dexterity as the content of what he had to say. Now, for the first time as an adult, I had the opportunity to speak to people who had actually worked with my father, or had been taught by him.

Conversations I had that morning with his former students and colleagues served only to confirm this impression. His students without exception remembered him with great affection, as a caring and stimulating teacher with a great command of the English language – a highly respected ability in Guyana – and an extraordinary memory for books and quotations.

'I found your father a brilliant lecturer,' said Azgar, an East Indian former student and friend, who was now working for the university administration. 'He did not confine his teaching basically to the classroom. Anywhere you see Bill Carr you could say "Sir" and he doesn't want you to call him "Professor". "Bill" goes for him anywhere, and he was very open to discuss whatever is your problem, be it academic or counselling outside of what you'd call normal university life.'

This accessibility and lack of pretension was rare among academics in my experience. It greatly endeared my father to his students, as did his habit of peppering lectures, seminars and even faculty meetings with a flow of four-letter words and pungent expletives. His reputation for swearing was so widespread that in one faculty meeting where he was listed as one of the 'discussants', someone crossed out the prefix, leaving the words 'Bill Carr – cussant' to the amusement of his colleagues. In other respects too he was unusual for an academic. He spent a lot of time in the company of non-academic members of staff, and included some of his students among his drinking companions. His predilection for alcohol was well-known, and his students often bought rum for him. He did not hesitate to take his students into his confidence inside the classroom, telling anecdotes from his personal life and denouncing the various conspiracies being hatched against him by his political enemies. As in Jamaica, his politics made him popular with his students, especially the ones who were in the PPP. One student fondly remembered my father dancing a jig in the crowded Walcott lecture theatre, in protest at the government's refusal to allow Walter Rodney to take up his post at the History department.

But it was my father's total dedication to the literature he was teaching that had had the biggest impact on the generations of students who passed through his classes. 'He was the most amazing person,' said Joyce Jonas, who had worked with him for more than twenty years. 'If you look back at the exams that he set, they were extraordinarily provocative. He never gave his students the kind of stereotyped questions you usually expect. There was always something to encourage them to make interesting links in their thinking. I think I remember him most as a Shakespeare expert. He always impressed me with his gift. Not only that he seemed to know most of the plays by heart, but that he was able to make them come alive. You would be sitting in your office and suddenly you would hear Bill's voice launching into some soliloquy, fully dramatized, and the entire Arts faculty had to listen, because Bill had a seriously loud voice, and the students in his class would sit absolutely mesmerized. From the moment that Bill walked in, he was acting, whatever play he was doing. He didn't teach a play, he acted it, it was a one-man dramatization of the play, and the students would be absolutely in awe of what was going on.'

It was not difficult to imagine my father's 'seriously loud voice' penetrating the thin wooden walls of the faculty building, or to conceive of the impact that such a theatrical teaching style must have had on his students, in a country where books were difficult to obtain, and where the classics are often better appreciated than they are in the mother country itself.

In effect, he turned himself into a kind of living text. The classroom became his own private theatre, in which he acted out different roles and characters for his students. Such behaviour might not have elicited highbrow academic approval, but certainly impressed young students, for whom the ability to make a book or a play come alive was more important than dry textual analysis. But there was more to his teaching than performance alone. Most of his colleagues remarked on his critical intelligence, his creativity and imagination, his 'razor-sharp mind', and his determination to raise academic standards and maintain the university as an independent and critical institution in the face of strong governmental pressure to convert it into another mouthpiece for the regime.

Not all his colleagues were equally impressed by his peculiar methods and personality. Jamaican-born Al Creighton was the dean of the Arts faculty in the last years of my father's life. As a schoolboy in Kingston, he had seen him give a talk at his school and had heard of his reputation on the Mona campus. The two of them had later worked together in university drama productions in Georgetown, but relations between the young Jamaican dean and the mercurial professor were not always harmonious. As charismatic as my father may have been inside the classroom, he remained throughout his life an administrative disaster, prone to losing students' exam papers and mixing up their grades. 'Towards the end of his life unfortunately, he did not consider me a friend because he thought that I was unfair to him in a number of ways,' Al Creighton explained diplomatically. 'Bill Carr was not known to be the greatest respecter of discipline and therefore we clashed occasionally on little matters in the faculty, and he felt that I was an enemy of his.'

Somewhat to his own surprise the man my father considered to be an enemy was asked to read a tribute to him at his funeral. Despite a temperamental aversion to funerals in general, he reluctantly agreed to do it, and something of the flavour of their occasional clashes emerges in this double-edged portrait:

> Life to William Carr was William Shakespeare, whose work he quoted so much, whose characters he imitated and taught for several years to several students. Yet if he heard any hypocrite like Goneril mouthing her devotion with, 'Sir, I love you more than words can wield the matter,' his response would be like Cordelia's: 'Love, and be silent.' But ironically Professor Carr could not be silent as he dramatized his role. Many times an uninitiated visitor to the faculty building might have been suddenly alarmed out of his wits by a loud theatrical bellow echoing across the hall: 'Get thee to a nunnery, go; farewell!' Or worse than that: 'Awake, awake! Ring the alarm bell! Murder and treason! As from your graves, rise up, and walk like sprites/to countenance this horror!' However, any member of the

English department would calmly tell the visitor, 'Don't panic, it's only Bill Carr having a tutorial.' Because Bill's speech was never 'unable' and none could use words to 'wield the matter better', so much so that there were also those in the faculty who would say to him, 'Bill, teach, and be silent.' I do not expect he will ever be silent. I am sure, for decades to come, you will almost hear his voice echoing Othello in Turkeyen corridors during blackouts late at night declaiming, 'Put out the light, and then put out the light!'

That morning I sat in the staff common room, discussing the ghost of Turkeyen with Joyce Jonas and Cicily Johns, a lecturer in linguistics who also remembered him well. The two women made an interesting contrast. Joyce Jonas was white, English and very serious. She wore a flowery, old-fashioned dress that made me think of a missionary or a Sunday School teacher. Cicily Johns was Afro-Guyanese, with a soft, dreamy voice that concealed a steely, sardonic wit. She was the only ex-colleague of my father's who remembered the events surrounding our departure in 1967, and she'd been close to the family of Sandra Williams, who had since changed her name to Andaiye. 'To tell the truth,' she said, in that slow, slightly mocking delivery, 'the girl he took up with, Andaiye, was very privileged yet very unhappy, and nobody could understand why he would leave a basically stable person like his wife for somebody like her, because we believe, you know, that people marry stable people — but then I gathered that he had done something of the sort in Jamaica, fallen in love or something.'

'More than once!' I told her.

'Yes. He was in the habit of falling in love.' She did not look particularly impressed at the thought. 'And people just did not take it seriously, and we felt that it was a rather ridiculous thing that he did, but I will never forget what he said: "Why did she go? She didn't have to leave." A week later.'

'A week later he said that?' I asked in amazement, 'about his wife?'

'Hmmm,' she murmured dreamily, with obvious amusement. '"Why did she go? She shouldn't have left. She didn't have to leave."'

Her voice was quietly mocking as she relished the absurdity of these declarations. What did all this mean? All the evidence had suggested that my father's psychotic behaviour was the sole reason for our departure. Yet now it turned out that only a week later he had been going round the faculty asking people why my mother had left. Was it another typical Bill Carr device to portray himself as the victim yet again and conceal his responsibility from himself and others? Or had he really woken up a week later from his delirium without any memory of what had happened to find himself without his wife and children?

I asked Cicily what the reaction on the faculty had been to these events.

'Well, the faculty wouldn't have known. Who would have known would have been friends of Andaiye and her father, who was a well-known doctor and had a lot of friends, because what your father did affected one of our promising young women, and therefore people were concerned about her role in the whole matter, and the victimization of your mother.'

'You knew about that?'

'Oh, yes. In fact you attributed it to the fact that he was drunk all the time. He deliberately got himself drunk.'

This was the first time I had heard anybody suggest what I had already come to believe myself – that my father's behaviour was not simply the result of his drinking, but that he had drunk precisely in order to behave in certain ways which his own conscience would not have been able to accept if he had been sober.

'It was just a scandal which had broken,' Cicily went on, 'and people felt that he had behaved in a very extraordinary way. He had been brutal to his wife, and people felt, what was the point? It was not going to last. They could foresee that their relationship was a pretext really, but nobody could really understand what it was really all about, because it seemed to us that neither Bill nor Andaiye was stable enough. In any case, if you want to start a relationship, there is absolutely no need to start it in that particular way.'

There was, I agreed, no doubt about that, but a pretext for what?

Joyce Jonas had begun working at the university in 1969, and she had known nothing about my father's past behaviour. She was clearly taken aback by what she had just heard.

'I found him a very gentle and gracious person,' she said, 'and I'm amazed to hear that he had that other side to his character. It's kind of difficult to imagine that, and it makes me wonder another thing about Bill, and that is that I very often had the feeling that he wasn't living his life – he was acting a role. I very often got that feeling. I remember one time he would come for quite a long period, a couple of months maybe, dressed all in black, and it was quite obvious that this was his Hamlet phase. And this was part of the Bill phenomenon, you know, that he was soaking himself in that part, and therefore he was now Hamlet, and one sort of learned to live with that, that you weren't really interacting with Bill, but with the character he'd currently assumed.'

My mother had also recently told me about this tendency of my father's to immerse himself in a character he was playing. When he was preparing one of his stage roles, he would identify so strongly with the part that suddenly she would find herself living with Iago or Macbeth. He did not start acting, on stage at least, until his second or third year in Jamaica, but his interest in the theatre was always much more than a hobby or an expatriate distraction; it was an existential need, in which the defining line between life and art was often difficult to locate. No matter what the situation was like at home, or which of his leading ladies he had fallen in love with, his wife and children were always expected to turn out for these performances, not that we minded. On the contrary we always enjoyed ourselves hugely, even though Anna once stood up at the end of *Othello* when Iago was being stabbed and shouted at the actors to stop hurting her father.

As a child I saw him in a number of amateur productions, including *Macbeth*, *Othello*, a Footlights-style pastiche of *Goldfinger* called *Silverthumbs*, and even, appropriately enough, a version of *Who's Afraid of Virginia Woolf?* whose rehearsals were carried out in our house in Stony Hill, with or without the other three actors. Even though I rarely understood the plots, I loved to watch him on stage and I was so awed by his ability that for a while I even wanted to become an actor when I grew up, like him.

My father's involvement in the theatre was another aspect of his egocentricity and constant need to be the centre of attention, but there was clearly much more to it than egocentricity alone. In a review of Samuel Beckett which he had written in the 50s, he praised Beckett's response to 'this mean world . . . which we do not like, but which we are obliged to live in'. Both on and off stage, he spent much of his adult life trying to be someone else, whether it was Che Guevara, Karl Marx, or the gallery of Shakespearian characters to which he returned again and again – Iago, Mercutio, King Claudius, Macbeth, the 'inverted Lear' that Kathleen Drayton had described. Again and again throughout his life he identified himself with fictional characters or real people, weaving their stories into his life as metaphors and role models. At other times he seemed to be writing his own script, making up a completely new character and pushing its emotions to melodramatic extremes, such as the crazed parody of insanity that he had put on for the two psychiatrists back in 1967.

As I imagined him walking round the campus dressed as Hamlet, I wondered whether he found in this compulsive role-playing an escape from that mean world which he wrote of as a young man – a dramatic intensity that was literally larger than life. But there was another possible explanation for this constant blurring of fantasy and reality, between the theatre and the world. For the first time I wondered whether the passion with which he buried himself in those other lives was the result of some form of incipient schizophrenia, and whether the extensive dramatis personae that he had played throughout his life had been the result of a fragmenting personality, especially after he began drinking heavily, when the line between fantasy and reality often seems to have disappeared completely.

'I always felt that he had a very strong sense of himself,' said Joyce. 'It sounds paradoxical, because here it is, the man is assuming a number of dramatic roles, but it seems as if once he was in that role, he adjusted to it so perfectly that he was fully self-assured in it. He never needed to apologize for himself.'

But didn't this constant need to adopt a new disguise suggest a man with a very weak sense of himself? I asked.

'You may very well be right, but the impression that one got at any particular moment, when he was in any particular role, was that here is a man who knows who he is, living consistently with that sense of who he is.'

The conversation went on, with each of us contributing our own observations and memories of my father in a mutual attempt to reconstruct his elusive personality. Both women had known him for longer than anyone in my family had done, and yet there seemed to be as many gaps in their knowledge of him as there were in mine. Unlike the conversation with Marjorie, there was no antagonism or hostility, and I felt as if each anecdote and observation that emerged was another piece in a puzzle that we were approaching from entirely different directions. On the surface Joyce Jonas could not have been more different from my father, yet she showed a real sympathy for him that was absent from Cicily Johns' more scathing observations.

'I remember he told me once he was a Roman Catholic,' she said. 'I'd never, never thought of him as being a religious person, and he told me, yes, he was a Roman Catholic, and at his funeral he'd chosen the hymn, "Morning has broken like the first morning", and I thought that was rather an amazing expression of faith in the Resurrection for a man I'd never associated with any kind of religion. There was obviously something going on in his own thinking that he could express what was clearly a hope in the Resurrection, and I found that very moving.'

I told her what I knew about his reconversion to the church in the mid-70s and his bizarre attempts to annul my parents' marriage.

Cicily laughed, but Joyce looked serious and intense, as if she was struggling to remember something important. 'What brought him to the West Indies?' she asked. 'I'm wondering if it was some sense of guilt in him, as a white person, some feeling of guilt that he had to in some way make amends for what Europeans had done to the people in the West Indies. I mean, is it possible that you represented something that was evil in his thinking?'

But I pointed out that my father's arrival in the West Indies was the result of practical necessity, and that the guilt, if it was there, would have come afterwards. I also told her that since coming to Guyana I had begun to wonder whether or not we had in fact been some bizarre kind of sacrifice.

'I remember towards the end of Bill's life, one used to be embarrassed and – ashamed for him,' Joyce said. 'Because he was a bit of a tramp, you know, a homeless person. He would be here on campus, and he would just sit down on the ground and wait for someone to give him a drop home. He looked shabby, and he would just be sitting there. If anybody hadn't known him they would just have walked past him thinking that he was somebody begging by the side of the street.'

'Even when he was still working, you mean?'

'He was still working, yes. As a department and faculty we would bend over backwards to accommodate him, because we were aware that he wasn't really doing his work properly, but Bill had given so many years, he was such an institution, that you couldn't just get rid of him like that, so we always tried to fill in the gaps. But I remember feeling dreadfully sad one day, to just see this man, who had impressed me so much — not that I respected him morally — I felt the drinking and so on, that didn't impress me — but there was something of quality there that was being thrown away, and it was almost as if he was deliberately throwing it away. That's why I liked your word sacrifice. There was almost a wanting to die, wanting to throw it all away, wanting to humiliate himself, to go down as low as possible. I mean, he didn't have to sit on the ground. Anybody would have given him a ride home. He just had to make the arrangement, but there was something perverse in him that made him want to sit down on the ground like some beggar, then you must come along and say "Bill, would you like a ride home?" It was very sad to see that — embrace of the disgrace that he brought upon himself.'

This was not the kind of sacrifice I had meant, but her interpretation of the word seemed entirely plausible. The peculiar phrase she had used to describe it — 'embrace of the disgrace' — reminded me of a word that Vanessa had used in connection with his last visit to England — penance. Had he deliberately allowed himself to go down so far, stripping himself of the last vestiges of dignity and self-respect in some gesture of public atonement that sounded like a scene from Hawthorne's *The Scarlet Letter*? Or was he just a ruined old drunk, who no longer had any self-respect left or even cared what anyone thought of him? Whatever was behind it, the grim spectacle of this public degradation was chilling and depressing. It was obvious that Joyce had been disturbed by it too, and now the unexpected appearance of one of his children from out of the distant past had helped her to come up with a kind of explanation for it.

'He always seemed to be so much a man of the world,' she said, 'a very worldly-wise kind of person, and I always got the impression that he looked on me as somebody who was rather naïve and rather virtuous perhaps, not that he particularly admired that. I was, in fact, a keen church-goer, and I remember one day, we were alone together, and he was looking at me in a strange way, and I suddenly got an overwhelming sense that he was seeing me as something virtuous, and that he was seeing himself very much as a toad, and I can't explain that very strong sense I had, but it stayed with me for a very long time afterwards.'

I had a mental picture of my father squatting toad-like by the side of the road, watching Joyce Jonas coming towards him on her way to church, the image of purity and goodness. It was a striking anecdote, with a kind of 'Beauty and the Beast' aspect to it, as if she had somehow managed to sense the Mr Hyde side of my father's character, in a brief, almost telepathic moment of intuition that she had not been able to explain to herself until now. Was it only her interpretation, or had he really seen himself as flawed and corrupted and carrying some secret burden, envious of someone who possessed the virtue and innocence that he had lost?

It was not the kind of conversation that any of us were used to having every day. Joyce looked somewhat dazed as she announced that her break was over and she had to go to a tutorial. 'I suppose anything is going to seem rather ordinary after this, isn't it?' she said. I agreed that it would. Afterwards I sat talking to Cicily for a little longer. We talked about children, their universality and innocence and their ability to remake the world for adults. The subject led to the recent killings at Dunblane, and she said that she could not think about the massacre without thinking of all those parents who were without their children. We also talked about the events of 1967. Although she was clearly sympathetic to my mother, she nevertheless expressed surprise at the fact that she had 'allowed' my father to treat her the way he had.

'If any man had done that to me, I would have broken a bottle over his head,' she said with feeling. I replied that my father had been a lot stronger than my mother, and that it would have been difficult for her to fight back. She shrugged. 'I would have waited till he was asleep and then smashed him on the head with it.'

I had no doubt that she meant it, but it was difficult to imagine my mother sneaking up on her sleeping husband and bashing him over the head with a bottle. My mother has always tended to implode when angry, expressing anger through looks and silences, rather than my father's explosive outbursts. I could not remember her even raising her voice, let alone using physical violence on anyone. She once admitted to me that she had thought of killing him in Jamaica as the only way of getting out of the relationship, but the wish never advanced beyond the fantasy. Many women caught up in abusive relationships have undoubtedly had similar fantasies, but only a few have actually carried them out, usually to a less-than-sympathetic reception from the courts. Even if she had managed to summon up the necessary violence to fight him on his own terms, she would almost certainly have had to kill him to avoid worse retaliation, and a jail sentence for premeditated murder would not have been much of a liberation.

Cicily clearly saw things differently. Her own marriage had ended some years before, and her experience of her husband seemed to have rid her of any idealistic notions regarding the male species, especially the Guyanese male. Nevertheless she had been shocked by my father's behaviour.

'In Guyana many men have two or even three homes,' she said, 'but they *pay* for them! And they don't treat their wives like that. Burnham used to ask his ministers not only for their home phone numbers but the numbers of the houses where they *really* were so that he could always reach them at any time of day, but these men would still be supporting their families and they wouldn't be violent.'

She also expressed disapproval at my father's marriage to Marjorie and said that he should not have married a black woman. When I asked why not, she replied that 'we' did not believe mixed marriages were a good thing. Whether 'we' referred to the PNC, the Afro-Guyanese, or the entire Guyanese population was not clear, but the fact that she could openly express such a separatist attitude to relationships without a trace of reserve or embarrassment was an indication of the country's sexual politics, and also of the stir that my father's second marriage must have created, in certain circles at least. There was no time to go into any of these issues, as her lunch break had now come to an end. 'Well,' she said, smiling as we shook hands, 'I'm glad to see you made it out in one piece!'

I walked around the campus for a while longer before taking a minibus back to town. All the way back to the hotel, I kept imagining my father sitting beside the road, a sad, wretched creature who had lost his way in the world, his shirt untucked, just as it had been the last time I had seen him alive, waiting for someone to take him home. It was impossible not to feel sympathy towards the man that Joyce Jonas had described. In the years that we had grown up without him, we had become used to regarding him as the villain and ourselves as the innocent victims. Now it seemed that he had been as much a victim of himself as any of us, and that what had happened all those years ago had been merely one episode in the long-drawn-out tragedy of his life, a tragedy that had continued after we had gone, right up to the last act.

*

My father's reputation as a charismatic teacher is something that began in the West Indies, along with his predilection for rum and Shakespeare. Before coming to the Caribbean he had never taught in a classroom or a lecture hall; his teaching had been restricted to the individual supervisions that he carried out while he was doing his research. Tony Scull had no memory of him as a particularly outstanding teacher, although he had considered him 'a powerful supervisor of great intellectual calibre'. In his teaching, as in other areas of his life, the Caribbean brought something out of him that was not evident before.

One of his friends in Guyana was the poet Ian McDonald, a Trinidadian 'local white' who edited the excellent literary journal *Kyk-over-al*, and also worked for the nationalized sugar company Guysuco, formerly Bookers, the powerful British company that had once dominated virtually every aspect of the Guyanese economy. A serious, gentle man with a distinguished air, he dropped round to the hotel and gave me some of his books of poetry as a present. One contained a handwritten tribute to my father's 'profound knowledge of good books'. Both he and my father had been educated at Cambridge at different times, and they had shared a common passion for literature and poetry. They had often lent books to each other and spent a lot of time together on the patio at Stone Avenue, where 'the ogre of the patio', as my father called himself, prepared his classes. Not surprisingly his memory of my father was indelibly associated with books and literature. 'I have a very vivid memory of Bill at home, reclined on a Berbice chair and absolutely surrounded with books. He'd have a stand and they were piled up there, and then there'd be a pile on the floor coming up next to the chair, and there'd be one on the arm of the chair itself, and of course he'd been reading one, and while we were talking he'd often pick out one, or put some aside, or bring one out of the pile and begin to leaf through it and quote from it, and so the hours would go by.'

Despite having been greatly impressed by my father's knowledge and insights during these literary afternoons, he had only seen him lecture once, towards the end of his life. My father was giving a special public lecture on Martin Carter, the Guyanese national poet. He had only recently come out of hospital and was still very sick and frail, but Carter had been a friend and he was keen to speak. The lecture generated a lot of interest beforehand and the auditorium was filled with an enthusiastic and expectant audience. 'I was absolutely astonished,' said Ian, 'because there he was. I knew he'd not been at all well, and he got up and he lectured for an hour without notes. All he had was Martin Carter's selected poems in his hand, and he lectured for an hour with absolute brilliance, and gave me perceptions of Martin Carter – and I know his work very well – that I'd never had before. He was lucid, he was brilliant, the love of the poetry came out enormously strongly. Everybody was absolutely enthralled, and I went away saying that this must be one of the great lecturers, if this is how he lectures all the time, and I'll always remember that day, because it was one of the most brilliant lectures I'd ever heard, and I was at Cambridge for four years, so I'd heard many great lectures.'

Listening to this, it occurred to me that both Ian McDonald and my father belonged to a literary culture that had existed before the dominance of film and TV, when writers were still considered by some to be the unacknowledged legislators of the world and 'good books' were believed to have a civilizing influence over society. What would my father have made, I wondered, of structuralism and deconstruction and postmodernism? How would he have responded to hip leftist academics who built their careers dismissing the work of 'dead white males' as politically and aesthetically irrelevant because they had not denounced sexism or imperialism in their novels? Would he have agreed that the writers he revered were in fact instruments of the 'dominant culture' and therefore indirect accomplices of racial and sexual domination? And what would he have had to say about some of the self-regarding icons of contemporary English fiction, who had reduced the writing of novels to a vacuous exercise in style and slick wordplay, in which real intelligence and moral passion were replaced by smirking cleverness and glib cynicism? Not much, I thought. At least living in Guyana had spared him that, because the fact was that the kind of writing my father believed in was becoming increasingly obsolete in his home country. Perhaps 'literature' had never had the moral influence on society that critics like Matthew Arnold and Leavis had once assigned to it, but there was no doubt also that its impact had been drastically reduced in the last half of the century. How many people in England looked to writers, especially novelists, to pose important questions about society? And how many writers even asked them in the first place? In an age where fiction rarely rose above the level of light entertainment or ego gratification for celebrity authors, both the writing and the reading of novels had become little more than an intellectual pastime, while literature remained a highbrow academic activity confined to the universities, where professors haggled over the political meaning of subtexts in the classics like convicts looking for a file inside a wedding cake.

The same sense of a bygone era hovered over my father's attitude to his teaching. In a highly technological consumer society, where the whole concept of an arts education as a means of widening the possibilities of the human personality was disappearing, a degree in English was rapidly becoming an anachronism. The idea that my father had 'touched students lives', which I heard so often in Guyana, was not something I had ever heard from anyone I had ever known who had gone to an English university, where professors were too often remote, inaccessible icons, dispensing knowledge and opinions that their students were often too awed by to question. This was the world that my father had wanted to return to, and I could not help feeling that he would have been as out-of-place within the English Academy as one of those Japanese soldiers who occasionally emerge from New Guinea decades after the war is over, only to find out that the enemy has won.

Apart from other people's impressions, the only evidence I had of his teaching ability was a copy of a radio lecture that he had given for Guyanese schools on *Romeo and Juliet*. The descriptions of his 'performances' in the classroom had sometimes made me wonder whether his theatrical teaching style might have had more value as entertainment than as education, but the tape provided a pleasant surprise. The lecture had been recorded in the studio, and the voice that emerged was something that I could not remember ever having heard before. It was an immediately likeable voice, without the Caribbean accent that I remembered from England, the voice of a wise old man of the world sharing his knowledge and experience with his younger listeners. The lecture itself was humorous, knowledgeable and insightful, and the evidence of the few quoted excerpts from the play suggested that he was a much better actor than I had imagined, as he slipped in and out of different characters and accents with ease and conviction. Only at one brief moment, when the gentle, professorial voice suddenly delivered Mercutio's dying speech, with passionate fury, could I hear the echo of the old Bill Carr carried down the years, roaring, 'A plague on your houses! Your HOUSES!'

However good my father may have been as a teacher inside the classroom, his academic reputation was severely undermined outside it by his lack of published work and his aversion to academic research. At the time he arrived in the West Indies, the concept of 'Commonwealth literature' was just beginning to gain critical acceptance in England. His first-hand contact with West Indian culture and society, and his personal acquaintance with most of the region's well-known writers, placed him in a unique position from which to build an international academic reputation as a specialist on West Indian literature. Yet throughout all the years he spent in the Caribbean he never published a single book on the subject. Despite occasional references in his letters to forthcoming books of criticism on Derek Walcott and the Jamaican writer John Hearne, these books never materialized. From the mid-60s onwards his output gradually dried up as his drinking intensified, so that he rarely published any articles at all, especially in the kind of literary and academic journals that might have helped to establish his reputation. Nor did he attend the conferences and symposiums through which academics exchange information and research findings.

All this meant that he failed to keep up with the new developments in criticism even within his specialist field. His lack of published work meant that his name was never really known outside the West Indies itself, despite his early pioneering efforts on behalf of West Indian literature when he lived in Jamaica. While former students of his went on to teach West Indian Literature at U W I, and other contemporaries and colleagues edited anthologies of Caribbean writing and secured professorships at English and American universities, he stayed in Guyana and drifted further and further behind, to the point when he was virtually unemployable in any university except U G itself. In 1976 he even applied for a special chair of West Indian literature at the university. Professor Bill Murray from Lancaster University gave him a dubious reference, mentioning my father's lack of published material as a negative factor against his appointment. Professor Murray described him as 'a lively and sensitive critic' at his best, but added rather dismissively that 'he does not seem to me to be, from his literary criticism, a man with much weight in the philosophical part of his intellectual life' because 'his convictions show through at all points and may perhaps, in the very firmness with which they are held, be a disadvantage to an academic critic'.

Whether this criticism referred to my father's political opinions or his general intellectual approach, it suggested that the qualities his students so admired did not necessarily appeal to his academic colleagues back in England. There was, of course, no obligation on him to publish anything, and it may be that, unlike many academics, he was more interested in teaching than he was in establishing an academic reputation. Nevertheless he did take himself seriously as a literary critic, and it was a paradox that someone who felt as strongly about writers and writing as he did could not motivate himself for long enough to put his ideas and feelings about them into print. Instead he saved his ideas for the classroom, the bar-room and the patio. However stimulating or entertaining this may have been for his listeners, the overall impression I had of my father's professional life was of a man who had failed to live up to the promise he had shown in his youth.

Perhaps he was afraid of finishing anything in case he was disappointed, but I could not help feeling that this failure to publish was yet another consequence of his self-destructiveness. Even on a practical level a few articles might have made a vast difference to his life. From time to time he did try to get out of Guyana and look for work abroad, but his job applications were rarely successful. The truth − although he could not see it − was that both his health and his lack of published work had made him virtually unemployable abroad. His description of himself as an 'Emeritus Professor' in his last letter to my cousin was one further indication of how far removed the 'Patio God' had become from reality.

It is one of the sad ironies of my father's life that his declining years coincided with the dramatic decline of the institution in whose achievements he had taken so much pride. Today the University of Guyana is in the grip of a profound financial and educational crisis from which it may not emerge intact, at least in the form that its socialist founders originally intended. Unable to pay teachers' salaries, buy new books or basic equipment or even maintain its crumbling infrastructure, the university is a shadow of its former self.

Academic standards were already falling consistently during the Burnham years as a result of poor working conditions, low salaries, and politically motivated appointments, but they are now so low that one lecturer complained to me that a U G degree is worth no more than a high school certificate. The decline has demoralized students and staff alike. On the same day as my visit to the campus there was a violent clash between police and students demanding the dismissal of a lecturer who had torn up his students' essays on the grounds that they were not worth marking. The students were also protesting against the deteriorating amenities of the university; the discovery of a dead dog in a lavatory was the last straw.

The origins of the crisis at U G can be traced to the general economic collapse of the country in the 70s and 80s, but it has now reached such a point that the university may be closed down or converted into a secondary school. The decay was already well in evidence before my father retired, and he often railed against the running-down of the university and the political interference that was turning it into 'a pseudo high school where the yawning bullies have absolute dominion'.

In one well-known incident he staged a typically self-destructive protest. The roof of his office needed repairing, and during the rainy season the rain would pour down directly on to his desk. Instead of moving to another office, or even moving his desk, he carried on working in the same place, letting the rain pour down on him till he was completely drenched. When staff members tried to persuade him to leave he insisted that he was in his place of work and was not going to move till the roof was fixed. True to his word, he stayed there, letting the rain pour down on him day after day, until he eventually became seriously ill and had to go to hospital.

I heard this story from a number of people, and it symbolized for me the peculiar combination of stubborn principle, attention-seeking and outright masochism of his life in Guyana. In a public act of political protest was also concealed a more private longing for death and punishment. 'I could never write an obituary on U G,' he wrote in 1985. 'Perhaps I am selfish. But then I feel I would be writing my own.' U G's obituary has still not been written, but the day may not be far off. And if the university does finally close, it would be a sad end to an institution that involved so much goodwill and dedication. Perhaps my father is lucky not to have to watch the finest achievement of his life crumble away.

Chapter Eight

One afternoon I went to the national zoo at the Botanical Gardens to look for the largest snake in the world. I had last seen it in 1967, a giant anaconda from the interior, lying in state in its own glass cage. Despite my snake phobia I used to spend hours watching the dormant reptile whenever I visited the zoo, waiting in vain for it to uncoil to its full length. Then, as now, the zoo had been one of the few places to go in Georgetown. I often went there with Bruce, crossing into the Botanical Gardens from the canal behind our house in the course of our jungle explorations. My friend Anthony Nunn worked for the zoo and sometimes I helped him clean the cages and feed the lions. One Sunday we even went there on a family outing with my father, the only time I remember us doing anything together during the whole time we were in Guyana. That day he managed to draw attention to himself as usual by fearlessly retrieving some ladies' purses from a vicious kleptomaniac monkey, which danced about on the end of its chain and tried to bite anyone who went near it.

The monkey and the largest snake in the world had gone, but there were still manatees, their pale fleshy bodies occasionally protruding momentarily above the surface of their pond like giant floating sausages. The zoo's main attraction was its spectacular collection of exotic birds from the Guyanese interior, clustered together on their branches in a dazzling array of brilliant colours like figures from a Rousseau painting. I wandered round the little compound looking at the varied assortment of lions, tapirs, wild hogs and snakes that I had once watched being fed with a child's fascination.

It was a place that I had never expected to see again, where nothing particularly outstanding or dramatic had happened, and yet it always came to mind whenever I thought of Guyana. Perhaps it was the zoo's association with childhood and innocence, and the intense excitement that these caged animals had once provoked in me that had made it stick so vividly in my mind. Or perhaps the largest snake in the world was simply one of those arbitrary, even banal bits and pieces that lodge themselves in the memory for no logical reason, so that decades later we still remember them with perfect clarity when far more important details about the past have become blurred or forgotten.

My father must have felt the same sense of familiarity and mild surprise on visiting the places in England associated with his youth and finding that they were still there, just as he had imagined them, and now here I was, on the other side of the world, peeling back layers of memory in an attempt to reconstruct the past. Every conversation, every meeting offered a new glimpse into my father's lost world, and also into mine, as the memories of my childhood continued to play over and over again in my mind. I was now emotionally closer to that period than I had ever been at any time in my adult life, as I tried to put all the pieces together into some kind of totality. But there was an element of wishful thinking. Part of me longed to construct an alternative past to take the place of the real one, in which my father's behaviour would finally be explained and forgiven, and there would be no more mysteries or blank spaces left. Closing the circle, I called it, without knowing exactly what I meant by that, although I knew it had something to do with assimilating and accepting a part of my life that had always seemed an unmitigated disaster and which I had always tried to put behind me.

It was a slightly unreal life I was leading back in Guyana. During the day I went all over the city, chasing up leads and visiting different people who knew my father. In the evenings I usually had dinner in the hotel restaurant, with its black-and-white engravings from the colonial era depicting an idealized nineteenth-century society of horse-drawn carriages, wooden churches, sugar mills without slaves, and men and women in top hats and long dresses. Nearly always there were more waiters than customers, and they performed their tasks with a kind of ritualistic solemnity and concentration, as if grateful for the chance to do anything at all, while an old man twanged the same dreamy, melancholy melodies on an electric guitar. Afterwards I usually had a couple of drinks and went to bed early, where I read through my father's articles and letters, and watched a flickering satellite serial about Rasputin and the Romanovs before trying to go to sleep.

Almost every night I had insomnia and had to take a sleeping pill, so that I woke up in the morning needing a few cups of strong coffee to restore myself to consciousness. I had only been in the country a few days, but already the past had begun to weigh down on my mind with a gloomy, suffocating intensity. It was during these hot, airless nights, when I would find myself lying awake for hours, listening to the din of a nearby air-conditioner, with my thoughts going round in circles asking questions that never seemed to have definitive answers, that the past seemed most oppressive and inexplicable.

Nevertheless it was pleasant to be back in the Botanical Gardens again. The sun had gone down, and the landscaped garden of trees, plants and lilies looked beautiful and soothing to the eye. A pair of lovers were snuggling up to each other near some bushes and a group of school kids in karate suits were performing martial arts exercises on the grass. I had already begun to appreciate these cool Guyanese evenings, when the streets slowly emptied and the light seemed softer and slightly golden after the harsh glare and heat of the day. In spite of its unhappy personal associations, there was a careless, ramshackle beauty in that run-down colonial town, with its canals and white buildings and careless, exuberant greenery sprouting up everywhere like a dream of the tropics.

In theory Georgetown was a recipe for urban chaos. The roads were scarred with potholes, many of the traffic lights didn't seem to work, there were no cops or buses anywhere, most neighbourhoods were subject to daily blackouts, and yet somehow the city seemed to function, and it was on evenings like this that it was at its most attractive and seductive, when the outside world seemed as remote from Guyana as Guyana did from the outside world, and the most logical and natural thing to do was sit in the shade with a bottle of Five Year and pour yourself an evening drink and watch the night come slowly down.

Perhaps this sense of isolation and introspection was a psychological effect of being stuck between the jungle on one side and the vast emptiness of the Atlantic on the other; more than any other city I have ever been to, Georgetown felt as though it were the only place on earth. The city functioned on a wavelength so different from anywhere else that it was difficult to know whether it was falling apart or slowly coming together. Even the familiar brand names and advertisements that give most cities a superficial visual uniformity were absent. Despite the ghostly satellite B-movies, the live NBA matches and the US commercials, somehow the world of Nike,

Coca-Cola and the United Colours of Benetton had passed Guyana by. It was as if the country had somehow become unhooked from the rest of the world during the Burnham era and been allowed to drift off on its own, at the same sluggish pace, without anybody even realizing that it had gone.

Near the main entrance to the Botanical Gardens stands Castellani House, the former Governor-General's residence that had later become the home of L. F. S. Burnham, the Comrade Leader. It was here that the lunatic I had read about in the newspaper had been found in the cupboard. Today the enormous white mansion has been turned into an art gallery; there was an exhibition of African painting and sculpture when I went to visit. Inevitably there were no other visitors, and I wandered through the labyrinthine sequence of doors and rooms, all of them made from the same luxurious combination of mahogany and tropical hardwoods. I was less interested in the exhibition than I was in seeing the house where the Comrade Leader had lived during his years in power.

From the upper floors I could see the large open field with the statue of Cuffee. A black slave, he had led the failed Berbice slave uprising of 1763, and had later been roasted alive by the vengeful planters. With a characteristic mixture of cynicism and self-delusion, Burnham and his cohorts had portrayed themselves as Cuffee's spiritual descendants, carrying the torch of black resistance to white domination into the twentieth century. Like much of Burnham's rhetoric, it was a fraud, but one that carried great emotional force in a country with a centuries-old tradition of slave revolts and guerrilla warfare against white rule. I imagined the great man now, looking balefully down at the large open field where every year, on the national holiday to commemorate the revolt, he would address the massed crowds gathered in his honour with a mixture of black nationalist and Third Worldist jargon.

In comparison with the bloodstained excesses of Bokasssa, Amin, the Shah of Iran, and other Third World tyrants who rose to power with the active sponsorship of their former colonial rulers, Linden Forbes Burnham was a minor monster, but a monster nevertheless. An Oxford Rhodes Scholar, he originally trained as a barrister before entering politics in the early fifties as a political comrade of Cheddi Jagan on the PPP executive, but his adherence to the Marxist PPP always owed more to personal ambition than to ideological conviction. In 1953, when the British responded to the PPP's overwhelming victory in the colony's first national elections by suspending the Guyanese constitution and sending troops to the country, Burnham sensed which way the Cold War wind was blowing, and declared himself an anti-communist. Two years later, encouraged by the British, he left the party to form the People's National Congress, supposedly because of his aversion to the PPP's pro-Soviet line.

The formation of the new party meant that Guyanese politics was now split along racial lines: while the PNC took the Afro-Guyanese population with it, the majority of East Indians continued to support the PPP. This was a dangerous situation, which was shortly to have dire consequences for Guyana.

Burnham's party whipped up racial hostility towards Cheddi Jagan's 'coolie-rice government', but continued to enjoy the support of the British and the Americans. This foreign support finally paid dividends in 1964, when Jagan, in what many considered to be a monumental act of political misjudgement, conceded to British and American pressure, and agreed to change the voting system to one of proportional representation in return for independence. The subsequent elections enabled the PNC to gain power at last, in coalition with a right-wing party led by a local businessman. Shortly afterwards, the former anti-communist Burnham embarked on an ideological U-turn in order to exploit the radical ideological currents spreading through Guyana and the Caribbean, reinventing himself as a black nationalist leader and anti-colonialist revolutionary.

Following the PNC's first fraudulent electoral victory in 1968, which gave it undivided power, the party embarked upon an ultra-leftist, ill-planned programme of nationalizations, with catastrophic consequences. There are few parallels in modern history, in peacetime conditions, to the extraordinary collapse that took place in Guyana under Burnham's misrule. In the two decades following Guyanese independence in 1966 the economy went into meltdown and what was potentially one of the richest countries in the Caribbean saw its standard of living slip below that of Haiti's. Agricultural production sank to a record low, the public transportation system virtually ceased to exist, the vital bauxite industry collapsed, imports dried up – except to the PNC elite – and basic goods like bread, sugar, cigarettes and rice became scarce or disappeared from the shops altogether. Hospitals, schools and factories were all sucked into the dizzying decline, along with most other institutions. As the streets began to overflow with madmen, beggars and criminal gangs, the most talented sectors of society fled the country en masse, a process which only intensified Guyana's spectacular downward spiral.

The deeper the country plummeted into the abyss, the more the PNC attempted to divert attention from its responsibility by resorting to shrill, nationalist rhetoric, blaming imperialist intervention and foreign pressure for the disaster. *Build Co-operative Guyana Through Self-Help... We Must Control and Own Our Own Resources ... We Shall Feed, House and Clothe Ourselves by 1976* ... The meaningless slogans continued to pour forth each year, clarion calls for non-existent programmes and policies that bore less and less connection to reality. Amid the mounting chaos and poverty, the Comrade Leader and his family continued to grow richer and his megalomania intensified. Like dictators everywhere, he was intent on making his country a projection of himself, naming towns and streets after himself and his family, organizing giant Chinese-style rallies in which massed ranks of schoolchildren would form his portrait. Articulate, well-educated, even intellectual, Burnham was never the stereotypical ranting tyrant. He emanated an icy self-control, delivering his wordy utterances in clipped, tight-lipped sentences, using extravagant phrases like 'the paramountcy of the party' and 'attitudinal metamorphosis' to describe his peculiar form of pseudo-socialist gangsterism. 'Which party can guarantee a happy new year every year?' asked Burnham in 1973, as the country continued to collapse around him. 'There is only one answer!'

Even though Burnham seemed to regard Guyana as his personal property, he still retained a lawyer's fondness for legalistic procedures, referendums and elections, however fraudulent, to legitimize his rule. To the outside world at least, this meant that Guyana was never quite seen as a dictatorship, despite the PNC's python-like grip on most areas of national life, and its selective use of violence and other repressive measures to intimidate the opposition. The Comrade Leader's revolutionary posturing even earned him a reputation abroad as a progressive, attracting the support of Castro and Angela Davis. A motley collection of phoney revolutionaries, crooks and outright madmen made their way to the Co-operative Republic – men like the Reverend Jim Jones, Michael X, the Trinidadian Black Power activist and multiple murderer, and the self-styled 'Rabbi Washington', a fugitive from the FBI, whose House of Israel sect would play a key role in suppressing and terrorizing the opposition to Burnham.

All these men shared the same, mostly fraudulent involvement with racial politics and black liberationism as a basis for their power and reputation. The hothouse racial atmosphere and corruption of the Co-operative Republic provided them with a natural home. In the ideological wonderland of Burnham's Guyana, the slogans and empty gestures easily blurred the distinctions between what was being said and what was actually done, allowing the charlatans and racial hucksters to blend easily into the political landscape.

The most notorious of Guyana's refugees from abroad was the Reverend Jim Jones, the deranged 'socialist' preacher from the United States, whose People's Temple carved a communitarian Utopia out of the wilderness, which eventually led to the holocaust at Jonestown. The revelations concerning the Burnham regime's close connections with the People's Temple would damage his reputation abroad, but were not enough to loosen his grip on power internally. And so Linden Forbes Burnham continued to rule the country until 1985, when he died of a simple throat infection because no hospital in Georgetown had the equipment to treat him.

In a small country like Guyana, it was never very likely that Burnham was going to remain unaware of my father's existence, even if my father had been more discreet in the expression of his political views. It was equally unlikely that my father would have ended up anywhere else except in the anti-Burnham opposition. Although there was a superficial similarity between the aims and language of the two parties, the PNC's style of government effectively meant a one-party state with a neutralized parliamentary opposition; by contrast Cheddi Jagan's People's Progressive Party remained a social-democratic party in Marxist-Leninist clothing and provided the only left-wing alternative to Burnham at that time, even though it was excluded from power by the PNC's vote-rigging machine. The PNC was also profoundly anti-white, as my father had already learned from his rum-shop brawling with the party's supporters.

When we were living in Guyana my father's political activity was restricted mostly to heated debates with his friends and colleagues at the university, but in the years immediately after our departure his involvement in Guyanese politics deepened and he moved gradually closer to the PPP. In the early 70s he began writing articles for the PPP party newspaper, the *Mirror*, at a time when the political atmosphere in the country was becoming more violent and repressive. In 1972 he wrote to my mother:

> *Guyana is a nasty fucked-up place to live and work in as long as Burnham and his bitches are in. A boy of fifteen was kidnapped, stabbed and wounded the other day because his father was a vendor of* The Mirror *and* Mirror *people are subjected to police harassment. What happens if you write for it? I have now had to use a pseudonym – Little Boy Blue – but I'm told that my 'style' gives me away. The PPP is all that one has left. Ah, well.*
>
> *Regards,*
> *Bill*

That same year 'Little Boy Blue' went one step further and actually joined the PPP. It was a risky step to take as far as his future in Guyana was concerned, when other foreign academics critical of the government were losing their jobs or even being deported. In effect he was almost challenging the PNC to do something about him. That he was well aware of the risks he was taking is clear from the following letter to my mother, written in the same year.

> *Everybody thinks that PPP-wise I have gone stark, raving mad. Not at all. I thought about it for sometime. Anyway they treat you like a human being not like a white bastard, a honky shit, etc. I got tired of being pissed on in a country full of bullies and cowards. Somebody had to run a risk and make some kind of sense. I think I'll survive, in which case some guys will look a bit embarrassed. Though God knows what will happen if I lose. They meet exactly a month from now – much too late for me to be able to get a job anywhere that is worth having. We'll see.*

As a political manifesto, this self-dramatizing fragment owes more to Marlon Brando or Alan Ladd than Karl Marx. Typically my father presents his membership of the PPP as a heroic individual gesture, with wider repercussions for society as a whole. It is the drama of the peace-loving man, finally pushed too far, who comes riding into town to sort out the bullies. The reference to a forthcoming meeting presumably referred to an attempt by the PNC-stacked university board to get rid of him, but in the event — as he always did — he managed to keep his job.

As melodramatic as his conception of it may have been, his membership of the PPP was not merely symbolic. In the early 70s in particular he was an active member of the party. He embraced its cause as his own, taking part in electoral campaigns and demonstrations and making public speeches denouncing the regime. At the same time his chief constituency was always the East Indian population, which made up the bulk of the PPP's support, and Burnham never felt sufficiently threatened by such activity to take serious action against him.

My father's attitude to Burnham himself was typically contradictory. He despised the Comrade Leader with the same visceral passion he had once reserved for Bustamante in Jamaica, giving full vent to his spleen in both private and public. At a time when many people were afraid to criticize the regime at all, he seems to have held Burnham personally responsible for the evening blackouts which interrupted his reading or his television viewing, and the inevitable electricity cuts would often provoke an explosion of 'Jesus fucking Christ — Buurrnhaam!' followed by a stream of curses directed at the malignant presence hovering over the city. His hatred was so intense and expressed with such monotonous regularity that Vanessa told me she used to wish someone would kill Burnham just so her stepfather would stop being so miserable. Yet when Burnham did die, my father went out on to Sheriff Avenue and wept at the sight of his riderless white horse in the funeral cortège, saying that this was not the way he had wanted to defeat him.

The two men met on various occasions. There is even a story that Burnham rode over to my father's house, during one of his many serious bouts of illness, with a bottle of plum wine to wish him a recovery.

At first my father's membership of the PPP provided him with a cause. Between his break-up with Andaiye and his marriage to Marjorie, his membership of the party seems to have been his main reason for staying in the country at all. As in Jamaica, his activity earned him a prominence and notoriety that he would not have achieved in England. Political life in Guyana was conducted on a more personalized and human scale than in a bigger country. Political enemies knew each other, lived near each other, and often came into contact socially, especially at the university.

My father was a member of the Jagans' local party group. He was not only on good terms with most members of the PPP hierarchy, but also knew many of the PNC leaders personally as well. This kind of face-to-face politics would have been very important for him, since his political choices were often as much influenced by the personalities he encountered as the ideas they held. He was never the kind of anonymous revolutionary described by Brecht as a 'blank sheet on which the revolution writes its instructions'. In politics, as in most other areas of his life, he needed to be on stage, with a more dramatic role than the mundane routines of democratic life in England were ever likely to provide, and for a while at least, in the long, bitter struggle against the PNC, he seems to have found it.

It was Janet Jagan – the wife of the president and long-time editor of the *Mirror* – who first put me on the trail of Moses Nagamootoo. I had called her up to arrange to visit the paper, and she recommended him as a former journalist and political comrade of my father's, who had known him much better than she did. She also said that he had once interviewed my father at length about his life before coming to Guyana. This was exciting news. I had talked to a lot of people, but apart from the few flashes of revelation contained in his letters and articles, I still did not have my father's version of his past. How had he presented the murkier episodes in his life to the world? How had he explained them to himself? Barring a ghostly Shakespearian visitation in my hotel room, it did not seem likely that these questions would ever be answered. Now the possibility had emerged that he might have answered them after all and I felt as excited as a historian suddenly presented with the existence of a new and potentially revealing document.

I called Moses Nagamootoo at his office at the Ministry of Information. He seemed as excited at the prospect of meeting 'Bill's son' as I was about meeting him. Not only had he written a series of long articles about my father's life, he said, but he had also recorded four tapes of 'beautiful' interviews with him. This was even better, or so it seemed. The problem was that he didn't have the transcripts and the tapes were now in the possession of Marjorie's sister, Joan. According to Moses, my father had had possession of the tapes, and some years ago had complained to him one day that his sister-in-law had got hold of them. Moses was too busy to go into this mysterious episode in more detail, but he invited me to come to the funeral of Romesh Walsil, one of President Jagan's bodyguards, the following day, and said that we could talk there.

And so the next afternoon I drove out to the funeral, which was being held near Ogle, a small town about twenty minutes out of Georgetown along the main road to the airport. At around 1 o'clock the taxi-driver turned off the main road and drove along a dirt track through an East Indian village with little plots of vegetables in the gardens and dogs and chickens running around among the cluster of stilted houses. The funeral was not hard to find. Outside one of the houses, an assortment of cars were parked, with chauffeurs standing alongside them. A small crowd was waiting patiently in the sweltering heat, including a military band in ceremonial white jackets, caps and gloves and a detachment of armed soldiers. In the garden a few hundred people were standing or sitting quietly on rows of benches beneath a plastic awning, mostly East Indian relatives and friends of the deceased. The older women were dressed traditionally in white veils, while the younger women wore smart Western clothes. The men were dressed in the informal Guyanese style, with untucked white shirts and black trousers.

A little aisle had been roped off between the benches, leading to a raised coffin, where the bodyguard's immediate family were gathered. An old woman who seemed to be a professional mourner let out shrieks and moans of anguish at key moments in the ceremony. I joined the queue of people waiting to pay their respects and stood briefly before the deceased. Romesh Walsil was lying with his arms folded, dressed in a smart black suit and surrounded by flowers. He was a big-shouldered, barrel-chested man with a thick black moustache who looked much too young and strong to be laid out in a coffin.

Unsure what to do with myself, I went out into the garden and mingled with the crowd. The occasion was obviously an important party event as well as a private funeral. Various members of the P P P hierarchy were sitting on benches, including the president and the First Lady, together with former comrades of Romesh. I also noticed some of my father's former colleagues from the university. The overwhelming presence of East Indians provided an accurate reflection of the party's ethnic base of support, but there was a sprinkling of Afro-Guyanese, including a towering bodyguard wearing dark sunglasses and a black suit, with a knife attached to his belt in a little sheath. I already had appointments with both the Jagans and there seemed no point in introducing myself to them now. Instead I drifted around the crowd, until a stocky, unsmiling East Indian, in dark wraparound sunglasses, appeared out of the crowd and introduced himself as Moses Nagamootoo.

Moses, who looked in his late forties, was short and stocky with a shock of black hair combed backwards. His thick forearms and heavy, slightly paunchy body gave one the impression of a wrestler beginning to go to seed. Besides being the Minister of Information, he held various other portfolios and, even though he wore his authority lightly, it was obvious from the way people kept coming up to him to hold discreet conversations that he was a man of influence in the party. He had known Romesh well and was clearly upset by his death. President Jagan's bodyguard had been only forty-seven years old and his death had taken everyone by surprise. He had been a member of the PPP for most of his adult life and had accompanied the president everywhere, as his personal servant, cook, masseur and escort in countless demonstrations, meetings and political campaigns.

Romesh had also received military training in Bulgaria in preparation for a possible armed uprising against Burnham, an option which Cheddi Jagan had rejected. He was a man who belonged to another era – to the PPP's harsh years in the political wilderness. He was a streetfighter who had grown up in a poor rural family and spent his entire political life in an atmosphere of violence and repression. Ironically, the PPP's belated electoral victory in 1992 and the subsequent normalization of Guyanese political life had left him feeling that he was without a role. He had retired from active politics to tend his garden and grow vegetables, and one afternoon, just a few days previously, the former bodybuilder had been chopping down some coconut trees in his back garden when he had dropped dead of a heart attack. The coconut tree was still there, lying in the garden behind the guests, a monument to the unpredictable workings of fate and the absurdity that often coexisted with the tragic. 'That man will be kicking his coffin tonight!' Moses said, shaking his head at his former comrade's death, as though discussing a cricketer who had thrown his wicket away with a foolish shot.

Moses introduced me to another member of Internal Security, a tough-looking, amiable black bodyguard called Harold Snag, who like Romesh had also been part of my father's circle. Harold had once saved his life during a political rally in Georgetown in the early 70s. According to his modest account some hundred-odd P N C supporters had come specifically in order to 'get Bill Carr'. One of them had pulled a knife and tried to stab my father, but Harold had intercepted the blow and thrown the weapon away.

The bodyguard, who had shared many similar scrapes with my father, remembered him fondly. 'He was a guy I respected a lot because he was very intelligent,' he said. 'He used to like a little drink, but he was a dedicated man for righteousness. He believed in the integrity and honesty of individuals. He believed that justice must be not for one person but for all. Once I asked him, "Are you a communist?" and he said, "If being a communist means fighting for what I believe in then I'm a communist." '

The bodyguard was clearly impressed by my father's definition of his politics, but the crackle of a voice on the loudspeaker put an end to his reminiscences. I moved nearer to the coffin, as the professional mourner let out a heart-rending shriek. On the far side of the coffin a young swami in a white tunic with the polished good looks of an Indian film star was standing by the microphone. He spoke a few words and then half sang, half chanted a beautiful Sanskrit prayer. The crowd echoed back the refrain, a sad, haunting melody that sounded like a farewell to the dead. The young swami then gave a rather rambling sermon on the need to account for our actions and perform our social duties and not to lose ourselves in self-admiration. When we looked back on our lives from our 'dark little corners', he said, it was important to be able to see our actions in a positive light if we wanted to avoid frustration, stress and heart failure.

Considering the manner of Romesh's demise, this message seemed somewhat inappropriate, but no one seemed particularly disturbed by it. Nor did anyone take offence when a government minister stood up to make a speech, and had to be corrected by members of the family when he got the number of Romesh's brothers and his date of birth wrong. The minister apologized and soldiered on. His speech was an unusual one for a Marxist politician, with its mix of Hindu religious philosophy and secular morality. He placed strong emphasis on the relationship between the individual and the community, and the need to place individual actions in the context of dharma. 'Death is inevitable,' he intoned, 'death does not discriminate. Death takes the young as it takes the old, the strong, the weak, the rich, the poor, but death in itself is a lesson. It is a lesson not for the one who has passed away but for those of us who are alive. It forces us to pose certain questions to ourselves. Of what purpose have we been to our community, to our people, to our country? What contributions have we made? Have we lived unselfishly or selfishly? Those are pertinent questions.'

They were indeed, and there were certainly not many politicians asking them nowadays in my part of the world. I wondered what the answers would have been in my father's case, as President Jagan himself now got up to deliver a tribute, which picked up the theme of the individual and the collective, as he recounted examples of Romesh's bravery and selflessness. It was people like Romesh, he said, who 'make up a country' as a result of their 'commitment, dedication, their hard work, never forgetting loyalty to the family and of course adequately providing for their children'.

I knew that the president had also spoken at my father's funeral and it was not difficult to imagine that he must have said something similar, although I assumed he would have left out the part about his children. Cheddi's dedication to his own family was well known, but even if he had been familiar with the 'dark little corners' of my father's life, he would have been unlikely to mention them. Funerals always tend to promote a certain discretion among the living, and political tributes are required almost by obligation to stress the exemplary lives of their fallen comrades and their dedication to the cause, whether or not it was the cause that had killed them.

'Long live Guyana! Long live Romesh Walsil!' Cheddi concluded, as the choir now stepped forward with clenched fists raised and gave a tuneless rendition of the PPP anthem, with its awkward rhyme and metre:

> We're building our Guyana free
> not half a slave or halfway free,
> give us a sign and forward go
> each one must be a he-ro!
> the people's fortress PPP
> will keep the red flag flying!

Listening to that song, and the almost naïve sincerity with which it was delivered, I had the feeling that I had arrived in a kind of ideological version of Conan Doyle's lost world, where vanished political creeds and beliefs were still preserved in their pure state. In no other country in the English-speaking Caribbean had Marxism had more impact than in Guyana, where as early as 1905 a Guyanese labour newspaper carried an enthusiastic report of the uprising in St Petersburg. Guyana's three main parties are all Marxist-Leninist and, at a time when former communists all over the world were hurriedly reinventing themselves as social democrats, neo-liberal entrepreneurs and nationalist warlords, the red flag was still proudly flying in this isolated little corner of the South American mainland, and history, it seemed, had not ended after all.

The coffin was now closed and carried out of the house. A procession of family members and mourners, the band and the soldiers, filed into the hot sun and walked along a dirt track towards the cemetery. Along the way Moses introduced me to more people who had known my father. One of them was a skinny, intense young political science professor from the university with a mop of black hair and glasses called Freddie Kissoon, who assured me that the only way to understand Bill Carr was to read Frantz Fanon and Erich Fromm. He spoke with great seriousness, as though he were delivering a lecture on an important socio-political phenomenon. My father, he said, was a quasi-Marxist who had tried to carry the white man's burden, by 'eschewing Caucasian women' and 'fleeing into blackness'. It was a phenomenon to which he had clearly given a lot of thought, and we agreed to meet later that week at the hotel, when he would have more time to make a proper analysis.

The procession emerged on to a flat, open plain, where a small Hindu cemetery was situated on the other side of a narrow drainage canal. The sun was directly overhead now and many of the mourners held umbrellas to provide themselves with some protection from the burning heat, as they filed across the narrow wooden bridge into the cemetery. I sought some shade from a nearby van and sat on the ground watching the burial from a short distance away. The sky was almost cloudless and the wide open plain stretched out for miles towards a distant line of coconut trees, giving a sense of space and distance which was absent in Georgetown itself. A few villagers had come out on to their verandas, and sat watching curiously as the band played the Last Post and the squad of soldiers fired their rifles in the air in a military salute to the fallen hero. As I watched the funeral, I thought of my father 'eschewing Caucasian women', and his obsession with my mother's blue eyes. I remembered another story of hers about my father in Guyana. He had been sitting around the house drinking, and, as rum spilled over his vest, he taunted her about how attractive he found his female Indian students, telling her, 'When you see those coolie girls sometimes you forget you're their teacher.'

As I sat by the van in the pulverizing heat looking out over the swampy plain, contemplating this morbid, psycho-racial melodrama that was now opening up before me, I wished once again that I had not come back to Guyana. Wouldn't it have been better to have left the past alone, as incomplete and inexplicable as it had always been? Even as I asked myself the question I knew that it was too late. I felt only more anxious to get hold of the missing tapes, to find some definitive evidence of my father's motivations from my father himself, instead of relying on other people's memories and interpretations.

After the funeral Moses picked me up in his chauffeur-driven car, and we drove slowly out along the crowded dirt road. 'Look at the state of this neighbourhood,' he said, disgustedly, as we passed the rows of dilapidated-looking wooden houses. 'The P N C have mashed everything up and now we have to try and build it all up again.' We drove towards Ogle and he talked a little more about the tapes and how they had encapsulated my father's entire life from his childhood to his arrival in Guyana. The more Moses described their contents, the more I regarded these missing interviews as my father's equivalent of the Watergate tapes, which would finally provide the definitive evidence I was seeking.

Moses' attitude to Marjorie's sister Joan was extremely hostile. He assured me that my father had personally cursed her out to him over the tapes. When I asked him what Joan, or anyone else, would want with four tapes of interviews with my father, he said that he thought she had been planning to write a book about him. This was yet another bizarre twist. Was Joan's interest in the tapes motivated by literary jealousy, to pre-empt Moses, or had she wanted to use their contents herself? Moses had no doubts about the matter. The tapes, he said, were in the possession of 'that family', and they rightfully belonged to me.

As curious as I was to hear the tapes, I did not see why I had any more right to them than Marjorie and her family, but the Minister was clearly in an emotional mood after the funeral. The death of his former friend and comrade, and the unexpected appearance of Bill Carr's son on the same day, seemed to instil in him both a sense of loss and also nostalgia for the vanished heroic past they had all shared together in the darkest days of the PNC repression. He wanted to drink and we drove to a bar at the nearby internal airport, a little hideaway where Moses liked to go when he didn't want anyone to find him. He greeted the barman with easy familiarity and ordered a half-bottle of Five Year and a bowl of ice. We sat outside near one of the aircraft hangars.

'One for Bill and Romesh,' he said, emptying the contents of the first glass on the ground.

I raised my glass to toast the absent dead and gulped it down. For the rest of the afternoon we sat drinking one rum after another and talking about Bill Carr. Like almost all the Guyanese I had met so far, Moses expressed himself with a fluency and a sheer relish for language that were not easily encountered back in the motherland, but which seemed to be an integral part of Guyanese culture. In a country where everybody liked to talk and appreciated those who could talk well, the Minister of Information was a star performer. His conversation was sprinkled with metaphors, images and broad dramatic statements that sometimes bordered on the histrionic. It soon became obvious that he had an extraordinarily high regard for my father, bordering on outright devotion. Although he had not seen much of him after 1985, the two of them had once spent a lot of time together, and Moses seemed to know a lot about even his very early past. 'I think that Bill's mother had everything to do with the life that I knew him,' he said. 'The point is he was so filled with hatred, bitterness, I wouldn't even say disappointment about her, and invariably he would be returning to the question of his mother from time to time, that the mother was the one who abandoned him. The mother would be drinking, and the reason why Bill hated gin, was because gin brings back something about the mother always. I got the impression that she committed suicide, even though he didn't say that in exact words. She put some pills in her glass or something like that.'

'He was still thinking about her after all these years?' I asked.

'Yes, and I think he was consumed by it. Invariably he goes back. It is his point of reference in life, at least that life that I knew him for twenty years.'

I told him a little about what I remembered of my father and his violence towards his first wife, and asked him if he thought my father's resentment towards his mother had affected the way he felt about women in general.

'He was escaping,' he replied, 'and the fact that he had conjugal relations with non-whites and embraced black women in his life was because he was running away. He was veering towards another type of existence – into the Caribbean, into a black existence, into a dark existence. He was plunging into an abyss, and I believe he was trying to discover himself in a reverse way, to go in an opposite direction to where he had started. He had felt this rejection, as if a world had closed on him, and he was sailing, one white man, in a sea of blackness, in the Caribbean Sea.'

This was not quite the answer I had expected, but the minister was in full flight now. In his eyes my father was an almost mythical figure, the shipwrecked white man, stranded in the tropics among an alien people, except that my father had reversed the role. To escape from the memory of his mother and his middle-class English background this twentieth-century Robinson Crusoe had reinvented himself as Man Friday. He had shed his race and nationality and become indistinguishable from the inhabitants of the islands. He had 'married into their family, abided with their company and culture and way of life, their kung fu and their dance and their language and their rhythm'. And this Crusoe was also Don Quixote, a roving knight-errant in search of a larger cause. He was the white Shakespearian scholar who had so identified with the character of Othello, the black Moor, that he had actually become Othello. 'And why not?' Moses asked, rhetorically, 'because in this part of the world Bill Carr had had a phenomenal transformation of his psyche. He *was* Othello. He was a black incarnation.'

It was heady stuff, but was it true? Was this the way Moses had seen my father or the way that my father had seen himself? In that moment, as the rum began to take effect, the truth seemed less important than the telling, as the Minister of Information retraced his relationship with my father as though re-telling some biblical epic. He had first met the 'black incarnation' in 1968, when both he and Romesh had been members of the Progressive Youth Organization of the PPP. Even though my father was then in his late thirties he spent a lot of time with the young PPP radicals, many of whom were students at the university. After joining the party he gravitated towards the Internal Security section, to which Moses and Romesh belonged. This group was opposed to the strategy of peaceful political struggle advocated by the leadership and dreamt of an armed uprising against Burnham, in line with the revolutionary tide that was sweeping Latin America and the Third World. The fiery young Moses had even volunteered to fight in Vietnam, and had got as far as Mongolia, only to be rejected because Guyana was considered to be too small and insignificant a country to provide volunteers to the anti-imperialist cause.

'Bill was very popular with that group because we were looking for leadership,' Moses explained, 'and he could talk about his military experience. Whether he could only have been exposed to a G3 or such antiquated weapons, it was new to us, because he presented himself to us as someone who had seen battle. We hadn't, and so he was always fresh among young people. He belonged to the left wing of the party that said, "You have to take these bastards out with the use of revolutionary violence if necessary."'

'You're saying that one of the reasons why some people gravitated around my father was because they saw him as some kind of military expert?' I asked incredulously.

Moses nodded. 'Yes, and theoretically also. He knew much more of national liberation struggles than we knew. He was a strategic planner. He felt there had to be a strategic response to what was happening in this country. I remember him going into villages in the West Coast of Berbice in '75, '76, and he had actually organized some groups, and he was teaching them how to defend their village, how to protect the ballot boxes on election day: "Don't allow anyone to take them away, defend them with your life."'

'He was teaching them how to defend their villages militarily?' I asked in amazement.

'Well, I didn't see any guns, but I suppose he must have been telling them, "If you have it, use it."'

This was pure Lord Jim, with a touch of *The Comedians* – the Englishman in the tropics, the refugee from Western civilization redeeming himself in the struggle against a local tyrant. Or perhaps it was Che Guevara after all. When I was a child, my father had often talked to me about weapons too, but as far as I knew he had not taken part in any fighting in Malaya, nor had he had any experience of national liberation struggles except when he was in the army and played a peripheral role in helping to repress them. But whether he had actually claimed to have military experience or had simply given the impression that he had, his aggressively militant behaviour had clearly impressed the young East Indian revolutionaries.

'When he joined the party, he pasted his party card on the wall of his office!' Moses said admiringly. 'He was a serious man! He believed that in this way he was not an outsider, and he had in a sense earned his perfect, harmonious blending in the Guyanese society, and it's amazing, he was very loved. Everywhere you go from Berbice to Essequibo and you walk into various communities and you ask, "Do you know Bill Carr, the white guy," you'll find an amazing response. He would come into these marches, into these demonstrations, he would march in the noonday heat, you're talking about 98 degrees, and he would be marching with me and Cheddi Jagan for fifteen miles. He would be sore. He would keep going, and people would throw garlands at him, they will hail him. He speaks up from the platform against the dictatorship and so on, and he became even more aggressive than us. We understood the society, Bill came with a kind of bravado. He refused to accept the fact that in Guyana he was a non-Guyanese.'

Moses ordered another half-bottle, which we quickly consumed, each of us scooping handfuls of ice from the communal bowl and filling our own glasses as he turned to the subject of my father's rum-shop brawling. 'He was British, he was white, and he was beaten for being white, so he would always say, "I am on the side of the oppressed, I am on the side of those who are fighting for democracy. If you beat me, it's not Carr the white man – you're beating one other person who is against this dictatorship." So in that sense he was inviting confrontation, because if you lure the PNC, mainly black, into beating a white man, and the white man is on the side of Jagan, on the side of the PPP, it makes the cause of Jagan even holier, like a holy crusade – that there are people of non-Indian descent who are here to fight for justice.'

Martyrdom, garlands, holy crusades, Moses' language was steeped in this kind of religious imagery, and his praises were becoming more extravagant as the rum continued to flow. I had not come across anyone in Guyana who seemed to hold my father in such veneration. Like Marjorie, he described my father as a prophetic figure, the white socialist who believed in 'a broader vision, egalitarianism, the happiness of all', and deliberately turned himself into a sacrificial lamb in Guyana, allowing himself to be 'beaten for being white' in order to awaken the consciousness of the population to the evils of the Burnham dictatorship.

It was becoming obvious that the Minister of Information and I were approaching my father from entirely different directions. Unlike Moses, I could not see the beatings that my father had suffered as some noble attempt to take the sins of Guyana on his shoulders, but as part of some dark, private drama of retribution and punishment for which politics had merely provided the excuse. When I suggested this possibility, Moses frowned and looked unconvinced.

'I was one time with Bill and Cheddi Jagan in 1973,' he said. 'There was this big crowd, and Bill came with what appeared to be some eggs to the meeting, and Cheddi Jagan was speaking and there were some thugs from the other side. And Cheddi Jagan was hit with one massive brick on his stomach. It felled him, and there were people who rushed him away from the scene. But Bill came up on the platform and seized the mike, and began to talk! There were stones all around showering down on him, but he took all of these eggs and he threw them into the crowd, he just pelted them! Now I don't know if he wanted the crowd to beat him or if here was a man who has got what it takes to be courageous. We would say, "Get down, Bill, let's go!" and he chose to walk! There was this big mob, a riotous, angry, murderous mob behind Bill, and they were hitting him at the back of his head with sticks, mostly women, poking at him. "You white bastard, go home!" You white this! You white that! And he was walking! I ran from where I was, I said I will not leave Bill alone, and I was backing him, I was taking on the crowd, I was taking the licks for him and I said, "Run, Bill, run!"'

But my father had naturally refused to run. He continued to walk impassively, with Moses behind him trying to protect him from the blows that the PNC mob were raining down on them. Then suddenly a particularly powerful blow caught the young PPP militant on the forehead and knocked him to the ground so that he lost sight of his friend. He was rescued by Harold Snag, the bodyguard I had met earlier that day, and bundled into a nearby vehicle and driven away. My father, meanwhile, had disappeared, and they went looking for him and did not find him until later that evening, sitting alone in a bar with the dried blood still on his face.

This extraordinary anecdote contained so many elements of my father's personality – the mixture of masochism, heroism and courage, the love of drama, the loneliness behind the public man. At the same time, I could not help thinking that everything – the eggs, the Christ-like walk through the howling mob, the withdrawal into the solitude of the bar without bothering to clean off the blood, knowing that his comrades would find him there later – was all part of a role that my father had been acting out for himself and others. The description of his slow, almost contemptuous walk through the crowd reminded me of the last scene in *Khartoum*, when Charlton Heston's General Gordon walks calmly down the stairs of the Governor-General's palace in his moustache and full-dress uniform towards the victorious Mahdi's baying followers, until a spear thrown by a cowardly native brings him down. The film was one of many my father and I had seen together which touched on the theme of masculine courage and heroism. At the time I had taken the imperialist assumptions of the film for granted, without questioning the role of the British as the good guys. Now I wondered if my father himself had retained that same image of British sang-froid, as he faced down the PNC mob.

'He was a guy who did not run away from a battle,' Moses said. 'He faced it. I don't think he's going looking for it. What he's saying is, "I have as much right to be a human being as you are. I have as much right to make sense of what this country is all about. You're going down the drain, you're killing this country, you have a dictatorship in this country. I'm telling you for your good – change your ways."'

Throughout the conversation Moses often lapsed into the dramatic present like this, as though he were relating scenes from a play or a film. Every actor needs an appreciative audience and my father seemed to have found one in the Minister of Information's dramatic imagination. But this vision of an essentially noble, heroic figure, motivated by grand ideals and a selfless commitment to 'the happiness of all', did not and could not correspond to what I remembered. It was not that I doubted my father's courage, or the sincerity of his political convictions, and I even admired the way that he had stuck by them so consistently throughout his years in the Caribbean. But unlike Moses I had lived with him in his own house and I had seen him behave in certain ways that entirely contradicted the grand liberationist ideals that he espoused in his public life. In his own home, with his own family my father had behaved exactly like the bullies and cowards he had so often railed against in Guyana, and had contravened his own moral codes, and mine. I asked Moses how he explained such a contradiction between my father's private and public life.

'Well, I wouldn't know about that,' he said guardedly. 'We met in 1968 and took an immediate liking to each other. You know what I saw him doing at David Chanderbali's home? Bill was dancing the tangero, or some Spanish music. So here was this powerful, strong, bearded man, an actor on the stage, an incredible user of the English language, who was loved on the campus because he was the man who gave life to Shakespeare, who gave life to the classics. If you met a man like that, your immediate response to this man is that he doesn't have a dark side in his family life, because unless you're saying that he's schizophrenic, he has an absolute split personality, there he was with all his friends endeared to him. And he makes everyone laugh and happy, and he goes home in this sadistic delight to inflict punishment on his family – I have to accept that he has to be a perfect masochist or sadist or schizophrenic that I could not discover in twenty years. How do *you* explain that?'

I replied that some form of schizophrenia or split personality was the only explanation I had been able to come up with so far. Moses did not look convinced. For some reason I felt slightly depressed by this unfamiliar image of my father dancing at his friend's house in 1968. Such gaiety and spontaneity had been mostly absent during the years when he lived with us. There had not been much of it around during that miserable first year in England either, as the reality of our rejection sank in, following the arrival of the crate from Guyana, with most of our books and belongings soaked and destroyed. Yet there was my father, the Falstaff of the tropics, gaily dancing the 'tangero' with his new-found friends, as if nothing had happened. The image suggested a man enjoying life to the full, a man liberated from his family and himself, yet it was impossible for me to contemplate it without seeing a kind of faultline underlying the gaiety. Had he really been celebrating his new-found freedom from the dreary coils of family life, or had he in fact been a man dancing on the edge of the abyss, drowning his own guilt even as he played the role of the life and soul of the party? It was impossible to know the truth, but it was obvious that Moses had not been aware of the dark secrets that lay behind my father's *joie de vivre*, and therefore had no reason to doubt that the performance was anything other than what it seemed.

It was getting dark and Moses called home on his mobile phone to check that there was going to be electricity that evening. It was around this point that I began to detect a change in his attitude towards me. At first he had been very open and keen to talk about my father, throwing open his memories like the gates to a shrine, in the apparent expectation that I had come to worship with him. Instead I had presented him with another side of my father that he had obviously been totally unaware of. He became increasingly suspicious and defensive, as though I had come to desecrate the holy place. 'You know, no one here will give a fuck about what happened to you,' he said suddenly, as we teetered unsteadily over to the ministerial car, where the driver was still patiently waiting. 'So Bill beat his wife and kids. So what? He did so much for Guyana.'

This outburst surprised me. I did not feel sorry for myself and I had not come to Guyana to elicit sympathy from anyone. Nor did I want to destroy my father's reputation. I saw no reason to dispute my father's genuine achievements in Guyana. I knew that my perception of him was incomplete, and that he had been a different person when he was not with his family, but it was equally obvious that Moses' perception of him had been incomplete too. His aggressive reaction was even more surprising in that I had so far only spoken about the past in the most general terms, leaving out the worst details. All the time I was in Guyana I was painfully conscious that I might be accused of vindictiveness or character assassination if I revealed too much of what I remembered about my father, and this tended to make me even more selective about what I said than I might have been with people who had never known him. As far as I was concerned, I was in Guyana to listen and to ask questions. I only talked about my own past when I felt that the person I was talking to either knew something about it already, or was at least able to consider what I said and perhaps shed some light on some of my father's 'dark little corners'. At the same time I knew I was not going to find out anything at all if I merely sat and nodded while my father's friends sang his praises. I needed to present them with what I knew also and see how they accounted for the contradictions of his personality and behaviour.

At first I had thought that Moses might be willing at least to consider some of the murkier areas of my father's personality, but it soon turned out that I had been mistaken. He was reluctant to accept any flaw at all in the saintly, noble image that he had consecrated to memory, although at the same time he was clearly bothered by what I had told him, and seemed to be looking for an explanation for it, just as I was. As his elevated conception of my father did not allow for any defects, he seemed to have decided that the responsibility must lie elsewhere. As we arrived at his house, he said, almost as if thinking out loud, that he could understand how Bill might have come home in a bad mood sometimes and taken it out on his wife and kids. I said nothing. Was this the booze talking? Was it a reflection of that more general acceptance that my father had once hinted at when he said that he had struck my mother 'as husbands do'? Or was it simply that as far as Moses was concerned, even wife-beating was excusable, as long as it was 'Bill' who was doing it?

It was not a promising beginning to the evening. We went upstairs and sat outside on the veranda in the cool evening, watching the darkness come down over Georgetown. A young adolescent boy appeared with an inane grin on his face, and Moses ordered him to fetch the inevitable ice, glasses and bottle of rum. The boy was obviously simple, and Moses said that his family had adopted him and given him a home, as he went inside and came out with a tray of drinks. This kind of charity appeared to be quite common in Guyana, and Marjorie and my father had taken children in off the streets from time to time and given them a temporary home.

Once again the ritual began. We scooped our handfuls of ice from the communal bowl and filled our glasses with rum and Coke as we talked about Bill Carr. We had now got through at least a bottle and a half, and I was surprised to find myself still sitting upright. The Minister of Information had a dull, glazed look too, as he leaned back against the balcony, his feet planted firmly on the floor, facing into the brightly lit house, where his wife and children were watching TV. He called for his wife, Sita, who appeared briefly to say hello and looked at me with mild curiosity when Moses introduced me as Bill's son. She came out barefoot, with large round eyes and long black hair that hung down to her waist, before quickly retreating into the house to make some food, while we continued drinking and talking.

Later Moses summoned his teenage daughter, who stood with obvious embarrassment in the doorway, as he said, 'Well? Isn't she pretty?' I agreed that she was, and her father allowed her to go back inside to watch TV to her obvious relief. Throughout the evening various people came and went. A young engineer from a gold-mining company in the interior joined in our drinking, sitting mostly in silence as the Minister of Information held forth. Moses was an entertaining and compulsive talker, slipping in and out of his Guyanese accent as he alternated his reminiscences of Bill Carr with a stream of anecdotes and political gossip, quotations from Byron and more psycho-racial philosophizing. Like Fanon, he believed that race and sex in the Caribbean were always interlinked and that sexual relationships were still trapped in the psychological mould of slavery, in which the feelings of self-hatred and inferiority associated with blackness had been internalized and whiteness tended to be excessively exalted. Thus each racial group wanted to marry someone of a fairer complexion. Black people wanted to marry mulattos, mulattos wanted to marry Indians and Indians wanted to marry Europeans or local whites, in a neurotic climb towards the promised land of pure whiteness. My father, on the other hand, had been moving in the opposite direction by marrying a black woman from a militant P N C family, a marriage that Burnham himself had personally tried to prevent.

The Minister of Information seemed to have an almost morbid fascination with my father's 'descent' into blackness. But it was difficult to tell from his lurid racial imagery, in which he talked of 'black abysses' and 'seas of blackness', whether he admired him for it or whether he shared Burnham's horror and disapproval. He was still holding forth on the subject when a young black man came staggering up the stairs and leaned unsteadily against the wall. His name was Earl and he worked as a D J for a local radio station, which had its studio under the minister's house. In a few minutes, he announced, with a foolish grin, he was going on the air. It was difficult to imagine what kind of programme it would be, since Earl, like everyone else, looked as if he was about to fall down the stairs at any moment, but he insisted that he was ready.

'I'm not drunk,' he giggled, crashing into the table and nearly knocking it over. 'I'm just a little in-eb-ri-at-ed.' He stumbled down the stairs laughing to himself. Moses told me that he was a St Lucian who had married a Guyanese East Indian girl. 'You see what I mean?' he said triumphantly. 'It's the way of the world. It may not be the way we like it, but that's how it is.'

A strong breeze was blowing over the darkened city, agitating the nearby coconut trees. I sat there in the vast tropical night, cocooned in rum, listening to Moses holding forth about abysses of blackness above the dull roaring in my ears. Once again I reached for the bottle and dug into the ice. The sight of that golden liquid cascading over the ice was almost as pleasant as the effect it produced. I sniffed the sweet smell of the white man's poison and felt myself approaching a new advanced state of drunkenness, in which the wildest exaggerations seemed perfectly believable and reality, rational observation, even memory itself, were being carried away in the flood of words and metaphors.

But I was determined to remain lucid and in control, and I was conscious of a battle of wills between Moses and myself that was going on under the surface. All the time I felt him watching me with increasing suspicion, like a detective trying to break my alibi. 'What are you searching for?' he asked, peering at me aggressively. 'What are you trying to restore?'

'What are you so worried about?' I responded. 'I'm not here as an avenging angel.'

'It's his father,' the young mining engineer said, in an attempt to mediate, as if the answer to Moses' question were perfectly obvious.

Moses sniffed derisively, and it was clear that this explanation did not impress him. His hostility surprised me. The question of why I had come to Guyana was one that I had still not fully answered myself. All I knew for certain was that I wanted to understand the personality of the man who had had such a disastrous impact on my family, and see if I could explain what had happened all those years ago. Given that metaphors seemed more important than facts that evening, I quoted the Zen parable about reality being like an elephant, in which one person sees the trunk, another sees the leg, and so on, without anyone seeing the whole animal. My father, I said, was like the elephant, and the different memories that I and other people in Guyana had of him all derived from the same man.

Moses scowled. 'No one here gives a jackass what he did to you,' he repeated. 'Your father was crucified more times than Jesus Christ!'

There was no arguing with that. In the Minister of Information's idealistic imagination, my father had now reached such transcendental heights that anything that might possibly diminish him could only be considered blasphemous or heretical. It occurred to me that he would probably not have tolerated my presence at all had I not been Bill Carr's son. And so the drunken dialogue of the deaf continued. Throughout the evening Moses asked me more questions about my father and then immediately tried to disprove my answers or find some mitigating circumstances to justify his behaviour, while I clung on even more tenaciously to what I remembered.

'There would have been a public outcry if Bill had really treated his wife like that!' he exclaimed, when I told him some of the details about our last few weeks in Guyana. I told him that many people had known about what was going on and that there had been a minor scandal, but nothing more.

'Look, you only knew him as a child, but he was my friend for more than twenty years!' he said. This was true, but if it was obvious that my perception of my father was limited by the fact that I had only really known him during my truncated childhood, it was also obvious that Moses' image of my father had been constructed on the basis of the person that he had known and loved. The trouble was that virtually everything he had been told about my father's past had come from my father himself. This was not the most reliable source, at least as far as his family were concerned. Like most of my father's friends in Guyana, Moses had met him after we had left the country, and the absence of witnesses to how he had treated us allowed his memory to be more 'convenient' than usual. Thus Moses had 'got the impression' that he had been abandoned and 'shipwrecked' in Guyana. He had not considered that my father himself might have caused the wreck or that there had been other passengers on board. The only violence he had ever heard my father talk about was some vague incident from his time in Jamaica when he had caught my mother having an affair with the gardener and 'slugged' him on the lawn.

I laughed. I remembered our old gardener Joshua quite well and it was difficult to believe that my mother or any other woman would have been attracted to him, at least when we knew him. The incident obviously referred to a brief affair that she had had with a Jamaican friend of my father's during the eighteen months in which they had been living apart. In his obsessive jealousy my father had taken to parking his car outside the friend's house, and the two men had fought on one occasion. As my mother remembers the incident, it was less 'slugging' than a clumsy, unseemly scrabble on the lawn that had ended without losers or winners. But this torrid Mandingo fantasy of the white woman having an affair with a black servant slotted neatly into a racially deterministic view of sexual relationships, while the idea of Bill Carr slugging the perpetrator fitted with the Hemingway tough-guy image that my father himself was so fond of.

The conversation careered onwards, Moses continuing to break off from his reminiscences to repeat the same questions. Why are you here? What are you trying to restore? How do you know it wasn't *your* fault? From time to time he returned to the subject of the tapes, insisting that they contained the truth about my father and that I should go and ask Marjorie for them. I assured him that I would. The Minister of Information was becoming gloomy and morose now, mixing rum with White Horse whisky, as Sita came out on to the balcony to bring us some food. 'Why you don't sit here with us?' Moses patted the bench beside us. 'We never talk like this, man.'

Sita neither refused nor accepted, but remained standing in the doorway with an enigmatic smile. I wondered if she had been listening to the conversation already and disliked its content, or whether she was simply unwilling to get involved in a male boozing session that was already sliding into rambling incoherence. She had been one of my father's students and remembered a Conrad lecture that had greatly impressed her. Moses had already told me that she was very fond of my father, and she talked about him with the same tenderness and almost reverential affection that he did.

'You remember when Bill used to come round here?' he asked her. 'He used to sit out here with those little feet of his and say, "You got some roti for me?"'

She nodded with a smile. I remembered those tiny feet too from my father's last visit. The warmth and affection that she felt towards my father were so obvious that I felt like an intruder who had no right to be there. Like the lunatic at Castellani House I was out of the closet, a walking skeleton from the past, the poor little white kid with his wretched childhood, getting drunk with my father's friends on the same balcony where the great man had sat. Suddenly the way I remembered my past seemed in danger of being swamped by the enormous legacy of goodwill that he had left behind him. As I felt myself spinning around in a swirling current of alcohol, I felt not pride but a kind of horror at his memory and the inexplicable legacy that he had left us.

Sita disappeared into the house and left us alone again, but the conversation was beginning to falter now and there was a sour note in the atmosphere as a result of the repeated sparring. Suddenly Moses seemed to grow tired of the reminiscing and cross-examination and abruptly announced that he would get his driver to take me back to the hotel. He lurched unsteadily to his feet, nearly falling over in the process, and accompanied me downstairs to the car, where the driver was still patiently waiting. The Minister of Information's eyes had the dull, repentant look of a man who had drunk and talked too much for his own good and was beginning to regret it. It had been a memorable evening. I shook hands and thanked him for talking to me. His face was hard and unsmiling and he grunted only a curt reply as I promised to call him again, before the car drove out into the almost total darkness, and back into the deserted streets of Georgetown.

Back at the hotel there was the usual ghostly silence emanating from dozens of vacant rooms. I flicked on the TV in search of some vacuous distraction to rest my mind and found two blurred male characters from a satellite B-movie standing in an industrial wasteland and shouting at each other across the flickering screen.

'I'll tell you what's on the other side of life!' cried one of them triumphantly. 'Nothing! Absolutely nothing!'

'You're lying!' replied his companion. 'That can't be!'

I sympathized with his disappointment, but already I felt a hangover coming on and I switched off and tried to write down what had been said and done that day. It was impossible to concentrate, as the usual questions swirled round and round in my head, floating on a choppy sea of booze.

Eventually I gave up and fell into a drunken slumber, only to wake up again a few hours later stone-cold sober with the alarming sensation that not only my past but also my present was slipping away from me and that I would never understand or retain it unless I wrote down everything. In the same moment it came to me, like a sloppy, rum-soaked revelation, that all that was left on the other side of life was what other people remembered, and that without those memories there was no record that anyone had ever existed at all. Immediately I began manically to write up all the stories, memories and incidents that I could remember from the last twenty-four hours, as if I were afraid that they too were going to disappear. For the rest of the night I wrote, my pen digging into the page, as if to give the words more weight and stop them flying off the page, leaving nothing but blankness and silence. I was still writing in the early hours of the morning, when the first birds began to emit their unfamiliar whoops and cries, and the sun slowly came up on another Guyana day.

Chapter Nine

There are few of us who have not at some stage in our lives imagined ourselves as characters in a book or a film. 'It was like something from a novel,' we sometimes say when we describe some strange or unusual event in which we were involved. On one level these comparisons are an implicit recognition of the absence of the exceptional in daily life, but they also provide a kind of fairground mirror in which our lives are lifted out of the commonplace and everyday into something worthy of fiction. My father spent a lot of time making such comparisons, as he consciously sought to live his life as an epic drama on the scale of those characters he consumed in literature and the theatre. But despite the prodigious energy he poured into the reinvention of himself he was never able to transcend the legacy of unhappiness and depression left over from his own childhood. In this sense his life was simultaneously stranger than fiction and more banal — the story of a lonely little boy abandoned by his mother.

There is little doubt that the origins of the great rage that marked so much of his life can be traced directly back to the mother who had failed to return the enormous love that he had once felt for her as a child, and which still persisted as an adult, but now alongside a new hatred and anger. Even his rejection of his past and his revolt against England and Englishness drew their emotional force as much from that childhood rejection as from his politics and guilt about the British Empire.

That same rage may also have influenced his treatment of his wife, the white woman he brought to the West Indies. In 1967, when the two psychiatrists came round to Canje Street to witness his Grand Guignol performance as Bill Carr the lunatic, my mother asked them in desperation, 'What have I done to make this man like this?' to which the Irish psychiatrist Frank Farilee replied, 'Nothing, my dear, you simply remind him of his mother.' This snapshot Freudian diagnosis, made on the basis of that single visit, was not exactly original, but the fact that my father had still been expressing his loathing for his mother decades after her death suggested that it may not have been entirely inaccurate either.

The woman who inspired such lifelong hatred from her only son was born Josephine Hanby in the early years of the century, the youngest of eleven children from a recently arrived rural Yorkshire family in Harrogate. As the youngest daughter, Josephine enjoyed an easier childhood than her siblings, but from an early age she was driven by a strong desire to rise above her humble background. Initially she trained as a secretary, but her attempts at social mobility were generally focused on the male species. She was, by all accounts, an attractive and glamorous woman in her youth, who knew how to make herself the object of male attention. As my cousin Pat put it, 'Joey liked men, and men liked Joey.'

In 1930 Joey married William Abbey Carr, a solicitor's clerk from Harrogate and a World War I veteran, who was some years older than her. The relationship has always been surrounded by a whiff of provincial hypocrisy and sleaze that often seems to cling to my paternal grandmother. During my father's visit to England he told me that his father had been obliged to steal money from work in order to pay for Josephine to have a series of abortions. Whether these abortions were the result of liaisons with other men is not known, but it would not have been out of character. When the thefts were discovered my grandfather lost his job, and the marriage broke up in such bad circumstances that Josephine refused to allow my father to have anything to do with her former husband, accusing him of drinking and violence.

My paternal grandfather has always been a rather obscure, almost anonymous figure in the collective family memory. Following the break-up of his parents' marriage, my father did not see him again until his late teens, but he would later describe him as one of the most 'delightful men I have ever met'. In one of a series of autobiographical poems he fondly described his father as a gentle, quiet man of 'dapper little suits . . . shining shoes and crisp small hat'. The same poem also refers to 'the filthy trench horror on which you would never let me draw you', and mentions a wartime disability that apparently prevented his father from playing the piano as he used to do. It ends with this tribute to the father he barely knew, in which he seems to see him as the emotional rudder that was missing from his own personality:

Emulate you? Could I but,
My brave small father, had I your calm
Maker of me!
But, lovely Yorkshire Lording
I'm still learning.

Josephine's refusal to allow my father to have anything to do with her ex-husband seemed to have stemmed more from malice and vindictiveness than from any concern for her son. No sooner was the marriage over than she sent him off to the first of a series of boarding schools. For the rest of his childhood he was either at boarding school or being looked after by his two aunts in the summer holidays, while Josephine virtually ignored him, but the boarding school which left the most indelible impression on my father's memory was the convent on the Welsh border run by the Sisters of the Order of Charity of St Vincent de Paul.

The school had been temporarily relocated to avoid the risk of wartime bombing, and it was run on exceptionally medieval lines, with a sadistic range of punishments being inflicted on the male pupils. My father would later tell his friends in Guyana how he had been made to eat pork fat, and suffered a ritual called 'stretching on the boards', in which boys were stripped naked and flogged over their desks in front of the mixed class. On one occasion the good Sisters told him that his mother was coming to take him away for the weekend. The charade was carried out with such zeal and conviction that he was told to get packed and dressed and taken outside to meet her, whereupon the nuns announced that she was not coming after all and took him back inside. This was their way of punishing him for some wrong-doing.

The effect of these humiliations at female hands can only be imagined. The brutality of the convent would certainly have compounded the sense of abandonment by his mother, and contributed to the anger and sense of injustice that became such decisive components of his character. Years later in bar-room conversations across Guyana he was still bitterly denouncing the indignities suffered at the hands of Sister Pauline and Sister Mary, his principal tormentors at the school. This particularly vicious experience of English boarding school life, coupled with the lack of parental love and affection, helped to create the anti-establishment rebel who would later turn his back on

England completely and seek to invent a new life and personality in the West Indies.

While my father languished in his boarding school Josephine continued to work as a secretary in London, enjoying a string of glamorous affairs. My father might have remained at the convent till the end of the war had his Auntie Peggy not rescued him on her own initiative. Even after starting at Dulwich in the last year of the war, he remained largely peripheral to his mother's life.

By the end of the war, Josephine's frenetic wartime activity had failed to translate itself into the long-term social ascendancy that she craved. She ended up marrying a paint salesman from a wealthy family, an amiable non-achiever who was as much of a disappointment to his own family as he was to her.

The gradual realization that her second husband was not going to be any more successful than the first finally turned Josephine's hopes towards her neglected son. Later she would boast how hard she had worked to pay his way through Dulwich, even though my father had in fact won a scholarship, as he also did to get into Cambridge. But his arrival at university revived his mother's delusions of social grandeur, and she now saw herself ascending socially as a result of her son's intellectual achievements, for which she claimed partial responsibility.

This fantasy was disappointed by my father's departure to the West Indies, and from 1960 onwards she had little contact with him. My family saw very little of her either, except for brief visits when we came back to England. My own memory of my grandmother is not the glamorous man-eater of her youth, but a rather unctuous, sinister figure, a cross between Maggie Smith in *A Private Function* and Bette Davis in *The Nanny*.

From the beginning Josephine considered my mother unsuitable for her son and her antipathy did not help my parents' relationship. Nor did her hostility lessen after our return from the West Indies. It was Josephine who played the pivotal role in turning my father's relatives against my mother. At first she pretended to be sympathetic, so that my mother rather foolishly told her everything that had happened in the West Indies, including her affair in Jamaica. With characteristic duplicity Josephine then twisted the story round and presented it to her relatives as the main reason for the breakdown of the marriage. Given her own prolific affairs, her occupation of the moral highground was somewhat spurious, but her version of events fitted in easily with the old-fashioned patriarchal values of my father's Yorkshire relatives, and Little Ian thus emerged as the wronged innocent, a position he continued to occupy in Yorkshire throughout his life.

My father's own feelings towards his mother fluctuated between opposite extremes. He was angry with her for much of his life and eventually came to despise her, but none the less she exercised a powerful emotional hold over him from which he never entirely freed himself. My mother remembers that he was very defensive of her in the early years of their relationship and that Josephine indirectly caused many rows between them. One Christmas Eve before I was born my parents arrived late at Josephine's house to find her glaring at them, accusing them of making her late for Midnight Mass. This caused a row between my parents when she had gone to bed. On another occasion my father angrily accused my mother of trying to compete with Josephine when she wore a smart dress to visit her mother-in-law's house.

My father thought of his mother at different stages of his life as both an ideal of female perfection and a whore, and was never able to dethrone her entirely from the glamorous pedestal on which he had placed her as a child. To some extent the evolution of his feelings towards her followed the classic stages of a disenchanted romantic infatuation, in which absolute need and devotion finally gave way to disappointment, hatred and fury at his betrayal. In one of his autobiographical poems he wrote:

> Movie star bright
> You were to me as child
> But near middle age
> Began to sound its warning
> Curfewed me into accidental knowledge

These last cryptic lines may refer to his discovery of the sleazy underside of the glamorous mother that he had once adored, but he also blamed her for the loss of his beloved father:

> Oh, if only I could say
> Our father! But then, there was only me.

Mother, to lose him
was to lose too much.

Whatever my grandmother may have felt in private, there is no evidence that she ever admitted any responsibility for the terrible rage and disappointment that was her lasting legacy to her only son. As devious as she was, she does not seem to have been a woman blessed with much sensitivity or insight, and there was clearly a lot of unhappiness beneath the youthful vivacity, which gradually came to dominate, as she settled down with bad grace into a sour, unsatisfying life of redbrick, lace-curtain mediocrity in Reading. Like my father himself, she saw herself principally as a victim. She often complained about how badly people had treated her, and accused my mother of trying to prevent her grandchildren from seeing her, even though none of us remember anything of the kind. As she grew older she became hypochondriac and manic-depressive. She was always suffering from aches and pains which remained largely undetected by medical science, but for which she nevertheless obtained a steady flow of pain-killing drugs. In her last years she was addicted to codeine, and spent much of her time in bed, complaining about her illnesses, while her hapless husband ran around looking after her.

On various occasions she deliberately took an overdose, in what seem to have been calculated bids for attention rather than genuine suicide attempts, since there was always someone around to save her, usually her husband. On Christmas Day 1968, however, the timing went badly wrong. The truth about my grandmother's death has never been fully clarified, but it seems that Josephine was left alone in the house while her husband went out to the pub for a Christmas drink. In the morning she had put the turkey in the oven in preparation for their Christmas dinner, but while he was away she took another overdose and went to bed. At some point she tried to get up, but she lost consciousness and collapsed on the bedroom floor, where her husband subsequently found her. Whether she was already dead is not known, but for some reason her husband simply covered her with a blanket and left her there.

Whether these scenes had become so common that he assumed she was unconscious and left her to sleep it off, or whether he himself was too drunk to know how to react, he did not call an ambulance until much later, by which time she was most definitely dead. Had Josephine mistimed another cry for help, expecting her husband to return earlier than he did? Or was it a genuine resolve to commit suicide? If she had intended to kill herself, why had she put the turkey in the oven? These questions have never been answered, and the coroner's inquest recorded an open verdict on Josephine's sordid and miserable end.

My father clearly believed that she had committed suicide. Years later he was still haunted by her death, and his conviction that she had killed herself may have helped to extinguish some of the hatred he had felt towards her while she was alive, especially after his reconversion to the Catholic Church. The fact that his mother died on Christmas Day also had special significance for him. In one poem, entitled Christmas 1978, addressed directly to his mother, the association between her death and the birth of Christ suggested a new kind of relationship with her:

> All known now and forgiven too
> Since that pristine shining day
> When Christ was born
> And you chose to die. Now years thence
> With sadness and some truth
> I whisper to your wandering ghost.
> It cannot be forgotten.

It was a reconciliation that had certainly never been achieved in his mother's lifetime. To some extent the hatred and resentment that he felt towards her was retrospective, the result of accumulated insights and 'accidental knowledge' garnered over the years. But given the lack of contact between them after he left England, it is difficult to imagine that he ever confronted her with his feelings. Instead he tried to cut her out of his life altogether, along with everything else about his past. Yet despite the geographical distance that he put between them, his disappointed relationship with his mother was the essential tragedy of his life, much more so than the loss of his own family. My father was very different from his mother in many ways, but he also inherited something of her deviousness, together with a powerful downward pull into depression and addiction, which destroyed him as it had once destroyed her.

The parallels between my father and his mother have sometimes made me speculate on the existence of a 'bad gene' in my family, transmitted from one generation to the next. Especially when I was younger the fear haunted me that I was going to be like my father, and the fact that I also had a tendency to depression and anger only sharpened this sense of being trapped in an emotional mould that had been created before I was born. But the intensity of these emotions diminished over the years, and I ceased to regard the past as a kind of Greek punishment which condemned me to repeat my parents' mistakes. My father, however, never forgot the disappointment and humiliation of his childhood, and the emotional burden of those years actually increased as he grew older.

It is one of the tragedies of his life that his self-pitying immersion in the past never led to the kind of self-awareness that might have enabled him to overcome its grim emotional legacy in himself. Instead of trying to understand the way his childhood had affected his behaviour as an adult, he was content to tell the stories of maternal abandonment and boarding school cruelty over and over again, in which he inevitably emerged as the victim, a Dickensian child hero, unloved and rejected by the world. This overwhelming sense of victimhood blinded him to his own cruelty towards others and enabled him to evade taking responsibility for it. Even at the height of his domestic rages in Guyana, there was something tortured and self-pitying about his anger, as though he were a hurt little boy with an adult's fists who was finally taking his revenge for some great, intolerable injustice.

Perhaps some form of psychotherapy might have helped him to free himself from his past instead of wallowing in the tragedy of it all, but he was not the kind of person to even admit that his self-destructive behaviour might have neurotic origins. Apart from the farcical charade that he had put on for the two psychiatrists in Guyana, he never received any professional psychiatric help. Instead he made his own way through the world, dragging the emotional wreckage of his childhood with him wherever he went, even as he tried to re-invent himself in a variety of different contexts. Yet despite everything, politics, religion, literature, the anaesthetic effects of booze and violence, the relentless projection of his dramatis personae out into the world, that emotional undertow of unhappiness and loss remained throughout his life, always pulling him back down when the gaiety and laughter were over. It was this unhappiness that really constituted my imaginary 'bad gene', and my father's failure to transcend it prevented him from ever achieving the lasting peace he always yearned for. In this way the burden of one shallow, superficial woman's neglect was unconsciously handed on to another generation, poisoning his life, and ours. And ten years after her death, the voice of that lonely, abandoned child could still be heard in his snippets of alcoholic verse, longing for a reunion with his absent parents, while his stepchildren celebrated the happy Christmas around him that he had never known himself, and had rarely been able to provide for his own children:

> *Perhaps we'll all meet up one day.*
> *Odd conference.*
> *Be then abiding*
> *and as gracious as you're claimed to be.*

> *I hear songs and children's voices*
> *The crackle of unwrapping paper*
> *These calm me, more or less*
> *But not my forty-seven years.*

Chapter Ten

The young black man stood on the sidewalk near Starbroek Market in his ragged khaki shorts and short-sleeved shirt, watching me come towards him, his face a mask of contempt. As I approached he assumed a more defiant, aggressive posture and his lips curled. 'You white motherfucker,' he jeered, as I came alongside him. I walked on, pretending I hadn't heard, momentarily disconcerted at finding myself an object of racial contempt. It was not the only time I came across such hostility in the capital. From time to time as I walked around the city centre or stopped to take pictures, mocking voices would shout out comments about whitey taking photographs or whitey with his camera, till I felt embarrassed about even producing the machine in public.

All this was harmless enough, but it was a symptom of the racial resentment that still lingered on in Guyana three decades after the formal withdrawal of white power from the colony. When we arrived in the country in 1966, the anti-white feeling had been even more evident – especially after Jamaica, where we had never encountered any racial hostility at all. My sister still recalls the threatening atmosphere on first arriving in Georgetown, even though she was only eight years old at the time. The memory may be related to an incident when my mother took us to a public swimming pool, where we were stared at with such universal hostility that we never went back. Once I returned from school and asked my mother what a 'limey shit' meant. Even Kathleen Drayton, an influential person in Guyanese society, had black friends who were embarrassed to go and see her because she was white.

The immediate cause of the anti-white feeling in Guyana was the long-drawn-out struggle between the P P P and the British government in the years leading up to independence. The British refusal to withdraw from the colony until the electoral defeat of the P P P had been assured was bitterly resented by many Guyanese as another example of imperial arrogance, and the delayed transition to independence had been made especially painful by the most savage outbreak of racial violence in Guyanese history. Between 1962 and 1964 the conflict between the PNC and the PPP began to take on the dimensions of an ethnic war between the Afro-Guyanese and East Indian populations. The country was engulfed by a wave of racial rioting, tit-for-tat killings and mutual atrocities, in which the centre of Georgetown was virtually razed to the ground.

The ferocity of the violence, much of it whipped up by politicians on the streets, shocked the Guyanese, as it did the rest of the Caribbean. Even though we arrived in the country two years after the violence had subsided, the memories of that two-year descent into race war were still fresh, and horror stories of riots and racial killings still circulated.

The origins of the conflict between the two largest ethnic communities in Guyana went back to the nineteenth century, when plantation owners in the Caribbean began to recruit large numbers of indentured labourers from India following the abolition of slavery in 1834. Seduced by the plantation owners' promises of land and a better future by plantation recruiters, thousands of Indians crossed the *kala pani*, the 'black water' of the Atlantic, to the New World only to find themselves bound to conditions of service that were little better than slavery. The willingness of the new 'coolie' immigrants to work for virtually nothing soon placed them in a position of direct competition with the newly freed black slaves. In the years following abolition thousands of Negro slaves abandoned the despised plantations and founded their own independent farming villages, but the lack of state support and the enormous difficulties involved in clearing and maintaining the swampy coastal land allotted to them soon made most of the villages economically unviable, forcing their inhabitants to look for work on the plantations once more. But now they found their bargaining power gradually undermined by the presence of the alternative, cheaper force of the coolies, a situation which forced the two communities into conflict with one another.

This characteristic British policy of racial divide-and-rule may have suited the white plantocracy at the time, but the long-term consequence of the resentment that ensued has been a festering racial division which has yet to be superseded. For more than a hundred years that original economic faultline has given rise to an accumulation of mutual prejudices, jealousies and fears between the two communities, in which each complains of discrimination and racism by the other. Whereas the Afro-Guyanese population has tended to drift towards the urban areas, occupying positions in the civil service and education, the East Indian population still dominates the countryside. Although poverty is not as race-related as PNC demagogues like to make out, the predominant East Indian presence in shop-keeping and rice-farming has led to the stereotype of the 'coolie rice' capitalist farmer, while in turn the Afro-Guyanese are often characterized by East Indians as lazy and criminal.

Marxist historians and politicians have dismissed racial conflict in Guyana as an imperialist invention, stressing the common class and national interests uniting the two groups. Yet even though there have been times when Afro-Guyanese and East Indians have joined together in common cause, such as the early years of the PPP, it was the mutual antipathy and distrust between them that enabled the British to split the anti-colonial movement in the 1950s and eventually impose their will on the colony. The full consequences of the country's division into two ethnically based parties were made horrifically clear in the carnage which finally brought down the Jagan administration in 1963, to which the British and American sponsorship of the PNC had indirectly contributed. Today, the spectre of racial violence still remains beneath the apparently calm surface of post-Burnham Guyana, waiting to be summoned forth. As late as October 1992, it briefly flared up once again, when PNC mobs went on the rampage in Georgetown, burning and looting Indian shops on the eve of elections.

This was the country to which my father brought his white family from Jamaica in 1966, a volatile, race-tormented society at the forefront of the radical politics that were emerging across the English-speaking Caribbean. It was a turbulent period in Caribbean history, which saw the bright hopes and aspirations that had accompanied the end of the colonial era begin to fade. The principal reason for this growing disillusionment was the continued poverty and economic stagnation throughout the region, as the miserable legacy of the sugar planters was compounded by local corruption, population growth and a lop-sided export economy that was traditionally more geared to the needs of the outside world than those of the region itself. While tourists came to Jamaica and Trinidad for their taste of paradise, and rich whites continued to live in the same luxurious enclaves as their slave-owning predecessors, the slums of Kingston and Port of Spain swelled with impoverished migrants from the countryside. The same pattern was encountered, in different degrees, throughout the region, with the black masses inevitably making up the poorer sections of the population, while the lighter-skinned middle classes tended to occupy most of the top positions in their respective societies.

In the past emigration had provided an escape route from West Indian poverty, but that outlet was being restricted by tough anti-immigration legislation from Britain: the country no longer needed unskilled labour to meet the post-war labour shortage and feared invasion from its former colonies. The result was an upsurge in political radicalism across the region, where the growth of anti-imperialist, pan-Africanist and black nationalist ideas found an increasingly enthusiastic audience among the angry, volatile mass of the urban poor.

These radical currents inevitably found expression on the university campus, where the future direction of West Indian society in all its aspects was being discussed. The new campus radicals drew their inspiration from the leaders of the African independence struggles as well as Caribbean intellectuals such as Franz Fanon, Aimé Césaire and C. L. R. James. Another surprisingly influential force in the new politics was Rastafarianism. From the mid-60s onwards this fringe religious sect developed into a mass cultural and political movement which articulated the new mood of black militancy and the rejection of white European values.

The black civil rights movement in the United States also had an enormous impact on the ideas, strategies and even the fashions of black radicals in the Caribbean, especially following the advent of Black Power. The fiery rhetoric of militant black ideologues like Stokely Carmichael, Malcolm X and Angela Davis struck a deep chord in Caribbean youth, particularly in Trinidad and Guyana, the two countries with the largest East Indian populations, where Black Power often had more than a hint of anti-Indian feeling.

Like their North American counterparts, young West Indian students began to wear Afro haircuts and adopt African names and denounce the generation of light-skinned politicians that had managed the transition to independence as 'Uncle Toms' and 'yard niggers'. After centuries of the racial stigma and contempt associated with slavery, to be black was now a source of pride and angry self-affirmation. There was talk of a black revolution incorporating the Caribbean, the black ghettoes of the United States, and the newly independent countries of Africa. Some looked forward to the creation of a 'new Caribbean man', while others dreamed of returning to Africa, either metaphorically or even, like the Rastafarians, physically.

This glorification of Africa often owed more to romantic mythology than to historical fact or logistical possibility, and was usually accompanied by a virulent dismissal of white civilization. In the most radical black nationalist circles, it was the white race, rather than any particular social or economic system, that was regarded as responsible for colonialism, imperialism, slavery and all the evils that had been heaped on the West Indies and the Third World. While some proponents of Black Power and Negritude expanded the concept of blackness to include the Vietnamese, Latin Americans, Chinese and all the other victims of white colonialism, there was never any doubt who the enemy was – the white man and his neo-colonialist descendants. To be white was automatically to be part of the problem rather than the solution. The solution lay in a conscious rejection of white Anglo-Saxon civilization, in a celebration of black power and black pride, in the triumph of 'black truth' over 'white lies'.

The angry, race-driven politics of the Caribbean presented a minefield of potential complexes for a neurotic left-wing intellectual like my father, whose socialist convictions were accompanied by a niggling sense of his own inauthenticity. Even before coming to the West Indies he had been acutely self-conscious about his middle-class, public-school background and feared exclusion from the oppressed masses with whom he identified. It was this desire for authenticity that led him to extend his national service in order to make contact with the working classes. But in the West Indies his sense of exclusion was intensified by the inescapable fact of his whiteness, which tied him to a colonial past that he despised and felt ashamed of.

No matter how left wing he had been in England, he always had more to prove in the Caribbean as a result of his colour. At a time when students at the University of the West Indies were even doubting the true blackness of native intellectuals, a white English professor was suspect before he had even opened his mouth. Throughout his early years in the West Indies my father's torment at his Englishness caused him to proclaim his anti-British sentiments even more loudly.

His early articles written in Jamaica contain numerous references to the pernicious nature of British colonialism and its destructive impact on the West Indies. 'Spain and France seem to have conceded some generosity of imaginative endowment,' he wrote in an article on the Jamaican writer Roger Mais. 'The British have supplied warehouses, religious forms, the law, ugly, barely functional cities (there are almost no towns in the British Caribbean that anybody can be said to meaningfully "live" in. Roughly speaking, people either make money in them or starve in them).'

The beginnings of the 'phenomenal transformation of his psyche' that my father experienced in the West Indies can already be detected in this early rejection of Britain and Britishness. But the transformation did not happen overnight. When he arrived in Jamaica the university was still staffed mostly by expatriates, who had little contact with the society around them. There were then few white leftists in the Caribbean and it was not difficult for my father to stand out from the English expatriate establishment, both through his personal behaviour and his vocal engagement with local politics. In this sense, the wife-beating, the heavy drinking, the public scenes, the general aura of turbulence and disorder, the glorification of his Yorkshire past, were all part of a conscious attempt to present himself as a different kind of Englishman. He even began to interpret his new life in the Caribbean as something predestined, and was proud of the fact that his initials W.I.C. stood for West Indies Carr.

While he could distance himself from his colleagues, it was not so easy to become fully accepted within Caribbean political circles, let alone by ordinary West Indians. His early attempts to speak patois were often the subject of amusement and ridicule, and his left-wing ideas were not always appreciated by the more conservative Jamaican peasants and workers who made up his potential constituency. No matter how much my father hung around rum shops or immersed himself in local politics and literature, his colour always made him a potential target for racially slanted attacks, in which his ideas could be undermined or discounted because they came from a white man.

In the racially sensitive atmosphere of 1960s Caribbean society he found it difficult to shake off the dreaded label of English liberal that tended to attach itself to any progressive white in the region. Even in the mid-60s an article on new developments in Caribbean arts in the *Caribbean Quarterly* mentions my father's name as one of a group of

English 'liberal' critics, along with Jerry Owens and Louis James, his colleagues at U W I. The definition was not intended as a compliment, with its suggestion that he was racially patronizing and out of touch with West Indian culture. Just as Black Power activists in the United States reserved special loathing for the white northern liberals, many Caribbean black nationalists regarded an 'English liberal' as a wolf in sheep's clothing, an even more contemptible and pathetic creature than the most reactionary English colonial official.

My father's situation was further complicated by the increasing conflict between his politics and his chosen professional field. As a left-wing intellectual seeking to gain a foothold in Caribbean society, he was obliged to demonstrate his anti-colonial credentials. At the same time he was a lecturer in English literature from the élite university background of Cambridge, a Leavisite cultural missionary teaching the classics of a 'dominant' colonial literature at a time when all aspects of European culture were being called into question.

Together with Jerry Owens and Louis James, my father became one of the pioneer English critics of West Indian literature in the Caribbean. Just as writers such as George Lamming, V. S. Naipaul and Derek Walcott were beginning to forge international reputations, he criticized the dominance of linguistics and Old English on the university syllabus and argued for the introduction of Caribbean authors on to the curriculum. Yet his Leavisite commitment to standards and quality left him open to charges of racial condescension from some West Indian critics, for whom an author's race or political views were often more important than any inherent quality pertaining to the work itself – especially if the work was European. Like his Cambridge mentor, my father believed that the best literature in the world *was* European, but the radicalization of Caribbean society in the 1960s saw the development of an Africanist school of West Indian criticism, which increasingly demanded that Caribbean literature should reflect African folk traditions and the revolutionary aspirations of the black masses. At a time when Jean Rhys' *Wide Sargasso Sea* could be written off by some radical West Indian critics as not being a West Indian novel because its author was a white Creole and therefore not 'relevant' to the Caribbean, the question arose as to how 'relevant' an English critic of West Indian literature could be, or indeed what right an Englishman had to interpret and criticize West Indian literature at all.

In effect, my father was teaching literature at a time when the first manifestations of political correctness were beginning to appear on the academic horizon. In both his articles and his conversation he was often scathing about the Africanist school, which he considered to be both a falsification of history and a crude politicization of literature. None the less he was uncomfortably aware of the conflict between the literary tradition that he came from and the new politically motivated standards of criticism that were accorded increasing importance in the West Indies. In an article written in 1961, entitled 'The West Indian Writer: Prelude and Context', his ambivalent attitude to West Indian literature is made clear. Quoting with approval Naipaul's famous dictum, 'History is built around achievement and creation; and nothing of value was built in the West Indies,' he described the dilemma in which he found himself:

> *When we are told that simple Jamaican cultists feel the historical loss of the spear and the coalpot, the developed ritual of West Indian tribal life, we are dealing finally with the author's subjective requirements and not with the rewarding detail of genuine observation. It is clearly dangerous for an Englishman to offer strong disagreement with the implications of this kind of manufactured background.*

And again:

> *In the main the society lacks both the time and the inclination to make sharp discriminations within and about itself. And when, as an Englishman, you are faced with what you judge to be a totally fraudulent reputation your task is not an easy one . . . In locating what you regard simply as a failure in sensibility you may be dealing with historical and emotional conditions which help to make the failure inevitable.*

Whether this meant that a bad West Indian writer was bad because of the colonial history of the West Indies and therefore could not be criticized, or that to criticize a 'fraudulent reputation' was to collude with colonialism, the discomfort is obvious. Much of the article is dedicated to proving that West Indian society lacked the 'complexity of manners' required by Henry James to produce great literature, while simultaneously attacking the historical conditions responsible for such cultural impoverishment. But even as he upheld writers such as Naipaul, Conrad and Hardy as models, he seemed to be looking nervously over his shoulder at legions of imaginary critics pointing the accusing finger of racism. The article concluded with an observation on the condition of exile of the West Indian writer, which was in retrospect an almost prophetic insight into his own condition:

> *The comparative anonymity of English life can have the pull of a magnetic attraction. Living in the West Indies is apt to have the effect a sunray lamp might have on a lizard — you can bask in the glow without realizing that you are being shrivelled.*

In my father's case that shrivelling process advanced inexorably throughout the decade, as he sank deeper into alcoholism and the pressures in both his personal and public life increased. As the political temperature heated up across the Caribbean, the possibility of exclusion or irrelevance on account of his colour loomed larger. Gradually the expatriate academics were going home, and university positions were being taken up by native lecturers and academics, many of them former students of my father's. One of them was the Jamaican poet Mervyn Morris. In the late 60s, he captured the atmosphere of the times with one of the key Caribbean poems of the decade, 'To an Expatriate Friend'.

> *. . . And then the revolution. Black*
> *and loud the horns of anger blew*
> *against the long oppression; sufferers*
> *cast off the precious values of the few.*
>
> *New powers enslaved us all:*
> *each person manacled in skin, in race.*
> *You could not wear your paid-up dues;*
> *the keen discriminators typed your face.*
>
> *The future darkening, you thought it time*
> *to say goodbye. It may be you were right.*
> *It hurt to see you go; but more,*
> *It hurt to see you slowly going white.*

My father believed the poem was written about him, even though Mervyn Morris later denied this. Whoever the real subject was, my father's reaction was another sign of the deep insecurity underlying his 'phenomenal transformation'. It is easy to imagine the effect the last two lines would have had on 'West Indies Carr', the Englishman in revolt against his own past, and, with 'the future darkening', fearing exclusion from a Caribbean society. But his reaction was very different from the anonymous expatriate in Morris's poem. Instead of turning white, my father moved in the opposite direction, shedding the most obvious symbols of his Englishness – his own family, and the place he chose to do it was the most logical place of all, the University of Guyana.

'I think he had a white man problem. I think he believed that the whites had treated civilization and the world badly, and that as a white professor he had very little to offer the white world.'

It was mid-morning at the Tower Hotel and Freddie Kissoon had come to make his analysis of Bill Carr. We sat upstairs in the empty hotel restaurant, among the idealized black and white prints of colonial Guyana. Freddie was in his mid-forties but he looked younger, and the youthful impression was enhanced by a fiery political radicalism more typical of students than university lecturers. He was immediately likeable. He spoke lucidly and passionately, his thin, bony hands perpetually moving in front of him as if trying to give concrete shape to his ideas. A former student at the university, he first met my father when he was sixteen years old, and was immediately drawn to him.

'I got to know your dad at the university and he would have been one of the persons there that young radicals like us would look up to. He didn't hobnob or socialize with the middle-class, and the light-complexioned class of the English-speaking Caribbean, and as the years go by, you watched Bill and you felt that he was carrying the white man's burden, which some evangelical, Anglican, or religious orders have done in the past. He was doing it with more honesty, and, I think, from an ideological viewpoint, and this led him into areas that were quite inexplicable – or logical, if you know his politics, that is, the ghetto rum shop: the intense – to use a common term from Guyanese sociological parlance – "liming" with the Rastas, with the lumpen, arguing with them, getting into fights with them. And he always came out on the wrong side of it. You know, when I think of Bill – was he carrying the white man's burden or was the man just a bohemian anarchist? Because bohemian anarchists behave like that. They go down in Turkey, they go down in India, they become Hindus, only Bill's thing was political.'

I had never thought of my father as a bohemian anarchist before, but the definition seemed as valid as anything else, even though, I tentatively suggested, the bohemianism was infused with a powerful streak of masochism.

'I didn't want to raise that,' Freddie replied, looking suddenly uncomfortable. 'And this is the fault of people like us, who have some kind of philosophical training. Although I think I'm being quite insulting and quite wrong to you, I should open up. Yes, masochism was part of Bill's politics and personality, and was discussed by us many times, but I don't know how you tell a man's son that he was a masochist.'

Sensing that the turning-point in the conversation had arrived, I replied that I did not need protecting and that he could tell me whatever he wanted. Freddie still looked guarded and uncomfortable. 'Fine,' he said. 'I'm only trying to protect a man who I felt was my friend, who I felt was one of the anti-dictatorship liberationists of Guyana, and who I felt had contributed to some kind of intellectual shaping of the generation that has emerged in Guyana after 1970, of which I was one.'

'I totally accept that,' I replied, 'but do you protect a man by mythologizing him?'

'It's wrong, but then I'm a product of a long anti-dictatorship struggle in which we protect people. Unlike you – you come from British democracy. You guys probably open up freely, there's nobody you saw who got killed. I saw Bill get beaten up, and here I am talking about him, and this emotional attachment to the man: "Don't say he was a fool, don't say he was wrong." I can see that I was wrong in that.'

This was an honest admission to make, which touched on one of the mysteries I had so far encountered in trying to understand the gulf between what my family and other people remembered about my father – the strange refusal even of people who must have been aware of his destructive tendencies to say anything negative about him. Sometimes this reluctance seemed to stem from an awkwardness at dealing with the darker aspects of his personality with one of his children, based on the apparent assumption that I was likely to be offended. There was also the natural tendency not to speak badly of the dead, a tendency which was particularly pronounced among former comrades of my father's like Freddie Kissoon. Nevertheless, I could see that the self-destructive streak in my father's personality had disturbed him, and I asked him how he responded to it at the time.

'You couldn't speak to him,' he said, 'because he would protect himself with intellectual profundity, and you feel, this guy's lecturing you, this guy's your senior, maybe he knows best. You know, when you come to him, you say, "Man, just cool out. What are you doing? Why you drink so much? Why you get into these fights?" And then he will quote some writer or philosopher. Look, you mediocre in relation to this guy, you haven't asserted yourself philosophically, you tend to back down. If Bill was alive now, I would tell him that what he was doing wasn't helping the non-white race, wasn't helping his family, wasn't helping us to overthrow Burnham!'

'Can you remember any particular examples when you might have said something to him after a fight? I'm trying to imagine how he might have justified himself.'

'He justified it in terms of ordinary sociology. He would say, "The guy was ob-no-xious! He was being a fool! He was stupid! And I just went over there and kicked his ass up!" He would put it like that, so you got no political explanation.'

The description of this tough-guy posturing was another variation on the ghetto rum-shop theme, with its echoes of Hemingway and Roger Mais, the hard-drinking bar-room intellectual, settling disputes with his fists. It was also a kind of twentieth-century extension of my father's perennial Falstaff role, brawling in taverns like some Elizabethan poet, 'kicking the ass up' people he disagreed with, except, as everyone had testified so far, it was my father himself who invariably got his ass kicked. Behind the role-playing and the 'intellectual profundity', however, I was still convinced that he had been using these situations, in part at least, to inflict punishment on himself because of his behaviour towards his family.

The fact that young, idealistic students like Freddie Kissoon found such masochistic behaviour so inexplicable was hardly surprising, since he apparently knew nothing about my father's past and did not even know that we were ever in Guyana. When I told him now about my family, and my belief that my father's sense of a white man's burden had led to our expulsion from Guyana, he looked shocked and incredulous.

'Well,' he said, 'my first reaction is that if Bill did that, then I don't think he did it consciously, and if he did it consciously then there is a very sad part to him. I guess the way you put it, it could be a logical explanation. I don't know what happened in the family. I don't know if he thought his wife wasn't complementing him politically and he thought, "Look, maybe I should go down to the Third World and do this thing without getting my family involved." I don't know.'

What about his theory about my father's involvement with Africanist women and his rejection of Caucasian women?

'OK,' he conceded, 'you can tie that in to what you're saying, but then there aren't many Caucasian women in the West Indies. All right, he could have taken up with a light-complexioned Asian woman, but you've got to understand that he was involved in radical politics and the West Indies do not produce blue-eyed, light-complexioned Indian women in radical politics, or very fair-skinned radical African women. The other thing to note is that maybe the whole Caucasian women thing is a myth. Maybe he did like Caucasian women. Both the Africanist women he got involved with were involved in his field of scholarship, so it could just have been an accidental meeting. Maybe if his field had been politics or economics, he could have met someone else, but I want to believe that he probably had very little admiration for the Caucasian women of the West Indies. I couldn't see Bill having a relation with a white West Indian woman. I could be wrong, man, these things . . .'

His voice trailed off. He seemed embarrassed and appalled at the possibility that my father's rejection of Caucasian women might have had the kind of consequences I had outlined for this English family whose existence he had only now found out about. Yet even as he played down the importance of his own theory, he wanted to believe that my father had little admiration for the Caucasian women of the West Indies. It was symptomatic of the tangled relationship between race, sex and class in Caribbean radical circles that even one's choice of sexual partner could be an ideological as well as an emotional decision, so that a relationship with a Caucasian woman could be seen as an act of political betrayal. It was not surprising, I thought, that my father had lost his bearings in this claustrophobic, hothouse atmosphere, where the colour of your wife's skin could be interpreted as a litmus test of your political integrity.

Whatever his initial feelings on coming to the Caribbean, my father must have come to perceive his wife and family as an obstacle to the kind of life that he wanted to lead in the West Indies. We were, in effect, the most visible symbols of his Englishness, permanent reminders of the white colonial past that we wanted to escape from. My mother most of all, with her scepticism, her vaguely liberal views, her temperamental aversion to my father's loud, declamatory politics, above all, her whiteness, was clearly not a suitable companion in the brave new world of anti-colonial struggle that he saw opening up before him. In a society in which white women could be both desired and despised, she was potentially a political liability, and my father certainly seems to have seen her as such. When once in Jamaica he heard that some black nationalist members of Bustamante's ruling Labour Party had been joking in a Kingston hotel about how they wanted to 'fuck Bill Carr's wife', he flew into a rage, not with the politicians, but with my mother.

The more exciting his public life became, the more he found his wife and children an emotional burden as well as a political embarrassment. His children anchored him to a mundane, everyday world that he wanted to get away from. He and his friends could sit up all night on their verandas, drinking and holding forth on literature and politics and all the great Utopian projects for changing society that came and went during that revolutionary decade. But we were always there in the morning – his four little English brats, with our mumps and measles and childhood ailments, demanding attention, wanting to go to the beach or the cinema, needing to be taken to school and then to be picked up again in the afternoon. When he sat in his study in his world of books and quotations we ran around the house and garden shooting guns and playing loud games. We had temper tantrums and fights and children's accidents. We fought each other and threw up in the night and were scared of the dark. All this was not the kind of activity with which great men are expected to concern themselves in any society, but it must have seemed especially petty and mediocre in comparison with the heroic destiny that my father now saw unfolding before him.

The burden of his wife and children seemed to become heavier throughout his years in Jamaica, as his involvement with the Caribbean deepened and he moved further away from his own English past and everything it represented. But it was not until he reached Guyana that he was able finally to rid himself of his family. At first he tried to keep his public and private lives separate, as he set about establishing himself in his new country with his usual manic energy. Well adapted by now to Caribbean mores, he quickly made an impact in both his teaching and his social life. But at the end of each night he would have to stagger back to the house, in his Mr Hyde role, to his failing marriage and his children.

If anything, his whiteness was a bigger disadvantage in Guyana, where more than anywhere else in the West Indies white people in positions of authority tended to be objects of resentment and suspicion. A white sociologist who was teaching at UG at the time later remembered an incident in which a PNC member of staff printed a list of expatriates working at the university on the staff noticeboard, and demanded that they leave the country. Only three expatriates had been excluded from the list as 'honorary Guyanese', and my father was one of them. As flattered as he must have been by this positive appreciation, he was also clearly aware of the fact that it was not universally shared. One story suggests the pressure he felt himself to be under and the impact it had on his domestic life. After my mother's short-lived, but successful experience of working as a solicitor in Jamaica, she now found herself confined to the house once again in Guyana. In an attempt to break out of her domestic isolation she looked for work, and was offered a minor administrative position at the university. But before she could even take up the post, the PPP newspaper, the *Mirror*, found out and printed a story with the headline: *Lecturer's Wife Takes Guyanese Girl's job.*

As far as my mother knew, the job had not been taken from anyone, but the front-page story, in the PPP newspaper of all places, was guaranteed to incur my father's wrath. As usual his anger found its outlet in his wife, when my mother showed him the newspaper herself, knowing that he would find out about it anyway. Needless to say, she did not take the job, but the whole episode was another indication of the prevailing atmosphere in Guyana. The university was then probably the most radical place in the English-speaking Caribbean, where the intellectual influence of Black Power and pan-Africanism was most strongly felt. For many Guyanese East Indians the slogans of Black Power had more to do with black supremacy than Third World liberation, but the movement's angry rhetoric and vague political programme suited the PNC very well, and the government would later roll out the red carpet for Stokely Carmichael when he was invited to speak at the university in 1970, and told students, 'You must learn how to kill.'

*

One Guyanese student who came under the influence of Black Power was the woman who had a decisive impact on my father's life, and indirectly, on my family as well – Sandra Williams, later known as Andaiye. After we left Guyana they lived together for four years, until Sandra left him in 1972. A furious, wounded, letter written by my father to my mother, shortly afterwards, provides an explanation for the break-up:

> *During the year before she left me I sensed Sandra getting more and more restive, black/white, betraying her people etc . . . Also she had a lot of internal female problems . . . In my view she merits compassion not anger from me though there is no need for you to agree. One person who does not, however, is the yard nigger who took her away. A pig of a Svengali who works the same techniques on every woman who looks worth it – how he has been hurt by white people (meaning usually me), how he will address himself to solving the problems etc . . . Highly intelligent women fall flat on their backs with open knees and when he's gorged himself he leaves them. As the character Shaft has it, faced with a similar type in the States: 'Revolution, my ass. All your's doing is finding a new way to get pussy.' . . . He'll hurt Sandra but there's nothing I can do about it. She'll just have to take it. By the way there are two categories in the US and Guyana – black people and niggers. She is a black person. He is an all-time, permanent nigger.*

This torrid document has always seemed to me particularly revealing, not only because of my father's amazing insensitivity in relating the sordid details of his break-up with Sandra to his ex-wife, of all people, but also because of the extraordinary use by a white man of Black Power jargon like 'yard nigger'. The ferocity of the language made me even wonder occasionally whether he was really some kind of closet racist, smuggling his contempt out of the West Indies in letters to his ex-wife. But it was not until I had come to Guyana that I realized the real significance of the letter, *that it was not really written by a white man at all*. In effect, my father had changed colour, or at least thought he had. The 'phenomenal transformation' had taken place, as the following fragment from the same letter makes even clearer:

> *I am sick and tired of being fucked around by niggers and idealistic black men/women. I don't doubt the integrity of Sandra's convictions*

*— just the bloody sacrifices she demanded from herself and me. I
ended up as a sacrificial object on the altar of her sincerity. Walking
out on me was her gift to her brothers and sisters — many of whom
are niggers and likely to remain so. A black person is there as a
human being. But you can rarely salvage a nigger. I might sound
like Enoch Powell but I am only using contemporary Black Power
jokes.*

Whether this letter was an accurate description of Sandra's motives,
it certainly seemed to provide a glimpse into my father's own thinking,
in which people could be discarded or thrown away as a political
gesture. Had his own family also been a sacrificial object offered up
as proof of his sincerity and commitment to her brothers and sisters?
Had his head been so spun around by all the endless rhetoric about
yard niggers, Uncle Toms and 'honky shits' that he had finally needed
to demonstrate that inside he was as black as anyone else? Did he, in
fact, *feel* so black that he had come to regard his white English family
as an alien presence in his life?

The idea that my father might have offered up his own family as a
symbolic act of atonement for the crimes of the white race was clearly
not part of Freddie Kissoon's theory of the white man's burden, but
it did not seem at all far-fetched to me. Whether he had *consciously*
intended it as such was not the point. Many of my father's more
extreme actions were the result of powerful eruptions of feeling rather
than calculated intellectual decisions. During our last few weeks in
Guyana he was in an advanced state of inebriation most of the time.
The evidence suggests that the inner tensions and external pressures
of his years in the Caribbean finally exploded with such force that he
decided to jettison his family for good.

It may be, as Kathleen Drayton had suggested, that he did have a
streak of insanity and that his rejection of his family was one of the
occasions when it revealed itself. Yet there was an underlying method
and logic to his madness. When he stood on the balcony that last
afternoon and waved goodbye to his children, he must have known
that he was probably saying goodbye to us for ever, and that in doing
so he was leaving an entire phase of his life behind. Had he wanted,
we could have stayed in Guyana, and my parents could have separated
and lived apart. We could even have gone back to Jamaica, but the

speed and urgency with which our expulsion was carried out made this impossible. It is difficult to avoid the conclusion that West Indies Carr did not even want us in the Caribbean. He was effectively jumping ship, shedding his nationality, his past, even his race, in exchange for a new image of himself, a Caribbean Che Guevara performing a painful but necessary act of excision in the name of a higher cause.

There were, of course, other possible interpretations. He may have been just another egocentric male tired of the responsibility of looking after his children. There was also the fact that his children were material witnesses to a side of himself that he did not want to be reminded of. We had seen the way that he had treated his wife and would have been an embarrassing reminder of his imperfections had we stayed in Guyana or the Caribbean.

Yet all this, so far, remained in the realm of speculation, especially since there was still no evidence that he himself had really tried to explain his own motivations to anyone. Despite his undoubted intellectual gifts, he seems to have been curiously devoid of any capacity for self-analysis, and his gift of language often seems to have served as a kind of psychological smokescreen, in which the stream of words and quotations did more to conceal his real motivations than it did to reveal them.

So far I had not found a single person in Guyana to whom he had confided the motives underlying his behaviour during the months we lived there. The whole period seemed to have been airbrushed from the historical record, so that many people did not know we had been there at all. This tendency of my father's to make an abrupt and total break between different periods of his life was another disturbing feature of his personality. It was as if he needed continually to wipe the slate clean and start again, so that he would not have to face up to his past mistakes and disappointments. During those last crazed weeks in Guyana he had gone much further than usual, pulling down the entire structure of his domestic life in an act of destruction that was also one of dramatic creation. And he had done it. To all intents and purposes the scholarship boy from Dulwich had broken the external links with his English past and reinvented himself as a Guyanese in spite of his colour.

To people like Freddie Kissoon he was even a national hero. 'I guess nobody in Guyana would have seen Bill Carr as non-Guyanese,' he said. 'When you mix with people freely, your friends walk in and out of your home, and then you become a household word among them, the colour is lost. When he died, both Dr Jagan and his wife went to his funeral, and had he been alive now, when Dr Jagan was in power, he would have been offered something very substantial.'

'Even though he wasn't Guyanese?'

'Even though he wasn't Guyanese. At his funeral I stood up in church and I told my wife, "History has robbed this country of this man. This man should have lived to take over some aspect of literature and arts in Guyana." But that wasn't to be.'

It was not, and I felt sorry for Freddie Kissoon, that I had presented him with my own bleak memories of the man who had impressed him in so many ways. He was a nice guy who seemed genuinely shocked and upset by what I had told him. Once again I felt guilty and even apologetic for remembering my father the way I did. I wished instead that I could accept the positive image of him that was being continually presented to me. But no amount of eulogies could wipe out the past. If anything, the glowing descriptions of my father only made it worse, since I could not help wondering why we were the only ones who had such memories in the first place. I tried to explain my motives for coming to Guyana to Freddie and he seemed sympathetic. Before parting, he wished me luck with my investigation, and said that I seemed to be carrying 'a weight'. He was right, although I had not really realized it until coming to Guyana. Now that I had come, it did not seem to be getting any lighter.

Chapter Eleven

It is doubtful that many British people even knew of the existence of an obscure corner of the Empire called British Guiana until 1953. That year the Churchill government took the drastic step of suspending the Guianese constitution and declaring martial law in the colony after the electoral victory of the People's Progressive Party. Although various unconvincing and mostly spurious justifications were put forward for this intervention, the real reason was more succinctly defined by a cabinet minister at the Conservative Party conference that year. 'Her Majesty's Government are not going to allow a Communist State to be organized within the British Commonwealth,' he declared. 'Our friends can take that as a definitive statement, and our enemies can attach to it all the importance that I think they should.'

The man who had struck such terror into the British establishment was a young East Indian dentist and sugar estate worker's son called Cheddi Jagan. An orthodox pro-Soviet Marxist, whose ideological influences also included Roosevelt, the British Labour Party and the Dean of Canterbury, Dr Jagan must have been surprised to find himself accused of being a threat to democracy. Despite the PPP's Marxist language, and its passive support of the Soviet Union, it was essentially a nationalist, anti-colonial party that had won power through legitimate democratic elections sponsored by the colonial administration itself. But in the era of McCarthyism and the high Cold War, such a government was not considered suitable. So the PPP found its electoral victory dissolved, and tiny British Guiana became, for the first time in its history, the centre of an international crisis, and a threat to the security of the free world.

The suppression of democratic rights in British Guiana transformed the colony into something of a *cause célèbre* for the British left, and Cheddi Jagan overnight became an anti-colonial leader of international repute. That same year he and Forbes Burnham travelled to Britain, where they met various Labour Party politicians and well-known figures involved in anti-colonial politics, and spoke at public meetings about the situation in the colony. One of these meetings was held at Cambridge University, where they were invited to speak by the Cambridge University Socialist Club. Among the members of the audience that night was a young idealistic student of English literature in his first term at Cambridge: William Ian Carr.

My father did not speak to Jagan or Burnham personally, but he was so impressed by what he heard that night that he later told people in Guyana that it was Cheddi Jagan who was responsible for his coming to the West Indies. While this may be another example of his rewriting his history, there is no doubt that Cheddi Jagan did make a great impression on him. Not only did the two of them eventually become close personal friends, but they also campaigned together and spoke on the same political platform, often in the atmosphere of violence and intimidation that Moses had described. My father mentioned Cheddi in his letters many times. In one particularly grim, despairing missive from the early 70s, he even described him as the main reason for his staying in Guyana:

> *Life in Georgetown is much as usual. I have been robbed yet again and various arrangements for accommodation fell through. The familiar combination of muddle and hopelessness. And yet somehow it remains interesting and there is always Cheddi. Leaving everything else out of it, I have at last met a politician of whom I am personally fond. After I got a rock in the head and a paling stave beating at one of our meetings (Cheddi got a rock too) – I picked it up when it bounced off him and gave it to him as a parliamentary souvenir – he came round to where I was living – no guards, no bullshit – put his hands on my shoulders and said, 'Bill, how you feeling?'*
> *It was as small as that and as large. He really cared.*

This kind of affection and respect for the PPP leader seemed to be fairly general. Everybody, it seemed, liked Cheddi. Even those on the left who criticized the PPP as a racist East Indian party tended to exempt Jagan himself from such charges. He had a reputation for decency and integrity that was unusual in politics, even though some left-wing critics accused him of being politically naïve. The charge of naïveté was also echoed by the right. In a famous passage from Arthur Schlesinger's book, *The Thousand Days*, the former Kennedy adviser describes how Jagan's almost ingenuous honesty actually brought about his own downfall during his ill-fated trip to Washington in 1961 to obtain a US loan. Kennedy and his advisers had already been alerted by the British to the demon dentist's supposedly communist tendencies. They questioned Jagan closely about his political influences in a somewhat farcical attempt to determine whether or not he was a Marxist. Cheddi failed the cross-examination. Irritated by the questioning, he declared in a press conference that he was a Marxist but not a communist and cited the British socialist Harold Laski as an influence on both himself and Kennedy.

The reference failed to impress the strongly anti-communist president or his advisers, who now regarded Guyana as a potential Cuba. As a result Jagan returned home without the loan he wanted, and unaware that Kennedy had issued secret instructions to the CIA to depose him and decided to give US support to Forbes Burnham. The rest was a sordid, minor chapter in Cold War history, which has been obscured by bloodier destabilization operations elsewhere in Guatemala and Chile. In 1962, using funds channelled through a phoney office in London, the CIA helped support anti-Jagan trade unions in what became the longest general strike in Guyanese and international trade union history. With his country rendered virtually ungovernable and torn apart by racial violence, Jagan finally succumbed to British pressure to change the constitution. The colony was freed from 'communism' and handed over to Forbes Burnham, the man both Schlesinger and the British had described, correctly, as 'a racist and a demagogue'.

The PPP's 1964 electoral defeat was the beginning of a thirty-two-year period in the political wilderness, and it is one of the ironies of Guyanese history that during the PPP's years in opposition, the Marxist Schlesinger had doubted was 'recoverable for democracy' remained faithfully committed to the democratic process, while Burnham and the PNC set about building a de facto one-party state. The grim conditions in which Cheddi's party had to operate would certainly have stretched anyone's faith in parliamentary democracy, but his moderate line prevailed. Throughout the years of opposition he had argued against the PPP militants calling for an armed insurrection, even when the electoral process had been rendered virtually meaningless by the PNC's massive vote-rigging. It was not until October 1992 that this patience had been finally rewarded, and the PPP returned to power in free and fair elections under international supervision.

My father died only months before the belated electoral triumph of the man who had had so much influence over his own political and personal destiny, and in whose party he had fought and campaigned for so many years. Not only had Cheddi influenced my father's life, but if what he said was true about his reasons for coming to Guyana, then the PPP leader had also indirectly influenced the course of my own. And so I was interested to meet him, to find out what he thought of his English friend and comrade, and to see what qualities had so impressed my father on that distant Cambridge evening, forty-one years before.

I met his Excellency, Cheddi Jagan, the president of Guyana, at his office the day after his seventy-eighth birthday. That morning I had seen pictures of him and his wife in the newspapers, smiling as he blew out the candles on his birthday cake. In most of the pictures I had ever seen of Cheddi he seemed to be smiling like that, and he was smiling now, as we shook hands and sat down. Listening to his speech at the Romesh funeral, he had not struck me as the most obviously charismatic of politicians; close up he seemed more like an amiable uncle, with his broad, open smile and receding white hair. He was dressed in a long-sleeved shirt, hanging loosely over blue trousers, and he spoke with the same deep voice and slow, leisurely delivery that I had heard at the funeral.

After all the spontaneous Guyanese outpourings I had heard so far, Cheddi was surprisingly restrained and unforthcoming on the subject of my father. He responded to my questions with short, rather bland utterances that seemed to die away before they had even begun. Whether he felt constrained by the formality of the situation, or whether he felt awkward about discussing my father with one of his children, he seemed strangely guarded and elusive. I began by reminding him of the meeting he had addressed in Cambridge in 1953 and asked him if he was aware of his influence in bringing my father to Guyana.

He shook his head and smiled politely. 'I'm afraid not.'

Could he remember how my father first became involved in the party?

'Well, he was involved in many things here. He was a dramatist and an actor, and I remember my wife and I went to a Shakespearian play they had in one of the high schools, and we were very impressed with his performance, and we got to know him better than that, and gradually he came into the PPP's activities. He used to write a lot, and he used to attend our party group, and so he got more actively involved in the work of the party.'

I asked him if he recalled the political campaigning that they had done together, including the violent incident my father had mentioned in his letter, but he said there had been so many meetings like that that he could not remember any particular incident. My father had written in the same letter that Cheddi had told him afterwards to restrict his campaigning to the countryside since he was more likely to be attacked in Georgetown as a foreigner. Although there had been a few foreigners involved with the PPP in the 60s, they had all left by the time he became involved with the party, largely as a result of the PNC's increasing xenophobia. 'The more the PNC got into power,' Cheddi said, 'and began exercising full power, they took on more of a racial position, using racial discrimination as a way of attacking their opponents.'

Had the PNC ever directly used racialist language in their attacks against him?

'I don't think it was overt, but you did have that in many other ways, like for instance the harassment they gave him at the university.'

My father had spent a lot of his time with the more militant factions of the PPP, and I was curious to know how the reportedly puritanical leader of an orthodox Marxist party regarded his more eccentric forms of political activity. I asked him if he had been aware that one of his party members was going around picking fights in situations that were not directly related to his work with the party. Again the answer was statesman-like and non-committal. 'Well, basically he was a fighter, you know, and he stood for his rights and his principles and he was prepared to speak out, and that was anathema for the ruling party then.'

But didn't he think he had taken unnecessary risks? I persisted.

'Well, I wouldn't know all the movements that he did personally, you know, but when he went with us he had the protection of the party and whatever security we had.'

I could hear the shutters coming down, and I asked him if he thought that my father's drinking had affected his political work. On this issue the president was a little more forthcoming. 'Yes,' he replied. 'I believe he could have played a much bigger role in the whole development of the struggle, to which he was committed, but I believe, you know, that some people get so frustrated, especially as our struggle was so long and so drawn out, and all kinds of things happen, and in the context of his own background and what not, this may have affected him and led him to drink more and more.'

The idea that it was 'the struggle' that had made my father drink did not seem to me entirely convincing, since he was already well into his alcoholism before he became involved with the PPP, but it was possible that watching the slow inexorable disintegration of everything that he had believed in politically may have contributed to his sense of hopelessness and despair. In what way did his drinking prevent him from playing a fuller role?

'In the later stages, you know, he almost became immobile.' The president paused. 'He drank too much, I would say.'

I could not tell whether Cheddi was being diplomatic or genuinely critical, but this bland observation seemed such an extraordinary understatement that I could not think how to respond to it. Instead I asked him if they had had a relationship outside politics.

'Oh, yes. I used to visit him at his house and have long talks,' Cheddi replied.

'About what?' I asked.

'About politics, and art and literature, and things like that.'

Cheddi was not exactly wasting words, and I realized that I was not going to get any insight into the dynamics of the relationship between the two men from the president himself. On the evidence of this meeting, at least, the laidback, apparently unflappable PPP leader and my tempestuous, manic-depressive father seemed like polar opposites. If Cheddi reminded me of Conrad's 'gentle apostle' Michaelis in *The Secret Agent*, with his unshakeable optimism and his rationalist belief in human progress, then my father seemed to me like Little Stevie, drawing 'circles, circles, circles, innumerable circles . . . the symbolism of a mad art attempting the inconceivable'. Throughout his adult life my father was often drawn towards men who possessed qualities of calm and discipline that he felt he lacked in himself, whether it was Matthew Arnold, the Paul Scofield of *A Man for All Seasons*, or Cheddi himself. These were, of course, the qualities he had always associated with his own father, whom he had barely known. I wondered now whether there had been an unconsciously filial bond in his feelings towards the serene PPP patriarch underlying the ideological affinity.

Cheddi talked with a little more warmth and feeling about my father's funeral, which he had addressed, but even then his description of him sounded oddly impersonal. 'These events are sometimes, for me, traumatic, because he was a dear friend, and a colleague, a person who was committed to struggle, and it really touched me a lot that he had passed away.'

'Could you sum up the contribution he made to Guyana?'

'Well, I think he was doing a good job, first of all at the university, because everything was put under control so to speak, at the political level, at the social level, at the academic level, and therefore not only was he brave, but also in terms of ideas and principles and so forth, he was making an impact on his students at the university, and that's another reason he was attacked.'

'But he didn't live long enough to see the P P P come to power. Do you think there would have been a role for him if he had lived?'

'Yes, I'm sure we would have had positions. We've brought, for instance, two academic people into the government, including one ex-P N C member, so I'm sure there would have been a place for him.'

Once again I wondered if he was being diplomatic, since it was difficult to imagine my father holding down a ministerial post if he had been as immobile as Cheddi described. Time was running out, and the conversation turned briefly to politics. For the first time, Cheddi began to loosen up and hold forth about the party to which he had dedicated his life. He talked about its early ideological influences, and the P P P's first administration, reeling off a string of statistics of high economic growth rates to show how successful it had been before the destabilization campaign had brought it down. 'At that time they hate us on the grounds that when we get independence we will set up a regime on the model of the Soviet Union, in other words a one-party state, whereas in a multi-party system we were winning elections and we would have won the 1964 election too had they not changed the system. In other words, what we are saying is it's not the philosophy of Marxism which is wrong, but the way its being applied, and if our experiment had been allowed to continue, perhaps we wouldn't have had the kind of débâcle we saw in Eastern Europe and the Soviet Union.'

The idea that what had happened in little British Guiana all those years ago might have influenced the future of humanity and prevented the fall of the Berlin Wall seemed somewhat far-fetched, but Cheddi seemed quite convinced of it. Listening to him expound on the virtues of 'scientific socialism', I thought that Guyana must be one of the few places on earth where a political leader could be found who used the term without irony or embarrassment. For a man who had spent virtually his entire career in opposition as a result of using the word Marxist too freely, he seemed quite unaffected by post-modern ideological doubt and predicted confidently that the problem of world poverty could be solved within his lifetime.

Such optimism was even more remarkable given the bleak national and international prospects for the kind of politics that he believed in. History had not been kind to Cheddi, or to Guyana. He had been driven from office as a result of the Cold War, and now that it was over, he had been returned to power only to find himself faced with the enormous task of repairing the damage left by the party that had cheated him out of the presidency for more than three decades. His government had inherited a wrecked economy, the crippling loss of the skilled people who were needed to rebuild the country, and an enormous debt burden that continued to eat into its revenues. Everywhere small Third World countries like Guyana risked being marginalized by global economic forces more concerned with prising them open for their own benefit than in contributing to local development.

Like his Jamaican counterpart Michael Manley, with whom his career has some parallels, Cheddi had been forced to bite the ideological bullet and go begging at the IMF and the World Bank, accepting loans in exchange for tough economic austerity programmes aimed at promoting 'growth'. Yet despite the unfavourable circumstances in which he had come to power, Cheddi was surprisingly hopeful about the future and even predicted a gradual evolution of Guyanese society towards socialism. He was equally optimistic about the international situation, and before I left he handed me a copy of a pamphlet containing proposals that he had made at the United Nations for a 'New Global Human Order'. He was smiling again as he explained his blueprint for eradicating world poverty and creating full employment. Once again, with the enthusiasm of a butterfly collector showing me his collection of favourite species, he reeled off statistics to show how world military spending outstripped expenditure on basic necessities in health and education, how the creation of an international poverty dividend would help to redress the imbalances between north and south, and how a just economic order was the only alternative to a world riven by ethnic and political violence.

The proposals were all perfectly rational. There was not a single thing he said that I could have disagreed with. Yet I was left with the impression of a man insulated by ideology, whose optimistic faith in human progress was not matched by a realistic perception of the forces ranged against such ideas. In the era of ethnic barbarism, resurgent fascism and rabid neo-liberal economic theory, I found it difficult to share such clear-eyed faith in the possibilities of scientific socialism myself, but Cheddi was clearly a man who knew how to wait. Perhaps it was that same combination of ideological conviction and calm, smiling confidence in ultimate victory, that had once inspired my father as a young man all those years ago to leave the bleak post-war political landscape of Europe and turn, like Mercutio, to that 'dew-dropping south', in search of a Utopian dream of peace, love and justice that the sugar-estate worker's son had still not abandoned.

One of the consequences of Cheddi Jagan's early visit to Cambridge was an article entitled 'Democracy in Crisis', which he wrote for the first issue of a new university student journal called *Cambridge Left*. The journal had originally been founded in the 1930s by the communist poet John Cornford. In 1953 it was relaunched as the house journal of the Cambridge University Socialist Club, a discussion group whose membership was open to 'all socialists, from Fabians to Marxists, Syndicalists to Anarchists, and mere "intellectual riff-raff" and those simply curious about the nature and working of socialism'.

In many ways *Cambridge Left* is a period piece, representing a vanished tradition within the English left, with its earnest concern to bridge the gulf between what one of its editorials described as 'the ostrich-like burial of heads in sands of academic speculation' and 'the jungloid reality of factory and mill'. For a leftist student publication, it often produced writing of a surprisingly high standard, and was unusual in its non-sectarian approach to politics, and its attempts to combine political commentary and analysis with socialist cultural criticism. Like its original founder, many of its contributors were students of English literature, and the journal has a strong literary bias, with poems and book reviews alongside the political articles. The lurking presence of F. R. Leavis can also be detected behind the discussions of morality and politics, which often sat rather uneasily alongside the more orthodox Marxist perspectives on the issues of the day, from decolonization and the Formosa crisis to the rearming of Germany and the 'alienation of the leadership and rank and file within the Labour Party'.

Much of the writing also reflected the general sense of alienation from existing political structures and the discontent with a moribund English society characteristic of 50s intellectuals. Thus my father's friend Simon Gray, in an article on Suez, angrily denounced 'the spectacle of a nation shuffling into further muddle by a refusal to face up to its own idiocy', while my father railed in a similarly Osbornian key against 'a nation in which at least 25 per cent of the electorate are so indifferent to who governs them that they are too inert even to cast a vote'.

Even the advertisements reflected this odd combination of socialist orthodoxy, moral questioning and 50s gloom. 'Why has Western Civilization lost its nerve?' asked a group calling itself the Ethical Society, alongside an advert for Canon Stockwood's 'I Went to Moscow'. The Society For Friendship With Bulgaria offered readers the chance to 'know more about this interesting Socialist People's Republic', while a peculiar organization calling itself the Panacea Society warned of 'the menace of S A T A N I C   E V I L   and A N G E L I C E R R O R now combining in the effort to gain W O R L D D O M I N I O N'.

A notice informed readers that 'correspondence relating to the magazine should be sent to: W. I. Carr, Pembroke College, Cambridge'. In the Michaelmas term 1954 my father's name appeared for the first time as the more proletarian 'Bill Carr' in the list of editors. On the same page he reviewed *On the Waterfront*, one of the first films he went to see with my mother. Although not entirely dismissive, the review's grudging praise is hedged in with dogmatic political objections. Thus Elia Kazan is taken to task for asserting that 'love and affection, the relationship between Terry Molloy and Edie Doyle, are the only significant responses to . . . the fundamental social issue, the breakdown of capitalist methods of industrial control'. My father accuses Kazan of 'the classic liberal let-out, the use of personal relationships as a refuge from social relationships', all of which has rendered American society 'immune from the criticisms Mr Kazan might have made'.

His heavy-handed Stalinist critique drew a response from a reader called Margaret Roberts the following term with the sternly Leavisite title of 'Critical Standards'. In it she accused my father of allowing his own political and ideological standards to undermine his aesthetic appreciation of the film and failing to understand that 'those aspects of human activity which derive from man's spiritual life, his imagination, his intellectual creativity and his "vision" cannot be circumscribed by anything but their own limits'.

Always sensitive to criticism, my father struck back the next term, accusing Miss Roberts of having 'effectively paralysed the critical faculty, and . . . greatly limited the conscious application of its function'. At the same time he reiterated his criticism that Kazan had failed to show 'an awareness of the interconnection of experience' between personal relationships and society. 'We do not go the length of saying that all problems are in effect the same problem,' he declared, 'but we do say that all personal and social activity is judged primarily by the question how to live? And how to live at the moment covers every imaginable problem from a love affair to the situation in Formosa.'

The question of how to live was indeed one that was to occupy my father for most of his life. The answers he came up with would probably have surprised Miss Roberts and many of the other people with whom he came into contact at Cambridge, but their seeds can already be seen in these early articles. In another highly favourable review of an independent American film called *Salt of the Earth*, he took up the theme of the relationship between society and the individual once again. The film was a fictionalized account of a Mexican miners strike in 'Zinctown, New Mexico', and made a great impression on the young Cambridge intellectual, who contrasted its gritty portrayal of working-class solidarity and capitalist class relations with the 'bourgeois liberalism' of *On the Waterfront*:

> *Personal relations are microcosmic images of social relations (a fact that is lost on Mr Elia Kazan) and* Salt of the Earth *shows the development of the ordinary human emotions of love, affection and esteem in socialist terms.*

These emotions would later turn out to be mostly conspicuous by their absence in my father's own home, whether in socialist or any other terms, nor had they been particularly prominent in his own childhood, but this absence did not stop him from believing that they existed *somewhere else*. As many have done before and since, my father was in effect linking personal happiness to a different social system. In these early articles the crude Marxist assumption that flawed and oppressive personal relationships would automatically be remedied by the overthrow of capitalism was also accompanied by a tendency to idealize the working class in general. Thus, in a review of two sociological accounts of English working-class life, he contrasts the 'bleak social ethic' of a 'middle-class estate layout' with 'the moving accounts . . . of the archetypal events in Bethnal Green life . . . – the rallying round at childbirth and the compassionate description, based on a living sense of people, of a local wedding'.

The fact that even at that stage in his life my father's response to childbirth was something less than 'rallying round', and his knowledge of working-class family life was mostly theoretical or second-hand, does not detract from the underlying romanticism and sense of yearning in these early articles. The workers, it was clear, did the essential things in life better despite their class oppression. It is impossible to know how much this sentimental image of the English working class matched his own limited experience. Despite the fact that he extended his national service precisely in order to deepen his knowledge of the working class, he did not keep in contact with anyone from his army days after going up to Cambridge.

This lack of continuity is surprising, since a few working-class acquaintances would certainly have enhanced the image of the proletarian socialist intellectual that he was already trying to cultivate. The only document of his national service days is a photograph of him in uniform, smiling and looking fit, one of a group of soldiers leaning against a tank. Did he really find the masculine, classless comradeship that the photograph seems to suggest? Or did he remain an outsider, excluded from ordinary human emotions and a living sense of people by the same rigid English class barriers that generations of downwardly mobile middle-class intellectuals have tried in vain to overcome?

Whatever the truth, his attitude towards the English working class did not remain so starry-eyed. As the 50s ground miserably onwards, his earlier romanticism was beginning to give way to a generalized disenchantment with English society, for which neither the old nor the new left offered a cure. ' "Working class this and middle class that," ' – he complained, bad-temperedly, in a contemptuous review of a famous collection of New Left writings entitled *Out of Apathy*.

'It may be a preliminary to understanding, but one that needs to be quickly dispensed with ... how aimless to play off one against the other, particularly when it tends to conclude in an offensive egocentricity.'

The review of *Out of Apathy* is characterized by an extraordinary and at times barely coherent outpouring of disgust and contempt directed at some of the representatives of the New Left. Richard Hoggart, Raymond Williams, the young Stuart Hall and E. P. Thompson are among the most notable targets for my father's relentless wrath. The barrage of insults and criticism does not seem to be based on any obvious political disagreement, since E. P. Thompson is criticized, of all things, for his failure to understand the importance of original sin as 'a useful enough hint at the dark complexity of motive and purpose within us'. The link between the scattergun criticisms is more clearly expressed in the following diatribe:

> *Is it really necessary ... to have bleak rationalism or the sniggering unintelligence of public school left-wingers, the pathetic dishonesties of middle-class socialists out on the limb of class-consciousness, earnest grammar school boys, talking about 'areas of experience' and 'our reading' of a novel and busily separating the sheep from the goats, and the drizzling rain of socialist humanism ... It is not an attractive prospect that opens in front of us – a prospect in which those who ought to be representative of the best consciousness of their time are prostrate before their own metaphors and fenced in by a gimcrack series of references.*

The fact that my father was himself both a public-school left-winger and a middle-class socialist did nothing to balance the ferocity of his contempt for others in the same category, and may even have intensified it, since the underlying assumption in the article seemed to be that he was authentic, whereas the intellectual heavyweights of the New Left were not:

> Out of Apathy *has so little that is truly personal, so little that is a matter of independent personal insight. Instead we are steeped in a tepid bath of good intentions, and I find myself in the ironical position of saying to a group of Socialists – you are not radical enough, you don't go deep enough, you dodge and evade, and take comfort from abstractions. It's well enough enthusing about the values of*

'people' but what if you don't show much knowledge of what people are like?

It is hard to know exactly what my father was complaining about, since he gave no concrete examples of the weaknesses he described, nor did he explain himself what people were like. The political vagueness at the heart of this furious polemic was symptomatic of his own inner confusion. Throughout his life what he really believed in was often overshadowed by his angry denunciations of what he was against. The expression of his political views owed more to his temperamental anger than his ideas, leading him to take up contradictory positions, depending on what mood he was in or who he was arguing with. At various times he could sound like an English Liberal, a dogmatic Stalinist or a lapsed priest.

Even his membership of the Communist Party had been motivated more by a need to rebel against his middle-class background than by a genuine intellectual conversion to Marxism. During his years at Cambridge he became alienated from most British left-wing political parties and organizations, all of whom were tarred with the same brush of inauthenticity. Where was such authenticity to be found? Where was the combination of drama and a great moral cause that he craved? Where could the 'ordinary human emotions of love, affection and esteem in socialist terms' be brought into existence?

They were clearly not going to be found in 50s England. At a time when British power was waning abroad, and British society was seen by many on the left to be in a state of moral and political asphyxiation, it may well be that, like many European leftist intellectuals, he began to project his revolutionary fantasies on to the only part of the planet where revolutions were still taking place – the Third World and the colonies. My father's Cambridge friend Tony Scull remembers that they often talked about liberation theology and the anti-colonial movements that were emerging after World War II. My father had been involved peripherally in the Malayan insurgency, on the wrong side, but there is little evidence of how the experience affected his political views, although my mother remembers him describing his shock at seeing beggars starving on the platform at Calcutta railway station while his unit waited to be flown across to Malaya. The one colonial crisis which did make an impression on him was not a Third World revolutionary struggle at all, but the vicious war between E O K A and the British in Cyprus. In the spring of 1956 he wrote:

> *You unfold the* Daily Mail *and the first thing you see is a photograph of a dead British officer. He is lying in a street in Nicosia and he has five bullets in his back. And you know, as you read, that you have to write an article on Cyprus. You can't afford to be ironic, or not too ironic anyway, and you can't afford to do what a socialist might do if he were not ironic – that is to say, you cannot conceal the body under a propaganda shroud by talking about freedom, or union with Greece, or self-determination for colonial dependencies.*

This ambivalent reaction to the Cypriot crisis, coming from an ex-national serviceman who might well have become a body under a propaganda shroud himself, is another example of my father's intensely moralistic conception of politics, and his sense of personal involvement and implication in larger political issues. Certainly no real Marxist revolutionary would have presented the Cypriot war in these terms. On the contrary a thorough-going Marxist intellectual like Sartre would not have been troubled by photographs of a hundred dead British officers, knowing that each corpse was another nail in the coffin of imperialism. My father was not Sartre, and his politics, as far as they could be identified at all, seemed closer to Camus. It was ironic that decades later this temperamental political misfit, who had rejected both the Communist Party and the 'bleak rationalism' of the New Left in England, would embrace the rigid Marxist orthodoxies of the P P P with such fervent conviction. At the same time it was absolutely logical. The P P P was authentic. Its members were not public-school left-wingers or middle-class socialists, but the salt of the earth. After so many years of searching for his brothers-in-arms, my father had finally found his way to Zinctown, New Mexico after all.

'Berbice! Berbice!' Every day as I passed the minibus stop near Starbroek Market I would hear the same eager, insistent cries, shouted at passers-by like a woman's name, as the drivers competed with each other to hustle enough custom to fill their waiting vehicles. For days I had been promising the same driver that I would be going to Berbice soon. Now I dutifully made my way to his van and sat waiting in the sweltering heat while the other seats slowly filled up with passengers. At last the vehicle pulled away, blaring loud pop music, and we drove out of the city in the direction of the university and the sea wall, past a small funfair with a large sign proclaiming: *Welcome to fantasyland, Guyana*.

Soon we had left the capital behind. The van was careering at breakneck speed along the increasingly bumpy, potholed coastal road, through a mixture of East Indian and African villages which were mostly poorer, unpainted versions of the stilted houses in the capital – bare, dirt yards underneath, and dogs and chickens running about outside. Occasionally we passed squatter settlements of more recent construction. Rows of tiny raised huts were laid out neatly on stretches of wasteground, with a wrecked bus lying by the side of the road, a testament to the wrecked public transportation system that was another of the Comrade Leader's lasting contributions to Guyana. Once a railway and a functioning bus service had connected the capital to Berbice, but there were now no more buses on the roads anywhere, the railway tracks had been torn up and sold to Zambia, the occasional disused railway carriage left standing in the middle of a field the only evidence they had ever existed.

The official reason for the closure of the railway was that it was too costly, but there were those who said that the real reason was racial discrimination against the rural East Indian population who had used it most. Berbice was the centre of East Indian prosperity, and the birthplace of some of the country's greatest cricketers, like Rohan Kanhai and Basil Butcher. It was also the political heartland of the PPP, where Cheddi Jagan himself had been born on a sugar estate near Port Mourant. My father had campaigned in Berbice during the run-up to the 1973 election, after Cheddi had advised him against speaking in the capital to avoid the risk of being physically attacked. His membership of the PPP also coincided with a worsening of the political situation in Guyana, when the PNC was beginning to move beyond electoral fraud to a more overt use of violence and intimidation to keep itself in power. It was during the 1973 elections, when my father had been campaigning in Berbice, that Burnham used the army for the first time to seize ballot boxes and keep opposition voters away from polling stations, a new strategy in what the Comrade Leader termed 'the year of the breakthrough'. That year, on 21 November, two days before my birthday, he had described the violent Georgetown meeting where he and Cheddi had spoken in a letter to my mother. He ended with this message:

We campaigned in the country once or twice and if you stone me in Berbice you'll probably get lynched. Tell Matthew and give them all my love.

The letter was signed 'Bill', but the name and address on the envelope was given as 'Henry James, University of Guyana, PO Box 841'. I could not remember my reaction to this letter, but it is unlikely that I would have been as impressed by my father's exploits as he seemed to expect. Living in dreary, strike-bound Britain, with its power cuts and three-day week, trying with some difficulty to find my way into the secular world after four years at boarding school with the Jesuits, neither Guyana nor my father had been uppermost in my mind, let alone Berbice, a place I had never even heard of. By the time I had left school, I had ceased to look up to my father, and my adolescent correspondence with him on the Cuban Revolution, Che Guevara and apartheid had virtually ended.

And so it was only now, after all these years, that I had begun to understand the strangeness of his life in Guyana, and fill in some of the details behind his fragmentary references to distant political battles which for some reason he had wanted me to know about, even as I was moving away from him.

The early 70s were the high-water mark of my father's radicalism. This period coincided with the two years between his break-up with Sandra Williams and his second marriage. His decision finally to join the PPP may even have been partly a reaction to the end of the relationship, and an explicit rejection of Sandra's Black Power politics. Certainly the timescale seemed to fit, since the letters announcing his membership of the party and his break-up with Sandra were both dated February 1972, and eight months later the letter bearing Che Guevara's revolutionary farewell to his family was sent to my brother, by which time he had become an active party member.

The same period also corresponded with one of his most intense periods of drinking, when he was reportedly getting through some four or five bottles of rum a day, and he was diagnosed as having cirrhosis of the liver. As usual my father was living several contradictory lives at the same time. Even as he was preaching the gospel of international proletarian revolution, he was wilfully drinking himself to death. In his early forties and single again, having been ditched by the Guyanese woman he had left his family for, he felt lonely and adrift. 'At least you have four hulks jumping around you,' he wrote enviously to my mother. His ostensible reason for staying in Guyana was his work at the university, but he had now put his job under threat by openly declaring his political loyalties.

While all this was going on he continued to play the role of pen-father to his kids, his occasional blue air-mail envelopes wending their way across the Atlantic, with the inevitable excuses, apologies and paternal advice.

All these details were going round in my mind as we drove through the flat countryside along the coastal road, separated from the sea wall by a few hundred yards of swampy wasteland and patches of cultivated ground, past farms and villages interspersed with clusters of coconut and banana trees. It was my first real glimpse of rural Guyana and I enjoyed being out of the capital, despite the driver's reckless speed. Soon we turned inland, crossing wooden bridges over narrow muddy rivers into a heavily cultivated landscape, with fields of sugar cane and rice stretching towards the green wall of rainforest in the distance. Most of the villages were East Indian now. Peasants and farmers were everywhere engaged in the laborious task of emptying sacks of rice to dry by the edge of the road. Occasionally the van stopped to let off passengers and pick up new ones before roaring off again. During one of these brief halts, I noticed a sign outside someone's garden warning that the world was going to end in 1997, which may have explained the driver's haste.

After two hair-raising hours we reached a dilapidated wooden jetty at the edge of the Berbice river, its wide muddy waters lined with dark green mangrove on both banks. On the far side of the river I could see the distant outline of New Amsterdam, the provincial capital, where I had arranged to meet the PPP regional secretary Rohil Pessaud an hour before. I parted company with the van and went down to the jetty where an old, battered-looking hulk of a ferry was still filling up with cars and passengers. The same ferry is mentioned in V. S. Naipaul's *The Middle Passage*, where Cheddi Jagan complains to the author about its lateness and inefficiency. That book was written in the early 60s, but the ferry did not seem to have improved its service, as it sat waiting, for no apparent reason, for another forty minutes before finally pulling away lethargically from the pier. Then it promptly broke down and drifted listlessly in the choppy brown water for another half an hour before the engine finally coughed into life again and chugged onwards towards the distant bank.

Finally the boat moored at an even more dilapidated jetty on the other side. The whole structure looked as though it might fall into the water at any moment and the general appearance of decay was enhanced by the various bits of machinery discarded in the mud at its feet, which included a giant propeller and a wrecked police launch with wild plants growing out of it like a giant flowerpot.

New Amsterdam was just a few hundred yards away at the end of the road. It was Guyana's second city, a combination of frontier and market town, with a population of 20,000, but one or two bustling streets failed to alleviate the general atmosphere of sleepy tranquillity. I got off the boat and went straight to Freedom House, the local P P P branch, in search of Mr Pessaud, but the regional secretary was not there. Since I was nearly two hours late it was hardly surprising that I had missed Mr Pessaud and I sat waiting in an office with a picture of Lenin on one wall and the smiling Cheddi Jagan on the other, while a party worker tried to locate him for me.

After a few minutes I was directed to the Berbice regional party headquarters nearby, where Mr Pessaud greeted me warmly and took me into his office. He was chubby, moustachioed and balding. He spoke highly of my father, like most P P P members. 'It was a privilege for me to campaign with Bill,' he declared. 'We did several public meetings together on the East coast and in Berbice, and he was always very impressive, very friendly to our people in opposition. While a lot of people were scared to identify with the P P P then, because of the Burnham regime, very vindictive, Bill always identified with us, with the working class, and I was always very happy, very proud to have him campaign with me, and we were very close.'

Rohil remembered two incidents during the 1973 campaign in Berbice when the police had tried to intervene and prohibit P P P internal meetings. On both occasions my father had stood up and ordered the police to leave on the grounds that their presence was illegal, and the police had actually backed down. While these stories demonstrated my father's fearless defiance of the regime, they also revealed a crucial difference between the kind of low-intensity gang-sterism employed by Burnham and the indiscriminate use of terror and violence practised by other regimes on the continent. The difference is important in understanding my father's political activity in Guyana, since his undeniable courage was to some extent made possible precisely by the kind of regime that he had chosen to confront. While most PPP members consistently referred to the Burnham regime as a dictatorship, it was also a peculiarly Guyanese dictatorship, in which the blatant abuse of power co-existed with elections, however fraudulent, and therefore allowed considerable political space in which the opposition could organize and campaign. In Haiti or El Salvador, for example, not only would there have been no such meetings in the first place, but the police would certainly not have meekly retired, and my father would very likely have been taken out and shot, along with everyone else present, for this and for many of the other things that he said and did in Guyana.

The PNC's limited tolerance for its opponents was undoubtedly due more to the fact that it did not feel threatened enough to resort to such methods than to any democratic convictions. One reason for its sense of security was the political stalemate caused by the racial division between the two largest parties, in which each party continued to appeal to its own ethnic constituency without trespassing on to the other's territory. For all its socialist ideology, the PPP was never able to transcend its East Indian base of support and make significant inroads into the Afro-Guyanese vote, while the PNC's election-rigging ensured that the larger Indian population could never translate its superiority in numbers into a parliamentary majority. Even in Berbice, for example, the PNC was regularly winning elections during the Burnham years, despite the fact that more than 70 per cent of the population was East Indian. As long as these methods worked, therefore, the regime was never obliged to resort to wholesale repression and mass murder to keep itself in power, and they continued to work right up to 1992, when external pressure finally forced the PNC to fight genuinely open elections, which the party then lost.

All this did not mean that political opposition in Guyana was free of risks during the Burnham era, and there were countless incidents of mob intimidation, selective beatings, not to mention the murders of Walter Rodney and others, to show that it was not. At the same time the kind of 'repressive tolerance' practised by the regime did create a peculiar situation in which a white foreigner like my father could order police to withdraw from an opposition meeting and be obeyed, and, above all, stay in the country year after year even after he had become a prominent and influential member of the PPP.

'Bill was always outspoken,' Rohil said. 'He was part of the political organization and he helped us tremendously during those repressive years, and he always spoke for what he believed in. At that time, you know, socialism was on the agenda, and he was always talking about his experiences, about socialism and the working class in Guyana.'

My ears pricked up at the mention of these 'experiences'. Was this another example of my father's self-mythologizing? I asked Rohil what kind of experiences he had talked about.

'He used to make mention of the struggles of the coal mines in England. I think he was born in the area, I'm not too certain. But he used to talk about the struggle of the coal miners, and he used to draw references with the struggle against the ruling leadership in England, and how the working class in every part of the world would face the same kind of bad working conditions, and so it was not only in Guyana where we fight against the dictatorship or the ruling class but in other places of the capitalist world.'

These struggles in the coal mines of England were an aspect of my father's past that I had certainly not heard about before, and as far as I knew none of his relatives had either. It was true that he had been born in Yorkshire. But he had been brought up in staid, provincial Harrogate, not a coal-mining village. There was no record of his ever having had any first-hand knowledge of coal-mining or miners beyond the pages of *Sons and Lovers*. This could qualify as an 'experience' to the extent that literary events often seemed to be as real to my father as historical ones, but it was certainly not the type of experience that Rohil seemed to believe had informed his vision of the international workers' struggle.

It was impossible to know whether my father had actually fabricated his own past, or whether the regional secretary, like many other people I had spoken to in Guyana, had innocently invented it for him. 'He was very convincing,' Rohil went on. 'He was a very good speaker, and over the years he had learned some of the ways the Guyanese speak, the dialects, and the Guyanese way of talking, and he would talk simple, like a farmer or a fisherman talking. You know, he never used to use any of this high language, because he was an English teacher, but when he reached down there to an ordinary farmer and peasant he used to use their language. Wherever Bill went, wherever he go, there was always a clamour for him, people wanted to listen to him, because as a European, supporting the People's Progressive Party, our people out there was very proud of that. Here, a European, what we say "a white man" supporting the struggles of the PPP, and a friend to the leadership of the PPP.'

This pride in having a European or a white man in the ranks of the PPP was another aspect of the complex racial attitudes in Guyana, where anti-white sentiment could co-exist with excessive respect for white people. The mere presence of a white man seemed to give added lustre and legitimacy to the PPP's cause – so that Moses Nagamootoo could describe my father's presence on a demonstration as the inspiration for a 'holy crusade'. This reverence for Europeans and their culture also accounted for the constant appreciation of my father's 'excellent command of the English language' and his knowledge of 'the classics'. He may have suffered racial persecution among PNC supporters, but his whiteness did clearly enhance his prestige as far as the PPP's constituency were concerned.

I asked Rohil if people had ever felt resentful about having a white man preaching politics to them.

He shook his head. 'We have a history of colonialism in Guyana, of British rule, but having a friend in Bill Carr, they didn't see him as a white man, although he was white in colour. When he died we lost a good friend, and personally too I was very sad and shocked when I heard of his death. I attended that funeral, so he was really a friend to the PPP and to our country, and he played a part, for whatever we are enjoying now.'

I had hoped to look around New Amsterdam, but I had to be back in the capital that afternoon, and there was only one more ferry, which was leaving in an hour's time. Rohil offered to drive me down to the dock, but first he wanted to have a drink with me in memory of my father. 'Bill always like to have a beer or two when he came down here,' he said conspiratorially. I told him that I was not surprised, as we drove out past the local hospital, which Rohil said, without irony, his administration had been patching up.

As the bar where my father used to drink on his visits to Berbice had since been turned into a Chinese restaurant called the Golden Dragon, we went to a bar immediately opposite. We stepped into a cavernous wooden interior with sky-blue walls, decorated with various cheap Chinese paintings. A short, dumpy Chinaman in shorts and vest brought us our beers. The bar was virtually empty, and we sat by the window looking out over the quiet main street and raised our bottles in a toast to my absent father.

Rohil looked sad as he remembered his former friend and comrade, as if my presence there had reminded him of the loss. He remembered an incident in which a Cuban speaker had come to Guyana and given a speech to a PPP branch meeting on Che Guevara. The speaker had been very boring, he said, and after he left my father had amused everybody by making jokes about him and then given his own speech on Che Guevara, which had been far more interesting. Rohil shook his head and smiled at the memory. Looking at the restaurant across the road which had once been my father's old haunt, he told me how my father would sit at a table in the bar and people from other tables would gather round to hear him talk about politics, literature and life. It was as if Rohil could still see the scene, as if those invisible customers were still there, pressing in around the table, listening to the white man holding forth. It often happened in Guyana that people would point to physical objects associated with their memories of my father – a sitting-room couch, a bar counter, the chair in his patio – as if he had only just left the room. Almost everyone who had known him remembered him in terms of some striking visual image. Each time I would try to imagine what they had seen and to reconcile that image with what I remembered. And so I tried to imagine him sitting at one of those tables now, the holy drinker entertaining the customers with a rambling mixture of literature, politics and anecdotes, mixing fact and fiction freely as he recalled his past, going over the same old themes – his mother, boarding school, Yorkshire, the moors, Geoff Boycott, coal miners – as if he were bent on consecrating his history in the minds of his listeners.

I did not tell Rohil what I remembered about him. His warmth and affection for my father were so genuine that I did not want to spoil his small tribute to the memory of his friend and comrade. So we finished our beers and he took me down to the ferry, which was due to leave in twenty minutes. In the event it remained docked for another two hours, while a line of cars manoeuvred its way on board with excruciating slowness. During the long wait I met a young Indian rice farmer who had studied economics at the university. He had heard of my father although he had not known him personally. He lived in Georgetown but had come to New Amsterdam to negotiate a credit loan for his farm in Berbice, and he offered to drive me back to the city when we got to the other side. He was very friendly and gregarious and the long wait gave us plenty of time to talk about a whole range of subjects, from the pros and cons of privatization and Guyana's dealings with the IMF, to the rice harvest and the jaguar attacks on cattle at his family farm near the jungle.

He was good company, but after reaching his car I began to doubt the wisdom of accepting the lift, since his driving was demented even by Guyanese standards. He overtook without looking at what lay ahead or behind, blissfully oblivious to any vehicles or people in his path as he roared down the bumpy road, only narrowly managing to avoid decapitating the untethered goats and cattle grazing on the rice paddy by the roadside. As we hurtled back towards the capital, he held forth on the subject of Guyanese race relations. He was not a racist and had nothing against the Africans personally, he assured me, but he believed the races should remain separate, and he would certainly not want any of his own daughters to marry one of them. To pass the time he told a few Guyanese racial jokes, in a mixture of English and patois, chortling with delighted laughter at the end of each one, as though he were hearing each joke for the first time.

Some of the jokes were quite funny, but others were blatantly racist. One of them went something like this. One day God decides to parcel out all the jobs and responsibilities between all the different races in Guyana. The white man goes to God and says, 'What you got for me God?' God says, 'You can administrate, you can govern, man.' After that the Indian asks the same question, and God says, 'You can have some land and cows.' Next comes the turn of the 'Portugee' and the Chinaman, and God says, 'You can have a business and you can have a shop.' Finally, at the end of the queue, the black man goes to God and asks, 'What you got for me God?' and God says, 'Nothing. I got nothing left for you, man.'

I waited for the punchline, but the farmer chortled happily and I realized that I had just missed it. Virtually all the jokes contained some kind of putdown of the Afro-Guyanese. He assured me that each race had similar jokes, and he was probably right. But after a while I began to find them depressing to listen to, and I was glad when the capital appeared up ahead once again. The sun was going down and there was a local cricket match in progress next to the highway. I stared out of the window at the fielders crouched down in readiness. The ground was on former swampland that Dutch settlers had drained some three hundred years ago before bringing the first slaves to cultivate it. It now belonged to a local Indian team, the rice farmer said. As I watched the retreating flashes of white standing out against the surrounding green, I thought how often I had seen that same sight in the English countryside. I wondered at the process of history by which the game had found its way across the ocean as a form of recreation for the colonizers and remained long after they had gone, the favourite sport of East Indians and Afro-Guyanese alike. As always I found the silence and the slow movement of the game soothing and peaceful. I strained my head to watch as the bowler ran in and the batsman began his backlift. In that moment they seemed like symbols of history's long reach and also of the fragility of things, as they acted out the eternal ritual of the English summer against the background of the sea wall, while the brooding waters of the Atlantic, which had brought their ancestors to the country, crashed relentlessly against it, always threatening to wash the whole place away.

Chapter Twelve

Even before coming to Guyana I had expected to encounter a different image of my father to the one I was used to, yet the more I found out about the person he had been after we left the more I felt compelled to re-examine my own memories of him. This was a difficult and mostly unsatisfactory process. It was nearly thirty years since I had lived with my father. During that time my memories of my childhood had remained more or less unchanged, but had suffered a gradual process of erosion that made them hazier and more fragmented as time went on, inexorably wiping out more details, till the blank spaces outnumbered what I actually remembered. In the process many of the childhood emotions I had once felt towards my father had either disappeared or become so completely alien to my present life that it was as if they belonged to someone else.

I knew that my own relationship with him had always been conflictive, much more so than it had appeared in the affectionate, paternal letters he wrote to me after we had returned to England. As the eldest son I was exposed to demands and expectations which my brothers and sister were spared. My sister was always his favourite, and the main object of his affection, while he tended to ignore my brothers because they were so young.

Affection certainly was not something that I ever associated with my father. There was very little intimacy in our relationship. Unlike my mother, he was always a rather remote, absent figure, the object of mixed feelings of awe, fear and hero worship. He seemed never to be able to give me the approval I wanted and always seemed to be speaking from a height of knowledge and experience of the world that I could never hope to reach.

I often had the feeling that I angered and disappointed him, and failed to measure up to his standards. In Jamaica he once used me as an example of the inarticulacy of children on the TV show *Brains Trust*, quoting with much amusement an incident when in a fit of temper I called my brother a 'dirty toilet'. I certainly felt inarticulate compared to him. I was an awkward, intense and self-conscious child, immersed in the world of my imagination and at the same time acutely sensitive to my parents' predicament, and my mother's distress in particular. I was also subject to wild mood swings, which I could never understand or express properly. My father, on the other hand, always had something to say about everything, his knowledge of the world impossibly vast, and he expressed himself with an impressive stream of words that always left me feeling I hadn't quite understood him.

At the same time there was always a mutual element of competition between us. We often seemed to be engaged in a battle of wills over large and small things. One of the main areas of conflict concerned my intellectual development. My education began early. Even as a toddler Tony Scull remembers that my father was in the habit of teaching me 'clever phrases of current political and lit-crit significance, which caused much laughter when cutely repeated'. The houses I grew up in were always filled with books, which both my parents treated as if they had some mysterious ability to make me a better and more intelligent person. As a child I found this veneration of books and literature rather alarming. I often looked at the intimidating rows of paperbacks out of which my father mysteriously made his living, full of names that meant absolutely nothing to me, names like Saul Bellow, Victor Reid, Graham Greene and James Baldwin. I was always curious about the covers but rarely wanted to look inside them.

The only books I took much interest in were the ones with sections of photographs in the middle, usually books on war and violence, such as Lord Russell of Liverpool's books on German and Japanese war crimes, *The Sword of the Swastika* and *The Knights of Bushido*, and Ludovic Kennedy's *10 Rillington Place*. Fear was always a dominant emotion in my childhood, and these black-and-white images of atrocity and murder provided graphic evidence of a cruel, murderous world lurking on the fringes of my 'zap! pow! bang!' consciousness that I would one day have to defend myself against. I was very curious about the war, and my father often used to talk about it, reminiscing about the doodlebugs that dropped on London when he was at Dulwich and how he and his classmates would hide under their desks.

I remember one night my parents came home in a state of emotional shock after seeing Sidney Lumet's powerful evocation of twentieth-century cruelty *The Pawnbroker*. My mother's vivid description of the plot only confirmed my belief that the wider world was indeed a terrible, frightening place, in which the worst things would always come true. In this way history filtered its way into my childhood imagination, in the form of black-and-white and mostly horrific realist images on the one hand, and the more heroic and attractive mythologies offered by epic movies like *Khartoum*, *Zulu* and *El Cid* on the other. My father tried impatiently to deconstruct these films for me, pointing out the historical truths that lay behind the myths, especially when they concerned British or American imperial history. From him I first learned about the Black and Tans and the Easter Rising, the ignominious fall of Singapore, and the unheroic truth of Custer's last stand. Yet I always preferred the heroic version of history to the real thing, and perhaps, in spite of himself, my father did too.

When I did read, it was usually Ian Fleming, Willard Price's adventure books or *The Hardy Boys*, about two teenagers who wore football sweaters and went around solving fiendish espionage conspiracies. I was so absorbed in these books that their plots and characters became woven into the games and role-playing that Bruce and I were constantly inventing. My father did not regard such reading material as suitable, however, either from a literary or a political point of view. He wanted me to like Shakespeare, Dickens and Mark Twain. My lack of interest irritated him, and seemed to convince him that I was going to grow up to become some kind of philistine thug.

Occasionally I read classics like *Treasure Island* or *The Coral Island*, but *The Man from U.N.C.L.E.* and James Bond were generally more appealing. Even worse than my aversion to literature, was my insatiable appetite for comic books. I preferred images to words, especially the splashy, colourful kind to be found in American comics. My heroes were Prince Namor the Submariner, the Green Lantern, the Phantom and the Incredible Hulk, rather than Nicholas Nickelby and David Copperfield, but I also read English black-and-white comics called *War* and *Commando*, in which blonde English officers proved their manhood on the battlefield by sten-gunning shaven-headed Germans inevitably called Fritz or Hans, who shouted '*Ach, Himmel!*' and '*Donner und Blitzen!*' as they died.

Both my parents were concerned about the long-term effects that prolonged exposure to this kind of material would have on me. My father had a particular loathing of American comicbooks as well as most other aspects of American mass culture. For a while he banned them from the house and I was allowed to read only the English comics *Eagle* and *Swift*, which he considered to be intellectually and artistically superior to their American counterparts. This attempt at intellectual censorship only drove my comicbook obsession underground so that I began to hide them under the bed and read them under the bedsheets.

When I discovered an American comicbook series called 'The Classics', I was able to take a crash course in great literature and learn the plots without having to perform the tedious task of actually reading the books. But needless to say, my father regarded this approach to literature as heretical and, although the ban on comicbooks was eventually lifted, he never stopped trying to raise my critical standards with Leavisite zeal, reacting with impatience to any sign of intellectual slowness on my part. My mother, who shared many of his concerns, was generally more patient. Friends often assumed that my father was the main intellectual influence on his children, but in fact my mother often talked to me about books and films in a way that made them seem more appealing and comprehensible than my father could make them sound – perhaps because she approached them from a more personal and less academic perspective. Many of the books in the house were in fact hers, and she often used to read us poems from an old anthology called *Iron, Honey Gold*, which eventually turned up in Cambridge tattered but still readable.

If my mother tended to treat me more as an equal, perhaps too much so, my father always had an ability, whether consciously intended or not, to make me feel somehow inadequate or inferior to him. As a result I tended to resist his pressure to read books, and it wasn't until after I returned to England that I actually began to read for myself, and wrote asking him for advice on books and writers. Like my school history projects on the Cuban Revolution that I wrote to him about, this short-lived literary correspondence was a belated attempt to earn his respect and prove to him that I had not turned out the way he had expected.

Another by-product of American cultural imperialism that my father regarded as potentially damaging to my mental health was my obsession with the Wild West, or rather that version of it presented by Hollywood and comics like *The Two-Gun Kid*, where there was never any blood and the bad guys grunted, 'Muh gun hand!' as their Colts or Winchesters went flying into the dust. Like Billy the Kid and Jesse James I always carried a gun, and spent hours listening to records of Frankie Laine's kitsch cowboy ballads, the story of the Lone Ranger and the ballad of Davy Crockett. Virtually every Christmas and birthday I would ask for a rifle or a pistol. This fixation with weapons alarmed my parents, even though they usually gave in to my demands. In 1963, when we were living in Jamaica, my eighth birthday occurred on the day after Kennedy's assassination, and I was given a rifle as usual. That morning I came running into the sitting-room, where my parents were both tearfully watching re-runs of the assassination, gleefully shooting off my new weapon. This unintended act of solidarity with Lee Harvey Oswald seemed to confirm my parents' fears that I was turning into Cro-Magnon boy, the incarnation of mindless barbarism. My father angrily took the gun away and sent me to my room for the rest of the morning.

My parents did their best to cure me of my Wild West obsession. One birthday they bought me a huge book called *A True History of the Wild West*, full of photographs and daguerreotypes of famous outlaws, marshals and extremely unglamorous-looking cowboys with drooping moustaches and floppy hats. Many of the outlaws had been photographed on the mortuary slab and looked quite fetching and peaceful. There were bad, dangerous men like Joachim Murietta, the half-caste Mexican assassin, the Dalton Brothers, shot to pieces in a civic ambush in Coffeyville, and Oliver Harding, the Gentleman Bandit, who wore a derby hat and a waistcoat and robbed trains with a derringer, and eventually blinded himself with nails in a fit of religious mania after his arrest.

Although it was intended to demythologize the West, this grainy, hard-boiled realism only intensified my fascination with gunfighters and outlaws, and it became one of the key books of my childhood. The other was a comicbook album about an imaginary Western town called *Four Feather Falls*. Years later I could remember nothing of its contents, but the vague recollection of a magical world within its pages evoked a strange feeling of nostalgia. Sometimes I would go looking round my mother's house in Cambridge for *Four Feather Falls*, as though it were the buried entrance to that lost world of fantasy and wonder which had, in spite of everything, been part of my childhood.

*

My father chiefly objected to my interest in guns and Westerns because he feared an unhealthy attraction to violence and the wrong kind of hero. He therefore took it upon himself to disabuse me of any falsely romantic notions that I had about the West. He would tell me how General Custer was a cold-blooded Indian killer, how the Colt .45 was inaccurate even at short range, how Billy the Kid was a cowardly psychopath who usually shot his victims in the back. My father's own attitude to Hollywood was oddly ambivalent. Recognizing that it was impossible to break my fascination entirely, he divided Westerns into good and bad Westerns, a categorization which owed as much to their political and moral content as to their cinematic qualities. One 'bad' Western was *Major Dundee*, an early Sam Peckinpah film starring Charlton Heston, which was set in Mexico during the disastrous attempts by the French to set up an empire south of the border. My father took me to see it in Jamaica with my brother and sister, but halfway through the film, during a shootout on a river, he suddenly stood up and ordered us out of the cinema, shouting at the audience that they were a bunch of fascists. Mortified, we trooped out behind him to the car, where he proceeded to harangue us all the way home on the subject of American imperialism and the falsity of presenting Americans as defenders of Mexican sovereignty.

The list of acceptable Westerns included *High Noon*, *The Man Who Shot Liberty Valance*, *3.10 to Yuma*, and especially *Shane*, which my father considered to be the greatest Western ever made. All these films were concerned with the same themes of cowardice and bravery, of individual conscience and heroism. Whether it was Gary Cooper facing the bad guys alone in *High Noon*, or Van Heflin's farmer risking death to bring an outlaw to trial in *3.10 to Yuma*, their heroes were quiet, unassuming men, who acted alone, responding to their own inner morality rather than the demands of society, and who recognized the futility of violence, turning to it only reluctantly. This, I dimly understood, was the model that my father wanted me to emulate.

However different our perspectives, this shared interest in the Western had been one of the few points of contact between us, and I had felt proud when he took me with him to see *3.10 to Yuma*. As usual I wanted to like it because he did, but I found the film slow and boring and lacking in gunfights. What I had not realized then was the extent to which my father himself identified with the classic Western hero. Many years later, in one of the faded copies of *Cambridge Left*,

I came across one of his articles entitled 'S'posin I Lost My Fair-Haired Beauty', in which he expounded on the way that Westerns were 'symbols for certain types of politico-social behaviour, allegorical versions of social problems with which we are confronted', in particular, 'problems of violence and social morality'. Behind the analysis, however, was an allegorical version of my father himself:

> *A new hero has recently begun to dominate the Western. He is not of the generation of Bill Hickock, or Wyatt Earp, or Billy the Kid . . . but tense, cryptic and persecuted, he remains socially anonymous, emerging from a blank past into a doubtful future . . . This hero is always alone, never a member of a social group and permanently unable to enter into normal human relationships. He is always a tragic hero, in so far as he represents an attitude that is no longer socially acceptable, but which society nevertheless cannot do without; men like Shane are simultaneously scapegoats and heroes, sacrificial objects, carrying the burden of social guilt and social fear.*

'Tense, cryptic and persecuted . . . emerging from a blank past into a doubtful future . . .' This was not entirely different from the way that Moses Nagamootoo had seen my father, or the way that my father had seen himself. He had clearly been preoccupied with heroism, and 'problems of violence and social morality' long before he talked about them to me. As his eldest son, I was naturally inclined to see him as a hero, and he correspondingly found in me a mirror in which he wanted to see his own heroism reflected, as his reference to me in the letter about Berbice made clear. There is no doubt that I did look up to him, and even idolized him, as a child. I was so in awe of his abilities as an actor that I would watch him even in plays that were way above my head, and I loved his reminiscences about the war and his army days, as well as the brilliantly imaginative fantasies with the ridiculous names that he made up.

It was never entirely possible to see him as a hero, however, especially when his behaviour in his own home disintegrated and his disavowal of violence was constantly being contradicted by his own actions. In fact the verbal and physical violence that he unleashed was a far more dangerous model for his children than my Wild West and war fantasies, but if he realized this he did nothing to hide or restrict it. 'They don't drink my rum, they don't have to use my language,' he once told my mother, when she complained about him swearing in front of us. Nor was this violence only directed at his wife. In the last few years in the West Indies, I was often on the receiving end as well. Always quick-tempered and impatient when any of his children refused to do what he wanted, my behaviour in particular often drove him into a raging fury.

One Christmas Eve in Jamaica we were staying in a friend's house by the sea. I knew, or at least strongly suspected, that I had been given a James Bond detachable machine-gun with a plastic suitcase, the kind used by Sean Connery in *From Russia with Love*. At some point in the evening I sneaked into the presents cupboard for a preview. My father found out and went berserk, flailing out with his arms and fists and screaming at me that I was an S.O.B., an insult that for years I believed had something to do with E S S O service stations. The next morning I walked miserably along the isolated little beach outside the house, dismally firing the plastic bullets that plopped into the sand a few yards away, as yet another day had been plunged into gloom by my father's endless, unjustified rage.

These beatings were not the kind that my mother got. I have no memory of being given black eyes or being punched in the face. They were nevertheless painful and frightening, since he was usually swearing loudly and seemed to be completely out of control. They were also frequent enough for my mother to lie about my misdemeanours in order to protect me from his wrath. Even though I learned to anticipate the kind of things that were likely to annoy him, I resented the way that the atmosphere in the household was always dependent on his moods and sometimes I even deliberately provoked him as well. Often he seemed to be merely looking for an excuse, and the only option was to run away into the garden and wait for him to calm down. At Stony Hill there was a trapdoor in my bedroom, and I sometimes used to run out into the garden when I saw one of these beatings coming until it was safe to come back, but my father eventually nailed it up and cut off this means of escape.

One of the worst incidents occurred when we were travelling back to England on a cruise ship for a holiday. During the voyage Bruce and I were playing on deck with some friends we had made. We were jumping around on lifeboats when my brother fell and hit his head. There was no cut, but he was crying, and a bump was already beginning to appear. Nevertheless I was so carried away with the game that I let him find his way back to our cabin by himself, and continued playing. When I got back to the cabin my father fell upon me, cursing and thrashing me round the cabin while the others looked on helplessly. It was a wild over-reaction, like so many of his responses to his children's real or imagined wrongdoings, and he then compounded the punishment by dragging me into the dining-room to eat, even though I was still tearful, where I presented such a spectacle that many of the passengers stared at our table.

The anger and sense of injustice that these beatings provoked were an integral part of my memory of my father. I was often filled with fantasies of revenge, which were undercut with guilt and a longing to be close to him. Sometimes I imagined coming to my mother's rescue and cleaning up the town like one of my cinematic heroes, but I was always conscious of my own physical weakness in comparison with my father. From my child's perspective, he was simply too powerful to be resisted. I envied him that power, and the freedom that it gave him simply to blast the world out of his way and behave as he liked without feeling any guilt.

But I feared that rage when I saw it in myself, and for years afterwards I would fight against it, not always successfully. Children often see more in their parents than they are able to understand at the time, but even as a child it was clear to me that there was a huge gap between what my father said and what he actually did.

Alongside the awe I felt towards him, I also saw him as a bullying tyrant, who failed to live up to his own standards. The gentler side of his personality occasionally revealed itself, when he felt like it, but these moments were too ephemeral and were always on his terms. For a man who spent so much of his life immersed in imaginative literature, my father showed an extraordinary inability to imagine the feelings of the real people around him, particularly those of his own children. Wrapped up in his alcoholic cocoon, convinced that I was my mother's ally and therefore 'against' him, his flashes of humanity became more fleeting as time went on. The distance between us increased, so that today only the faintest memory of that softer side remains.

There is no trace of the angry battle of wills that characterized our relationship in the affectionate, almost tender letters that he wrote to me in England. Spared my physical presence, he was able to offer a version of himself that had been rarely present in real life. At first I was pleased with the warm, loving tone of these letters, but some years later, as I realized that he was never coming back, I began to see them as an attempt to substitute words for himself, and it became virtually impossible for me to take seriously his little homilies on violence and morality. It was only now, after twenty-nine years, that I had come back to find that the father who tried to get me to hang up my guns all those years ago had really wanted to be Shane all along.

Even before I had come to Guyana, many people had mentioned to me the name of Martin Carter in connection with my father, and the visit to his home produced yet another of the bizarre revelations that seemed to occur on an almost daily basis. I knew that he was Guyana's most famous poet, with an output of work that stretched back to the early 50s. I also knew that he had been very active in Guyanese politics. He had been one of the original members of the PPP and had been imprisoned by the British. Later he joined the PNC and then left that party too. His imprisonment by the British as a young man had resulted in *Poems of Resistance*, one of the seminal works of Caribbean anti-colonial writing, with its famous, often quoted outpouring of black rage:

> *I come from the nigger yard of yesterday*
> *Leaping from the oppressor's hate*
> *And the scorn of myself;*
> *From the agony of the dark hut in the shadow*
> *And the hurt of things.*

My father was a great admirer of Martin Carter's poetry, and the two of them had been close friends and drinking companions since the late 60s. Carter had been best man at my father's marriage to Marjorie, and a frequent visitor to their house. He had also spoken at his funeral. Everything suggested that he had been a key figure in my father's life in Guyana and that he might be able to fill in some of the gaps concerning his early years in the country especially.

I met him at his home in Lamaha Street, a noisy wooden house built to allow the cooling breeze to circulate through it but not to keep out the din of traffic from the busy main street outside. The once angry, rebellious poet was now older and more subdued. A big soft-spoken man in his late sixties, he was still recovering from a serious stroke, which had forced him to give up writing poetry. It had the effect of making him seem shy and slightly distant. He spoke hesitantly, and with occasional difficulty. His wife Phyllis was with him. Light-skinned and white-haired, she was very welcoming and friendly. We sat at their dining table, next to a wall decorated with gourds and basket weavings collected on their travels. I told them how similar Georgetown looked to what I remembered.

Martin nodded, with a look of resignation that I had already become familiar with in Guyana. 'That's right,' he lamented, shaking his head sadly. 'This country doesn't change. It doesn't change.'

My father often used to come round to their house, Phyllis said, and with a fond smile pointed to the couch where he used to sit and 'hold forth'. She had worked at one of the Georgetown hospitals and remembered various incidents when she had seen him in hospital, and even occasionally looked after him. Once she had an argument with him when he accused her of telling the doctor not to let him go home for Christmas.

I asked Martin and Phyllis if my father had struck them as a self-destructive person.

'In the later stages when he was more dependent on other people,' Martin replied. 'He had a tendency to stray from one idea and then it would come back to him again, so that is the sort of memory I have of him – a straying.'

Did he mean that my father's intellect was failing him?

'To some extent, but this doesn't really cover the whole thing, because he was still very bright, there's no doubt about that. His acumen was unusual for a person in that condition, and he always remained a very perceptive person. He was – what's the word? – cranky. He became cranky, you know. He would have ideas that people would not accept easily.'

'Cranky' seemed an appropriate enough adjective to describe the man who had come back to England in 1987. We talked about his 'straying' and I commented that even in his early articles, he had left me with the impression of a mind that tended to shoot off in all directions.

'Oh, yes!' Phyllis agreed. 'He certainly did!'

'A loose cannon,' added her husband. 'That was it.'

Had they ever talked to him about what made him so angry?

'At one time we did have a long talk about it,' he said. 'About what fired him, so to speak, and it never came out really. I think it was a matter of temperament more than anything else. He was a man of plenty fire, and the feeling just took command of him.'

Did they remember my father getting himself beaten up?

'Ohhh, yes!' Martin chuckled at the memory. 'Bill would do that!'

And what, I asked, did he think my father had been trying to achieve by this?

'I believe it was self-expression,' he replied, deadpan.

'He was getting himself beaten up as a form of self-expression?' I repeated disbelievingly.

They both laughed. 'I believe so,' Martin affirmed cheerfully.

On second thoughts this did not seem such an odd concept, given the confusion between drama and reality that marked much of my father's life. We talked a little about this aspect of his personality. I told them about the letters he had written comparing himself to Karl Marx and Che Guevara. They did not look particularly surprised.

'Oh, yes, that was Bill!' Martin said. 'He would do that! But I don't think it was correct of him to do it. He was . . . making a play more than anything else.'

As someone who had known my father since his earliest days in Guyana, I asked Martin if he could remember anything about his state of mind around the time of our departure from the country. He did not seem to know very much.

'The impression you have of it,' he said, 'is that his life was in certain respects not what he wanted to happen. I believe too that he felt out of place in this country.'

'Right up to the end?' I asked, surprised.

'No. In the early days. But after a while he became conditioned to it, you know.'

'Did he ever talk about his wife and children?'

'Oh, yes!' they both replied.

'It was three children, wasn't it?' Martin asked.

'Four,' Phyllis replied. 'It was four.'

'He always spoke about them,' Martin said.

'In what sense?' I asked.

'Very pleasant.'

Had he ever spoken about the reasons why we left?

'No,' Martin shook his head emphatically. 'I vividly remember that he never spoke about that at all.'

'Did you get the impression that he didn't want to talk about it, or the subject just never came up?'

'I think he just didn't want to talk about it.'

I detected an awkwardness in the conversation. I wondered how much they had heard from other sources and whether they felt uncomfortable talking about it as well. Once again it amazed me how my father could cast an absolute pall of silence over such a crucial episode in his life as the expulsion of his wife and children, so that even his closest friends did not have any idea of what had happened. Was there no one in Guyana to whom he had talked about it? It seemed not. Whether or not the Carters knew the full story, they did not ask me for any more details, nor did I offer any myself. Instead we talked about the last period of his life.

It was then that Phyllis Carter dropped her bombshell. They had last seen him alive about three days before his death when it was obvious that he was dying. 'Of course, you know what he died from?' she said in a casual tone. 'He didn't want people to know what he was dying from.'

I looked at her uncomprehendingly. 'What had he died from?' I asked.

'He had a cancer of the breast.'

'He had cancer?'

She nodded. 'Of his right breast.'

'Are you sure?'

They both nodded. 'It was the right, wasn't it?' Phyllis asked. 'The way he was lying? And he was in pain, but he didn't want people to know.'

'Three days he was in pain, eh?' asked Martin.

'Oh, more than three days,' she said. 'He had been to hospital and he asked to go home. And of course they said they could do nothing for him, and he did go home, and then Marjorie called and asked if we would come up, and he was there obviously in pain, and then she told me what the problem was, that he didn't want anybody to know that this was what he was dying from.'

I was stunned by this unexpected piece of news. No one had mentioned cancer before. Marjorie herself had told me that he had died of complications resulting from cirrhosis, that and the fact that he had 'given up fighting'. Now I remembered the terrible, short breathing that I had noticed in London: cancer seemed perfectly plausible. But it did not seem to be something to be ashamed of or to conceal. What, I asked, in complete confusion, was so wrong with admitting that you had cancer when you were actually dying of it?

'Well, of course, knowing what Bill was,' she replied, as if the answer were perfectly logical, 'how could cancer take him? You know, he was so vibrant and so – it was something that can't come to him. He probably would think that he had no right to die of cancer, more cirrhosis or something like that.'

'I thought it was cirrhosis,' I said.

'Well, he did have that. It was there – '

'But that's not the reason,' Martin broke in. 'The real reason was cancer of the breast.'

I shook my head in wonder. Right up to his death, it seemed, my father had been trying to preserve the myth that he had spent so much of his life trying to construct. But the idea that cirrhosis of the liver represented a more noble death than cancer was absolutely ludicrous. One of his role models in his early years in the West Indies was the Jamaican poet and novelist Roger Mais, whose turbulent life and passionate personality had impressed him greatly for, what my father called, 'the fullness with which he put himself into what he was doing'. A Caribbean renaissance man who had been many things in his life, Mais had died of cancer in the 1950s, and once referred to it as a 'fascist disease'. Had my father been trying to conceal the existence of this 'fascist disease' in himself, for the sake of some topsy-turvy Falstaffian moral system that equated hard drinking and a rotten liver with zest for life?

All these thoughts were going round in my mind, as I mentioned that many people were surprised my father had lived as long as he had anyway.

'Because of the cirrhosis,' Phyllis agreed. 'Once I went to Bill, he was in hospital, and his haemoglobin count was something like 6 or 4, and they never thought he would make it overnight, but the next morning he was there fighting right back.'

'And he did come back,' said Martin.

'Oh gosh, yes!' she chuckled. 'Came out of the hospital and abused everybody for keeping him in there! That was Bill!'

Did they think he had achieved any spiritual or emotional fulfilment at the time of his death?

'Umm,' Martin looked doubtfully at his wife. 'What you think?'

'Spiritual, yes. Because he had the Catholic Church. He went to the church – what was its name?'

I was only half listening now as they debated the name of his parish church and who had been his local priest. I was still dwelling on this latest twist in my father's mysterious demise. Had he known or suspected that he had cancer when he came to England? Had it really been cancer that killed him? Or was it cirrhosis, or a broken heart, or a combination of all three? As always there were too many rumours and subjective impressions, not enough facts. Even if there were always going to be unanswered questions about his life, surely it should be possible to discover the truth about his death? It sounded straightforward enough in theory, but as I stepped out into the noisy blare of traffic in Lamaha Street, I doubted that it would be. It was time to forget literature and politics for a while, and to seek the aid of medical science.

Chapter Thirteen

On 5 February 1973, a year after his break-up with Sandra Williams, my father sent a letter to my mother which included the following information:

> *Things have not been going well here . . . I have been ill again – as Mercutio might put it, 'I have it, and soundly too.' A touch of jaundice – which has now passed – and cirrhosis of the liver, which of course will not pass. It cannot be cured. It can merely be stopped, if of course . . . Who knows that the children may not pick up the pension money? None of this is said as an appeal to compassion – I am merely telling you about things as they stand.*

The conclusion to the unfinished sentence was obviously meant to be 'if of course I stop drinking', and the fact that he had left it unfinished was a clear indication that he had no intention of doing anything of the kind. Throughout his years in Guyana he was taken into hospital on numerous occasions, and was treated by most of the doctors in Georgetown at some time or other. Again and again he was told he would soon be dead if he continued to drink, but each time he went into hospital he emerged once again back on the street, having dragged himself back from the jaws of death through sheer force of will only to hit the bottle once again.

This grim struggle against the effects of alcoholism impressed many people in Guyana, as though his ravaged liver had been the site of some titanic Freudian battle between the life force and the death instinct. Perhaps my father interpreted it in the same way. There is no doubt that the enormous energy and willpower he invested in fighting off his disintegration was matched only by his determination to destroy himself in the first place. But the glorification of his heroic struggle against his various illnesses ignored the fact that he himself was ultimately responsible for them. Had he exerted the same degree of willpower against the causes of his alcoholism rather than just its effects, he might have lived longer and achieved a lot more in his life.

In one letter from the early 70s he announced that he had given up drinking, but this brief period of temperance was an exception. In a drinking culture like the Caribbean, where so many of his friends drank, it would not have been easy for a chronic alcoholic like my father to sustain the necessary willpower for very long, even if he had been able to summon it up in the first place. Again and again in Guyana, I heard male friends of my father's refer to his drinking with an affectionate, conspiratorial grin, as if it was one of the engaging things about him, even though it must have been obvious that he was slowly killing himself. Even one of the taxi-drivers outside my hotel remembered with amusement meeting my father some years before drunk in a bar, and being told, 'Why bother to get sober when you're only going to have to get drunk again?'

It was anecdotes like these that made my father a 'character'. Whether it was the students who bought him his quart of rum at the university, or the customers who had listened to him tell stories in bars around the country, it was clear that many people liked the person he turned into when he was drunk. Having seen the havoc that his drinking had wrought in his own home, I could not appreciate such affectionate amusement. Like many men, my father was proud of his capacity for hard liquor even long after it had become obvious that he was writing his own suicide note every time he poured himself a glass of rum.

There was no doubt in my mind that alcohol ruined my father, physically and intellectually, and was the main reason why his first marriage broke up in such appalling circumstances. But if his alcoholism was the cause of his disintegration, it was also the symptom of a deeper drive towards self-destruction.

Alcohol was an intrinsic part of the personality that my father had built for himself in the West Indies. Without it he would not have been the Bill Carr so many people in Guyana seemed to want – Bill Carr the story-teller, the raconteur, the bar-room philosopher, with his Shakespearian quotations and literary references, sending off sparks of light even as he hurtled downwards towards disintegration and death.

It may be that there was never really any other alternative route for someone like my father, that he needed alcohol to counteract the destructive emotions within himself. Perhaps the relentless punishment that he inflicted on his body gave him the sense of struggle he needed to give his life meaning, as he sought to stave off physical collapse. But whatever the reasons, I found nothing romantic or glamorous about such self-destruction. His drinking was the main reason why he had failed to realize his potential. The effects of his alcoholism had not been confined to himself. His family had not had the privilege of sitting in bars with him listening to the holy drinker inspired by alcohol. That was something I could experience only through other people's eyes. As a child, I had felt nothing but despair and anger, watching him get drunk and knowing what its consequences were going to be. As an adult, I regarded his drinking as a gratuitous and tragic waste of his life and talent. It had created both the wife-beating thug of my childhood and the physical ruin who had come back to England in 1987. Death comes to us all whether we drink or not, but my father's drinking had speeded up the process. And yet now it seemed that it had not been alcohol that had got him after all, but cancer.

At some point during his years in Guyana, my father seems to have spent time in virtually every hospital in the country, but the hospital to which he was admitted before his death was the Georgetown Public Hospital. I went there to speak to Dr Terence Morris, who had treated him in the last weeks of his life. Marjorie had given his name to me on the telephone and I spoke to him in a bare, sparsely equipped consulting-room just off the main entrance. The whole hospital had a deserted, lifeless feel as a result of a one-day nurses' strike, and Dr Morris seemed to be the only person on duty. He was, he said, the admitting officer who had taken my father into hospital in February 1992, but he was also a long-term friend of the family and had treated him before. The family connection immediately made me suspect his objectivity, and the conversation soon began to sound like a cross-examination of a medical witness. I began by asking him what state my father had been in when he had been admitted to hospital.

'When I first saw Mr Carr,' he began confidently, 'he had already developed some of the complications of alcoholic liver disease. He was known to have cirrhosis of the liver, and he was also at the time having bronchial pneumonia, as a result of which he was admitted to hospital for treatment, which also included blood transfusion.'

'I've been told that he had cancer as well,' I said, matter-of-factly.

'No.' Dr Morris looked evasive. 'That is . . . That is not confirmed.'

'It wasn't confirmed?' I repeated.

'No. It was thought of.'

I asked him what he meant by that, and said that I had been told he had a tumour in his chest.

'Well, from the clinical symptoms, the clinical presentation, that was one of the presumptive diagnoses made,' he explained, 'but it was not confirmed.'

Once again I could sense the facts slipping my grasp. I felt myself becoming irritated by this deliberate vagueness. Was it not possible to get to the bottom of anything in this country? Why had it not been confirmed? I asked him.

'Umm.' Again he looked evasive. 'I cannot give the exact reason why it wasn't confirmed because I was actually the admitting officer, I was not the attending physician, but what I would suppose is most likely – because of the lack of necessary facilities to diagnose such a condition.'

This seemed plausible enough. In a country where virtually nothing worked properly, where spare parts and simple technical appliances were missing from most areas of life, and where Burnham himself had died due to lack of basic hospital equipment, it was unlikely that the hospital would have been able to diagnose cancer, especially in a patient whose organism was already in such an advanced state of disintegration as my father's. And yet the doctor's evasiveness suggested that this was not the whole explanation.

'O K,' I said, 'so you're saying that cancer was suspected, then, but it wasn't definitely proven to your knowledge?'

'No, it wasn't.'

'As far as you know, what did he die of, then?'

'He died of complications of the alcoholic liver disease and bronchial pneumonia.'

'When you saw him what kind of condition was he in?'

'Well, I knew him before he became terminally ill,' he said. 'And he was always a jolly fellow, always willing to share a joke, but towards the end he gave up fighting. I think he was realistic. He was a very realistic man.'

Realism had never seemed to me to be one of my father's outstanding traits, and I asked him whether he meant this in the context of his health.

'In the context of his life and his death, and his illness. He faced up always to the truth, to reality, and he fought what ought to be fought against. I mean he couldn't have done anything else in the end.'

I asked him if he was surprised at how long my father had lasted. This elicited a brief lecture on the psychological resistance of different individuals to disease, and the importance of willpower in the struggle against it. This was no doubt true, but I felt the conversation straying into poetry once again, into illness-as-metaphor. I tried to steer it back to science, by asking him the precise symptoms that my father had presented to make the hospital think he might have had cancer.

'One, his presentation,' replied Dr Morris, with a hint of impatience. 'I remember he presented shortness of breath, a typical picture of bronchial pneumonia – but then the severity of it, and also, I think, because of the X-ray findings.'

'Did the X-rays indicate that he might have had a tumour?' I asked with equal impatience.

'Well, more clearly, he also had an abdominal mass. Yes, if I can remember, and that's why they thought of a possible tumour.'

'And what about his chest?'

'He had bronchial pneumonia.'

It was maddening and grotesque, this haggling over the state of my father's internal organs. And yet the more I sensed Dr Morris's vagueness, the more I wondered what lay behind it. Everything he was telling me confirmed what Phyllis Carter had said, yet I had the feeling that he was not telling me everything he knew.

'Hadn't the X-rays detected anything in his chest?' I persisted.

'X-rays can't – clearly – detect anything in his chest. And in that stage, in his condition – I mean, the surgeons also saw him, I think, and it was decided that it would probably have been worse to put him under the knife. Why? Because of the liver disease, one of the complications of which was a bleeding disorder.'

I vaguely remembered that my father had been unable to have a biopsy in London because he was anaemic, but I was beginning to come to the conclusion that I was not going to get the full story from Dr Morris. Without a medical dictionary, further interrogation seemed futile. Whatever else he had died of, it was certainly not a broken heart since his heart was one of the few organs that had been functioning properly on his admittance into hospital. Still, the cross-examination had not quite finished. I asked Dr Morris when he had last seen my father alive.

'I saw him the day he died,' he declared, emphatically, as though there were absolutely no doubt about it. 'Unto the day he died. I was there.'

'Can you tell me what you saw?'

'After he was admitted to hospital, his condition continuously deteriorated until death,' he replied, matter-of-factly.

Marjorie and everybody else had said that my father had gone home a few days before his death. Yet there Dr Morris was, claiming that he had died in hospital, and that he had been there on the day of his death. It was curiouser and curiouser.

'But he didn't die in hospital, he died at home, right?'

Dr Morris looked disconcerted. 'Was it at home? Yeah. I can't fully remember. I can't fully remember.'

I rested my case.

It was Marjorie who took me to the cemetery to see the grave. I had arranged to meet her at the teacher training institute where she worked, next to the university campus. We had not met since that first explosive exchange on my father's patio, and as the taxi turned into the drive, past the cows grazing by the roadside, I was already preparing myself for another abrasive confrontation. I had spoken to her on the phone a few times, and each time she had been coldly co-operative, emanating hostility even as she gave me the names and phone numbers. I found her in the classroom where she had just finished teaching. She greeted me coldly once again, speaking in the same clipped, short sentences, as if she had decided not to say anything more than she had to. This was an appropriate enough response to someone who she seemed to believe had 'killed' her husband, but I was beginning to resent what I felt more than ever to be an unjustified charge.

While we waited in the main office for a taxi, Marjorie introduced me to people who had known my father. A young student told me how much he had touched her life. I found it even more difficult than usual to share her enthusiasm, since I felt tense and was anxious to get the visit to the cemetery over with. I also suspected that Marjorie was trying to introduce me to my father's fans – to show yet again that he had been a wonderful person and that my memory of him was wrong.

As we sat stiffly together in the back of the taxi heading into town, she suddenly asked me why I had come back to Guyana. Once again

I told her that I wanted to understand the apparent disparity between the person his first family had known before 1967 and the person he became afterwards.

'No one will believe you here if you talk about the Bill Carr before,' she said. She seemed pleased at the thought. It was not shaping up to be a very fruitful conversation and the anger soon began to rise to the surface once again as we went over some of the tortuous terrain that we had already covered the other evening – the letters, my father's violence, his return to England. Even though the presence of the taxi-driver obliged us to keep our voices down, this restraint only increased the tension that emanated from the back seat, and I sensed that the curious eyes flickering in the rear-view mirror were not looking at the traffic.

'Everybody has the right to try and understand their own father,' I said impatiently. 'I just want to clarify things once and for all.'

'What do you want to clarify?' she asked suspiciously.

'Everything. You told me the other night I killed my father –'

'I said your letters were a contributing factor!' she interrupted.

This was not what she had said at all, but I was not prepared to accept even this lesser charge. I told her that it wasn't letters that had killed him, but cancer. That had never been proven, she said. In any case, I persisted, he had had enough things wrong with him without my letter being responsible for his death. She refused to accept this either. It was an impossible conversation. No matter what I said to her, she was determined to take the opposite position and refused to admit that my father had ever done anything to warrant any anger from me. Even when I talked about the past, and what had happened to my mother, she suggested that it was my mother's own fault for not having stood up to him. 'I wouldn't let any man hit me!' she vehemently declared. 'Once I had a fight with him and he slapped me, so I took a bottle and threw it at him, and God must have guided that bottle because it only hit him on the shoulder! But that stopped him!'

That was the only time he had ever tried to hit her, she said. When another time he had flown into one of his rages and started to rant and rave and throw things around the room, she had overturned a bookshelf and started to smash things herself.

'He said to me, "What are you doing? You're insane, woman! You need to see a psychiatrist," and I told him, "Now you know how it feels."'

After that she had always gone for his books whenever he flew into one of his 'real rages', and these pre-emptive strikes had kept him under control. I found it difficult to believe that my father could have been tamed so easily, and there was an irritating touch of self-congratulation in her attitude towards my mother. It was obvious that Marjorie was a more tempestuous and mercurial character, who was more able to respond to my father on his own terms. Nevertheless, the assumption that my father had been violent only because my mother had failed to stand up to him was a gross over-simplification, which neatly exonerated my father of any responsibility. There was no doubt that my mother had been unable to cope with his behaviour, but it was also arguable whether any woman could have dealt with the intense rage and hatred that he unleashed at that time. And why should anyone have had to? Did Marjorie really believe that male violence was some kind of inevitable natural phenomenon, which women had either to fight back against or go under themselves?

This was the second time since coming to Guyana that a woman had suggested to me that my mother had been partly responsible for what had happened to her because she had not been strong enough to stand up to her husband. This survival-of-the-fittest conception of relationships surprised and disturbed me. Whatever conflicts had existed in my parents' marriage, it was absolutely clear to me that my father's violence was unjustified and unacceptable and that he himself was responsible for it. As the physically stronger partner in the relationship, it had been up to him to resist the temptation to resort to physical violence during rows. Instead he had allowed himself to fall into a dark pit of behaviour that could not be excused and ended up becoming just the kind of bully he condemned whenever he encountered one of them outside his home. What was the point of anyone now denying this and trying to put the blame on his principal victim? My father's behaviour might have been unedifying to his friends and relatives who had not experienced it, but it was a great deal worse for those of us who had. Like the Minister of Information, however, Marjorie seemed unwilling to admit that such things had ever happened. Stung by her incredulity, I now described to her some of the worst incidents, to give her an idea of the intensity of my father's onslaughts, and she seemed genuinely taken aback for the first time.

'A lot of black men are very promiscuous,' she said, echoing what Cicily Johns had said, 'but they don't treat their wives like that.'

The taxi-driver's ears were clearly buzzing as the heated discussion of wife-beating, father-killing and domestic violence continued in the back of his car. He kept glancing at us in the mirror with the eager curiosity of a natural gossip, already looking forward to relating the conversation to his friends.

'You . . . er . . . doin' some kind of work here?' he asked me finally when Marjorie got out briefly to post a letter.

'Not exactly,' I hissed, glaring out of the window at the steaming-hot day.

I did not offer more information, nor did the taxi-driver ask for any as Marjorie got back into the cab and we resumed our bickering.

I was beginning to despair of ever reaching common ground on anything when the first few flashes of softness and understanding began to appear from behind the gloom. Couldn't I see any trace of my father in the person that so many people in Guyana had known and loved? she asked me with a note of tenderness and pleading in her voice. I told her that there were indeed traces of that man, but that these more positive memories were inevitably overwhelmed by the memory of his darker side and there was nothing I could do about it. I also said that the same question could be asked the other way round: wasn't there any trace in the man she had married of the father who had terrorized his previous family?

'He was a difficult man,' she conceded at last, 'but he wasn't violent.'

By the time we reached Le Repentir, the Catholic cemetery, these intermittent flickers of communication had become more frequent and some of the tension and anger began to ease out of the conversation. 'Bill always raged against the dying of the light,' Marjorie said quietly, looking sadly out of the window as the gate appeared up ahead. It was something that she obviously admired in him, but I could not help thinking that he had raged too much, and that often it was not at all clear what he was raging at. The cemetery was on the edge of town – a sprawling, densely packed mass of raised slabs and gravestones, dissected by tree-lined dirt roads with the usual watery ditches alongside them. Rows of coconut palms, many of them stripped of leaves, stretched away among the graves towards the low-lying mass of clouds above the distant green wall of rainforest on the horizon. A handful of grave-diggers and cemetery workers were lounging around by the main gate, watching our arrival without interest. Marjorie could not remember where the grave was among the complex sprawl, and we climbed some wooden steps to a little office, where a female assistant was sitting behind a worn counter. Marjorie asked her if she could tell her where William Carr was buried.

'Date of death?' she inquired officiously.

The assistant pulled a ledger from beneath the counter and began running her finger up and down the handwritten columns until she alighted on the surname CARR. Scrawling the lot number on a piece of paper, she summoned one of the older cemetery workers and a young black teenager and told them to go with us. We all climbed into the taxi and drove slowly out through Georgetown's crowded, semi-overgrown necropolis, following the cemetery worker's instructions. Finally he told the cab to stop on one of the dirt roads, and pointed out towards the cluttered graves on the other side of a ditch. Marjorie did not want to see the grave again and stayed in the taxi. I followed the teenager across the ditch, as he stepped lightly from tomb to tomb, checking each one against the numbers on the scrap of paper.

Most of the graves consisted of the same grey or white slabs, with tufts of wild grass protruding from the narrow spaces between them. Many were cracked or broken open, while others were partially overgrown. It was a haunting, strangely soothing place. The wind lightly stirred the palms as we walked along, using the graves as stepping-stones. There were a few horses grazing among the tombstones, and on one slab stood a large, heron-like bird.

Finally my guide paused by a flat raised slab of mottled grey concrete and announced that he had found the tomb. After all the eulogies that I had heard about my father and his contribution to Guyana, I was surprised and even mildly shocked at the miserable state of his final resting place. Lot B21 was unpainted, and already blackened by exposure to the elements. A large crack had opened up so that the head of the tomb was beginning to come loose. All around the slab the grass was uncut, and a creeper had grown across the top.

'Daar fall off arready,' observed the guide, critically, pointing at the cracked head from his vantage-point on a nearby tomb, as if he half expected my father to walk out.

I grunted a reply and knelt down, clearing the grass back to read the inscription, *W.I.C. 1931–1992*, which had been roughly scratched with a nail into the concrete. 'Until you see the grave it's not over,' my sister had said before I left England. I thought of those words now as I photographed the grave for her, as I had promised to do. I felt no sense of catharsis as I contemplated the site of my father's earthly remains. Nor did I feel any bitterness towards him, but only a mixture of sadness and regret at the thought of all that futile anger that he had unleashed all those years ago with such destructive consequences. In spite of everything I also felt a curious tenderness towards him – the remains of something that had once been much stronger. I wondered what he would have thought if he could have seen me there, standing by his grave. I thought of all the roles he had played in his lifetime and I remembered some words from Ibsen's *Peer Gynt* – that the soul of a man is like an onion, in which you peel layer after layer only to find nothing at its centre.

This was the centre, the endpoint of my father's life, a pile of bones, covered by a mouldering concrete slab with the initials W.I.C., and the dates that enclosed his time on earth. In itself the grave meant nothing to me. The real layers consisted of the memories he had left behind in the people that had known him, whether or not those memories contradicted each other, whether or not they corresponded with my own. Nothing else remained of the strange, tormented personality that those bones had once carried, Shakespeare's 'unperfect actor on the stage, who with his fear is put besides his part, or some fierce thing replete with too much rage, whose strength's abundance weakens his own heart'.

Now, in the presence of that worn monument to his earthly existence, I was more conscious than ever of the impossibility of being able to determine the truth about my father's life. 'Much love, all burnt,' he had once written to my mother, without saying who had done the burning or why it had been necessary to burn it in the first place. Even if I had come while he was still alive, it was difficult to imagine that he could have clarified things himself. What could he have said? That the crimes of the British Empire had weighed so heavily on his conscience that he had offered up his own family as an act of expiation on the altar of history? It did not seem very likely. In that moment I was not even sure if he had ever had any explanation himself for what had happened. Nothing I had heard so far, none of the letters or documents that he had left behind, suggested that he had really understood or attempted to account for the violent explosions of feeling that had dominated his life. Yet it was just possible that he might have some insights to offer, even beyond the grave, if I could only get hold of the famous tapes.

I turned away and walked back to the car, where Marjorie sat gloomily, clearly anxious to get away. We said nothing as we left the cemetery. When we did speak again, there seemed to be less rancour than before, and I used the opportunity to ask her about the tapes. She said that Moses had often mentioned some tapes, but she had never seen or heard them herself. The only tapes she knew about were some biographical interviews with my father recorded by . . . her sister. She didn't know why her sister had recorded these interviews, but she promised to look for them. I also asked her for copies of the letters I had written, the contents of which I had mostly forgotten, and she agreed to look for them too.

To my surprise when we arrived back at Stone Avenue she invited me into the house, and we sat talking on the patio once again. It was a very different conversation to the one we had had a few days before. The element of confrontation at last seemed to have disappeared. When Vanessa came back from work, we went into the sitting-room and continued talking for the rest of the afternoon. By the time I left, I had arranged to come back the next day and look through my father's papers. Peace, it seemed, had finally broken out.

The portrait of my father that Marjorie drew that afternoon was a more rounded and realistic one than that of the noble old lion she had accused me of destroying during our previous meeting.

She had met him in 1969 when she applied to study English at the University of Guyana as a mature student. He was then dean of the Arts faculty, and had interviewed her. Marjorie was already working as a full-time teacher. She easily passed the brief interview, which consisted of a few questions about Othello, and she subsequently attended his classes.

'Most of the students were afraid of him because he used to shout,' she said. 'He always used to feel that things were happening to him, that people were against him. I think Bill had this persecution complex, and he would sit in classes and say things that would get everybody around very sorry for him, and he would sit there being very sorry for himself, and I was the only person who never reacted that way. I said, "Well, if you want to be Jesus Christ and you want to be crucified, go right ahead."'

'What kind of things did he complain about?' I asked.

'Oh, right then it was the political situation in Guyana. Somebody from the P N C was doing this to him. When he was forty he was there moaning, "I'm going to be forty and what's going to happen?" And students would say, "Oh, don't you bother Mr Carr," and I think when he saw that I wasn't going to act like that maybe that was the attraction. I started to notice he was looking at me, and some of the students noticed it too, and then he invited me out, and after that things went on until we got married.'

The external circumstances were not exactly propitious for a romantic relationship between a white man and a black woman from a militant P N C family. Given Guyana's racial politics and my father's own political loyalties, the logical move would have been to marry an East Indian woman with P P P connections, but with characteristic perversity he embarked on a relationship that seemed guaranteed to provoke opposition. Not only was Marjorie's family strongly P N C, but her American brother-in-law Julian Mayfield was a well-known Black Power activist and writer, and an adviser to Burnham himself. Not surprisingly, her family was less than enthusiastic about Marjorie's growing involvement with 'Cracker Carr', a white man and a prominent P P P member into the bargain. Marjorie did not say much about her own feelings in the matter, but it was obvious that she must have been strong-willed to go ahead with the relationship in spite of her family's opposition. Nor was it only her family that disapproved. Burnham himself also made it known that he was not in favour of the marriage. Whether this Guyanese variant on *Romeo and Juliet* appealed to my father's Shakespearian sensibility or he simply did not give a damn if anyone approved or not, he managed to break through yet another set of barriers and overcome the family's opposition.

'They disapproved until my brother-in-law actually met Bill and they became such famous friends, and after that I got Julian's approval. Julian was the kind of person you didn't say no to. Everybody sort of looked to him for answers and that sort of thing. So when Julian approves, then I didn't have any problems after that.'

'Not even from Burnham?'

'He knew that I was going around with Bill but he didn't think I'd *marry* him!'

'And when you did?'

Marjorie shrugged. 'Nothing. Nothing came of it. I mean he had to accept I was married to him.'

Once again, it seemed, my father's refusal to be excluded from anything had taken him into what was to all intents and purposes closed territory. But according to Marjorie my father's conflicting political loyalties never caused any problems with her family, and the two of them never argued about politics. Nor was his whiteness an obstacle to her family's acceptance of him.

'Things would happen that would make him feel ashamed,' she said, 'and we would force him into positions like that. Once I didn't enrol Vanessa in time, so I said, "Bill, you have to come with me and get her into school," and he went and got her into school. Another friend of mine wanted to get her child into school and I said, "Take Bill with you – it'll happen." But each time it happened, we would get very annoyed and say, "You see in Guyana, as a white man, you get privileges we can't get in our own country," and he used to object sometimes and say, "You want me to do these things, and then you turn around and blame me and I am not responsible!"'

I reminded her that she had spoken before of my father's guilt about the British Empire and asked her if she thought he was ashamed of his past.

'He wasn't *ashamed* of it,' she explained, 'but it seemed as if he needed to apologize for it. That's a little different. He forced himself into a society of black people and East Indians, because, I felt, he wanted to make up for what you people did to us.'

I suppressed my irritation at the barbed use of 'you people'. Our relationship was still too fragile to risk an argument over my personal responsibility for the British Empire. Her previous defensiveness had gone now and she talked quite openly about some of the tensions and difficulties in her relationship with my father. Even though he had not been violent to her, their marriage had been characterized by many loud, furious rows, mostly over small things, in which my father would throw tantrums and throw the furniture around just as he had done in the past.

With two people as volatile and histrionic as my father and Marjorie, it was easy to imagine the levels to which these rows could escalate. My father once said that a marriage without conflicts would be boring. In one of his poems he described the two of them being swept along by an irresistible current towards some unnameable disaster. That final cataclysm never occurred, and the marriage endured right up to the end, despite its stresses and strains. A frequent cause of conflict was housework, which my father considered 'stupid'. He would often start swearing and shouting at Marjorie when she refused to put aside some household task to listen to a passage from a book he was reading.

'Sometimes he used to drive you up the wall,' she said with feeling. 'He sometimes did impossible things, but on the whole it was a good relationship. We could quarrel, but what I know about him, he never kept malice. He would tell you the worst things today, and tomorrow morning he'd smile at you and then I'd say, "Why are you smiling at me? I don't want anything to do with you," and he'd say, "I'm sorry."'

The idea that my father 'never kept malice' was new to me. He had not been in the habit of saying sorry to his first wife or his children. Yet the rages had certainly carried over into his second marriage, even if they never reached the same level of ferocity and viciousness as they had done with my mother.

Sometimes there was an element of madcap comedy to my father's stormy relationship with Marjorie. On one occasion he came home drunk and fell into the gutter. He then went upstairs and collapsed on the bed, reeking of sewage. Marjorie promptly moved out and went to live with her mother. When my father found out where she had gone, he moved in with Marjorie's mother too, and the two of them lived there for three months before returning home. After my father's death a family friend wrote an article called 'Scenes From A Marriage' in a Guyanese newspaper. In it he described an encounter on the patio with these two 'high-voltage personalities':

> They were in the midst of a quarrel and were hurling poetic sentences at each other. Joan, Bill's sister-in-law, was not helping matters by waspishly intervening with barbed insults which were intended to goad Bill's anger. 'Marjorie says that you have a bottle hidden and that you will not tell her where it is,' Joan said to Bill.
>
> 'Did you tell Joan such a thing?' Bill asked his wife, who had just stepped out of the house on to the veranda.
>
> 'Yes, I did. Because I have a passion for truth,' said Marjorie, hands stuffed into the pockets of her skirt and her face frowning in the direction of the garden.
>
> Bill Carr rose to his feet from the Berbice chair and enunciated with great dignity while staring at his wife Marjorie, 'I too have a passion. And I am looking at it!'
>
> As the combatants traded words and lines of exquisite prose, one could not help noticing the little demonstrations of affection between Bill and Marjorie. She never passed his chair without contriving to

touch him in some way. And when they took a break and she perched on the arm of his Berbice chair, he would tenderly put his arm around her waist, or rest his head against her.

Given my own experience of my father, I doubted whether these rows were always conducted in 'exquisite prose', but it was obvious that he had met his match in Marjorie, and that the two had complemented each other. Yet Marjorie's character still seemed an incomplete explanation for the difference between the two marriages. What Marjorie and Vanessa told me suggested that my father had himself undergone some kind of internal change, and had learned to exercise a self-control that had been absent when he was living with his first wife. There was nothing particularly surprising about this. Despite his inability to keep a vicious streak in check, I had never thought of my father as a sadist or a monster who enjoyed beating up women. Nor did I believe that he was ever proud of what he had done. The occasional references to the past in his letters to my mother made it clear that he was aware of what had happened, even if he did not try to explain it. Perhaps the real key to his transformation lay in his resolution in a letter to my mother that 'I must learn to live with the knowledge of what I have done and try not to do it again.' By the time he married Marjorie he was determined to put that resolution into practice, and despite his continued temper tantrums at last managed to keep his worst instincts in check. In this respect he was not the same person he had been during his first marriage. If he had been, I doubted whether 'going for his books' or anything else would have been sufficient to stop him.

There was also another reason for my father's self-control which Marjorie did not mention. In Jamaica and Guyana my father had been a white man beating up a white woman. As an expatriate in the West Indies, he was freed not only from the constraints of the culture and community he came from but also from the emotional pressure that his relatives in England might have brought to bear on him. The distance between his white family and Caribbean society meant that his behaviour could easily be written off as 'white man's business', but a white man beating up a black woman would have had very different connotations. In Guyana, as a white foreigner seeking entry into a black society, his situation was so precarious that he had no choice but to control himself or at the very least face social exclusion. It is difficult to imagine that 'Cracker Carr' would have been allowed to beat up his second wife without inviting immediate retaliation from Marjorie's militant family.

The fact that Marjorie was neither white nor English would also have exempted her from the intense anger that my father felt for his first wife. While that anger obviously had its source in the personality conflicts between them, and the unhappiness that he felt within the relationship itself, it is difficult to avoid the conclusion that my mother provided him with a convenient psychological outlet for his suppressed rage towards women and particularly towards his mother. Had he beaten the worst of that anger out of his system by the time he had married Marjorie? Or had he realized how dangerous it was and learned to repress it once again?

At one point in our conversation Marjorie asked me why I thought he had behaved so violently in his first marriage. I told her what the psychiatrists had once said about my mother reminding my father of his mother.

'No way could *I* remind him of his mother!' she laughed. 'No way!'

According to Marjorie, my father mellowed even more in his later years. His fits of temper became less frequent and intense, and he no longer raged at the mosquitoes when they disturbed his reading on the patio. Nevertheless, marriage to an alcoholic had demanded patience and devotion beyond the call of duty, and it was obvious that his drinking had been a constant source of friction between them. 'Bill was not one of those happy drunks,' she said. 'Each time he got drunk he would get very morose, and he would bellyache about several things that had happened, and who didn't like him, and who said this. What we used to quarrel about most of the time was when he said, "Buy me a drink," and I said, "No, you're not going to have a drink today," and that would cause him to get upset.'

'Did you drink yourself?'

'Yes! I mean, Bill taught me to drink. Every night he'd come home from work. He'd say, "Let's have a drink!" I always made sure I had a Pepsi in my glass and give him his drink. Then he discovered I wasn't putting any drink in my glass and he started to get me to drink too. I found that most of my friends around me whose marriages broke up never had a drink with their husbands. They couldn't understand why they needed a drink. He used to say, "Let's have a bedster, a pre-bedster, and then he went on to a sundowner . . ."'

'Post!' Vanessa interrupted her.

'That's pre-bedster,' Marjorie insisted. 'Sundowner. Then you'd get a post-bedster and the penultimate and the ultimate.'

I remembered Kathleen Drayton's description of Marjorie as being in a state of nervous exhaustion in the late 70s as a result of her attempts to control my father's drinking. This was not something that my mother had experienced, at least not in the same way. During his first marriage the destructive effects of my father's alcoholism had mostly made themselves felt in the way they affected his moods and behaviour. It was not until after we had left the West Indies that the physical impact of his alcoholism became evident and the pattern of hospitalizations and illnesses began. With my father unwilling or unable to heed his doctors' warnings, the responsibility for looking after him and trying to get him to stop or at least cut down his drinking fell largely on Marjorie. It was a long war of attrition, requiring considerable ingenuity and willpower. First she and her brother-in-law had persuaded him to stop drinking in rum shops and confine his drinking to home. She also took charge of his money, restricting his daily allowance so that he could not buy rum at the university.

Having achieved this minor victory, she then employed a range of tricks and ruses to prevent his drinking or to reduce its impact. These involved hiding bottles of rum in the garden, diluting his drinks with water, or dipping her finger in rum and wiping it round the edge of the glass so that he would get only the taste and smell. My father never noticed the difference. And sometimes when friends like Martin Carter came round for a heavy drinking session on the patio she would dilute their drinks too, with the same result. In this way she managed at least to restrict his alcohol consumption, even though she never succeeded in stopping it altogether. 'Lately people say, "Bill Carr drank so much,"' she complained. 'He didn't drink very much. He couldn't.'

'Any more,' Vanessa added.

'Any more.'

This did not exactly correspond to what other people remembered. Even in England, 'Little Ian's' consumption of beer and whisky had shocked his Yorkshire relatives during his 1987 visit, and I remembered watching with amazement as he drank an enormous tumbler of straight whisky in London that same year. I also knew that my father, like any true alcoholic, had found various ways of circumventing Marjorie's restrictions, from getting students to buy rum for him to persuading friends to smuggle bottles into hospital.

Nevertheless, despite the fights and the strain that his drinking must have caused her, she looked back fondly on the man she had known and loved for more than twenty years. 'We were very good friends,' she said. 'We liked the same things. We looked at the same movies. We read the same books. So then we would sit for long hours looking at the TV, or just talking about Bill's life in England, or asking me about what happened with mine. So it was a peaceful, nice existence – until the letters came.'

The letters once again. This time there was no anger in her voice – as if the episode had now become an objective, accepted fact that no longer needed to be shouted – but the message was the same: my letters had cut short this peaceful existence and cast a pall over their lives. And yet there was something about this that did not fit. Even by Marjorie's own account, her marriage had been stormy and I could not help thinking that she was letting the memory of their last few months together colour the way she remembered the whole relationship. It was not that I thought she was deceiving herself. On the contrary it was clear that my father had managed to find a measure of domestic happiness with his second family which had not been present with his first. But the blissful idyll that she described still begged the question why he had planned to come back to England alone. Even though Marjorie refused to believe that he had announced the date of his arrival to my niece, my letters were clearly written in response to some kind of overture from my father. How much had he actually told her? Had all his letters and phone calls been carried out behind his family's back? And what lay behind his apparent desperation to return in the first place? Was it yet another act of self-destruction, a suicidal uprooting of the life that he had built up over more than two decades? Or was there some other reason? These were questions that neither Marjorie nor anyone else had answered. Once again, it seemed, my father had kept his secrets, even from his own wife, and taken them with him to the grave.

The next day I went back to Stone Avenue to find piles of my father's papers on the floor of the sitting-room, which Marjorie and Vanessa had brought down for me. I had not expected to find so much material, and it would have taken at least a week to look through it all properly. In addition to letters, legal documents and critical articles, there were poems, short stories and unfinished manuscripts, including a play combining Richard III and Othello in one character, which my father had been writing on and off for years.

I had not long been trawling through this daunting array of material when a former boyfriend of Vanessa's called Lincoln Prince dropped round. Lincoln was in his late twenties and was now working in Spain as an airline pilot. He had been a friend of the family's since the early 8os, and shared a common interest in military matters and World War II with my father.

'Me, I've wanted to fly aircraft since I was a kid,' he said, in his twangy American accent, 'and to do that I had to get into the military here and I had to be an army lieutenant. And during my training, I would come over here at Bill's if I got assignments to write on military or other topics sometimes, to put it in a semblance of order, and he'd tell it to me. I'll tell you something, my parents, my dad and mom, I don't think they can ever have any place in my life like Bill Carr did. He was more of a father to me than my own dad.'

'Why was that?' I asked.

'Well, my mom and dad broke up and stuff like that, but even so my dad's still around, but I just can't communicate with him or my mom. I could not relate, I could not talk to my dad like I could to Bill. He was like, there. He just absorbs something that I've got to say to him, he digests it, and that gives me sumpn' to work on, and actually I still use things that Bill has taught me. I will use them for the rest of my life.'

This was exactly the way sons were supposed to remember their fathers, except that Lincoln was not his son, and I was. I wondered if Lincoln realized the irony of the situation. So this is what it might have been like, I found myself thinking, and in that moment it seemed only more extraordinary and inexplicable that not one of my father's own children remembered him in the same way. The things that he had taught me were entirely different. It was as if he had done everything all over again, with a different set of people, but this time done it all better.

A conversation afterwards with Vanessa confirmed this impression. Without her intervention it was unlikely that Marjorie and I would ever have been on speaking terms at all. Even during that first night she had tried to act as a mediator, and her own lack of hostility had had a calming influence on her mother. Like most of my father's second family, she was involved in education, and she taught art at a

242

local secondary school. She was a vibrant, engaging personality, with her heart-shaped face framed by long plaits, and large, intelligent eyes. Vanessa was genuinely curious and puzzled by what I told her, as we sat in the living-room comparing our two different childhoods under the same father, surrounded by his books and pictures, including a larger version of the Henry James photograph that his students had framed for him. To give an idea of the father I remembered, I showed her the mugshot photograph. The thuggish, combative face glared back at us, its tight mouth and severe haircut accentuating the aggressive, confrontational expression.

'That's Uncle Bill?' Vanessa said incredulously. 'He looks more like Paul Newman!'

I felt the same sense of surprise as she now showed me some of her family photographs. These were the only pictures I had seen of my father from the period after we had left Guyana. For the first time I was able to see something of his physical evolution during the years between our departure and his sudden, shocking reappearance in England in 1987. I stared wonderingly at these images of 'Uncle Bill' at home with his adopted family. There he was with a beard, looking relaxed and smiling in the back garden at Stone Avenue in an African patterned shirt; or emanating academic gravitas in his mortar board and gown as dean of the faculty; or dressed up as a pirate at a fancy-dress party with eye-patch, headscarf and make-up. Another picture showed him in the posture of a courtly lover, half sitting, half kneeling before a much younger Marjorie, who was smiling at the camera, resplendent in long plaited hair and a flowing African dress.

There were also some Christmas snapshots, showing him with his second family seated round the dinner table in festive mood, all of them smiling at the camera – no such photographs had ever been taken of our family. I felt not envy but incomprehension at the strangeness of it all. It was as though I were watching the continuation of my childhood in someone else. Yet it was as difficult for me to associate these images with my father as it was for Vanessa to associate my mugshot photograph with 'Uncle Bill'.

I asked Vanessa when the pirate picture had been taken. In the late 70s, she thought, when Uncle Bill had celebrated New Year's Eve by dancing to 'Saturday Night Fever'.

'Really?' I said. 'He never did anything like that with us.'

'He wasn't always like that,' she replied. 'Samantha and I had our times when we always used to be out at parties and having fun and never home and never taking anything seriously, and roller skates and boyfriends and he wasn't very tolerant of that. He was always tolerant of us when we got sensible, literate and talking about school and some film – he could like us more. But when the noise started and the friends came he used to move away.'

I told her about him emptying food on our heads. Had he ever done anything like that with her and her sister? Occasionally he threatened to do it but never actually carried it out, she said. Nor, as far as she could remember, had he ever been seriously violent with any of them.

'Each of us got a couple of slaps from him a couple of times,' she said. 'One time I remember is when I went out after school and I didn't tell anybody where I went and Mummy was frantic! And when I came home Mummy was off somewhere looking for me and the whole family was in a rigmarole and he put two slaps on me, on my arm. I didn't take it seriously because he didn't hit hard! I was just upset that he hit me.'

As with his second wife, my father seemed to have exercised a self-control in his treatment of his adopted children that he had been unable to manage with his own. But I doubted whether Marjorie would have tolerated any ill-treatment of her own children, especially from a man who was not their father. The very fact that Samantha and Vanessa were *not* his children would also have changed the way he felt about them. Fathers often regard their children as their own property, whom they are entitled to treat as they like in some kind of a return for bringing them into the world. The lack of blood ties between my father and his adopted children may well have worked in their favour, allowing him to give them the best of himself without that double-edged and often claustrophobic intensity that can characterize parents' feelings towards their own children. Whether my father's rejection of us had been an extension of his own self-destruction or whether we really reflected 'something evil in his thinking', as Joyce Jonas had put it, Samantha and Vanessa were not his, and they were not white. They were also both girls, and my father had always preferred daughters.

Uncle Bill first made his appearance in Vanessa's life when she was about two years old, but there was no trace in her memories of the irrational, frightening tyrant that his own children remembered. Neither she nor Samantha had ever felt afraid of him and she had no memory of living with him more traumatic than occasionally feeling nervous when she had not done her schoolwork or embarrassed when he came home drunk. The two girls had lived with him in various houses, which were usually crowded with children. Vanessa remembered playing noisy cowboy games with other children in the street and garden, ignoring my father when he shouted at them from the patio to be quiet.

The patio was Uncle Bill's private domain, where he prepared his classes and entertained his friends, and woe betide any child who crossed the boundary line and entered it when he was working. He would usually be there in the late afternoon when the two sisters came home from school. 'We never really bothered with him much,' Vanessa said. 'He would be out there on the patio, and Mummy would be somewhere around the house, in the kitchen or marking assignments. If she cooked, that could be a problem sometimes, 'cos he had a habit of wanting to show her passages from books or cartoons from newspapers when she was in the middle of working and that is when an argument used to start.'

After supper Uncle Bill would relax by watching television, usually movies and American cop shows like *Hawaii Five-O* and *T. J. Hooker* of all things. Then he would begin his 'bedster' ritual and retire early. Often friends would come round to the house – other 'uncles' like Martin Carter – and they would sit out on the patio and drink and talk and argue. Sometimes Uncle Martin would read poetry or play songs like 'Where Have All the Flowers Gone?' on the guitar and they would all get drunk together.

Vanessa had been aware of my father's drinking from an early age. She remembered watching her mother watering down his friends' drinks before taking them out on to the patio.

'Mummy rationed everything,' she said. 'What he ate, so he couldn't eat too much junk food, his cigarettes and his drinks. One night he came in and he asked her for a drink. She turned round slowly and she looked at him and said, "Nooo!" And she turned back and looked at her book and he stood there and put his hand on his heart and he said, "You've *cut* me!" and Samantha and I were rollin'! But we had to keep quiet because if he heard that would have been another story.'

I marvelled at how different life was in my father's second household, but there were also some familiar aspects – domestic fights and quarrels had been a routine part of Vanessa's upbringing.

'Whenever Mummy and Uncle Bill had an argument everybody in the street had to hear!' she remembered. 'You never heard her voice, because she was one of those people who used to hiss at you, but he would shout! So everybody in the neighbourhood heard it, and it would be kind of embarrassing. So it went from the stage of being scared they would break up when I was little, to being embarrassed, to just ignoring them.'

As loud as these rows must have been, Vanessa had no recollection of any physical violence, although my father often overturned furniture and threw things. 'He lost his temper a lot,' she said. 'It was easy for him to do that, but I figure Mummy was mostly our umbrella. He used to lose his temper a lot with one maid we had. She always used to sing songs from funerals and he used to be cussing out here and she would be singing.'

I laughed at the idea of my father driven mad by a maid singing funeral songs, and I asked Vanessa how she and her sister had dealt with him in these moods.

'Well, when we were younger, we just moved out of his way. We didn't go near him. That's what we did, because when we were older we could go out of the house and I don't think it bothered us that much. When I was younger I used to be scared that they would divorce, because remember, this is the father I knew, so it would have affected me as if he was my biological father.'

The community around them had also come to regard Uncle Bill as Vanessa's and Samantha's biological father, which, as he was white, placed his two stepdaughters in an ambiguous and sometimes uncomfortable position. 'Most people in Guyana unconsciously feel that white people are one step above them,' Vanessa explained, 'so therefore to be related to one, or to be a mixture, is to be better than them. Because of him I uncovered so many hypocrites, because you knew what they were like and when they got in front of him, it was like – sugar and spice. People used to get stupid when they got in front of him, because of his reputation partly, and because it was unfamiliar to have white people around. It was a strange thing. You had to see it to believe it. Samantha and I used to watch and laugh and he never noticed. He didn't know.'

Had she ever ever encountered any hostility or jealousy because of her stepfather?

'Yes! I remember when I was little at school I never spoke creole

English. I always spoke standard English and I used to get a hard time about that – how I was showing off because my father came from England and because he was white. I never noticed if it wasn't for other people. A man came here one afternoon, he used to do the yard work, and he asked for the white man that lives here. I said, "What white man?" And I was standing by the gate like an idiot, and then I said, "Oh, Bill!" But when I was at home I never noticed, and his accent – none of our maids could understand what he told them. I didn't think he had an English accent. I thought it was ordinary.'

She had been too young to remember much about my sister's visit to Guyana in 1978. It was not until the last years of Uncle Bill's life that she had begun to hear some of the details of his first marriage – especially after his return from England and the arrival of my letters in 1991. She believed what she had heard, even though she found it difficult to relate his behaviour then to the stepfather she had known. We both reached similar conclusions about my father's mostly successful attempts to control himself in his second marriage. 'He had to be conscious of what he did and therefore trying to make sure he wouldn't do it again,' she suggested, 'because I can't remember anything getting as bad as what you said.'

Vanessa went out soon afterwards, and I continued looking through my father's papers with Marjorie. In one of the piles I was surprised to find a letter that I had written to him many years ago, the only one of my letters that he seemed to have kept. Marjorie showed me a typed sheet in which my father thanked his sister-in-law Joan for suggesting the idea of a biography about his life. This curious document seemed to be a dedication from a book, although Marjorie assured me that no book had been written. She did, however, have one of the cassettes that her sister had recorded, which she allowed me to take away and copy. But there was no trace of Moses' tapes.

I also came upon my father's will. I was struck by the very precise requests for his funeral: he wanted the service to include three songs by Kris Kristofferson and one by Cat Stevens, and asked for 'a case of 26 oz. of XM Gold Medal Rum to be distributed among the pall-bearers and mourners'. He bequeathed his half-share of the house in Stone Avenue to Marjorie, together with 'all the residue of my real and personal property not hereinbefore disposed of', but to my surprise he had not entirely forgotten his old family. At the bottom of the page, there were five specific legacies, in which he bequeathed the sum of five pounds sterling to his first wife, and fifty pounds each to his four children by his first marriage.

These figures were so laughable that I had to read through the section again to make sure that I had not got them wrong. There was no mistake. The will was dated 1985, two years before he had come to England, when no one in my family had been in touch with him for years, but my father had not forgotten us. I stared at the will for a long time, trying to make sense of what it meant. How many times had Marjorie and others told me that Bill Carr never hated anyone, that Bill Carr loved and respected his wife and kids? Yet here was evidence of his enduring malice staring me in the face. None of us had expected to be left anything at all in his will, but this ridiculous legacy of five pounds sterling to his first wife seemed such a deliberate act of contempt that I could not quite believe he was capable of it.

Until that moment, against my expectations, I had begun to feel almost a certain affection towards the person so many people in Guyana described to me, but now I felt that old anger towards the father I remembered. Years after he had ceased to have any contact with his first wife, he had saved up one last mean little barb for after his death. What explained this petty, vindictive gesture? How could he have remained so angry after all those years? Was it some kind of black joke? I stared at the offending document, as in my mind one word – bastard – obliterated all the positive images that I had heard about him in an instant.

'He was always writing and changing wills,' Marjorie said, noticing me staring at it fixedly. 'That wasn't the final one.'

At first I was too furious even to talk, but I finally asked her why he had left this absurd sum of money to his ex-wife. Marjorie saw nothing unusual or untoward about it. She said that they had been advised by a lawyer to leave something as a 'legal precaution'. She did not elaborate, but it was obvious that the 'precaution' was intended to prevent my mother or any of us from claiming anything more, something that none of us had any intention of doing anyway. I had no intention, after all that had already happened, of getting involved in a sordid squabble over money, especially since it was not really about money at all. So eventually I left without saying another word about the matter, carrying a small pile of letters, poems and newspaper articles and Joan's tape, and feeling very angry indeed with Uncle Bill.

Chapter Fourteen

Perhaps it was the will or too many restless nights without sleep, but that evening I felt exhausted by both Guyana and my father's memory. I was halfway through my stay and I felt as if I had wandered into his head and got lost there. The more I tried to understand his actions and motivations, the more his life seemed a kind of psychological equivalent to Burnham's mansion – a labyrinth of rooms with doorways that kept opening on to other rooms, but lacking any centre or connection between them. Every time I felt myself to be on the verge of understanding him, I discovered a new room which had somehow to be fitted into the overall structure. The whole process was beginning to seem like a chaotic puzzle whose pieces would never fit together, and that night I decided to take a break. I went to see a Guyanese play called *A Diplomatic Blow* at the national cultural centre. Hardly had I left the hotel than a torrential downpour descended on the city, leaving huge pools in the potholed streets. We drove slowly through the rain to the theatre, where a line of taxis and cars were disgorging passengers into the downpour.

Inside the dimly lit auditorium, the seats were about a quarter full. Pop ballads from the sound system mingled with the muffled roar of rain outside. The Saturday night audience had dressed up in their best clothes for the occasion, the men in dark suits of crisply ironed pants and shirts, the women in light summer dresses and painstakingly sculpted hair, oozing a glamour and style that seemed oddly out of place in such a desolate, rainswept theatre.

The theatre was still less than half full when the music finally stopped and the performance began. Appropriately enough, the play was a bedroom farce about interracial sexual relationships, although the acoustics in the hall were so bad that I had to strain to hear what was being said. The stage set consisted of two scenes: a cheaply furnished room at stage level, and above that on a raised platform, a posh-looking lounge. The first scene introduced the principal characters. In the cheap room live a feckless, sexually voracious black Guyanese male and his put-upon girlfriend. Both characters were obvious stereotypes that the audience recognized. The put-upon girlfriend complains about her narcissistic boyfriend's inactivity; he lounges around with his shirt off, letting her do all the housework, and rouses himself from his lethargy only when sex seems to be in the offing.

After a leaden exchange between these two characters, a friend of the boyfriend's appears and invites him for a drink at the house of a female white diplomat working for the British Embassy. If the other characters had been stereotypical, the female diplomat was the kind of white woman Eldridge Cleaver or Michael X might have dreamed up in their most misogynistic fantasies. She was a crude racial caricature without trace of humanity, personality or intelligence, with her phoney middle-class manners, her posh English accent and her craving for black flesh. More than any of the other characters she was presented as an object of ridicule, contempt and also desire. The appearance of this vacuous cipher sent a ripple of excitement and amusement around the half-empty theatre. Without even a word needing to be said, the mere presence of the boyfriend and the white female diplomat in the same room produced sniggers from the audience, as though such physical proximity between a black man and a white woman was in itself a naughty transgression. The laughter intensified when the female diplomat began to flirt with the black stud, whose friend departed early and left them alone together on the couch.

Whatever potential this scenario may have afforded for irony and satire, there was little sign of either, as I strained my ears to catch the fragments of stilted dialogue floating round that cheerless, echoey hall. 'You Guyanese men are so romantic!' the diplomat cooed in her absurd BBC announcer's accent, as she cuddled up to the grinning protagonist on the couch. But to judge from the sound of growing laughter all around me, the play contained some kind of subtext that I was entirely missing. By now the boyfriend was grinning from ear to ear, occasionally slipping conspiratorial glances at the audience like a pantomime actor, and the scene culminated in a collective roar of laughter as the diplomat led the boyfriend to the bedroom, where he turned and raised his clenched fist at the audience in an unambiguously phallic gesture.

I was already beginning to find this witless farce faintly depressing, and the grim spectacle showed no sign of improving in Act II. The black hero comes home late and lies to his put-upon girlfriend about where he has been. Later he boasts of his conquest to the friend who invited him to the party: 'I scored!' he shouts.

'You lie!' the friend shouts back enviously, provoking another explosion of laughter from the audience.

At this point a power cut suddenly plunged everything into total darkness. The audience accepted the interruption as if it were entirely normal and a relaxed murmur of voices spread through the darkened theatre as they waited for the play to resume.

But I got up and left. I had had enough. I did not care how the play might end. Outside the rain was still pelting down, and a lake of water had formed around the main entrance. Eventually a taxi appeared, and the driver almost immediately began grumbling about the blackouts and the state of the roads and everything else as we splashed our way through the dark streets. 'This country's going from bad to worse,' he complained darkly. He talked of emigrating to England, where he had some relatives living in London.

Back in my hotel room I sat down to listen to the tape that Marjorie had given me. In spite of my gloomy mood, I still felt a surge of anticipation at the prospect of finally hearing my father talking about his life for the first time. I switched the machine on. Above the loud hissing of the tape could be heard a drunken male voice lazily slurring his words. Despite the poor sound quality I knew immediately that it was my father, even though the quavering, dipsomaniac voice did not match my memory of him from his visit to England. The background noise of birds and the occasional dog barking suggested that the interview had been recorded on the patio at Stone Avenue. The other voice I could hear asking questions – a woman with a Guyanese accent – was presumably Marjorie's sister.

The last time I had seen him really drunk had been in 1967. I had always associated my father's drunkenness with furious outbursts of rage, so it was strange to listen to this diminished version of him. The interview had been recorded in 1991 and even on that hissing tape the disintegration that had taken place in those missing years was obvious. Was it in this state that he had poured out his stories and anecdotes about his past in bars all over Georgetown? Had Joan deliberately recorded the interviews when my father was drunk in order to capture his famous story-telling powers in full flight?

Whether or not she had found the material she wanted, the tape was disappointing from my own point of view. Although drunk, my father was surprisingly lucid. There was a vivid portrait of Leavis lecturing at Downing College, a description of the Burnham/Jagan meeting in 1953 that had so impressed him, and a lot of analysis and description of the political situation in England during the 1950s, interspersed with little thumbnail sketches of well-known figures like Hugh Gaitskell and Nye Bevan. Marjorie's sister seemed particularly interested in my father's involvement in anti-colonial politics, and he talked about Ben Bella and the Algerian war with great authority, and mentioned the conflict in Cyprus as an important influence on his early political development.

The whole interview might have been entitled 'Bill Carr – the making of a revolutionary'. Yet my father himself remained a curiously blank, incomplete figure against the background of contemporary history that he described. There was little personal insight or reflection to be found among the stream of stories, anecdotes and evocations of the political atmosphere of the time. While I could believe that his life had been influenced by the historical circumstances of his time, Suez or the policies of Hugh Gaitskell did not strike me as an adequate explanation of his inner motivations. On the evidence of the tape, he had seen his life entirely in terms of political life or literary references, and there was no notion of the 'dark little corners' concealed in his past. There was no reference to his friends, relatives or wife. It was as if he considered his private life to be unimportant in comparison to the great historical events that he had lived through. What kind of person had he been at the time? What were his relationships like with other people? What did he feel about his family? What were his expectations of life?

These questions were neither raised nor answered. When the interview got to his decision to leave England for Jamaica, the tape ended abruptly. Anticipating his version of the crucial years, I eagerly whipped the tape over to listen to the other side, pressed the button, and . . . nothing, just empty hissing. I waited impatiently for a few minutes before pulling the tape out to check that I had not made some kind of mistake. I had just listened to 'Side three', clearly marked on the cassette, and 'Side four' was written in the same hand. Yet there was not a single word to be heard. I fast-forwarded, stopping continuously, but there was only the same infuriating roar. Side four had either never been recorded or been blanked out, and that brief, unsatisfactory account of my father's formative years was all I was going to get.

In the nine months my family had lived in Guyana I left the capital only once, when my mother arranged for me to go on a riverboat trip 'up the creek', as the Guyanese call it, to visit an Amerindian village in the interior. She thought it would provide me with a respite – if only a day – from the claustrophobic, pressure-cooker atmosphere at Canje Street. 'Up the creek' was a fitting metaphor for the situation in which my family found itself in those days, but that journey up the river has always stood out as one of the few bright moments in Guyana. I remember a group of us set off in the morning in an old wooden riverboat moored along the Essequibo. We chugged slowly along before entering a narrow, muddy tributary, wedged in on both sides by a towering, impenetrable wall of jungle. It was my first real glimpse of the Guyanese interior, and my first encounter with the jungle that Bruce and I had spent so many hours imagining in the Botanical Gardens back in Georgetown.

This was the real thing, and I remember being pleasantly intimidated by the sight of that dense, green wall and the thought of the dangerous animals and snakes within. I was more apprehensive about the prospect of piranha fish in the water, since I knew we would be going swimming when we reached the village. My brother and I had developed a real phobia about these vicious predators, which, we had heard, could strip a human being and an entire cow in minutes, and even died with their jaws open, ready to snap shut like a trap and take your fingers off.

Even as I warily scanned the muddy surface for any sign of piranhas or crocodiles and looked for anacondas in the overhanging trees, I felt happy to be moving in the opposite direction to Georgetown. The dense jungle, the swirling waters churned up by the propeller, the occasional squawking bird, and the hope of animals appearing at the water's edge, all contributed to the sense of freedom and adventure as the riverboat continued its slow, steady progress.

Years later I would dream about riverboat trips along the same kind of river, imagining myself being pulled towards a waterfall by an inexorable current, past banks teeming with bright snakes and exotic animals, as though the memory of those few hours had somehow imprinted itself on my subconscious. The Amerindian village consisted of a few huts in a large clearing next to the riverbank. We ate a picnic lunch on the boat, then dived with the other passengers off the back of the boat into the warm, sluggish water. For the rest of the afternoon I swam there in the creek, diving repeatedly off the back of the boat, not wanting it to end. In the late afternoon we turned once more towards Georgetown, and I left the jungle behind, and came back, like a prisoner returning from a day's parole, through the low metal gate into the collapsing world of my father's house.

I thought of that day in the jungle as I drove out to the internal airport at Ogle. I was to catch a plane to Kaieteur Falls, at 741 feet the largest single-drop waterfall in the world and one of the wonders of Guyana. I had booked a seat on a ten-seater plane as part of a tour agency package that included food and a trip to the Brazilian border. It was the first time I had been a simple tourist since coming to Guyana, and it was difficult to make the mental adjustment. Apart from Siobhan, the tour guide, the other passengers were mostly foreigners. They included a Guyanese computer operator who worked for Sainsbury's in London, and had not been back to Guyana since childhood; a young, clean-cut Englishman with a rugby player's physique, who was a representative of Price Waterhouse in the Guianas; and an American Tibetan scholar with a drooping walrus moustache and bald head who had come to Guyana to investigate the possibilities of opening a shrimp farm.

We waited at the airport for the other passengers to arrive from another hotel, chatting quietly in front of the bar where Moses and I had begun our boozy afternoon the week before. Finally the plane took off with a noisy roar of propellers and we were flying over the Demerara river. Soon rectangular strips of sugar-cane plantations and rice paddies gave way to the dense mass of the jungle, miles and miles of it, stretching out as far as the eye could see like a giant broccoli plantation. We reached the mouth of the Essequibo and flew inland, so low that we could see the outbuildings of logging companies, scattered villages and huts cut into the bank, and occasional canoes and motor-powered launches skimming along the surface. Dotted along the vast river were various islands, most of which were uninhabited and overgrown with rainforest.

We landed once again to pick up two other passengers, on a primitive runway cut into the jungle by a logging company, with piles of enormous tree trunks and the inevitable rusted, disused machinery alongside it, before following the Essequibo deeper into the jungle. We were now flying above one of the great unknown wildernesses of the South American continent. Below us the rainforest unfolded in a sea of green beneath the shifting curtain of mist and cloud, broken only by occasional rivers and darker patches where the forest suddenly dipped down into precipitous valleys. The jungle has often been associated with madness, fantasy and delusion in the European imagination and the Guyanese jungle was no exception. It was down there, concealed beneath the canopy of trees, that the English freebooter Walter Raleigh had imagined the location of El Dorado, with its mountainous piles of gold and glittering temples, whose Indian inhabitants were rumoured to be so rich that they ate their food with knives and forks of gold.

Raleigh had hoped that these fabulous riches would make his fortune and redeem his ailing reputation at Queen Elizabeth's court. Instead this exotic fantasy turned into an obsession that eventually cost him his life and that of his own son, who was killed in a raid on a Spanish settlement in the Guianas. His ships had moored at the mouth of the Essequibo while his soldiers ventured into the interior on one unsuccessful mission after another, until the old, broken pirate was forced to return to England, exhausted and discredited, to face imprisonment and execution in the Tower. Today the Guyanese jungle is still believed to contain riches. The more practical and successful heirs to Raleigh's fantasy are the intrepid Guyanese gold-miners, the 'porknockers', who spend months at a time living in the jungle, and the foreign mining companies who have to set up larger claims in the interior.

From that jungle also, in 1979, a cassette recorded in a place called Jonestown somehow found its way on to the international airwaves. On the tape the Reverend Jim Jones' tremulous and excited but oddly soothing voice could be heard coming through a loudspeaker, in an advanced state of lunacy and paranoia, telling his followers what a beautiful day it was as they queued up to drink poisoned Kool-aid. Their bloated bodies were found piled up on top of each other, together with Jones himself. In place of the Utopian socialist commune they had dreamed of, the mostly black men, women and children who had followed the messianic white charlatan from the ghettoes of the United States found only an appalling and meaningless death.

The Guyanese interior had also featured in the European literary imagination as a kind of blank screen for the projection of weird, exotic fantasies. It was there that Conan Doyle had set his *Boy's Own* yarn *The Lost World*, and that Evelyn Waugh's doomed upper-class hero Tony Last had met his absurd and cruel end in *A Handful of Dust*, an outcast in the jungle forced to read Dickens to a crazed English settler for the rest of his life. Conan Doyle had never even been to Guyana or South America, and Waugh had only passed through the interior on a journey to Brazil in the 1930s, but both writers shared the casual, routine racism of their class and period. In Conan Doyle's book the only black character is Zambo, the 'faithful' black servant of white literary tradition, who sits waiting for his gallant European masters like a loyal domestic animal, while Waugh's brutish, corrupt Indians eventually abandon the hapless Tony Last to his grotesque destiny.

Like Conrad, Waugh shared a perception of the jungle as something alien and hostile, a place where white men lost their moral bearings and drifted easily into madness. The Guyanese writer Wilson Harris had spent some years working in the interior as a surveyor and knew the jungle more intimately. In his books the rainforest figures as a kind of universal meeting place of cultures, an imaginative no man's land where dead and mythical characters mingle with living people and archetypes from Caribbean, Amerindian and Greek myth. His books contained a dense, impenetrable narrative structure whose prose style often seemed modelled on the jungle itself.

There had always been a strong element of fantasy in the way that Europeans perceived the Caribbean. From the earliest colonial days, the region was not an end in itself but a step on the way to somewhere else. The Europeans came, like Walter Raleigh, inspired by dreams of enormous wealth, to be obtained first by gold and later by slaves and sugar, wealth that one day would transform their social status and enable them to return to their own country as rich men of leisure. Many of them achieved that dream, and the wealth their slaves created helped to build cities like Liverpool and Bristol and pay for country estates and townhouses and fine mausoleums in English cathedrals.

Others stayed, and were ruined in the attempt, or died of boredom, syphilis or drink, having lived idle, useless lives, perpetually fearful of the slaves upon whose backs they lived, mimicking the customs of the metropolis within the corrupt, racist little world of Caribbean planter society. Together with the gold-diggers and slaveowners came the bureaucrats to fill the colonial administration, the clerks and governor-generals, the soldiers to man the garrisons, whose sole purpose was to prevent the ever-present possibility of a slave revolt, and missionaries from different denominations, offering the possibility of eternal salvation to the slaves as a compensation for their earthly captivity. But always amid this colonial traffic there was a trickle of liberals, abolitionists and social reformers, even revolutionaries – men like Reverend Smith, the 'Demerara Martyr', a white missionary who sided with the slaves during one of Guyana's many uprisings and died at the hands of the planters.

In the years since independence the Caribbean has continued to act as a magnet for European fantasies, bringing rich people to their eternal playgrounds, Jumbo jets full of tourists in search of deserted beaches, palm trees and even more exotic pleasures. In the tourist brochures the Caribbean is a kitsch version of one of the oldest European fantasies of all: the sensual, pre-industrial paradise of Rousseau and the Book of Genesis, untouched by time and history, complete with packaged hotels and steel bands, limbo dancers and swimming pools by the beach.

And there was also my father, who belonged to a category all his own. He had come to the Caribbean to teach 'the classics' at the tail end of the colonial era and stayed on when everyone else had gone back home. He had brought with him the psychological burden of empire and the equally heavy weight of his past. He was an exile from his own culture who simultaneously carried the icons of that culture with him wherever he went; who had left the beaches of Jamaica to come here to Guyana looking for 'Zinctown, New Mexico' somewhere down below in that improbable geographical mass of jungle and swampland, who had rejected England and everything it stood for, including his own family, yet at the very last moment of his life had lurched back once again to the 'frozen bosom of the north' in search of the same past that he had spent so many years trying to escape from.

As I sat in the aeroplane thinking about my father and looking down over the wild beauty of the Guyanese interior, with the drone of the propellers filling the little cabin, I felt hemmed in by the claustrophobic memories of my childhood. I could not get the will out of my mind – that miserable legacy of five pounds and the contempt it signified filled me with a useless, sterile anger. I had hoped that with this trip to Kaieteur I would escape my past for a few hours. But now I realized that it could be neither forgotten nor remade. No matter how many questions I managed to resolve or clarify, no matter how many positive accounts I heard about my father, they could not make those lost years seem any better. And the positive memories that so many people had of my father only made them seem worse. As the aeroplane passed into a mass of clouds and the forest faded from view, I silently cursed my father's name and wished that I had never come back to Guyana at all.

Soon we began to descend, and the dark green patches of jungle appeared once more through a swirl of clouds. About an hour and a half after leaving Georgetown we landed at the muddy little airstrip near Kaieteur. We stepped out of the plane into a thin drizzle of rain. Apart from a single dirt road leading into the jungle and a nearby hut, there were no signs of human habitation, nothing but the brooding, silent wilderness and the sound of the rain.

A park warden dressed in a green poncho, khaki baseball cap and army boots had been waiting for us. He was an eccentric character, who lived alone in the jungle all the year round. He emanated the self-sufficiency and polite indifference to human company of someone accustomed to long periods of solitude. Whether he was a natural mystic intoxicated by the wilderness, or whether his exuberance had more material causes, he seemed perfectly content living by himself in a little hut in the middle of nowhere. When one of the passengers asked him what he did with himself all year round, his eyes gleamed with amusement. 'I read!' he grinned. His usual reading material consisted of papers and reports on ecology and the natural world sent to him by the Smithsonian Institution. He spent the rest of his time walking in the forest, observing the animals and birds.

We drank a beer and followed Siobhan and the warden down towards the waterfall. We were quite close already, but Siobhan said that the bottom of the falls was so far below us that the crashing of the water could not be heard. We walked through the dripping forest until we emerged on a kind of rocky plateau, covered with weird, tropical vegetation. Directly in front of us, the fast-moving Potaro river swept down over into Kaieteur, pouring tons of water in an endless torrent over the edge of a cliff. A screen of mist hovered just below the level of the river. Peering down into the depths, we could barely see the mass of churning white water through the clouds of spray that were thrown up hundreds of feet into the air. Beyond the falls a steep narrow valley bordered by high cliffs fell back towards the jungle. It was a vision of such spectacular power and natural beauty that the entire party experienced a kind of collective elation.

We stood for a while admiring the falls, creeping as near as we dared to the wet slippery edge, and taking pictures of each other to record our individual presence at the falls for posterity, to remind ourselves in our old age that we had once been to Kaieteur, one of the wonders of the world. Afterwards we climbed upwards into the forest to get another view. Everything was wet and dripping, and the forest gave off an intoxicating smell of damp, rotting vegetation. Here and there huge tree trunks had fallen across the path, and craggy rocks trailing with creepers and liana protruded out of the forest. It was such a wild, exotic landscape that I was half expecting one of Conan Doyle's freakish dinosaurs to lumber out of the forest towards us, when suddenly the warden put his finger to his mouth and pointed into the undergrowth. About twenty yards away, a gorgeous, flame-coloured bird with a yellow coxcomb, stood perched perfectly still on a branch, standing out against the surrounding green like fire. We stared with awed fascination. Some members of the group fumbled for their cameras, but the bird was clearly not disposed to permit such sacrilege, and it vanished into the depths of the forest before they could even focus.

Siobhan took us to a ledge from where we could look directly down into Kaieteur. It was even more spectacular to see that great sheet of water from a distance, cascading into the boiling waters down below. In that moment, it was a real pleasure to be there, in that dripping wilderness, and for the first time that day I forgot why I was in Guyana, as we walked back across the rocky plateau towards the waiting plane. We took off once again and soon left the rainforest behind. Now we crossed over a different kind of landscape – low, bare hills and grassy plains where there was hardly a tree to be seen. This was the savannah, another part of Guyana that I had read about and seen pictures of in my school geography books in Georgetown, but never actually been to. It was desolate, monotonous country, hardly populated at all, except for the occasional cattle ranch and Amerindian hut. After about half an hour we landed at a makeshift airstrip by a small river which Siobhan informed us marked the border between Guyana and Brazil. We ate a picnic lunch in a thatched shelter, watched by a dour, expressionless Amerindian woman and her two children, then went down towards a layered waterfall, where we swam and clambered around for an hour or two before flying back to the capital.

By the time we got back to Georgetown in the late afternoon I was feeling pleasantly tired and relaxed, but it did not take long for my earlier gloom to return. I rang Moses Nagamootoo to thank him for his hospitality the previous week. He sounded sullen and hostile, replying mostly with gruff monosyllables. When I told him that I had not been able to find the tapes, the hostility became more overt. The reason I had not found them, he snapped, was because I was not really interested in finding out the truth about my father.

'Your father was shipwrecked and you've come here to persecute him! If you really wanted those tapes you would do anything to get them! You would subpoena that family!'

This was nonsensical. It was true that I wanted to hear the missing tapes, but the idea that I could subpoena my father's Guyanese family was absurd. And whatever had happened to them, I doubted whether they would reveal much more of the truth about my father than the one I had already heard.

Having placed me in the role of persecutor because I refused to accept his ludicrously inflated view of my father, Moses now seemed to regret our previous meeting. He told me that he had said some 'obscene' things about my father. I replied that I could not remember him saying anything that had struck me as 'obscene' and that as far as I was concerned he was just being honest, but this did not mollify him.

'I cannot continue this conversation,' he said.

'Why not?' I asked, irritated by his hostility. 'What are you so afraid of?'

'I will not continue this conversation,' he repeated with more determination.

'That's up to you,' I said, 'but if you ever want to talk again, you know where I am.'

The receiver clicked down. The Minister of Information was not offering any more information and I had the feeling that he would not be calling back.

*

260

In October 1967 my father sent me a letter with the following quotation and comments:

> 'Trust me that honest is as common a name as the name of a good fellow, that is to say a drunkard, a tavern hunter, a gamer, a waster; so are among the common sort all men honest men that are not known for manifest naughty knaves . . . follow not therefore the common reputation of honesty: if you will seem honest, be honest or else seem as you are.'
>
> The writer is a poet called Sir Thomas Wyatt, who lived when Henry VIII was king. This must have been written about 1533. It is surprising how little certain important things change. This doesn't mean you are not honest — it just seemed to me a point of view you might learn to find interesting — and it is a change from the karate boys.

The concept of honesty was always a crucial element in my father's perception of himself. It was honesty that got him beaten up in the rum shops. It was honesty that made him speak his mind so publicly against the government when he would have done better to keep his mouth shut. And it was honesty that he wanted his children to respect him for when he finally came to visit them after twenty years, so that even his last letter to Bruce was signed 'Bill — it's an honest name'.

Apart from Sir Thomas Wyatt's definition, it is not clear what my father actually meant by honesty, but the concept often served as a justification for the bullish way he charged at the world, turning his private life into a public drama, apparently indifferent to what anyone thought about him. In this way he turned his vices into virtues, so that his fits of temper, his public love affairs, the almost exhibitionist 'embrace of the disgrace' of his last years that Joyce Jonas had described — all could be explained under the general rubric of honesty. 'Honest Bill,' he might have been called, had Shakespeare actually written a part for him.

There is no doubt that my father sincerely believed that he was honest, according to his own subjective understanding of the word, but like his memory, his honesty sometimes tended to be selective, at least as far as his own family were concerned. At times he displayed a deviousness and duplicity that enabled him to say one thing and to do exactly the opposite without even noticing the disparity. Nothing illustrates this tendency more clearly than the way he continued the

261

process of divesting himself of his own family in the years after we left Guyana. Among his papers I found a clipping from a Guyanese newspaper. 'Ex-Wife Sues U.G. Lecturer for $14,000,' read the headline. The short, matter-of-fact article explained how University of Guyana Lecturer 'Wilfred Carr' was being sued for more than 14,000 Guyanese dollars in arrears of maintenance for herself and four children. This was not strictly true, since my mother had never claimed any maintenance for herself, but for her children only. In any case the hearing had been adjourned when the judgement summons came up in bail court because 'Carr, an English lecturer, failed to appear', a curious word order that seemed to suggest that my father's profession was somehow responsible for his non-appearance. The journalist also reported, correctly, that the money was due for the period 1974 to 1976 on the basis of an order made at Cambridge County Court on 29 January 1974, and that my mother was asking the court for judgement against him.

These bare, unadorned facts did not seem especially startling or sensational in themselves, but I was surprised that 'Wilfred Carr' had kept the cutting, since his role in the divorce did not seem like something that he would have wanted to record for posterity.

When the divorce proceedings were actually taking place, I was only dimly aware of the concrete details. But I knew enough to appreciate that my father was refusing to meet his commitments. The entire process had lasted seven years, and its general trajectory can be traced in the few remaining letters between my parents. From the beginning my father was eager to obtain a divorce as soon as possible, while my mother was determined after everything that had happened that he would pay the costs involved, and that adequate financial arrangements should be made as far as maintenance and provision for the four of us were concerned.

The process was dragged out and protracted, partly because of the geographical distance between the two people involved, but also because my father gave little evidence that he had any serious intention of fulfilling his obligations. At that time the divorce laws permitted a marriage to be dissolved on the grounds of cruelty or adultery. My mother did not want to accuse my father of cruelty because she did not want herself or her children to be involved in a sordid public court case. For his part my father did not want to state adultery because he considered it dishonest to cite his affair with Sandra Williams as the reason for the breakdown of the marriage.

My mother therefore began divorce proceedings in London, in order to keep the whole process away from Cambridge. Her lawyer also believed that my father should pay the costs involved, and that he should give some sign of good faith, as far as maintenance provision for his children was concerned. In the first few years after our return to England, he sent sporadic payments, his letters containing various references to cheques that had never arrived, or complicated excuses that may or may not have been true. Considering the delirious state he was in for much of the time during those years, these lapses were not entirely surprising, since at times he barely seems to have been aware where we were. 1972, in particular, seems to have been a bad year:

February 1972:

I'm not lying about the pre-Xmas letters. I can only suppose that some bloody thieving sod at this end opened them, found there was nothing he could use and so simply threw them away. I must look for the slips. But check at your end. I did address them wrongly.

May 1972:

As for money I will do my best. You would have had it long ere now but daydreaming at the wheel three weeks ago I collided with three cars. Nobody was hurt but quite a lot of damage was done . . . Some bastard in the atmosphere has scant regard for me.

19 July 1972:

I don't imagine my name is exactly a household word. I tried to find you when your message was left and all I got was a village called Cambridge which is apparently in Gloucestershire. You must visit it one day. Somebody I suppose will laugh. Probably the oldest inhabitant . . . I don't know what else to say. The money will come when I have it. O the pity of it, Iago, O, the pity of it. Man, you are hard to talk to and in very large measure because of me. Take care.

The impression of chaos and disorder that emerges from these letters was clearly an accurate reflection of my father's private life in Guyana at the time, but it was also obvious that he was not entirely living on another planet. Most of his remaining letters to my mother are chatty and pleasant, inevitably concluding with an expression of 'respect and admiration', and congratulations on doing a good job with the children. Occasionally however, the tone changes, such as this letter written to her lawyers in 1970:

> Dear Sir,
>   I would remind you that your client and I separated on May 20th 1967. Your client subsequently offered me a divorce in December 1969. I would like to suggest to you and to your client that there has been enough delay. A number of people's lives are involved and they are in no way assisted by the present practices of you and your client, practices that I can only describe as a combination of snide innuendo and deliberate procrastination . . .

While my mother waited in vain for my father to pay his share of bringing up his children, the law changed, allowing for a divorce after five years' separation. My mother now handed over responsibility for the divorce to her own firm in Cambridge. In 1972 the Decree Nisi was granted at Cambridge County Court, and a maintenance order was subsequently made requiring my father to pay seventy pounds a month in alimony. He seemed to accept these conditions without complaint:

> I've received two days ago the divorce proceedings from your firm. I am contesting and quarrelling with nothing and I hope I've filled in the forms correctly . . . The only thing that made me bawl was the dreadful legality of it all. It has to be done and I guess that is the best way of doing it. The terminology has some kind of professional integrity. It's just that the two people become irrelevances and the four children sound like ghastly accidents. I'm not being sarcastic – it's just a little difference in seeing things. 'When we shall meet at compt, that look of thine will hurl my soul from heaven. Girl, girl, art thou cold?' (Othello, Act V) I hope I haven't done you too much damage and you have four bloody nice children. One day we'll talk about it – as friends.

Despite the verbal agreement, the monthly payments failed to arrive. My father blamed various factors – car payments, government currency restrictions, his own financial difficulties and his inability to handle money. Even though there may have been an element of truth in some of these excuses, his inability to pay *anything* was beginning to seem like bad faith. Finally, after various letters and phone calls across the

Atlantic, my mother refused to apply for the Decree Absolute, to my father's obvious frustration in the spring of 1973:

> *Will you please now, I think that this is what I wanted to say, terminate this ghastly process? Send the Decree Absolute. That is what you promised insofar as I think I can guess who the legal draughtsman actually was. You would have to go back to the Hundred Years War or the Thirty Years War to find an equivalent.*

In November that same year, he reiterated the same demand, together with an unusually precise and optimistic financial prognosis:

> *I have authorized the immediate forwarding to you of $600. Next week I shall have a further $600 forwarded to you and before Christmas I will send you $1200 . . . I hope this constitutes good faith. At any rate it is the least I can do. I can neither reinstate nor reconstitute the past and it has worn the hell out of me living with it. At no stage did I ever feel proud of myself or pleased with myself either and I have paid in certain ways for much of what I did that was wrong. But the Henry James invisible silken halter is throttling me and we are both entitled to its severance. Both of us, I think, will benefit. Like the Roman Governor let the decree be made absolute – by mutual consent.*

One reason for his urgent desire to cut the 'silken halter' was that he now wanted to marry again, although no one in England knew this. My mother rather precipitously accepted his promises as evidence that he was prepared to meet his commitments at last and agreed to apply for the Decree Absolute. By the following January none of the promised payments had arrived, but nor had the Decree, to my father's obvious frustration:

> *You will by now have received my promise . . . You now have to honour yours. This awful thing has now obviously gone beyond the bounds of nightmare and it should be terminated. I have many regrets, no reproaches – and, after seven years, no apologies. I will do what I am required to do and what I am permitted to do. You, I believe, will do what you must. Revenge is a bad meal that destroys everybody who eats it.*

That same month the Decree Absolute was granted, and my parents' marriage was finally dissolved. With my mother's agreement the full details had been watered down, so that the worst incidents were not actually mentioned during her brief appearance in court, and precise details about my father's violence were subsumed into the general charge of 'drunkenness'.

But still none of the promised payments materialized, and so my mother applied for a court order to retrieve the money which failed to elicit any response from Guyana either. In July 1974 she wrote a sharp letter to my father, the only one of her letters of which she kept a copy:

> *Dear Bill,*
>
> *My firm wrote to you on the 16th May pointing out that there was 500 pounds then owing in respect of the Court Order, which you will recall, you consented to this year. I gather there has been no reply, and of course, the amount now owing is 750. The person dealing with the divorce for me has checked into it fully and we can enforce it in Guyana. Because of the difficulties you have had, and I presume, still have, I have not at this stage tried to make matters more difficult for you there as I am sure you can appreciate. However, I am beginning to feel more than slightly taken advantage of, having complied with all your wishes at no expense to you and I urgently need the money which is, of course, for 'our children'.*

My mother then proposed a new financial arrangement, in which the two of them would divide the financial responsibility for the four of us, so that he would pay for my sister and me, while she would look after my two brothers. She then closed with the following barbed plea:

> *As you know, I have largely supported the children myself since I have been back in England, and as they are getting older and more expensive, I am finding it increasingly difficult to manage . . . You must appreciate surely the difficulties we have all had and although there is not much you can do in connection with most problems I do feel that at least you could help with the financial side.*

This letter was followed by a few weeks of silence before my mother's lawyer received the following bizarre document in September:

> *CARR versus Carr*
>
> *The Carr in capital letters is clearly your client. The Carr in small letters is clearly me. The facts of the case, as I apprehend them, are as follows:*

1) I do not have the resources, at the moment, to meet the obligations that I voluntarily entered into. I intend to meet them as soon as I can.

2) I have remarried. I would suppose that even the most stricken husband has that measure of entitlement.

3) The involvement of two children in a market deal about money seems to me unnecessary. But then it hardly comes as a surprise. Matthew and Anna, if they wish, and provided their mother and the Court agrees, are more than welcome to live with my new wife and me. It is not finally a matter of finance, but a matter of trust and concern. I am not proposing to 'take the children away'; which, of course, might save your client some embarrassment with her bank manager. I am saying simply that they are invited. They are not pawns in a game and your client does not play the game very well.

4) Please inform your client that I wish no further personal communication with her. When writing to me please be kind enough to write in your professional capacity only. In human terms CARR versus Carr is over.

It was checkmate. Having got his Decree Absolute at last, my father was now reneging on all his agreements with the casual disdain of a Balkan diplomat. Gone were the chatty, concerned inquiries about my mother's health, the expressions of respect and admiration and congratulations on doing a good job. Nor were there any more promises of presents and letters for his children's birthdays. The hypocrisy, deviousness and bad faith of this fraudulent, wretched document are breathtaking. He was effectively abandoning the last vestiges of responsibility for his own children, whom he had already physically removed from his life. Yet at the same time he had the audacity to claim that *he* was the one who was really concerned about us, while my mother was only interested in 'a market deal about money'. The offer to me and Anna to come and live in Guyana was only sincere as far as my sister was concerned, even though she had never expressed any desire to move to Guyana permanently. My father knew this perfectly well, despite his 'trust and concern', and it is difficult to believe that he ever seriously imagined that the offer would be taken up.

This was the sordid history behind 'Wilfred Carr's' non-appearance in court. In the event my father never made any of the maintenance payments he had agreed to. But the saga was not over yet. Although my mother did not realize it, her court proceedings in Guyana gave her lawyers the legal power to prevent my father from buying property at the very time he was trying to buy a new house. This obliged him to reopen channels of communication. In 1977, in the middle of one night, he rang her up and pleaded with her to withdraw the court order, promising that he would fulfil his obligations as soon as he had a roof over his head. He then wrote a desperate letter, with the following melodramatic prediction:

> I can well understand your ignoring me. But I must again humbly profess my request. If you do nothing at all about it the gravest consequences must ensue. I mean by that you will have sentenced me to death in this fascist country and as I said before I do not think I deserve that fate. So please oblige — at least as far as you can.

My father often used local conspiracies and reasons of state as an excuse for evading his personal responsibilities, whether it was not coming to England to visit his children or failing to send money. Exactly what the 'gravest consequences' were he did not say, nor did he elaborate on why he should be 'sentenced to death' for paying the alimony he owed. And nor did it mention that his father had left him what he himself later described in the interview with Marjorie's sister as 'a considerable amount of money' in his will, which had enabled him to buy his house at Stone Avenue. Nevertheless my mother took pity and withdrew her petition. My father bought his house, and the promised payments never arrived.

It was this kind of behaviour that made it difficult for me to take seriously what Marjorie had told me about how much my father loved his children. It was true that he had said as much to various people in Guyana, and I had also heard how he had cried when he heard my youngest brother had developed a rare bone disease in his leg that had put him on crutches for a year. But not once had he done anything practical to help him. He had not even rung him up or written him a letter. In fact my youngest brother never received a letter from my father in his entire life, but that did not stop 'Honest Bill' from using his illness as a way of making people feel sorry for *him*. This was the essence of my father's love for his children. It was an emotional pose to make him look good in front of his friends, which had no repercussions or obligations in the real world.

My mother once wrote to my father, in a lighter moment, that she preferred him four thousand miles away. The comment amused him, but he agreed with it and clearly preferred to have his children four thousand miles away as well. He was not unique in this. Fathers often like to talk about the children they have not seen for years as if they were still 'theirs'. The existence of children scattered around the place, preferably at a safe distance, provides such men with a confirmation of their masculinity and the continuation of themselves into the next generation. My father had not come to see us even for the briefest visit, when it actually mattered to us, when there was still the possibility that some kind of relationship might have been salvaged. On more than one occasion my mother had asked him to visit us and each time he claimed that some P N C conspiracy was preventing him from leaving Guyana. Yet I had found out since coming to the country that he had in fact been abroad on various occasions, and had even gone to Canada and the United States. In the end, of course, he had come back, but only when it suited him, and by then it was too late.

The shock of his rejection and the brutal, unequivocal manner of its execution had been a catastrophic episode in all our lives, but it now belonged to my emotional pre-history. However intensely children may be aware of their parents' lives, they still tend to see them through the narrow frame of their own emotional needs. I had ceased to mourn the loss of 'Dad' a long time ago. As an adult I could accept the fact that people were weak and fallible and that perhaps he had made a mistake in his marriage. I could even accept that he did not like his children – or at least that he had discovered too late that we were incompatible with the kind of life he wanted to lead. But nothing and no one could ever make me believe that the way he had behaved towards his family had anything to do with love, even if he had apparently succeeded in making other people believe it.

In the end my mother did recover the maintenance arrears, but not from my father. In the late 70s his Aunt Peggy died, and my mother applied for an Equitable Receiving Order on her estate, and successfully obtained his share of her inheritance, which was then distributed between the four of us. It was a minor victory in a long history of defeats. Neither during the marriage nor after it had she ever been able to respond to my father in his own terms. She had not been able to shout back at him or hit him over the head with a bottle, nor had she been able to bring herself to deliver the *coup de grâce* even when she had him on the ropes with the court order. But always she had been determined not to be beaten on the issue of maintenance. It was for her a fundamental matter of principle and self-respect. In the end she had won, and years later, when it was all over, my father left the wife he respected so much the sum of five pounds sterling. Whatever else could be said about such behaviour, it was not honourable. And it was not 'honest'.

Chapter Fifteen

One of the mysteries surrounding my father's life in Guyana that I had yet to clear up was how he had been able to stay in the country for so long, given his outspoken opposition to the PNC. Why had the government not expelled him? How had he managed to keep his job at the university when the board of governors was packed with government appointees? How seriously had Burnham actually regarded him as an opponent? The logical place to find the answers seemed to be the headquarters of PNC itself, and so I duly rang it up and asked to speak to Desmond Hoyt, Guyana's president before Cheddi Jagan and Burnham's successor as leader of the PNC. A surly secretary informed me that Comrade Hoyt was out of the country. So I asked instead to speak to Hamilton Green, the former prime minister, and ex-mayor of Georgetown. Comrade Green, the secretary replied coldly, was no longer a member of the PNC and had formed his own party, 'Good and Green for Guyana'. It sounded more like an environmental pressure group or an advertising slogan for the Body Shop than the name of a political party, especially one run by Hamilton Green, a politician who had been particularly feared and loathed by the opposition.

Despite the grim curriculum attributed to him, he was also known as a 'grassroots man', a politician with a secure constituency among the mostly Afro-Guyanese population of the Georgetown slums. Even without the PNC, Mr Green still seemed able to move his people around like chess pieces, and was rumoured to have been behind the recent land occupation by black squatters in an Indian-dominated neighbourhood of the capital.

My father had singled out the formidable ex-prime minister as a special target in his *Mirror* articles, and his contemptuous defiance of the second most powerful man in the country was still talked about admiringly within PPP ranks. Needless to say, it did not endear him to Mr Green himself. So as my father's most active political adversary

Mr Green seemed just the person to answer some of my questions, although I doubted he would be prepared to speak to me.

I dialled his party offices, expecting a curt refusal.

'Good and Green!' answered a cheery male voice.

I asked to speak to Hamilton Green, adding that I was Bill Carr's son. A moment later Hamilton Green introduced himself. He spoke in a slow, lazy drawl. I explained that I was in Guyana and asked if he would be willing to speak to me about my father. To my surprise he agreed without hesitation, and told me to come to his house in a few days' time. He lived in the Lodge area of Georgetown – 'where the poor people live, man' – and he said that no address was necessary. 'Everybody knows me. Just ask for Hamilton Green.'

A few nights later I arrived at the appointed time in a desolate, run-down part of Georgetown where I had never been before. As Mr Green had predicted, the taxi-driver did not need any directions, although he did not seem to relish going to the Lodge area at night. I was not looking forward to the forthcoming encounter with Mr Green myself. From the stories I had heard about him, I had constructed – mistakenly, as it turned out – a mental image of some kind of Duvalier-style thug, surrounded by machete-toting hoodlums with dark sunglasses. My unease intensified as the houses began to thin out and we drove through a sparsely populated area where there did not seem to be anyone around on the streets.

Finally we stopped outside a high-walled compound on the edge of a barren strip of wasteground. On the other side of the wall stood a large house. Mr Green may have lived 'where the poor people live' but he was clearly not one of them himself. The barbed-wire fence running along the perimeter walls suggested a man who had a lot to protect. I got out of the cab and called out through the metal gate. Apart from the frogs croaking in the gutter there was no sound at all, and there did not seem to be any sign of life from within the darkened compound.

But after a few minutes two burly black guards emerged from an outbuilding and approached the gate. When I told them who I was, one of the guards grunted, went back to the outbuilding and then re-emerged to tell me that Mr Green would see me soon. He opened the gate and led me to a porch alongside the main house. I sat on a couch and waited in the clammy heat, listening to the croaking frogs and trying in vain to keep the voracious mosquitoes at bay. The porch contained all the paraphernalia of the populist politician. There was a large gong hanging from the ceiling, a lectern and a desk: it was obviously where Mr Green conducted his political business, receiving visitors and petitioners. Some forty minutes passed. I was beginning to wonder whether the whole visit was going to be a waste of time, when the door opened and a short black man with high cheekbones and slightly mocking eyes appeared in the doorway. 'Mr Carr?' he smiled. 'Hello, I'm Hamilton Green.'

For a man with such a controversial reputation, the former Prime Minister did not look particularly threatening. He was physically unimposing, with a slight build and quick, restless movements. His whole demeanour emanated brisk politeness, the sense of a man in a perpetual hurry who was doing a favour by speaking to me at all.

He apologized for being late and ushered me inside. The house appeared to be empty, and most of the lights in its numerous rooms were turned off. I followed him through a hallway decorated with African masks into a large sitting-room, whose walls were covered with similar masks and carvings. Apart from the zebra-skin rug on the floor, the leather couch and various musical instruments scattered round, the house looked more like a museum of African art than a place where people actually lived. The gallery-like appearance was enhanced by the total silence emanating from the rest of the building. Hardly had I sat down than Mr Green's mobile phone rang and he announced that he would have to leave me for a few minutes.

About ten minutes later he came back and apologized once again for being called away on political business. He had dropped the Guyanese accent now, returning to it only now and then when he picked up his mobile phone to deliver some short, clipped instructions to whoever was at the other end of the line. He spoke like a man accustomed to giving orders and seeing them obeyed, and exuded a secure sense of his own power and authority. At the same time he had a politician's ability to switch instantly between different personalities according to whom he was addressing. Talking to me, he was suave, polished and expansive, flashing his white teeth frequently and letting his voice linger at the end of his sentences as though caressing them.

Whatever hostility he had felt towards my father while he was alive, there was no sign of it now, as he spoke about his former opponent in the florid, jargonistic English that Burnham himself had been fond of and which his protégé obviously revelled in. 'I first met Bill when I had to interface with the university as a minister,' he began. 'At that time there was a great ferment within the university, as I think happens with every developing society. We were trying to address the questions of the role of the university in developing Guyana, and naturally we felt that the university should play a more developmental role and therefore should sort of . . . step in line with the needs, the demands and the aspirations of the elected government. Like all university people, Bill was opposed to governmental interference. He headed a group that said, "Look, we're going to do our own thing and we would brook no interference of any sort from any government, and you just pay the bills and we'll do the job."'

This did not seem to me an entirely unreasonable position, and was in fact the position of most universities throughout the world in democratic countries. The suggestion that the PNC had been fairly elected and therefore the group in favour of university independence was going against the wishes of the 'elected government' was laughable to anyone with even the most cursory knowledge of Guyanese politics. But Mr Green did not bat an eyelid as he explained how the government's search for a more 'developmental role' in the university had led to 'areas of confrontation'.

One of these points of conflict concerned the issue of compulsory national service, whose purpose the PNC's opponents believed was more concerned with inculcating loyalty to the regime than protecting the country's national sovereignty. The military training camps set up by the PNC in the isolation of the Guyanese interior had once enjoyed a notorious reputation as vehicles for filling new recruits with party propaganda. My father was among the staff members of the university who opposed students interrupting their studies to go into them. Mr Green, however, claimed that the real objective of these camps had been to 'reconfigure the socio-economic conditions of the people' by exposing Guyanese youth to the 'hinterland'. In this way the PNC's youthful pioneers would come to understand the meaning of 'development in the Third World' and avoid 'the pressures and prejudices inherited from the colonial system'.

I was still trying to decide whether Mr Green really believed what he said when he described another 'area of confrontation' between my father's group and the government, over the content of the university curriculum. Once again he offered Third World rhetoric as a justification for government intervention.

'We felt that there should be much greater emphasis on the sciences, as distinct from the arts, because you grew up in a British society where the British said to us, "You either be a lawyer or a doctor or you're really nobody in society," and there was not sufficient emphasis on the agricultural, even social sciences à la the Third World. And so we were trying to, as I say, reconfigure the whole society to meet the demands of society as it then was.'

This attempt to use the university to 'reconfigure' society was bound to arouse my father's opposition, even if the PNC had been sincere in these high-minded objectives. It conflicted with one of his most deeply held convictions – that the university should be an independent critic and observer of society. His belief that the government's interference was really aimed at neutralizing opposition and perpetuating the PNC's control over Guyanese society would only have intensified his hostility.

Despite his vocal opposition however, Mr Green was full of praise for his former opponent. 'I found Bill as an Englishman extremely courageous to really take a position,' he drawled, 'which was out of character with the other English people who came here. They tended to line up with the existing old imperialist bureaucracy and the remnants of the plantocracy, but Bill tended to empathize with, and to want to work with, the masses. I got the impression that he really genuinely felt that he was part of that exercise. As sometimes happens in every society, sometimes we all get caught up in rhetoric and you're fighting like hell, but really fighting for the same damn thing' – he chuckled at this amusing thought – 'and ultimately, that's what it turned out to be. Before his demise, I talked to him a couple of times and I think he had changed his whole approach and tended to be less aggressive, both in language and in dealing with matters.'

'But in the past you *had* found him aggressive?'

'Oh, yes,' Mr Green nodded meaningfully, and the magnanimous mask momentarily slipped. 'Bill could be *very* aggressive.'

'Can you give any examples, as far as it affected you personally?'

'Well, I've not had any personal run-ins with him,' he said amiably, 'but certainly when there were issues at the university campus, for example he would get out there and demonstrate that the staff should have a greater say, and that the government should not be able to appoint excess of numbers on the university board. And you know, he would make no bones about his position, publicly, on campus. Other lecturers tended to be less vocal.'

It was difficult to believe this was the man to whom my father had been so vociferously opposed. There was plenty of evidence to show that he had indeed been 'very aggressive' towards Mr Green, and yet it now seemed that he did not have a single bad word to say about his former enemy, and had even admired him during their years of confrontation.

'With our colonial history an Englishman is an Englishman no matter what form he comes in,' he went on, 'and by that time we had very few Caucasians in the system at all, because remember before independence the British rapidly reduced the people who functioned in the bureaucracy, and in any case they'd been training the locals to take over that aspect, and so it was only in technical things on the sugar estates that there were any English people left. Burnham was very strong on this question, we started to decolonize the entire system.'

Mr Green did not mention that one of the aims of this decolonization had been to put Burnham and his cohorts in permanent control of the former colony, which they had subsequently ruined and nearly destroyed completely. In the PNC's worldview, however, black was always beautiful, even when it was wrong, and colonialism provided a readily available historical alibi for its own disastrous misrule. Yet even while this racial purification of Guyanese society was taking place, my father seemed to have exercised the same fascination for the former prime minister as he had done for so many other people in the PPP.

'Here was this little white guy comin', sword in hand, shield in hand, into the fray of what was, essentially, a black cause' – he shook his head and chuckled once again – 'but Bill was never seen as white. Certainly I never saw him as white. I just saw him as this strange cat who came in and makes a lotta noise. We agreed with him sometimes, didn't agree with him sometimes. Really, we never regarded him as being a handful or dangerous.'

'In spite of his outspokenness?'

'Nnn-no. We never regarded him as being dangerous, because we had no evidence, unlike some others, that he was plotting anything, like to overthrow the government. Because of his openness. He said all he wanted to say and there was no undercurrent. That's how I saw him, and in that respect I didn't have any difficulty with him at all. There were others . . . like the Rodneys and all these, who we knew were planning activities of a much more serious nature.'

Mr Green did not go on to describe how the PNC had reacted to supposedly subversive conspiracies. It seemed impolitic, in the context, for me to mention the PNC's alleged methods of dealing with dissidents. Nevertheless, there seemed no reason to disbelieve what he had said about the regime's attitude to my father. What other explanation was there for the fact that he had been able to stay in the university and keep his job for so many years? Had he really been a serious threat to the regime, he could have been removed first from the university and then the country without too much difficulty. After all, the PNC had prevented Walter Rodney from working at the university, despite his academic reputation, and had weathered the subsequent international outcry even after his death. My father had no reputation at all beyond the Caribbean, and yet the regime had allowed the renegade Englishman to stay on at the university, loudly advocate the PPP's cause, even letting him become dean of the faculty at a time when the 'system' was being purged of 'Caucasians'.

'There's a lot of wrong stories spread about the government at that time,' Mr Green said, in an attempt to explain this apparent paradox. 'In spite of what they say about Burnham, Burnham liked people who disagreed with him, and in spite of his rhetoric about not being an intellectual, he was one of the brightest people we've ever had in this country, and so basically he was an intellectual and he liked intellectuals deep down in his heart.'

Whether Burnham really had respected my father or regarded him with amusement as a kind of court jester, both he and his prime minister had clearly got used to his presence.

I asked Mr Green what he had meant earlier about the 'change' he had observed in my father's later years.

'Well' – he smiled once again – 'his whole demeanour seemed a little different to me. With Bill Carr you expect to see somebody coming at you with the boxing gloves on, but he'd come out with a whole different approach.'

'As if he had stopped fighting?' I suggested.

Mr Green looked mildly offended by the expression. 'I don't like to use that kinda language. Not stopped fighting. The way I'd put it, he'd seen life, his own life in Guyana through a new prism, so to speak, which perhaps was saying "Look, I don't need to be this aggressive to achieve what I want to achieve." '

I changed the subject and asked him why he had left the PNC to form his own party. The cause was a longstanding personality conflict with Burnham's successor Desmond Hoyt, which dated back to Hoyt's nomination as party leader after the Comrade Leader's death. Mr Green had coveted the position himself and had not been happy about his defeat. Afterwards he and Hoyt clashed over a number of issues. Mr Green felt marginalized by the new leader and excluded from the decision-making process. He was particularly offended by Hoyt's acceptance of the conditions demanded by Jimmy Carter and the U N observation team during the 1992 elections. 'As one who had been back in the independence struggle I felt personally aggrieved that he should make decisions based on what an outsider dictated for us,' he explained with feeling.

Given that the U N's conditions were intended to create the circumstances in which genuinely free and fair elections could take place for the first time since 1964, and that they had subsequently ended the P N C's illegal monopoly on power, it was ingenuous of Mr Green to play the nationalist card. The sincerity of his opposition to 'outsiders' was further undermined by his indignant complaint that he had not been allowed to meet Carter during the elections. He claimed also that he was offended by Hoyt's attitude and cult of the personality, even though the name of his own party suggested that he himself had no aversion to personalized campaigns – the only reason I could see for the existence of Mr Green's party was the personality of Mr Green himself. So the conflict with Hoyt clearly owed more to personal ambition than political differences.

Following the P N C's defeat in the elections, Mr Green had asked the party to re-examine Hoyt's role, and Hoyt had been so annoyed by his criticisms that he had 'contrived a commission' to have him expelled. In late 1993, after an unsuccessful attempt to protest the expulsion in the appeal courts, Mr Green bounced back by forming his own party and winning the mayoralty and twelve seats on the Georgetown city council. 'This came as a surprise to Hoyt,' he said with undisguised satisfaction. 'He underestimated my own personal popularity, even if I say so.'

What, I asked, did his party actually stand for?

'Well, since the collapse of the Soviet Union, I've always been very careful to define what socialism means and conservatism means, and these terms really mean nothing when you get down to the bottom of it, in our part of the world. My party has advocated what I call a moral and spiritual revival, and we consider ourselves a strong environmental group. Now whatever ideological label you want to put on us, I don't like to use labels. Are we middle of the road, am I left?' He smiled once again. 'What is left, these days?'

What indeed? Nevertheless I was always suspicious when politicians started talking about moral and spiritual revivals, especially a politician like Mr Green, whose party had engaged in massive vote-rigging throughout its years in power.

It was getting late. I wanted to call a taxi, but to my surprise Mr Green offered to take me back to the hotel himself. On the way we drove along the only new road that I had seen in the country so far. When I commented on this, he smiled and said that he had had the road built himself, during his term as mayor. Coincidentally the road led through Albouystown, one of the poorest areas in the capital, and one of the former prime minister's main bases of support.

Without being asked he suddenly offered to give me a little tour of his constituency. We drove off the road, into a wretched huddle of shacks, hovels and little hole-in-the-wall rum shops. Everything about Albouystown testified to long-term urban poverty and advanced social deprivation, from the mean, shabby houses to the rubbish-strewn pavements. Some streets had no lighting at all, while others were feebly illuminated by occasional lamps, which cast a dirty yellow glow across the unpainted weatherbeaten houses. The inhabitants of this little urban hell seemed to be entirely black, and they hung around the crowded pavements, in small groups like prisoners in an exercise yard.

'This is the worst area of Georgetown, Carr Junior,' Mr Green said almost proudly. 'People don't like to come down here.' Most of the inhabitants of Albouystown, he said, were descended from sugar-estate workers, and much of the property was owned by absentee landlords. Mr Green was full of such sociological observations, together with plans for civic rebuilding projects to improve his fiefdom. He seemed to know everybody, and everybody seemed to know him. He kept stopping the car to shake someone's hand and to exchange a few words in Creole, cracking jokes, making arrangements, giving instructions. 'Y'all doin' business?' he teased two women who were standing in the street.

'Noooo!' they laughed coyly.

Mr Green cruised slowly on, without smiling, his eyes flickering restlessly back and forth across the crowded pavements as he talked. A part of his brain seemed to be constantly attending to party business, renewing contacts and fixing meetings, even as the flow of observations and commentary continued. One minute he was stopping his car to remind some women to be at a meeting the following Sunday, the next pulling up alongside a group of teenagers, who all but jumped to attention and clustered round his car with expressions of rapt devotion. Mr Green had the entire neighbourhood eating out of his hand, and he seemed to be enjoying the opportunity to demonstrate his popularity to the son of his former enemy.

Despite the ex-Mayor's civic plans and quasi-Marxist sociological observations, however, I could not help thinking that the wretched inhabitants of Albouystown were probably of more use to Mr Green than he was to them. But it was impressive to watch this ghetto king out among his subjects. Whatever he was responsible for, Mr Green had style. On the evidence of this performance he was indeed the grass-roots man that he claimed to be, and would be a presence in Guyanese politics for a long time to come. Who could say that he would not one day occupy Burnham's position? It was not an inspiring prospect, but like Cheddi, Mr Green was a man who knew how to wait, albeit for entirely different reasons. 'Well, goodbye, Carr Junior,' he said shaking my hand, as we arrived outside the hotel. I thanked him for the tour, and the busy ex-mayor flashed his immaculate white teeth and drove off once again into the Georgetown night.

Apart from public speaking and demonstrations, my father's main contribution to the PPP consisted of the articles he wrote for the PPP newspaper the *Mirror*, both under his own name and the pseudonym 'Little Boy Blue'. These articles were written at a time when the paper was coming under increasing pressure from the regime. Although the *Mirror* was never actually banned, the PNC tried to prevent or at least restrict its publication by various subterfuges, such as preventing it from importing ink and newsprint, refusing to allow it to import a new printing press from the United States, and physically attacking the paper's street vendors.

The articles of Little Boy Blue were something of a legend among the PPP members I had spoken to, and one morning I arranged with Janet Jagan to visit the *Mirror* offices and take a look at them. I was driven by an amiable, lantern-skulled Chinese taxi-driver whose family had come to Guyana at the end of last century, along with thousands of other Chinese. His lined, bony face and misty eyes testified to a long and difficult life, and I was not surprised when he told me that seven of his nine children had died. He had been working as a taxi-driver when Guyana had been flooded with international reporters in the wake of the Jonestown massacre. It had been a hectic two weeks, he recalled, driving various star journalists all around the city. Those two weeks had been the only time in Guyana's history when the country had ever attracted so much international attention, and life had not been so hectic again for Georgetown's taxi-drivers. My driver's job had occasionally brought him into direct contact with some of the weirder strains of human fauna that had drifted into Guyana, including the Reverend Jim Jones himself, whom he remembered as 'a nice, quiet-spoken feller'.

The *Mirror* offices were in a large warehouse near Albouystown. There was a blackout in progress when I arrived, so that neither the printing press nor anything else was working. A receptionist led me to an upstairs office, where I found Janet Jagan laboriously typing on a manual typewriter. The woman who had once been accused by the British press of 'teaching hate for Britain' was now in her seventies, grandmotherly and white-haired, her American accent totally unaffected by nearly fifty years in Guyana. She was a Marxist, like her husband, with the reputation of being a tough, steely character. Some said she was as important and influential a figure in the P P P as Cheddi himself. As a white woman involved in Guyanese politics, a thick skin was an essential quality for emotional and political survival, but toughness was not a word that I found easy to associate with either of the Jagans. Only a few days before I had seen a photograph of her in the newspapers, smiling as she popped a piece of cake into Cheddi's open mouth at a public reception to celebrate his birthday. That homely domestic image seemed to sum up the essentially benign aura that both the Jagans emanated.

'So, you're going to write up your father,' she said approvingly as we shook hands. This was not exactly how I would have put it myself, but I nodded vaguely. 'Your father was a great man,' she declared. As always I felt slightly awkward in the face of such fulsome tributes to a man I had never regarded as great. It seemed hypocritical to agree and mean-spirited to say anything to the contrary, so instead I asked her how well she had known him. Very well, she said, both as member of her local party group and as a columnist for the paper, which she edited. Like everybody else, she had little idea of his personal life before he came to Guyana although she was aware that he had children in England. 'I knew he was married before,' she said, 'but he had settled here, it seems.'

'He certainly had,' I agreed.

Whether she caught the unintended note of irony in my voice or noticed my earlier hesitation, she gave me a more searching look now, as if suddenly she doubted that I really had come to 'write up' my father. 'People do make mistakes in life, you know,' she said meaningfully. I agreed that they did, but this did not seem to be the moment to go into the mistakes I thought my father had made. I changed the subject to his contributions to the *Mirror* and she talked appreciatively of the moral support that he had given the party by writing for the paper at a time when most intellectuals and academics had been too scared of the P N C to lend their active support to the opposition.

Had there been any particular articles that he had written that had annoyed the regime? I asked.

She thought for a moment and shook her head. 'I can't remember, but I know they detested him. Of course they used race against him and everything else.'

'How?'

'Because he was white! Race is race! They used it in all directions, against whites, against the Indians. Being white too, I was subjected to a lot of their nasty references to being white. They used to pull that one on me and on him.'

My father had once mentioned the distinctive style that enabled people to recognize his Little Boy Blue articles, and I asked her what it was.

'Well, he was a great wit of course,' she replied, 'and a beautiful writer. You know he had a book that he wanted to write? I don't know if you know about it. He used to tell me that he had this book that he kept postponing and postponing. He was a great writer and I felt that he should write it. So I organized a summer holiday for him to go away into the interior where no one would bother him, and he thought about it but unfortunately he didn't take it up. As far as I know, he never wrote the book.'

'What kind of book was it going to be?'

'I'm not sure. It had to do with literary life, but I'm not sure if it was fiction or literary comment, but he used to say he had this book and he wanted to write it, and I provided him with a very beautiful place and he didn't take it up.'

I vaguely remembered my father telling me about some timber concession in the interior where he had stayed for a while in the late 6os, but he had not mentioned that he was doing any writing there and it was clearly not the same place. Whatever this book was going to be, it had failed to materialize, like all the others. I asked about the articles and she asked a young staff journalist to bring out the heavy bound volumes of the *Mirror* now and left me alone at a nearby desk to look through them.

Like the university journals that I had unearthed in the Cambridge University Rare Books department, the *Mirror* was like a window opening on to a vanished intellectual and political landscape that my father had once passed through. The paper was an odd combination of party broadsheet and Indian family newspaper, mixing kids' stories, essay prizes, reviews of Indian films and film stars together with local news and foreign news articles eulogizing the situation of German women in the GDR or announcing 'Big Prospects for Education in Bulgaria'. There was little evidence of the moral soul-searching and 50s angst of *Cambridge Left* in this mixture of Third World revolutionary fervour and uncritical support for the Soviet Union and the 'People's Democracies'. On the contrary the worldview contained in the *Mirror* reflected the revolutionary optimism of the late 6os and early 70s, the highwater mark of Third Worldism, when many on the left were predicting that the graveyard of capitalism was to be found not in the industrialized countries of the West but in the anti-imperialist guerrilla wars opening up across the South. Even in Guyana Che Guevara's famous call to arms of 'two, three, many Vietnams' still echoed – as in this prophetic poem by a youthful *Mirror* journalist called Moses Nagamootoo in 1968:

> *Battles like flaming thunder will light the Andes*
> *And hefty arms of brotherhood will bridge the seas*
> *Every land and city will be a Sierra*
> *Every red banner echo 'Viva Guevara!'*

Che Guevara was also mentioned as the subject of a lecture given by Bill Carr at the University of Guyana in October 1972, the same month and year that he wrote to my younger brother sending Che's revolutionary farewell to his children. The journalist described how 'Mr Carr' referred 'wittingly' to the making of a motion picture about Che and called the Cuban revolutionary 'a kind of saint, a romantic focus for the genuinely underprivileged and those who merely think they are'.

I wondered in which category my father would have placed himself, as I flipped the pages over until I found the first of his columns, written in the same year, under his own name. The columns were headed by a little photograph of my father with a beard, looking not entirely unlike . . . Che Guevara. It was another image of him that I found totally unfamiliar, showing a friendly, intelligent, fun-loving face, slightly tilted to the side and resting in one hand, with a mischievous half-smile. Unlike the severe, backward-combed military-style haircut from the mugshot photograph, his hair was now curly and he also seemed to have a blackened left eye.

It was easy to see why my father's style was so recognizable. His abusive, wordy polemics stood out instantly from the dour orthodoxy of most of the *Mirror*'s political journalism. The main targets of his wrath were the PNC and its leaders, and his articles were sprinkled with personalized insults and contemptuous nicknames which made the paper's other references to the government seem polite and deferential by comparison. Thus Burnham was 'Mose' and Hamilton Green 'Hammy'. One article described the PNC's newspaper, the *New Nation*, as 'the PNC's Sunday jack-off', while another referred to the party itself as a collection of 'hacks, suckers and thugs' headed by 'Archbishop Burnham, that noted equestrian cleric'. Mr Green was a particular object of my father's spleen. In one piece he wrote of the 'calculated beam which Hammy proffers as a smile, the lascivious smirk over his left shoulder'.

Not all the columns dealt with the PNC. There were also articles on literature and society and my father's own life, some of which provided little glimpses of how he saw himself in those years. 'At Cambridge I suppose I was something of an agitator,' he revealed in one column. This was a somewhat exaggerated label to apply to a left-wing student, but the same definition of himself later appeared in another article describing his political activity in Jamaica. 'I wouldn't call myself exactly a fan of Oscar Wilde's,' he wrote, in a review of Wilde's 'The Soul of Man Under Socialism'. 'I respect (and I suppose this is a kind of giveaway) the kind of masochistic courage he possessed.' Elsewhere he lambasted the 'rum bums', the PPP members who wanted to overthrow Burnham by force. They were 'pseudo-intellectuals who advocated revolutionary violence when they didn't know how to shoot', whereas he had been in the British army for four years and knew how to operate Sten and Bren guns and mount tripods and bipods. 'Revolutionary activity is as hard and painstaking as growing rice or planting cane,' he solemnly informed his readers, using the kind of rustic imagery that Ho Chi Minh would certainly have approved of. 'Meetings must be held, organizations have to be formed, serious men have to grow old in the work and possibly die while working.'

This was the disciplined, paternal voice of Cheddi Jagan, rather than Bill Carr, who had in fact had little experience of revolution or rice-growing and who showed little desire to 'grow old in the work'. On the contrary, both Moses Nagamootoo and Freddie Kissoon had told me that he had actually been an inspiration to the same radicals he was condemning. Yet here he was advocating political maturity and restraint with apparent sincerity, even though he was something of a rum bum himself. He was, it seemed, all things to all men, and perhaps to himself as well.

I came upon an even more bizarre example of the lack of inner coherence that so often marked my father's life, in a meditation on the theme 'Suffer the little children to come unto me,' whose real subject was the social consequences of capitalism on family life. In a reprise of the 50s sociological books that he had once reviewed in *Cambridge Left*, he angrily denounced the 'broken homes – broken by rum and unemployment (the two have a habit of going together), faced with tense and strained parents trying desperately to catch up with the spiralling cost of living'. Whatever else made my father drink, it was certainly not unemployment, and even as he was lamenting the impact of capitalism on the nuclear family his own 'tense and strained' wife was trying in vain to enlist his help in taking care of his own children on the other side of the Atlantic. 'Be wary of the unillusioned scepticism of children, especially Guyanese children,' the article concluded portentously. 'One day they will be adults.'

As my father's adult son, looking back on his life and ours, I found more than a touch of irony in such statements. Had he been so lacking in self-awareness that he did not notice the irony of these words when he was writing them? Was this extraordinary gulf between what he wrote and what he did due to hypocrisy, or the result of some fragmentation within his own personality, that enabled all the different parts of himself to coexist at the same time and operate independently of one another, without any apparent conflict between them? Almost everything he had said or done at one time in his life found its exact opposite somewhere else. His articles merely multiplied the impenetrable swarm of ambiguities that his life contained. What had really been driving him all those years? Where was the common thread that bound all his ambiguities together? In that moment I doubted whether I would ever find out and I wondered if it even existed.

His columns ended in 1974. I continued to look through the volumes in search of Moses Nagamootoo's interview with him but without success.

Before I left the *Mirror*'s offices, Janet Jagan gave me as a souvenir a copy of the photograph that headed my father's column. I left her pecking steadily away at her manual typewriter, and, stepped out into the hot afternoon, with the words from the Kris Kristofferson song 'The Pilgrim' that my father had chosen for his funeral going round in my head:

> *He's a poet, he's a picker, he's a prophet, he's a pusher,*
> *He's a pilgrim and a preacher and a problem when he's stoned.*
> *He's a walking contradiction, partly truth and partly fiction,*
> *Taking every wrong direction on his lonely way back home.*

The third party in Guyana's Marxist-Leninist triangle is the Working People's Alliance, the party formed by Walter Rodney and other Guyanese left-wing activists in the late 70s. At one time the WPA was seen by some on the left to be a party capable of breaking the racial division in Guyanese politics, under Rodney's leadership, but its electoral impact has so far been minimal, even after the dismantling of the PNC's vote-rigging machine in 1992. This similarity in language, ideology and ostensible aims between the country's three main political parties is confusing for outsiders, and has sometimes meant that politically active Guyanese have been members of all three parties in the course of their lives. On more than one occasion it has even led to a convergence between the two main parties, such as when the PPP decided to adopt a position of 'critical support' following the PNC's nationalization programme in the early 70s.

From the beginning the Working People's Alliance was conceived as a non-ethnic socialist party, and Walter Rodney's prestige and charisma, together with his impeccable black revolutionary credentials, immediately defined him as a possible competitor to Burnham in his own Afro-Guyanese constituency. The truth behind Walter Rodney's assassination has never been resolved, and the PNC ignored calls by Amnesty International and other human rights groups for an independent investigation into the murder. Today the WPA is led by Rupert Roopnaraine, an MP in the Guyanese parliament and a longtime friend of my father's. I met him in his office in the party headquarters at Rodney House, where our conversation was frequently interrupted by phone calls from party members or his constituents. An articulate, precisely spoken, left-wing intellectual in his late forties, Roopnaraine described himself as 'bookish', and the WPA appeared to be an unusually literate party. One wall of its headquarters was covered with books, a fact that would certainly have impressed my father. 'Bill was the kind of person who would have been more at home with the WPA than the PPP,' he said. 'The WPA is really a home for people of all kinds of different views. We don't have and never have had any kind of tyranny of a single line or ideology, and of course we're also a party with a deep interest in culture and literature, and these were the aspects of society that most interested Bill. So that while he was organizationally connected to the PPP, it was with the WPA and the people of the WPA that he spent most of his time.'

Before turning to full-time politics, the bookish MP had been a lecturer at the university, where he became a friend of my father's. He had worked with him on various projects and initiatives intended to halt what they both regarded as the university's intellectual disintegration during the Burnham years. 'This was a period when the university was very politicized,' he said, 'and it seemed as though if you ever saw two people together on campus, the one thing you can be certain of is that they were not discussing ideas. It was in that environment that we were attempting to work and I would say that Bill was essentially a force for making the university the kind of community to which we were accustomed, committed to knowledge, curiosity and all those things.'

This intellectual affinity had been cemented by shared political interests, even though the two of them had not been members of the same party. My father, Roopnaraine said, was a man 'wedded to working class values' with 'a fundamentally humanist vision of the world', which reflected itself both in his internationalist political perspective and also in his private life. 'Bill was not a man who was happiest with the elite, with whom he could have spent his time as a professor at the university. He had a very easy relationship with people on the street and was on very good terms with the ordinary workers at the university. You would go into his office and you are as likely to find him in deep conversation with the sweepers and the cleaners as you are likely to find him in conversation with the students. And I think he had that kind of common touch, a feeling of real comfort with grass-roots people of the working class.'

It was this commitment to 'working class values', he believed, that had originally brought my father to Guyana, with its reputation for radical politics and a labour movement with a strong Marxist influence. None the less, the W P A leader did not believe that my father was ever a systematic Marxist in his political ideas.

'It was always with him a very moral business, above all. I think that his attitudes in this regard were less ideological and intellectual than they were moral and personal. There was a real way – I don't want to call it such a strong word as shame – there was a sense in which he came out of a situation of real responsibility for the degeneration and exploitation and all of that, and felt that as a member of that group or race or class, or whatever you want to call it, he had a particular moral role to play and something to excise.'

'What class did he say that he came from?'

'He never talked to me about which class he came from.'

'Did he ever talk to you at all about the past?'

'Nooo.' He thought for a moment. 'In fact, we never had long discussions about it.'

'He never talked to you about his other family?'

'No. I think once we got into some discussion about that, but frankly it was a long time ago, and I don't want to be precise. We did not have sufficiently intimate conversations about those things. I must say that at the time I knew him, he did not seem overly preoccupied by those things, but you know Bill was a very complex man. He had clear areas of privacy that he maintained, even to close and intimate friends. It's quite possible that those were such areas.'

I was by now familiar with the way my father had managed to conceal his past, even from his closest friends. It was obvious that

Rupert Roopnaraine had greatly admired him and shared the personal affection towards him that so many others seemed to feel. He remembered him fondly coming down the street to visit his house, an exuberant, extroverted figure, 'always carrying on, so that you always heard him before you saw him'. At the same time Roopnaraine had not been unaware of a darker, more irrational streak underlying my father's 'fundamentally humanist vision of the world', and occasionally his 'areas of privacy' had made themselves known in all their inexplicable horror.

'I remember one episode,' he recalled, 'which was a very painful one for me. One afternoon Bill had been out somewhere, and he had been drinking, and he was not supposed to have been drinking, and he had actually collapsed. And I remember that myself and another friend had to virtually carry him in our arms and tend to him that afternoon, and I think I came to – not understand, that would be too presumptuous. I developed a certain kind of awareness of some compulsive anguish that he was undergoing, which I could not put my finger on.' He frowned at the memory, as if he was still trying to put his finger on it. 'I spent a lot of time with him that afternoon and when I saw him in that kind of condition I said to friends that I did not expect to see Bill alive again. He was, frankly, spewing up his liver. I mean he was in terrible condition, and lo and behold! he was on his feet very soon after. He had clearly the constitution of an ox, because he really ought to have died a long time before.'

It was strange, I thought, that despite the many hours he had 'rambled on until the night' with my father Roopnaraine had never discussed the possible source of that 'compulsive anguish', nor speculated on the possible motives for his self-destructiveness.

'He was a person of enormous flair and extroversion,' Roopnaraine said now, 'but of course, as we know with a lot of people who are like that, there is the zone of private impulse and compulsion, which one day I would like to hear explained by those who knew him better and more deeply, and I would benefit from understanding it a little more. I don't claim to understand it. I recognize some of its elements and some of its features.'

As with many of my father's younger friends, I had the feeling that Roopnaraine had observed this 'zone of private impulse and compulsion' from afar, and had perhaps been too respectful of my father to know how to approach him about it.

'My last visual image of him is with his stick, walking down the railway line,' he continued. 'He was a great figure to the people who lived there, the squatters and small farmers and so on. It was a very dangerous place and he was set upon, I believe, on one occasion. And he was staggering along, essentially in a world of his own, and I could not at that time really understand what it was that drove Bill either to stay alive or to destroy himself. Clearly that force was operating in both directions – the same force that was leading him to self-destruct was also keeping him going, and I could never put my finger on what it was, largely because I don't spend a lot of time psychoanalysing my friends.'

For someone who didn't like to psychoanalyse his friends, this was a penetrating insight, which touched on the essential duality at the core of my father's personality – Falstaff and Iago, the one force pulling him towards life and health, the other dragging him down into chaos and destruction. I remembered that last time I had seen him alive, walking over the railway bridge towards Chalk Farm station, and as I pictured him staggering along the disused railway track, I felt once more that same mixture of horror and pity at the thought of him lurching onwards through life, consumed by the different voices within himself, a lone player in some private drama that nobody had ever really understood, not even my father himself.

Chapter Sixteen

Despite my father's lifelong commitment to the left, he was never entirely on the same ideological wavelength as the political movements that he associated himself with. While he absorbed some tenets of Marxism into his own thinking, he was temperamentally and intellectually at odds with the cast-iron rationalism of 'scientific' socialism. Instead he belonged to a tradition of left-wing intellectuals for whom Marxism seemed to offer a kind of secular substitute for lost moral and religious values. As early as 1950, there is a review in the Dulwich school magazine by W. I. Carr of *The God That Failed*, a collection of essays by disillusioned intellectuals formerly connected to the communist movement, including Richard Wright, Arthur Koestler and the Italian novelist Ignazio Silone. Even then the idea of communism as a kind of secular alternative to the vanished religious impulse interested him. He was particularly impressed by the intellectual journey of Silone, who 'commenced as a member of the Roman Catholic Church, subsequently joined the Communist Party, and has since returned to Roman Catholicism'. The review combines a cautiously approving attitude towards Marxism with a distinctly un-Marxist nostalgia for a pre-industrial past and the religious values it once contained:

> *The streams of experience upon which Christianity imposed a spiritual pattern do not flourish in an industrial environment . . . Christianity flourished in its most vital form in a society that was almost entirely agricultural, it organized rural experience, and harnessed to its use impulses released upon the archetypal pattern of experience — the rhythmic movement of the four seasons. Although compressed within a narrower horizon than that made possible by industrial development, they possessed an abundant vitality making for an atmosphere far more congenial, emotionally speaking, than the present day.*

The search of this more congenial emotional atmosphere is one of the connecting threads in my father's life, and to some extent his own intellectual journey parallels Silone's. In his youth he was exposed to a Catholic education, in its most brutal and fanatical form, at the hands of the sadistic nuns at St Vincent de Paul, an experience that left him with a visceral resentment towards the Catholic Church lasting well into adulthood. At the same time, like many disillusioned Catholics, he never entirely rejected the Church's teachings, and his anger towards its earthly representatives was part of a deeper emotional attachment which reasserted itself in later life. Unlike Silone, his reconversion to Catholicism was not accompanied by a rejection of his earlier political ideas, but dialectical materialism clearly provided him with an inadequate explanation of 'that dark complexity of motive and purpose' that he was so conscious of in himself, and his emotional and intellectual fascination with the Church intensified as he grew older.

The first inkling we had in England of my father's spiritual transformation was a letter to Anna describing Sunday mass as a 'green oasis' in his life. This was later followed by his bizarre attempt to have his first marriage annulled. I did not discuss religion with him when he came to England, but I had the impression that his visit to the site of Nicholas Ferrar's monastic community at Little Gidding was intended, in part, as a kind of religious pilgrimage. Then there was the poem written shortly afterwards advising us all to 'brace, before the hands of the living God'. Many other poems that I retrieved from his house also contained religious references, like this verse written on Christmas Eve 1978:

> *Pleased to see the silence of the night*
> *Eventual bed with gratitude.*
> *Happiness still, our Lord,*
> *But still, our cry remains,*
> *O come, O come,*
> *Emmanuel.*
> *Redeem thy captive Israel . . .*

This yearning for peace and rest was a recurring theme in my father's poems, but he never achieved it for long. Often when I read them in my hotel room, I would imagine him sitting out on the patio at Stone Avenue with a drink in his hand, contemplating the tropical night sky during another blackout, dreaming of the chapel at Little Gidding amid the madness of a collapsing Guyana. In those moments I could almost forget and even forgive everything that he had ever done wrong. I would find myself wishing that time could be rewound back to our life together so that everything could be started again. Knowing that it was too late, I wished him peace with his new-found God, and I hoped that those brief moments of epiphany had consisted of more than just poetry.

My attempts to retrace the Catholic side of my father's life in Guyana began with a visit one morning to the presbytery opposite the Catholic cathedral in Brickdam, where I had arranged to meet Father Montrose, his parish priest. I was taken to a high-ceilinged study, where I sat looking at a large and oddly eclectic collection of books, whose titles included works by Lenin, Cardinal Newman and even a copy of *Lolita*. Finally Father Montrose arrived. He was young, bearded, and informally dressed in a white shirt and black trousers. We shook hands and sat down and he asked me how he could help.

I had hardly begun to ask him about my father when he looked puzzled. 'What did you say your father's name was?' he asked. I told him and an expression of surprise appeared on his face. 'Bill Carr?' he said. 'But I didn't know him personally, I only knew him through his articles in the papers.'

It turned out that there had been a mix-up on the telephone. He had assumed that the father I wanted to talk about was another alcoholic Englishman, whom he was looking after, a former engineer and virtual derelict, who was living on church charity. I wondered how many other white Robinson Crusoes had come adrift in Guyana, as the priest explained that the man I wanted to speak to was Father Rose, the parish priest in Campbellville.

Accordingly I set off for Campbellville, arriving shortly afterwards at St Theresa's Church, a pleasant whitewashed wooden building with a green lawn and low wooden fence. Next to the main entrance a large tree thrust its branches outwards like a splayed-out hand, casting an intricate pattern of shadows across the neatly cut grass. The church was shut and I went into the presbytery next-door, where I found Father Rose in his office. My father's priest was a sallow and alarmingly thin Englishman, in his early sixties, with a gaunt, cadaverous face and the troubled, preoccupied expression of a man immersed in some private world of the spirit, for whom earthly life was more a problem to be brooded over than celebrated. This sense of otherworldliness was enhanced by his soft, ponderous voice, so quiet that I had to strain to catch what he was saying above the noise of a workman carrying out repairs.

His secretary, Carol, who had also known my father, joined our meeting. She was almost as thin as the priest, but had a sweet, compassionate face that contrasted with his gaunt, ascetic visage. Father Rose was wary about discussing my father, but agreed to talk about him on condition that the conversation was restricted to religious matters. He had first met him, he said, soon after he had come to Campbellville in the late 70s. Then my father was already a well-known member of the parish, and being so well-educated used to come and read at mass. The two men also used to meet on other occasions when they would discuss religion and Shakespeare.

'I knew him as someone who was a very genuine Catholic,' said Father Rose in a ghostly, ethereal murmur, 'who really wanted to discuss religion at a high intellectual level, but his ill-health and his work and the fact of his wife not being a Catholic gradually drew him away from me, so towards the end of his life I didn't have much to do with him, but I did see him often. When he was dying I gave him the sacrament of the sick, and then he was in very good disposition and very friendly. We parted on good terms.'

What aspects of religion had they discussed during these theological conversations? I asked.

'I just thought he was looking for an intellectual response to some of the problems, of the Blessed Sacraments, the Holy Eucharist, and possibly the devotion to Mary which he found in our church, because in our church we are very devoted to Our Blessed Lady, and he liked to discuss that with me. He liked to know why we were so keen on praying to Our Blessed Lady, why we put so much emphasis on remembering her at every mass and every funeral service. He liked to go into those sorts of questions, not in a nasty way, but really trying to see what we saw, or what I saw, at any rate, in our devotion to Our Blessed Lady. I don't think he'd come across that very much in his former Catholic life, and I really felt that he wanted to share with me in loving Our Blessed Lady, as the mother of Our Blessed Jesus.'

Whether he had managed to share it or not, the priest did not say, but there seemed something symbolic about this fascination with the Virgin Mary, the embodiment of female purity and maternal compassion – the antithesis, in fact, of everything that my father's own mother had been to him. Had they ever discussed the concept of sin and penance? I asked.

'No. Hardly.'

'Did he strike you as being a happy and fulfilled man?'

Father Rose thought about this for a moment. 'No, not really. He struck me as a man who was seeking something intellectual. He was seeking some intellectual response from the people he was teaching and he didn't always get it. I feel that he felt that the intellectual standard of the people he was teaching wasn't up to the intellectual standard he was used to and had himself.'

Had Father Rose known about any attempt of my father to annul his previous marriage? There was an even longer hesitation. 'I don't think so, no. He was a very religious man, but he never discussed his marriage with me. I think with his wife living so near he didn't want to embarrass her, and the fact that she wasn't the same nationality as he was might have embarrassed him too.'

This answer was not at all what I had expected. Father Rose did not seem entirely clear about which marriage I was referring to. Why, I asked, would the fact of his wife's nationality have embarrassed him?

'I'd rather not say, but –' He seemed to be on the point of revealing his opinion after all but then to think better of it. 'I'd rather not say,' he repeated.

All this was mystifying to say the least. Father Rose went on to say that he was aware that my father had had children by a previous marriage, and that he had brought them up as Catholics. Since none of us had ever gone to mass with my father, it was obvious that he meant Samantha and Vanessa, and that he had not been aware of the existence of any other family. I also realized from when he said he had come to Campbellville that he had probably not been in Guyana when my father had carried out his attempted annulment.

Carol, who had been listening to the conversation, now suddenly joined in and described how she had first become aware of my father's religious convictions. 'I was very surprised when he came forward and wanted to join in our Easter and Lenten celebrations,' she said. 'He was very interested in the Passion, and we read the Passion on Palm Sunday, and he wanted an important part in it. I think he was the narrator. He did it very well, and it seemed to do something to him, because after that he continued to come to church, and especially the Easter vigil. How he got down here and how he reached the church we don't know, but he was able to read the scripture very well and put a lot into it.'

It was not surprising that these elements of Catholic ritual should have attracted him back to the Church. It was appropriate also that even in his religious life there should have been an element of theatre and role-playing. Once again, as in his political life, I had the same sense of a man living out his own private drama within a larger ritual, whose real meaning was concealed to those around him.

I asked Carol why she thought he had been so attracted to the Passion.

'I don't know, and up to now I don't know, and what I know about him up to then is that he was a bitter person and he was against the Church. When you talked to him he had nothing good to say about the Catholic religion. Something changed and he came forward, and I really don't know up to now what it could have been.'

I suggested the obvious symbolism of the Resurrection.

'Yeah, but you see something has to lead to the Resurrection. You have to suffer, and that's the whole point of the Resurrection, and I think he had gone through suffering. He was a sad man, there was no doubt about it, but most of it he could have done something about, but he didn't. I mean, he was partly responsible for the position he was in.'

I had no disagreement with that, but the fact that suffering was self-inflicted did not necessarily make it any easier to cope with. Like Malcolm Lowry, my father had found some kind of hell inside himself that he carried with him everywhere. The Church helped him to alleviate the burden while he was alive, and also offered the possibility of ultimate deliverance after his death. After that first decisive partici-pation in the Passion, said Carol, he would drift in to mass in such a shambolic state that many people had been surprised that he was even able to find his way to the church.

'You mean he was drunk when he came to mass?'

'Well,' she smiled, 'he'd obviously had a morning after the night before. He had a hangover, but his thinking was clear. You knew that he'd been at it the whole night. It was a little upsetting because there was nothing you could do to help him. We tried.'

'In what way?'

'You have to join organizations that can deal with the problem that he had. He didn't want to do that. That's what we find with a lot of people like him. They need their family and they need people to help them. The family have to be involved in it. Outsiders can't really help. I don't think his wife did anything to help with that.'

This did not coincide at all with what other people had told me about Marjorie's attempts to stop my father's drinking. When I asked Carol why she thought that his wife hadn't helped him, the only example she could give was that he had not joined A A. This was hardly Marjorie's fault, and I sensed that something was not being said. Was there some kind of hostility towards her because she was not a Catholic and A A was a Catholic organization? But neither she nor Father Rose seemed willing to go into this any further, and so I asked her instead what she had meant by my father's bitterness.

'I don't know what you mean by bitter. I mean "against" — that something caused him in his religion not to want God and accept the teaching of the Catholic Church, but it happens to a lot of people. The Catholic Church has a lot of harsh things, you need a lot of faith to accept them.'

'Do you think he had that faith by the end of his life?'

'I think he definitely did,' she replied with conviction, 'because he wanted the sacraments, he wanted the priest.'

My Catholic morning continued with a visit to the nearby house of Roxanna Kaiwal, an East Indian parishioner who Carol thought might be able to tell me something about my father. The house was in an affluent East Indian neighbourhood, and Carol drove me there herself in a rickety old car. Roxanna was a former deputy editor of the Guyanese *Catholic Herald*, who had worked in Guyana for Amnesty International. She was a feisty, courageous journalist who had been involved in some quite dangerous work probing into the sleazy connections between the P N C and the House of Israel sect. Her investigations had resulted in her house being ransacked by a group of Burnham's thugs. She was now a housewife, she said, and her beautiful daughter roamed restlessly around the sitting-room as we talked.

Roxanna described herself as 'small, brown and Third World'. She talked at great speed, frequently bursting into laughter, punctuating her sentences with exclamations of 'Oh my!' She had studied in Germany for six years in the early 80s, and retained a lot of affection for Europe and Britain in particular. She was a great fan of the B B C

World Service and British culture in general, and concerned about the negative cultural influence of the United States on Guyanese society, particularly the endless satellite B-movies which made up most of Guyana's TV programming.

'It used to be that all Guyanese immigrants went to Britain,' she complained. 'Now they all want to go to the States and Canada and – Oh, my! Should I say this? – I think American culture is trashy! It's just violence and lack of depth, and it's having an effect on the children, because they don't read books any more. There's a lot of functional illiteracy in Guyanese schools. I'm very worried about it. It's a violent culture, a drug culture and it's a very materialistic culture.'

She came from a very literary background, and the sitting-room was piled with books, where she had been sorting out her shelves. She had known my father through his articles and his reputation in the local cultural and literary scene, but her personal contact had been largely restricted to his appearances at mass. 'When he was sick he used to come to St Theresa's Church,' she said, 'and I always made a point of saying, "You're very welcome and I'm very glad to see you," and also because he used to live around the corner, and he used to go to this corner shop there. It's quite a famous liming place.'

The liming place was called Leo's. It had been such a regular haunt of my father's that Marjorie had once gone there and begged the owner not to sell him rum.

'They didn't bother with her, of course,' she said, 'because a sale is a sale, so sometimes after church on Sunday I would see him there and I would make a point of going to say hello to him.'

'So you're saying that he used to go there after church?'

She giggled. 'And have a drink there.'

'That's having your cake and eating it too, isn't it?' I suggested.

'Don't be so harsh!' she exclaimed indignantly. 'I think that's very naughty of you!'

Roxanna's most vivid memory of my father was his performance in a Derek Walcott play in the early 80s, 'the one about Robinson Crusoe'. A female friend of hers was putting on a production of the play at the cultural centre, and Roxanna suggested my father for one of the parts. 'My interest in getting him involved in this was really the crusading bit,' she explained. 'I thought, therapy, you know. Eventually she did take him in and he did quite a good job, although there was a problem. He had a hernia at the time, and she's trying to get him not to dress the part half-naked. She thought this would look very embarrassing, this hernia bouncing around on stage!' She giggled. 'But she didn't know how to say this to him! And she's doing it in a nice way, and he's saying, "No, no, no, I'm going to go through with this," insisting on playing the role, and I was in the audience, and there was a bit of a murmur, but after that people forgot that and got involved in the play itself.'

I remembered the same bulge in his stomach when he visited England and I winced at the thought of him showing off his hernia to the audience in a characteristically perverse display of honesty.

The conversation turned to the subject of my father's guilt. I told her about the semi-religious imagery people had used to describe him, in which the word guilt was often used to account for his political actions. I commented that it seemed an odd motive for such behaviour.

'Oh!' she disagreed. 'That is often a motive for political action.'

I said that the fact that it was common did not necessarily make it acceptable. I had always thought of guilt as an essentially selfish emotion, distinct from genuine altruism or solidarity. In my experience people who engaged in political action because they felt guilty were more interested in alleviating their own consciences than in effecting real change on behalf of others. I told her that while I could understand why an Englishman could despise the British Empire and feel ashamed about the crimes it had committed, I could not understand why he should personally assume the guilt for events that he had not directly participated in.

'That must have been his religious instinct,' she said confidently. 'It's like forgiveness. Can you forgive a murderer who's murdered somebody else's children? When I was in Germany we were discussing this with the Jesuits, and they were talking about Hitler and everybody else who had done wrong, and someone was saying, "It can't be you that forgives, it has to be the father or the mother of one of the victims," and I was thinking, it's the Catholic theology – if you're the body of Christ, that person who is also the body of Christ has also done something wrong and therefore it's very important that you, as the body of Christ, can forgive also. And I think it's a very important principle, although it sounds very complicated and may be a bit airy-fairy. I don't know if you understand what I mean.'

'Ummm,' I said doubtfully, unsure how much of any of this had to do with my father.

'So I think, yes, you must forgive other people who have done wrong to other people. It is a perfectly valid principle, and I think this is what your father was doing. He was not just forgiving, he was feeling guilty. It's like collective guilt. You are responsible for other human beings. It's Cain and Abel, you are your brother's keeper. Yes, of course you are.'

Once again my father was being presented to me as the Jesus Christ of the tropics, even by someone who admitted that she hardly knew him. Yet even stripped of its Catholic imagery, her exposition of guilt did not strike me as a very convincing explanation for my father's motivation, even if he had believed it himself. It was not that I thought the association between the Holocaust and slavery was misplaced. The industrialized extermination of six million Jews and the enslavement and mass transportation of millions of Africans to the Caribbean were both historical crimes of enormous dimensions, originating from European myths of racial superiority. The fact that the horrors of slavery belonged to the more distant past may have lessened their moral and political impact, but it did not make them any less real or barbaric. While slavery may not have been explicitly genocidal, the trade in human chattels destroyed millions of lives, both physically and spiritually, and remains one of the most evil chapters in European history.

Nevertheless, I did not see collective guilt as a theological concept of forgiveness, but as a concrete historical charge which aimed to establish national responsibility for the crimes of the Third Reich. While the Final Solution was rightly held up before the Germans as an episode worthy of national shame, the barbarism of the slave trade and the poisonous racial attitudes it engendered have never been fully assimilated or expunged by the countries that had once benefited from it. Even in my schooldays, it was Britain's key role in the abolition of the slave trade that had been stressed in the history we were taught, rather than the crucial British role in developing and expanding the trade in the first place, or the contribution that slavery made to the industrial revolution. In this way abolition was presented to us as another example of the triumph of Anglo-Saxon liberal values, while the centuries of slavery that had preceded it were relegated to a minor historical episode, and its legacy in the present was ignored completely.

Nowadays the educational emphasis on historical achievements and the diet of costume dramas and heritage reproductions of the past tend to obscure the more unsavoury aspects of British imperial history. In the West Indies however, it was precisely those aspects that stood out most in the popular memory. With his intensely moralistic attitude to politics, and his sense of personal implication and responsibility, it was perfectly possible that my father had reacted to his country's imperial past with the same disgust that some young Germans felt about the Nazi genocide, that he had felt a need personally to make up for it. The recent memory of World War II and the Holocaust may well have intensified his disgust at European racism, and his sense of coming from a bankrupt civilization to which he had nothing to contribute. Such an attitude was admirable, certainly preferable to the vacuous and dishonest celebration of British 'achievements'.

It was not the nature of the crime that I questioned, but the irrationality of my father's response to it, the way that the rejection of his country's past had been accompanied by the rejection or reinvention of his own. Even if the sacrifice of his family had really been inspired by the noble motives that Roxanna and others wanted to attribute to him, the fact remained that to treat his wife and children the way he had done because of what the British Empire had done was an act of pointless, destructive lunacy that benefited no one except my father himself, and it was doubtful, in the long run, whether it had even helped to relieve his own tormented conscience.

Resurrection. Sacrifice. Atonement. It was turning out to be another Guyanese morning. I decided to visit the nearby liming place where my father used to stop off on his way after church to meet the owner who had ignored Marjorie's pleas not to sell rum to her husband. Roxanna said that it was only a few minutes' walk away. She came out to give me directions from her front gate and shook her head in dismay at the sight of the withered water lilies floating in the storm drain outside. 'My lilies!' she said sadly. 'I only put them here a few weeks ago and now they're dying!'

I found Leo's rum shop on a dusty street corner just around the corner from St Theresa's Church.

Outside Leo's rum shop an advertisement for El Dorado rum bore the self-explanatory logo of a golden bottle. This was my father's little city of gold, where he came to refresh himself after mass. The shop itself took up the bottom floor of a two-storey wooden building, with a little counter hatch looking out on to a sheltered porch, where there were two tables and some chairs. I went to the counter and asked for Leo, expecting to find some fat petit bourgeois trader with a rum-soaked vest and a hard glint in his eye, a man in whom all human feeling had been extinguished through his complicity in the ruin of his customers. But in Guyana nothing turns out exactly the way you expect. The real Leo turned out to be a soft-spoken, laidback East Indian in his mid-forties, who was handing out free sweets to some poor local kids. He was wearing spectacles hanging from his neck by a cord, a pair of stripey shorts and a Nike T-shirt with a jagged pattern. I scanned his face briefly for the tell-tale signs of greed and corruption, but he seemed thoughtful, friendly and compassionate.

When I told him who I was, he stopped what he was doing and came round from behind the counter to talk to me. He spoke slowly, his voice fading to a murmur towards the end of his sentences as though he could barely be bothered to finish them. He came originally from a village in East Demerara, he said, about twenty-six miles from Georgetown, and he had heard of my father long before he met him.

'I've heard the name Bill Carr since I was a little boy,' he said. 'I remember growing up and people saying "Oh, Bill Carr is in the village," and everybody wanted to know. Someone famous was coming to the village. It was like Bobby Moore coming to visit.'

'Why was he so famous?'

'Probably because of his academic skills,' the rum-shop owner explained. 'That's what he was famous for, but he was very respected. He was looked up very high in society, even in the rural areas.'

Bill Carr had gone on to become one of his regular customers, he said, and often stopped by in his church clothes, although he had never paid any attention to which church he went to. He stood up facing the hatch with his back to the dusty street and both hands on the counter in front of him. 'I can still see him standing here like this,' he said, smiling at the memory. 'He would just purchase his drink and go away most times. Very rarely, when he bought a bottle, he say, "Leo, can I have one drink here and then leave?" and he would open the bottle and I would give him a cup and he would pour, probably one or two drinks, put his stuff in his bag and go home. He wasn't the kind of person who would drink and behave in such a way as to pick an argument with someone. He was always friendly, always loving, always kind. He always shared his knowledge.'

'Did he used to talk a lot when he came here?'

'Oh, yeah!' he drawled. 'We used to talk a lot! He will tell me about his university life, and sometimes he will tell me about his home in England and where he was raised. He would say, you know, that he wanted to probably go back there someday. I don't know if he felt probably his time was drawing near. The call, the inner call was there in him to go back there some time, you know? I had the feeling he had a family home, the way he used to speak, that he had some sort of attachment back in England.'

As I listened to the philosophical rum-shop owner talking about my father's 'inner call', as though his desire to return to England had been part of some universal rite of passage, I wondered if Guyana itself contained something of that 'congenial' atmosphere that my father had once projected on to the past; a pre-T V society where talk and friendship were still important and people still paid more attention to each other than they did to the stream of images and vicarious experiences being pumped into countless living-rooms elsewhere in the world. It also seemed to be a society in which human weaknesses were accepted and not judged or condemned, so that a chronic alcoholic like my father could be regarded with compassion and even tenderness by the man who sold him his rum.

Certainly Leo spent a lot of time observing people from his little cornershop hatch, and his worldview was imbued with a philosophical, almost Buddhist fatalism not usually encountered in a local cornershop owner. As I imagined my father reading the scriptures at St Theresa's and then telling stories about his past to the rum-shop oracle sitting in his hatch like a priest in the confessional, I warmed towards him once again. Even though Leo talked about his ruined customer with a kind of tenderness and affection, he had reportedly refused Marjorie's urgent requests to stop selling rum to him. I asked him whether he had noticed my father's physical deterioration.

'Bill was always easy-going,' he said. 'He never complained of any ill-health. I knew he had quite a big pouch really, and I used to look at it and I was a little disturbed by that pouch, but he never complained of no pains.'

Did he remember any encounters with my father's wife?

'Yeah.' He sighed and shook his head. 'Well, his wife came one time and she started off, you know. There were times when Bill did come and spend some time. I remember one time he did drink, and he fell down, and I couldn't see him, because he fell down below the counter, and when I came out I saw him there and I asked a guy to help me take him home. So his wife did come round and she started to quarrel, and Bill was very "Do you know this lady?" He used to ignore her.'

'He used to say he didn't know his own wife?'

He laughed. 'Yeah. He used to say, "You know this person?" And I said no. You know. She was aggressive to me.'

'But you continued to sell him drinks, even after she came?'

'Well, now and then really, right?' he murmured, a little defensively. 'But he left me and used to go to some other store, because I didn't want any trouble and I used to tell him, "Please, I don't want any trouble," so he left me. I lost him really. I missed him. What I liked was Bill coming round and talking and being together, it was even more than the sale. The sale didn't matter to me really. It was the company I used to appreciate so much. Sometimes I felt guilty, because when I saw him and he drank, I felt to myself, "I should say no!" But then he used to be very, very out of place. If you'd have turned Bill away, you would be sorry even for your own self that he will walk away without getting the alcohol. So I was torn a little bit between two things, trying to make Bill happy one way and making him unhappy another way.'

'Did he have many friends?'

'No. Bill wasn't a guy who had lots of people around with him, at least when he came here. He will walk with his bag, and then he will go back. He used to buy, remember, not only booze, he used to buy groceries too.'

The limited selection of goods visible through the hatch did not give the impression that Leo's grocery trade was exactly thriving. He mentioned that he had another shop on Sheriff Avenue and I asked him how business was going.

'Not too well,' he said indifferently. 'But I don't mind. I've achieved my goals in life. I know who I am and I'm contented. Now I just want to share my knowledge with others.'

There was a serene smile on the rum-shop oracle's face, the smile of a man who had freed himself of material attachments and found his place in the world. I shook hands and wished him well, and walked away, down the hot, dusty street where my father had once dragged his wasted flesh in his alcoholic haze, along his private Via Dolorosa, towards the green oasis of St Theresa's Church, where the Virgin Mary waited to receive him with outstretched arms.

Chapter Seventeen

Almost every day in Guyana I would pass St Stanislaus College, my old school on Brickdam, next to the main cathedral. The original L-shaped building was still there, with its familiar sky-blue lining and its elegant wooden arches above the main entrance, but an ugly concrete annexe had been added in the courtyard where the playground used to be. It was there on Brickdam, virtually in front of the school where he taught, that my old maths teacher Father Darke was murdered by a member of the House of Israel in 1979.

I could not remember much about him, beyond the fact that he had once been generous enough to give me 10 out of 200 for neat drawings in a maths test, instead of zero. At the time I lived in Guyana the Jesuits had not been especially political, and it was not until the early 70s that they began to involve themselves directly in the opposition to Burnham. The main forum for Jesuit dissent was the *Catholic Herald*, which in the early 70s began publishing articles critical of the regime's election-rigging and human rights abuses.

Father Darke had been a photographer for the *Herald*, even while he continued to work at the school. On the day he was killed, a big demonstration had been held outside the city courts to protest the arrest of Walter Rodney, Rupert Roopnaraine and others on trumped-up charges of arson. Suddenly the demonstration was attacked by members of the House of Israel and Father Darke ran back into St Stanislaus to get his camera. He returned to find some members of the sect beating an assistant editor of the *Herald*. He began to photograph the scene, when the gang suddenly turned on him, pursuing him down Brickdam, where they stabbed him to death with a bayonet a short distance away from where my father and Martin Carter were standing. The House of Israel rarely carried out such attacks spontaneously.

The P N C had later excluded the Catholic Church from education in Guyana and now St Stanislaus was no longer run by the Jesuits. But I often thought of poor Father Darke when I went past my old school on my trips across Georgetown. My two terms at St Stanislaus were among the few good memories I had taken with me from Guyana. I used to cycle there each day from Canje Street, crossing Sheriff Avenue and cycling along Brickdam. Apart from a Canadian diplomat's son called Edwards, I was the only white kid in the school, but despite the racial atmosphere in Guyana I was accepted on equal terms by the other pupils, and I enjoyed being there more than any other school in my childhood.

The only hostility I encountered came from an East Indian kid called Madramootoo, who was my tormentor during my first term. Whether Madramootoo had a grudge against white people or simply took a personal dislike to me, he did his best to make my life miserable. I had never had any trouble with such school bullies before, and as a result I was too intimidated to do anything about it, so that my first few weeks at the school gradually became a daily humiliation.

Madramootoo's bullying raised the issues of violence and physical courage that were so dear to my father's heart. As usual, he had a literary answer to my problem. He told me to read *The Red Badge of Courage* and *Tom Brown's Schooldays*. The latter so stirred me with its ending, when Tom Brown finally takes on Flashman and wins, that a new heroic possibility now opened before me. Both my father and the book seemed to be telling me to fight back, but the prospect of actually fighting someone seemed as terrifying as it was attractive. For days I tried in vain to work up the courage to stand up to Madramootoo. Then finally I went into school one morning, seething with pent-up aggression with the image of Tom Brown defeating Flashman fixed firmly in my mind. Madramootoo was sitting next to me in class, exuding sneering malevolence, waiting to resume his daily torment. As usual he picked up my pencils and threw them on the floor, in a symbolic assertion of his power over me. Until then I had meekly submitted and picked them up, but now, to his amazement and mine, I reached over, grabbed his pencils and, looking him straight in the eye, dropped them on the floor.

I had thrown down the gauntlet and the look he gave me in return left no doubt as to what its consequences would be. All that morning I sat next to him, hardly able to concentrate on my lessons as I contemplated the moment of reckoning. The fight took place during the mid-morning break, when we normally went to the school shop to eat roti and hot sauce. Hardly had we come out on to the playground when Madramootoo and I tore into each other, flailing and swinging our boyish fists and wrestling each other clumsily in the dirt, to the cheers of the other boys. Much to my own amazement, I emerged dazed but victorious from this ineffectual scuffle, and found myself being acclaimed by my classmates. It was just like the book. After that Madramootoo never bothered me again. This convergence of literature and life filled me with such a sense of my own invincibility that I subsequently tried to repeat the performance with Roger Mendonza after he had beaten up my brother Bruce, only to take a serious hiding outside the front gate in Canje Street.

My relations with the Jesuits and lay teachers at the school were very good. The priests in Guyana were young, idealistic and liberal in their outlook. Educational standards were high, we were not force-fed with religion, and there was no corporal punishment. The only conflict I ever had was with my art teacher, a blonde English Jesuit who once asked us all to paint a picture of how we imagined the Virgin Mary. This was not a very wise decision as far as I was concerned, since I could not draw and ended up painting a monstrous old hag. In what I thought was a witty recognition of my lack of artistic ability, I entitled this creation 'The Beautiful Virgin Mary', with a question mark after Virgin. In fact I had no idea what the word virgin meant, and assumed it was some kind of synonym for beautiful. I certainly did not know that I was challenging the immaculate conception, but when the young priest saw the painting and its title, his normally cheerful face turned beetroot-red and he tore the picture to pieces in front of the class and never spoke a friendly word to me again.

In my last few weeks in Guyana I took part in the only real game of cricket I ever played in the West Indies. It was an internal school match in the courtyard, and as I put on pads and gloves for virtually the first time in my life I was extremely nervous. Some of the teachers tried to reassure me and to demonstrate the basic techniques, but when I went out to bat I was bowled out immediately without even making contact with the ball. I trudged disconsolately back from the crease, painfully conscious of my clumsiness. My French teacher Mr Duprée commiserated me and gently explained to me what I had done wrong. Afterwards we sat together and watched the rest of the game and I felt better. Most of the teachers behaved with the same humanity and accessibility. Under the enlightened direction of the headmaster, Father

Hopkinson, they took a personal interest in their pupils and conducted their classes with authority that was never tyrannical, which made them liked rather than feared. I was sorry to have to leave them.

It was an entirely different story at the Jesuit boarding-school that I went to in the north of England in 1968. Like everybody else in my family, I remember the year of our return from Guyana as a period of dislocation, sadness and confusion. Our world had effectively fallen apart, and the adjustment to life in England was slow and painful. My mother managed to buy a little house on a newly built estate in Cambridge. It was the end of a fifteen-year ordeal for her, but now she had the enormous task of trying to patch up our bruised psyches and to find a way to support us.

The circumstances were not exactly helpful. The house had barely been finished when we moved into it and we hardly had any furniture. None of us really had any idea why we were in England at all, or whether our father was coming back. There were conflicts with some of our neighbours, who looked down on a woman bringing up kids by herself. They took every opportunity to exert their authority over us when my mother was not around and even when she was. I despised those small-town bigots who sat in judgement upon us – like Mr Pierce who told my mother he was going to 'fix' me in such a way that no one would ever find out about it. I was moody and resentful with everybody, with a tendency to hysterical rages. Like my father I took to wrecking rooms and throwing things. I fought constantly with my mother and my sister in particular.

All this was in contrast to the self-control I had displayed when we flew back from Guyana, which lasted for a few weeks afterwards. Then I had tried to assume the role of 'the man of the house'. But finally the role demanded more than I could put into it. I have sometimes thought of my disintegration during those first months back in England as a kind of delayed shock, a violent reaction against all the guilt, anger and unhappiness that was the legacy of my parents' marriage, and yet for some strange reason which neither I nor anybody else has ever been able to explain, I often seemed to be trying to copy my father.

I never mentioned any of this in my letters to him, and if he knew about it he never referred to it. After trying various options, which included a short period living at a friend's house, my mother finally accepted Father Hopkinson's recommendation and sent me to Mount St Mary's College, an obscure Jesuit boarding school in Derbyshire. She assumed that the two schools would be similar, but they turned out to be at opposite ends of the scale. If my first experience of irrational male authority was living in my father's house, the second was at the hands of the Jesuits in England. While my father exerted his power over his children through unpredictable moods and explosions of temper, the Jesuits were calmly systematic, but equally tyrannical. Unlike their progressive counterparts in Guyana, the staff at the Mount were mostly reactionary gargoyles, who looked down on the pupils in their charge from some remote Jesuitical plateau enforcing discipline with clinical regularity and strictness.

Both the priests and the lay teachers dispensed corporal punishment freely, using leather straps, the back of their hand or even cricket bats, but the most common instrument of punishment was the ferula, a shoe-shaped instrument made of whalebone and rubber, usually applied to the hand. These 'cracks' were issued in the form of a 'cheque', which the offender had to fill out with the number of blows to be received and the Latin initials 'A.M.D.G.', signifying 'For the greater Glory of God'. At the appointed hour each week, a queue of offenders would be found outside the ferula room, where the cheques were signed and the cracks administered.

The organization of the school was strictly hierarchical. After the teachers came the prefects, who could also inflict a range of punishments. And below the prefects each school year exerted what power it could over the year below, a situation that permitted all kinds of bullying and semi-licensed brutality. In this violent, prison-like atmosphere, some 400-odd adolescent boys underwent the initiation rites of the English middle classes, shunted back and forth between the chapel, the cadet corps, the playing fields and the classroom under the watchful eye of St Ignatius's grotesque soldiers of Christ.

As removed as it was from the twentieth century, the school could not insulate itself entirely from the outside world, and I soon found parallels between the various youth rebellions erupting elsewhere in the world and the situation in which I found myself. I became obsessed with revolutions and revolutionaries, and read about them constantly. I saw the school as an oppressive state which had to be resisted. Any sort of disobedience from missing mass to robbing the school kitchen seemed like a blow for freedom. My heroes were no longer Charlton

Heston and Jeff Chandler, but Che Guevara and Malcolm McDowell, shooting his teachers in the last scene of Lindsay Anderson's *If . . .* I was constantly in trouble, and when I left at the age of sixteen the Jesuits were no doubt as glad to see me go as I was to leave. By that time the worst of that earlier anger seemed to have burned itself out, or perhaps it had simply found a more legitimate target. And so I passed from an absurd childhood to an absurd adolescence, ready to begin my life in an adult society whose values I regarded as largely false, hypocritical and oppressive.

But still to this day the teachers at St Stanislaus School remain among the few representatives of adult authority who I am able to look back on with warmth and respect, and I never passed it without wondering what my life would have been like if I had stayed there.

I finally visited the school on my way to the presbytery, where I arranged to meet Father Malcolm Rodrigues, S.J., the former vice-chancellor of the university and a prominent member of the Jesuit opposition to Burnham. The school was now mixed and the Jesuits were long gone, but as I watched the boys and girls mingling in the playground I felt nostalgic for those nine months I had spent there. I introduced myself to the headmistress and asked if any of my old teachers from that period were still around. She coldly informed me that the Jesuits had 'withdrawn their services', in a way that made it clear she had not been particularly sorry to have seen them go, and said that she didn't think there were any of them left in Guyana.

There did not seem much else to talk about, and I went on to the presbytery to see Father Rodrigues. He was a light-skinned Guyanese in his late fifties, with none of the pale, bloodless severity of the Jesuits I had known in England. On the contrary he reminded me immediately of the priests I had known at St Stanislaus, with his intellectual energy, open-mindedness and youthful air. In addition to his work at the university he had the reputation of being an activist-priest, with political leanings towards Liberation Theology, and I knew that he had been closely involved in a strike of sugar workers in the 1970s. He had also been a friend of my father's, and had officiated at his funeral service. They had first met in the course of their political activities, he said, and later got to know each other at the university. He remembered my father as an outstanding academic and a gifted public speaker, not only at political meetings, but also at the university trade union, where he used to articulate the concerns of ordinary, non-academic workers.

Over the years the two of them had many conversations about religion, and I asked him if my father struck him as a man who was looking for some ultimate meaning that Marxism had failed to provide.

'I wouldn't put it as an ultimate meaning,' he replied. 'He was one who was always searching for a meaning that went beyond the immediate – the immediate referring to particular issues. He was always very conscious of that, and I think that is what eventually led him right back to the practice of his religion, to accept back once more, that there may be values, there may be truths, there may be certainties, which cannot just be established by the normal scientific analysis that we engage in at present. I got that sense of him as time went on. He never gave up the search.'

I told him about my father describing the mass as an oasis in one of his letters and commented on how surprised his family in England had been to learn of his reconversion. When I mentioned his attempt to annul his marriage, Father Malcolm looked as blank as Father Rose had done. It was beginning to look as though the annulment would have to be filed away amongst the many unsolved mysteries of my father's life. Had the whole episode been another of my father's attempts to unhook himself from his own past? Certainly, the annulment would have meant that as far as the church was concerned his family had never existed, but it was clearly not a mystery that Father Malcolm was able to shed any light on.

'I think that one of the things that allowed us to gravitate together was that I myself had been very active in the movement,' Father Malcolm said. 'Because of my activity we met, and he used to refer to me as "the Marxist priest", and I would correct him and say, "No, justice is part of the Church's teaching and I am just practising what I believe in. Justice and human rights have to be struggled for. If in the struggle for that I line up next to a Marxist, I have no problem with that." Now I think this is the sort of thing that began him thinking that maybe the Church had much more to offer than just to be this Sunday mass-goer, and I think he began to pose new questions and to see new meanings, even in the Sunday mass – the oasis aspect.'

Even though there was a clear connection between my father's intellectual fascination with Liberation Theology and his later conversion, it still did not explain to me his more emotional attachment to such elemental Catholic symbols as the Virgin Mary and the Crucifixion, which the more other-worldly Father Rose had described. I asked if my father had seemed like a man suffering from guilt.

'I think he had a major problem,' Father Malcolm replied with obvious reticence. 'Of course you know the problem, and he battled with it, but in the circumstances it was very difficult for him to deal with it.'

I had not heard any evidence to suggest that my father had ever seriously battled with his alcoholism, and I asked about the 'circumstances' that had apparently impeded him.

'Let me put it this way. Normally with that particular problem, the support within your immediate circles is absolutely crucial, and his wife was not a support to him in that sense.'

I told him of Marjorie's attempts to stop my father drinking, and her desperate visits to Leo's rum shop.

'Well, that may be true earlier on,' he conceded, 'but certainly in the latter period . . . I've been to their home and, you know, they were both smelling heavily of alcohol. And for Bill, he should be in no place, if you really want to overcome it, where that is going on.'

I was not sure what to make of this. Marjorie herself had admitted to me that she had learned to drink from my father. Perhaps she had had her moments of weakness too, but she could hardly be held responsible for my father's alcoholism, when he had never really tried to fight it himself. I had often asked myself since coming to Guyana whether there might have been more social pressure on my father to seek a cure if he had lived in England. It was a question that was impossible to answer. Certainly it was difficult to imagine that he would have been treated with the same kind of extraordinary tolerance at an English university that he received at U G.

'I think in the latter years definitely the tolerance was exceptional,' Father Malcolm agreed. 'But I think it was correct, because alcoholism is a sickness, it's not just somebody behaving bad. But the problem about that treatment is that the patient has to assent to it. Now I think that that explains the tolerance. When Bill came to lecture, he normally came quite normal, as far as alcoholics call normality. And he normally lectured very well, and I think people appreciated that. I always felt very sad at the end, because I would see him coming down, and by then he was using a walking stick, and he looked very bad, because of course it affects your face and the rest of you, and I always felt that he had so much to give and there was so much more that could still be given, but this particular illness was obviously taking its toll, not only on his capacity to give it, but on his life.'

For a moment Father Malcolm seemed on the verge of shifting responsibility for my father's failure to seek treatment on to my father himself, but even as he described his alcoholism as a sickness, he seemed convinced that its causes lay in the external situation around him. This seemed to me to ignore the psychological reasons for my father's alcoholism. But the progressive priest seemed unable to accept that a man with my father's political ideas and social conscience could harbour self-destructive tendencies. 'Once or twice I gave him a lift on campus and I would discuss his illness. He began to look very ashen as the liver began to give out, and I think he was hoping to go to England for awhile, have a total break and maybe have himself looked after. He needed a complete change and maybe get some treatment, and in my mind a complete break meant getting totally away from the context here, which could have been contributing towards the alcohol. I mean, we mustn't put Bill out of a context. He was in a context which, for a professional non-Guyanese, although he was very much in the Guyanese situation, was very oppressive, and somebody with that kind of character could well find it almost intolerable, and they might drink.' This was no doubt true, but my father had started drinking long before coming to Guyana, when his circumstances were not nearly so unfavourable.

The first time Father Malcolm learned that my father's illness had reached a new and possibly terminal phase was when Marjorie rang him two weeks before my father's death, asking him to come round. He found my father lying in his bed, weak and barely conscious. 'He was very, very sick, there was no doubt about it. I said to him, "Bill, you don't look very well. Would you like me to bring you the sacrament of the sick to anoint you?" and he said yes. So I went off and I got the oils and I anointed him.'

Father Rose had also told me that he had administered the sacraments of the sick to my father. Assuming that the memory of both men was correct, it now seemed, perhaps inevitably, that my father had in fact received extreme unction twice, from two different priests. Perhaps he himself had not realized what was happening as he moved closer towards death and his faculties had begun to shut down.

'The second visit when I got there,' Father Malcolm went on, 'his breathing was bad and the eyes wouldn't open, and he clearly couldn't articulate, and I told him that I would say some prayers and so forth, and I think I said, "Squeeze my hand if you hear me clear." I was right down there and I got the squeeze from him. He was still conscious, and I said the prayers for the dying, because to me he was clearly dying.'

That was the last time the priest had seen him alive. The next day my father died and Father Malcolm was asked by Marjorie to take care of the funeral arrangements. He had wanted to avoid making the funeral a mournful occasion, he said, and had tried to make the service a 'thanksgiving in the widest possible sense' – for all my father had contributed to Guyanese society. Unlike Father Rose, he thought that my father had died a fulfilled man, satisfied with his achievements, whose only regret might have been not to have lived to see the 'creativity of the many coming to the fore' after the 1992 elections. I had no doubt that my father would indeed have liked to see the PPP's belated triumph, but I was not at all convinced that he had died a contented man. Did Father Malcolm really believe this? Or did he just think that it was what one of Bill Carr's children would want to hear? Despite everything, I would have liked to believe that my father had on his deathbed looked back peacefully and contentedly on a lifetime's achievement, knowing that he had done all he had wanted to do. But precisely because he was my father, I could not believe it.

That evening I got a phone call from Roxanna Kaiwal at the hotel. She had been talking to a friend of hers, who remembered being shocked to see my father and Sandra Williams drinking and smoking in public in the early 70s. She had also been reading about a white plantation owner called John Smith who had destroyed himself through rum during the last century. Perhaps, she suggested, my father was part of a tradition. Perhaps he had found his heart of darkness in the Caribbean.

I agreed that it was a possibility. Over the years I had often looked upon the image of Kurtz in Conrad's novel as another of the metaphors that I had used to explain my father, the white man removed from the constraints of his own society and the identity that his past confers upon him, who discovers the fatal flaw in himself and willingly tumbles into it. But if he had found his heart of darkness in the West Indies, he had also found drama, intensity and laughter, and a community that had accepted him and even given him a position of prestige. He had excelled as a teacher and fulfilled his youthful vocation to 'help someone else discover what he really feels' many times over. In the process he had won many friends and admirers. He had in Marjorie and her children found a family with whom he seemed reasonably happy. Yet at the end of his life, just when the situation in Guyana was improving, just when he should have been looking forward to a peaceful retirement in the society where he had made his home, he had apparently been preparing to give it all up.

Chapter Eighteen

In the early 80s my father played the part of the Englishman Harry Trewe in Derek Walcott's two-man play *Pantomime*. This was the play that Roxanna Kaiwal's friend had directed, and my father's involvement in it, despite his worsening physical condition, was partly a labour of love. He always loved Derek Walcott's writing and once told Ian McDonald that Walcott was writing so much good poetry that it was impossible to keep up with his output.

The part of Harry Trewe could almost have been written for my father. *Pantomime* is set in an unnamed Caribbean island, where expatriate hotel owner Harry Trewe asks his black servant Jackson to act in a cabaret version of Robinson Crusoe, with the roles reversed, so that he, the white man, will play Man Friday and the servant will play Crusoe. Initially intended by Trewe as harmless entertainment, the 'pantomime' turns more serious and dangerous when the two begin rehearsing and improvising, and the reluctant Jackson begins to play his part too convincingly, allowing Walcott to reverse the master/servant role and make various ironic observations on the tragic history of black/white relations in the Caribbean.

This was the play Moses Nagamootoo had recalled when he described my father as a late-twentieth-century Robinson Crusoe shipwrecked in the tropics, and the image seems to have been drawn as much from the character of Harry Trewe as it was from my father's own life. Perhaps in his later years my father also saw himself as Harry Trewe, the ex-English liberal, the former music hall actor, the Englishman stranded in the tropics, cut off from his own past, who cries out despairingly, 'Where is the wife from whom I vowed never to be sundered? How old is my little son? If he could see his father like this, mad with memories of them . . . Even Job had his family. But I am alone, alone, I am all alone!'

Like Walcott's fictional character, my father spent much of the latter part of his life yearning for his native land, if not his family.

His vision of England had evolved over the years from his earlier feelings of bitterness and alienation into nostalgia. Perhaps, as some people had said, this nostalgia was sharpened by the madness that overtook Guyana during the 70s and 80s. Or perhaps the change in his attitude towards England was simply the natural consequence of time passing, and that strange tendency to idealize what is no longer retrievable and go back to the beginning, which often overtakes human beings as they get older.

Exactly what my father's intentions had been during his aborted attempt to return to England was something that nobody in his Guyanese family seemed able to clarify. Both Marjorie and Vanessa insisted that he had never intended to go by himself, and that despite the endless arguments and discussions about it, no concrete plans had ever been made for him to go back with anyone else either. Even the vague plans that were discussed, Marjorie said, had never involved him coming to live with any member of his first family. Yet the letter that my father sent to my niece had clearly stated that he was coming back by himself, with his suitcase full of books, and he had even given a date and time for my sister to go and meet him at the airport. And since the letter had not mentioned an address where he would be staying, and since we knew that he was too ill to look after himself, it seemed obvious that he intended to stay with her.

It now seemed clear to me that the letter to my niece had been written and sent without anyone in his Guyanese family knowing about it, but this still did not clarify the mystery as to why he was intending to come back in the first place. Apart from Marjorie and Vanessa, the only other person who knew anything about my father's attempt to return to England was Compton Abrams, a long-term friend of Marjorie's and my father's, who had lived with them in the same house for many years. I met him in the secondary school where he was headmaster. As we talked in his office, the din of children playing during the morning break could be heard in the background. Like most of my father's friends, he was immediately likeable, humorous but also reflective as he delivered his words with care, in his rich, sonorous Guyanese accent. I had met him briefly that first night at Stone Avenue. He was cool but co-operative now, even though he knew about the letters I had written. He told me how he had first met my father in the early 70s, when he had started courting Marjorie.

'One night I heard singing outside the house,' he said, smiling at the memory, 'and someone was playing a guitar and singing "Guantanamera", and Marjorie came running into my bedroom and she said, "Oh, my God, Compton! Go outside. It's Bill Carr out there and if you don't go he'll wake up the whole neighbourhood!" He had come round there with a friend and a guitar, and this I'm telling you is about after midnight, and he's singing "Guantanamera" and the other chap is playing the guitar! So this was the kind of humour that he had. From the time we became acquainted it seemed as though a mutual bond of love was struck up between us, so that we remained friends until the day he died. It's not to say that things were always nice and smooth between us. Bill could be very difficult sometimes. We had our little ups and downs, but the downs were so small that you don't even remember them, but they were a part of the whole relationship. Bill didn't have the heart and guts to go out and kill a chicken. He could make some noise when he wanted to but, you know, I suppose he studied too much literature.'

The fact that my father had studied too much literature had not had much effect on his violence in the past, and my sister herself had told him some of the incidents that she remembered. Compton had spent a lot of time with her during her visit to Guyana in 1978, and he was familiar with the stories of my father's 'other side', yet he still seemed to regard them with the same incredulity as everyone else.

'One night Anna and I were talking,' he remembered, 'and she's telling me how he had slugged your mother, and she came home one day and saw your mother with a beefsteak over her eye. And I'm saying, "Well, who did it?" And she says, "You don't understand what I'm telling you." But it's like, you know, that's not the person that I have seen!'

Didn't he think it was strange that there had been such a transformation?

'Yes, but the transformation was not an overnight transformation. We will agree that there'd been a period of time. And as a man gets older, he tends to reflect on his actions and attitudes, right? I mean, you're not going to continue making the same mistakes all the time. It did hurt him a lot with you children, you know. I suppose one of Bill's problems early on was that he couldn't jolly well look at you and say, "I love you." You know we got some men like that. They'd feel it inside, but they can't say it, because for them to admit it would be a sign of weakness, and your father in his early days was a robust, manly man, and that was the whole problem with him.'

As far as I was concerned, this kind of masculine 'strength' was in itself a weakness, and it certainly wasn't a satisfactory explanation of my father's drastic disengagement from his family. Listening to Compton's loyal defence of his friend, I wondered once again why he had wanted to give up the close relationships that he had built up over the years and return to a country where he really had nothing but memories, and a family that he had virtually lost contact with.

'He always said that he had no intentions of ever returning,' Compton said, 'and I would say, "Now you're saying that, but I feel everybody should return to their roots to see what it's like." And then I went to England and I had a book that a friend had written called *London before the Blitz* and I showed it to him, and it was bringing back memories of all sorts of things, you know, and he started to develop not an interest, but a curiosity, and time passed and he went to the States, he went to Canada, and I said, "What about England? I mean you really should go back and see what the place is like." '

I commented on how much his feelings towards England seemed to have changed when I met him there. Compton nodded in agreement. 'Yes, because he had mellowed a lot. He always talked about Yorkshire and the Moors and that sort of thing, and all this nostalgia. And I suppose it's the fact that he was getting on in years and in strength as well, and maybe like – which fish does that, the salmon or the trout, return to the same water every year?'

I couldn't remember either, but the image was appropriate. From the moment he had started talking about going back to England, Compton remembered, Marjorie had advised him against it, pointing out that he had no family to go back to and that he couldn't expect his children to look after him, but my father's obsession with England continued to grow.

'He had hoped he would get a workshop at Downing College or something,' Compton explained, 'where he would get a small room to live in with enough money to keep himself going, and he would not be a bother to anybody.'

This was not the way that my father had eventually announced his reappearance, but the pieces of the fantasy were beginning to fall into place, since it was at Downing where Leavis had held court. Compton did not know of any practical steps that had been taken to realize this absurd scheme. I mentioned the letter that he had sent to my niece, and pointed out that some practical steps did appear to have been taken, and that my father even seemed to have booked a flight. Why had he made these plans without telling his Guyanese family and friends? I asked.

Compton looked blank. 'I can't really answer that question. I don't know.'

'And what about what happened later? Why did he decide not to come?'

'Shouldn't you tell me?' he asked ironically.

It sounded like an accusation. I knew that he was referring to the letters I had written, and I reiterated the circumstances behind them yet again. He said that Marjorie had not known about the letter to my niece, and agreed that my father must have written it and sent it without showing it to her. This still did not answer the question as to why he had written it in the first place. No one, it seemed, had the answers to that, and no one seemed to want to speculate. There were eerie parallels between this attempted reappearance and our expulsion over twenty years before. In 1967 he had told us that we were going back to England and that he would be joining us the following year. And in the letter to my niece, and the phone calls to my cousin, he had also said that he was coming to England alone and that his Guyanese wife and children would be joining him the following year. Once again, he seemed to have been trying to invent a new life for himself by distancing himself from his immediate past, regardless of the consequences for anyone else.

I asked Compton whether he remembered my father's reaction to my letter.

'Before that letter came, right, he started to pack up. "These books I'm taking with me, these books I'll be giving to the university. Compton you look yourself and see whatever you want, right?" It's as though he was dividing up his possessions and I spent every Sunday with them you know, and he'd talk. He'd tell me about his favourite lecturer, was this man Leavis. It's as though he pictured himself as a Leavis, and going down to his college, and got my set of students and so on.'

This did not make any sense at all. Compton had just assured me that my father had taken no practical steps to go to England. Now he remembered watching him packing up his books. Either he had been preparing to go, or he hadn't. And if he hadn't, then there seemed little point in packing up his books when he had nowhere to go, unless he had been so immersed in his own fantasy world that he had lost all contact with reality.

'Was it a fantasy or an erring judgement?' Compton wondered, 'It's not that he was fantasizing, he honestly intended to go, but the circumstances were not going to be able to — it's like Marjorie said: "You're not going to be able to stand their climate, you've been away too long. You're not young now, you can't really work to look after yourself, and you know that you got to have somebody to look after you, and I am *not* going." So she put every sort of block in his way, but he still had the idea, it's as though, "All I need to do is to get back to England and everything will be all right."'

'But it was crazy,' I said, aghast at my father's lunacy. 'It was a crazy idea.'

'It was crazy! I mean for me, you, Marjorie and everybody else, yes it was crazy!' His voice softened now. 'But he didn't see it so.'

Compton spoke gently and indulgently, as though he found something endearing about my father's desire to return to England. Like Marjorie, he could not understand why my father's family on the other side of the Atlantic was so upset by the prospect of his return. We thought the whole episode a continuation of the way that he had always behaved towards us in the past. And nothing I had now heard in Guyana changed my view. I still thought it incredible that he could have expected to come back after all those years and be looked after by one of the children, as though he had some kind of natural right. Had he learned nothing during all those years, that he still believed he had a right to ask any of us for anything? Or had he been so immersed in his fantasy reconciliation with his homeland that he had simply made the phone calls and written the letters without ever really doing anything concrete about it at all? Had the booked flight and the stated date of his return ever really existed?

Compton had now got round to describing how my father had received my letter. One Sunday he returned to the house to find my father refusing to talk to anybody. 'I said, "Wha' happened?" and he just made two cuss words, and I said, "Arright, by afternoon you'll cool off and ketch yourself." And he just sort of withdrew, and it's as though he went through another metamorphosis, and it was like —

how could I put it? – the disappointment that he felt was so great that it sort of broke his spirit. He never ever mentioned it, and Marjorie said, "It's the letter, you will see the letter." And I said, "That's the letter that got him? I don't want to read it, then. It might depress me." So I never read the letter. And it's like after that, he was, "What's the point?" I ain't got no place to go. I might as well just . . .'

He did not finish the sentence, but the meaning was clear. 'But if he was so happy in Guyana, if he had the happy family life that he had before, why this intense need to go?' I asked. 'I mean he was risking giving up his family, right? If Marjorie wasn't going to go, and he was, what was he going to do, give her up?'

Compton smiled tolerantly. 'You are young. Maybe when you get older you might understand probably what he felt. I cannot understand it, either, what was this desire to return to England. I cannot understand it.'

No one, it seemed, could understand it, and probably nobody ever would. Had he been preparing to abandon his new family, just as he had abandoned his old one? Or had he decided to come by himself as a way of putting pressure on Marjorie to join him? Had the whole process been a gratuitous, self-destructive manoeuvre intended to provoke precisely the kind of rejection it eventually received? They were questions that I had been trying to answer ever since that initial conversation on the terrace with Marjorie, and it now looked as though I would be leaving Guyana without the answers.

Years ago, sometime in the mid-70s, when my feelings of betrayal by my father were at their height, I once sat down and wrote him an accusing, recriminatory letter telling him what I thought of him. No sooner had I finished writing it than the whole exercise seemed suddenly pointless and self-indulgent, and I tore it up without sending it. The letter that I sent in the autumn of 1991 was much shorter, but it contained something of that original tone:

> *Dear 'Dad',*
>
> *I didn't think I'd be writing to you again after the last exchange and I can't say it's an activity that gives me much pleasure. The news of your impending visit, however, gives me little choice. You really are a calculating, manipulative bastard. Either that or you are completely insane. Do you really think that after everything that*

has happened that anyone wants to see you again or have anything to do with you? Let me assure you, no one wants to see you, let alone look after you. It might have been different if you had ever shown the slightest remorse for, or even recognition of what you did in the past, prompted by a desire for a genuine reconciliation . . . But no, nothing . . . You pathetic fraud, do you think you can still treat us with the same contempt you always did and get away with it? Do you think everyone is going to feel sorry for you and take you in? Probably you do, judging on past behaviour. There is nothing for you here. No job, no house, no friends, nothing. I will not let you parasite off my sister or anyone else, is that clear? I don't care what mess you've made of your life in Guyana, it's nothing to do with any of us. So come to your senses for Christ's sake, and stay put. However bad Guyana is, it couldn't be any worse than it's going to be here. In the end, words cannot express my absolute contempt for this latest piece of gratuitous selfishness. I am ashamed to be related to you and appalled at the disgusting spectacle you have made of yourself . . . I repeat DO NOT COME . . .

    Yours,
     Matthew, your 'son'

 It was probably the angriest letter I had ever written to anyone in my life. Now, when I read it in Guyana, after all the conversations I had had with Marjorie and everyone else, I wished I had torn it up too. The sight of this furious tirade filled me with a heavy sense of depression and regret whenever I thought of my father retreating into his room at Stone Avenue like a wounded animal. In the light of his death, those angry words now had the force of an accusation directed not at my father but myself. I could still recall the state of barely controlled fury in which I had written the letter, weighing each word up for its maximum impact, determined to bring him to his senses and stop him from coming back. Would a calmer and more reasoned letter have achieved the same effect, without causing such a drastic reaction? The question was impossible to answer. In retrospect I would certainly not have written the same kind of letter, but hindsight always provides a false perspective. At the time I was convinced that I was dealing with a selfish egomaniac who did not care what emotional havoc he caused. A man capable of announcing his forthcoming return to a thirteen-year-old girl who barely knew him, I reasoned, was clearly impervious to normal means of persuasion and in need of shock treatment.

In one of our conversations Marjorie told me that no one in Guyana would have turned their father away like that, no matter what they had done. But the idea that my father had been turned away by his English family and that we were heartless and ungrateful was a wilful distortion of the truth. As far as we knew, he already had a house and family of his own in 1987, which he was voluntarily giving up. I did not accept a value system which claimed that fathers were always right, no matter what they did, and that blood ties conferred some kind of lifelong obligation on their children to receive and treat them with respect. Children were not born to be their parents' servants, and my father had never done anything to deserve the kind of love and respect that Marjorie thought we owed him.

It was nevertheless characteristic that he should have sunk into self-pity and acted like a man with nowhere to go, rather than consider how his own actions might have led to such anger in the first place. Once again he had behaved with crass disregard for his own family yet miraculously emerged as the wronged party. Now his victimhood had been consecrated by his death, and so too was my role as his 'killer'. I did not believe that my letter had killed him, but it was a sad, pathetic way to end a relationship that had been mostly dormant for more than twenty years beforehand, and would have been better off left that way. If only he had not come back to break that long silence, he might have lived out his last few months in Guyana in peace. But it was too late now. Everything was too late.

The other letter of mine that I had written to my father dated back to around 1974, two years after I had left boarding school. Its tone could not have been more different:

> Hi Dad,
>   It's me and I hope you're well. Let me know what you're doing now if you would, 'cos I hear only vague rumours about you writing in the bush somewhere . . .

The letter contained a brief description of my life at the time, which was not going particularly well. I had just left home and was planning to take my A levels, after dropping out twice. The letter was steeped in teenage angst and written in the self-consciously ironic style of someone trying to sound older and more worldly-wise than he actually was. It also included a plea in support of my mother's suggestion to divide the maintenance money between the four of us, before concluding with the following request:

Tell me about yourself. Tell me your thoughts, about life, about you and us back here, about living, writing, people. I would love to know them. I will send you volumes on my favourite subject – myself, but I will tell you whatever you want to know about anything. This I ask you, write me, and I'll write you back telling all. We'll publish them, titled LETTERS FROM BIG FOOL TO LITTLE FOOL – we'll be made!

I don't know what this letter seems like to you, it seems strange to me. But now it's late. My next letter, and may God strike me dead if I don't write one, will say more. Till then, goodnight, father.

I read my own words with a sense of unfamiliarity. It was my handwriting, but the sentiments seemed so alien to the way that I had felt about my father for years that it might have been written by another person. And yet I had written the letter, and he had kept it all those years, and reading it now I felt like an archaeologist who had discovered the foundation stone of a building that was no longer standing, as I tried to imagine the shape and structure of the emotions that had given rise to those unexpectedly intimate words. It would have been one of the last letters I wrote to him before his reappearance in 1987. I could not remember whether he had replied to it or not, but I doubted it since it was around that time that we had finally stopped writing to each other.

We had never had that dialogue about 'living, writing, people' or anything else, not even when he came back to England. Dialogue and understanding had never been features of our relationship. At some point between that teenage letter and the one that had stopped him coming to England, the hopeful desire to re-open communication had withered away and the word 'father' had become an ironic term that I could write only between quotation marks. As adults there were a lot of things we might have talked about, in politics, literature and history, but if we were bound together by the past we were also separated from each other by it. The ties of love and affection, if they had ever really existed, had faded with the years until I could no more address him as my father than he could talk to me directly as his son. Perhaps some kind of reconciliation might have been possible, but the initial gesture had to come from him, and he never seemed willing or able to make it. Whether as children or adults, he seemed incapable of seeing us as independent human beings with feelings of our own. Right up to the end he had been tearing up the script of his life and trying to write another, and expecting us to indulge his fantasies. The result was that bitter, raging letter, which now seemed so glaringly redundant in the light of his death. Throughout my childhood my father had done all the shouting. For the first and only time in my adult life I had given full expression of my anger towards him, and in doing so I had given him his last major role – *King Lear* rejected by his ungrateful children.

My father died on 22 February 1992 in his bedroom in Stone Avenue. He had gone into hospital that month as he usually did after the boozy Guyanese Christmas celebrations. A week later he discharged himself and returned home, where he retired to his bedroom. At first he was well enough to receive visitors, but one Sunday afternoon, a few days after returning home, he began not to recognize people. Compton suggested to Marjorie that they call Father Malcolm. For the rest of the afternoon he continued to slip in and out of consciousness. At one point he asked Marjorie whether she loved him or not, and she said yes. He asked her to kiss him and she did. He then told her that he wanted to read, but he was unable to hold the book. Marjorie offered to hold the book for him, but he told her not to bother. 'But why is it so dark?' he asked her, even though it was daylight. 'It's so dark in here.' Marjorie offered to turn on the light for him. 'Please do,' he told her.

Even then he complained that it was still dark and that there was a clock ticking somewhere in the room. 'It just keeps ticking,' he told her. Soon afterwards he told her that he could see a bridge across the sky. It was, he said, a beautiful bridge, and there was a rainbow across it and the sun was shining brilliantly. 'Don't you see it?' he asked her. Marjorie, humouring him, said that she could. She said it was a lovely bridge. Shortly afterwards he slipped into a coma. Before losing consciousness he began calling repeatedly for his mother. 'Mummy, Mummy. Wait for me, Mum. I'm coming.' Those were his last words on earth. He continued to repeat them over and over for nearly an hour, and then he was silent.

*

The funeral service was held three days later at Brickdam Cathedral, the ugly grey concrete building just down the road from St Stanislaus School. The congregation represented all the different areas of Guyanese society that my father had been involved in over the years. PPP activists, colleagues at the university and former students, friends and ordinary workers. All came to pay their respects to the white professor whose life and personality had woven themselves into Guyanese society in so many different ways. As Father Malcolm had intended, the service reflected all the main strands of my father's life in Guyana, the religious, the cultural, the political and the academic. Cheddi Jagan gave a personal and political tribute. Martin Carter read his poem 'Death of a Comrade'. Ian McDonald spoke of my father's knowledge of literature, his brilliance as an academic, his courage, and the 'unflinching Catholic faith' that had enabled him to endure his illnesses. He closed by quoting the following words from Cardinal Newman:

> *May he support us all the day long, till the shades lengthen, and the evening comes, and the busy world is hushed, and the fever of life is over, and our work is done! Then in his mercy may he give us a safe lodging, and a holy rest, and peace at the last.*

As my father had requested, the congregation sang 'Morning Has Broken', led by the U G choir. The reading was from John 15:

> *I am the true vine, and my Father is the husbandman. Every branch in me that beareth not fruit, he taketh away: and every branch that beareth fruit, he purgeth it, that it may bring forth more fruit . . .*

It was an appropriate tribute from the country that my father had made into his home and his stage, and where he had indeed brought forth fruit. Only a few discreet references in the tributes hinted at the darker side behind the public figure. 'It is sad to think how much more he might have achieved if he had allowed himself to be at his best more of the time,' Ian McDonald said in an oblique reference to my father's 'problem'. Telegrams and letters of condolence were sent to Marjorie from members of her family and my father's friends in different parts of the world. A telegram from a Guyanese friend in Nepal thanked him for 'the craziness of these last 20 years and the laughter – the laughter of a good man and my good friend who always walked bravely'. From his own family in England, however, there were no messages at all. It was not until the following day that Anna received the telegram with its cold, almost sarcastic announcement: 'Your dad's dead.'

I remember feeling nothing at all when I was told the news later that day, but my mother said she felt as if she had been punched. Two days later Anna emerged from hospital with her second daughter. She subsequently wrote to Marjorie and Vanessa three times with her condolences and requesting more information. In one of these letters, dated 6 February 1993, she tried to explain the circumstances surrounding the last bitter exchange with my father, ending with this plea:

> When exactly did he die and what caused his death? Where is his body now? Was he buried or cremated? Do you have any newspaper cuttings or photos that you could let me have? Do you have a small keepsake that I could have? Please, please try and understand things from our perspective, and however it may seem, I loved him and always will. Whilst he didn't seem to care about us, he and I did have something special and I am so sorry that he didn't live to see what his beautiful new granddaughter looks like.

That letter, like the others, received no reply.

The day before leaving Guyana I went back to Stone Avenue for the last time. I met Vanessa just as she was on her way to mass at St Theresa's Church, where Father Rose was conducting the service as usual. After saying goodbye I went into the house to give Marjorie the letters and documents that I had photocopied. She had found another of Joan's tapes and agreed to let me take it with me.

I did not stay long. Even though hostilities had ceased between us and she was no longer angry, an undercurrent of tension still remained. In spite of everything that had happened, I liked her, as I had done when she had come to England, and I regretted the way things had turned out between us. She had been helpful to me in many ways, but the memory of that first furious meeting on the patio still rankled, and the whole 'father-killing' melodrama had created a wall between us that neither of us seemed to be able to cross. Just before I left she gave me my father's old drinking glass and a little plastic bird that he had once worn round his neck as keepsakes for Anna. I did not expect to see her again and we shook hands stiffly, as if we were both embarrassed and regretful about the anger that had passed between us – two people who hardly knew each other, linked by the common memory of Bill Carr.

'You know, about Anna's letters,' she said suddenly, 'it wasn't that I was deliberately not writing to her. It's just that I'm a very bad letter-writer.'

I looked at her in surprise. The anger that she had unleashed that first evening made this explanation seem not entirely convincing. Someone could have written to Anna during those four years to tell her what had happened, especially since I was the one who had written the angry letters that had annoyed her so much. Whatever it had all been about, it was too late to go into now. My stay in Guyana was almost over, and there had been too much emotion already. I left, as usual, in a taxi. I took one last look at the concrete house, past Marjorie standing by the gate, towards the little kingdom with its glass bottles where 'the patio God' had once held court surrounded by his books. Then we clattered round the corner along the potholed road towards Sheriff Avenue, and my father's house faded from view for the last time.

That night I listened to the second cassette Marjorie had given me. It was not much more revealing than the first one had been, but there were some little flashes of illumination. The interview covered the first part of my father's life, from his childhood until his arrival at Cambridge. My father talked briefly about his relationship with his parents and his unhappy childhood, and his succession of boarding schools. He also talked about the books that had influenced him as a child, including *Swiss Family Robinson* and Ballantine's *The Coral Island*, the same ones he had once recommended to me. Dickens had also been an important influence, he said, especially *David Copperfield*, with whom he had strongly identified. But one of the biggest literary influences on his childhood had been the *Boy's Own* adventure yarns of G. A. Henty. As a boy, he had devoured these heroic imperialist yarns, despite the fact that 'the values are distorted', since, he explained, the growth of the British Empire could not be seen 'purely in terms of gallant, heroic Englishmen'. And he expressed other reservations. Girls lacked substance in Henty's novels, because 'they never did anything, they never were anything, they were always the passive image that the young man bore with him when he went off to the North-West Frontier or the West Indies or whatever. Of course no coloured people were treated with any sympathy at all. They always tended to be the bad guys.'

So the obsession with heroes and heroism that had marked so much of my father's adult life went right back to his childhood. Had his later involvement in the West Indies also had its origins in those distant boyhood fantasies? Had the lonely, bookish child fantasized a heroic role for himself to compensate for his experience of rejection and humiliation? As an adult he had become a kind of Henty hero in reverse, going off to the tropics at a time when the Empire was contracting, not expanding. Where Henty's 'gallant, heroic Englishmen' had pushed back the frontiers of British civilization or subdued the 'fuzzie-wuzzies', dervishes and Pathan tribesmen, he had lined up with the Empire's victims, like the Reverend Smith. But the need to play a heroic role had never disappeared; it had simply found a different context and setting. In spite of the self-destructiveness that so often pulled him down throughout his life, he had finally received what amounted to a hero's farewell from his adopted country.

The tape confirmed my original impression that the interviews were research for a biography of my father, linking his life to the politics of his time and West Indian independence in particular. As he worked his way through the 40s and 50s, from the same descriptions of V2 bombings of London that he had told me as a child to the more pleasant memories of his schooldays at Dulwich and his national service days, I was beginning to think that his family had been airbrushed from the official biography once again. Then towards the end of the tape the following exchange occurred, as he turned to his Cambridge days:

> 'You got married while you were at Cambridge?'
> 'Yes. In 1955.'
> 'Who did you marry?'
> 'Uh. An English girl. She was that! She was only twenty-one.'
> 'You met her at Cambridge?'
> 'I met her at Cambridge. She wasn't a student there, she was bred and born in Cambridge.'

This was followed by a digression on the differences between Oxford and Cambridge and a description of my mother as an 'exceedingly good lawyer'. Then Joan brought him back to the subject of his wife and asked him where she had been educated.

'Oddly enough, at a Roman Catholic convent in Cambridge,' he laughed. 'Oddly like mine, but fortunately for her, hers was a day convent. People in the main, institutions, will usually not be as cruel to women as they are to men. She hated the school period and she used to talk about it badly, like me talking about mine.'

There was no trace of bitterness or sarcasm in his voice, unlike the tone that he had used to talk about his mother or the 'bitches' at St Vincent de Paul. There was in fact no indication that he had felt anything towards his first wife at all. There was no impression of what she was like as a person, how they had met, why he had been attracted to her, what their life had been like together, what their expectations had been, just a few brief biographical details that revealed nothing. Even Neville Chamberlain emerged with more humanity from his descriptions. Like Henty's women, it seemed, my mother had never been anything either. It was as though the relationship in which my father had been involved for fifteen years had been completely irrelevant to the course of his life, or perhaps it was all too long ago to remember. The only reference to his children was even more cursory.

> 'How many children did you have?'
> 'Four.'
> 'Four children?'
> 'Yes.'
> 'Your children were all born in England?'
> 'No. One was born in Jamaica.'

And that was that. No names. No personalities. His children were no more than a minor biographical detail. Whatever the interviews were intended for, his family were clearly not an episode that he wanted to include in any public account of his life. Was this reticence the result of shame or embarrassment? Or was it that we were simply not a significant enough factor to warrant further mention? For now it was back to Hugh Gaitskell, Nye Bevan, and Cambridge, the great man and his times, before the recording abruptly stopped and my last hope of hearing my father's version of events faded.

The next morning I took a taxi to the airport, along the same awful road that I had come bumping along two weeks before. It seemed as though I had been in Guyana a lot longer, and now that I was leaving I felt a mixture of relief and regret. I would miss those long, slow sunsets in the afternoons, and that crumbling potholed city with the jungle stretching out behind it. Soon it would be Easter. Over at St Theresa's

Church they would be preparing to celebrate the ritual of the Crucifixion and the Resurrection that my father had once narrated. All over the city boys could be seen flying little kites, some of them hardly more than sheets of paper on short pieces of string. At sunset on Easter Monday the sky above the sea wall would be filled with hundreds of kites of all shapes and colours, with pieces of paper tied to their tails carrying the wishes and prayers of their owners up to heaven.

To my surprise there was some work going on along the highway, although it was not clear whether it was a major attempt at repairs or just another case of 'patching'. As we drove alongside the river the Indian taxi-driver and I had another of those Guyana conversations, which began with the state of the roads and the electricity and turned inevitably to the subject of politics and race. At one point I said that I thought Guyana's problems would never be solved until a way could be found to bridge the country's racial division. The taxi-driver solemnly agreed that this was true. The problem was that the Africans spent all their time smoking ganja and committing crimes instead of looking for work, he said, and they were so lazy that it was difficult to get them to do anything. I felt he had not quite seen my point, but I let the subject drop. As we approached the airport, an advertising poster by the side of the road declared: *Guyana: the sweet smell of excess*.

At the airport I bought a bottle of rum as a souvenir, just as my mother had done twenty-nine years before, and watched the West Indies–New Zealand one day international until the inevitable blackout temporarily shut down the airport. The lack of electricity did not interfere with my flight departure, however. My plane was the only one on the runway, and an hour later I was looking down at the strip of muddy water along the coast as we pulled away from South America and headed towards Trinidad and the blue Caribbean Sea.

After Guyana it was something of a culture shock to emerge in Barbados airport once again, and find myself surrounded by hundreds of American tourists dressed like golfing professionals. I was back in the world of Nike and the global economy, with its identical hotels and identical-looking people and its expensive restaurants filled with rich whites, but my mind was still very much in Guyana. It was as if I had just emerged from another world and was only now returning to the present.

*

There was one more person I still had to visit. Sandra Williams, or Andaiye as she was later known, had not been in Guyana, but her mother had given me her phone number in Barbados, where she was undergoing treatment for cancer. I called her from Georgetown and she agreed to see me when I arrived in Barbados. Her illness was serious but had gone into remission. For years I had known little about Sandra Williams, beyond the fact that she was the woman 'Daddy' had left us for. As a child I had understandably felt a certain animosity towards her, even though I could not remember actually meeting her. I knew that she was the daughter of a well-known Guyanese doctor who had been living in England for some years, and that she had been a student in Jamaica when we lived there. She and two friends had once rented our house at Mona Heights, when my mother and the three of us were in England on holiday, leaving my youngest brother in the care of my father.

As far as anyone knew, however, her relationship with my father began only after we came to Guyana – the catalyst that made him finally break with his family. Their relationship by all accounts had been turbulent and explosive, and her eventual rejection of him in 1972 for a cousin of Hamilton Green propelled him into one of the worst bouts of drinking in his life. Andaiye was, in effect, a bridge between the past we had shared with my father and his life afterwards. She seemed uniquely well-placed to give some insight into what had been going through his mind that famous Sunday night after the lecture.

That same day I went round to see her at a little bungalow on the edge of Bridgetown. Andaiye opened the door herself, wearing a long patterned African dress, and invited me in. She was still a striking woman, in spite of her fifty-three years, with high cheekbones and large brown eyes that looked at you directly, almost challengingly, from beneath her braided hair. Only the dark shadows under her eyes, and her slow, tired movements, gave any indication of her illness and the chemotherapy that she had been receiving.

Her first memory of my father dated back to 1961 or '62, when she was a young English student at the University of the West Indies. She remembered that he had supported the students in some university political issue, and she had been sitting at the end of a long dinner table as the students banged their plates and cheered the Englishman who had taken their side. Later she had met him from time to time when she and her friends were renting our house in Jamaica. Their relationship began after she saw him give a speech at the university in Guyana. She remembered that they had stayed up afterwards till the middle of the night drinking and talking. As someone who had always felt 'weird' and out of place in the privileged circles in which she had grown up, she was excited by the disorder of my father's life, even though she dismissed their actual relationship as 'a piece of nonsense'. She could not remember when they had actually decided to live together, and the only memories she had of the Sunday night when he had stayed over at her house was a vague recollection of a lot of ranting and raving.

Had he ever said anything afterwards about his family to indicate what he felt about them? She shook her head. There had only been incoherent explosions of feeling. 'He didn't leave your mother because of me, you know . . . He used to talk about you as if *you* had left.'

I asked her what she thought of my theory that my father's rejection of us had been a kind of racial sacrifice. She said she thought it was true. Both she and my father were then heavily influenced by Black Power, and the movement had 'driven my father wild'. Nor was he the only one. There had also been a white Englishwoman called Jackie, who had been living in her house when my father used to go round there. Jackie also seemed to have undergone a 'phenomenal transformation', and her identification with the black cause had reached such an extent that she had once made a public speech in Guyana, condemning the white race for what they had done to '*us*'.

My father had spent a lot of time round her house with her and Jackie in the run-up to our 'expulsion', usually drunk, and it sounded as though there had been a lot of 'explosions of feeling' from everyone concerned.

Andaiye came from a respectable middle-class Guyanese family, and her involvement with my father was not well-received by her parents at first. When she announced that she was going to live with him, her father refused to speak to her for days, and her mother condemned her for getting involved with a 'white man, and a disorderly white man at that' although her father had later become one of my father's closest friends in Guyana.

After her early involvement in the Black Power movement Andaiye became one of the founders of the W P A. I asked her why she had changed her name. She said it was a personal rather than a political decision. As a child pupils at school used to taunt her, singing, 'Your daddy's rich and your momma's good-looking,' because of her background, while at the same time she had always felt that she was treated differently because she was darker-skinned than the rest of her family. Once she had gone to a school party in Scotland, where nobody would dance with her because she was black, and the headmaster had to intervene to find her a partner. This sense of being different left her with a legacy of humiliation and anger which later found its outlet in Black Power. 'It was a way of vomiting up and dealing with a certain rage,' she explained. 'You really felt that bad. I don't suppose I would have done it if others hadn't done it, and I only read about imperialism later.'

This overlapping of personal anger and political action had been a feature of my father's personality too, especially in his youth, and the two of them seemed to have spent a lot of time 'vomiting up a certain rage' together. She could not remember any physical violence, she said, even though they had often fought verbally and shouted at each other, mostly about writers and politics. On this point Andaiye's memory seemed to be failing her, since a former friend of my father's who had stayed with the two of them in Guyana remembered that the atmosphere had been 'charged with tension and violence'. As usual with my father, the arguments would involve the whole neighbourhood, and she remembered that the unfortunate neighbours would grumble, 'The white man starting up now', when he threw open the windows and started shouting at the night in what came to be an almost nightly ritual.

'A lot of our relationship didn't have anything to do with him and me as people,' she said. 'It was always political. There was almost nothing that we could talk about that didn't come to this. I always thought I was reacting to something that was coming from him, but the only time he would admit that anything was his fault was when he had driven you to the point of absolute hysteria.'

In spite of these conflicts, she found him 'very entertaining' and continued to like him even after they had split up. At the same time she considered him emotionally self-indulgent. Like everyone else, she remembered him raging against the good sisters of St Vincent de Paul. 'He used to cry sometimes when he told me stories about some fucking kiss-me-ass pig of a nun, but you can't spend your whole life feeling bitter and angry about something like that.'

The evidence of the tape I had heard the night before showed that he had indeed continued to feel bitter and angry about it up to the end of his life, and it was typical that in the aftermath of our exodus from Guyana he should have been weeping over the injustices that he had suffered as a schoolboy.

Andaiye remembered that my father had helped with the housework, unlike other men she had known, but in general she had found him impossible to live with, as he filled the house with cats and never slept and always caused public scenes wherever he went. 'He used to give me the impression that he wanted recognition for his books,' she said, 'but he was always using up his intellectual capital in ways that had nothing to do with writing. He used to go to rum shops to drink liquor and get into political fights and arguments! Imagine! A white man sitting in your bar telling you to vote for the PPP! I learned to drink from him. He used to drink a bottle a day and I remember one night I sat and thought, "Let me see if I can drink a part of this." It was better than being sober.'

She admitted that living with a white man had been a problem as far as her political friends were concerned, but she denied that she had broken off the relationship as 'a gift to her brothers and sisters', as my father had alleged.

'Everybody thought that,' she said. 'When I left him Martin Carter said to me, "You've destroyed a human being for a black abstraction." Because he fell apart visibly and I didn't, they thought I wasn't damaged. The real reason I broke up with him was because I couldn't get any sleep! I was tired of Martin and Bill and the whole pack of them coming home drunk every night.'

I commented on how much I had been struck by the tolerance that had been extended to my father's drinking in Guyana, and asked her if she thought that it was a Guyanese trait. She agreed that it was. 'In Guyana we are very tolerant, but in the name of tolerance we don't give people support. Too many people were turned on by Bill's chaos. I was too.'

I sensed that she was getting tired, and I asked her if she could call a taxi for me. Afterwards we sat talking for a little longer while we waited for it to arrive. Like most of the people with whom my father had associated himself over the years, she came from an arts and teaching background, and she had not done very well out of it in material terms. She had once been a headteacher in Guyana, but she was now making a precarious living doing bits and pieces of freelance journalism, when she was well enough to work at all. 'You don't want to get mixed up with books if you want to make a decent living,' she joked.

I told her it was too late. A half-hour conversation was not much time in which to make an assessment of somebody's life, but it was obvious that hers had not turned out the way she might have expected all those years ago, in those distant angry days when the rum and conversation had flowed freely on the verandas and everyone had been vomiting up their rage together. The revolutionary tide of the 60s had ebbed here, it seemed, as it had everywhere else, leaving its survivors washed up on the shores of their own lives, facing the familiar problems of old age, mortality and economic survival. My father's 'phenomenal transformation' was also a product of those times, and his life had not turned out the way he must have imagined it either when he had peered angrily into the future through a haze of rum and seen the revolution coming.

The taxi arrived and I said goodbye to Andaiye. It had been an unusual conversation, which neither of us had ever expected to have, and we parted on good terms. Whatever had happened all those years ago, it was obvious that she had not been responsible for it. Now, as I drove back to the hotel I wondered if anyone had. I thought of my family in that little corner of the 60s, unaware of the storms of racial anger and guilt that were raging around us, which 'Daddy' had brought back with him into our front room. It was only now, nearly three decades later, that I was able to see what had happened from the outside, as though it had all happened to someone else. My re-encounter with the Caribbean was nearly over, and already the prospect of returning to my own life made the past seem suddenly lighter.

The next day I would be returning to my own family. As I thought of my daughter back in England, I sensed that I was leaving a part of my past behind for ever and that a new phase in my life had begun. That afternoon I swam in the sea for the first and last time before going back to England. As I waded out through the transparent, crystal-clear ocean, I remembered a distant day many years ago before the fall, when I waded into that same ocean off Negril Beach and looked back to see my mother and father lying there and felt a mixture of pleasure and safety at their presence. I looked back once more at the white sand and palm trees and imagined us all there, my parents, my brothers and sister and I, before I turned away and plunged into the warm, enclosing sea.

Epilogue

The following day I arrived back in London. It was a cold grey morning that seemed little different from the one I had left two weeks before. Once again I contemplated the paved roads and rows of identical suburban houses with neat gardens and curtained windows, as the high-speed train hurtled into London. The physical journey back to the lost world of my father had come to an end, but the memory of Guyana continued to haunt me like a strange dream from which I hadn't fully awoken, and I knew that the internal journey to the past was not yet over.

With the passing of time that feeling has been confirmed, and the process of unfreezing my father's memory has continued. For those who do not believe in a cosmic ledger where all human actions are written down and judged, the subjective and often incomplete memories of other people remain the main instrument available for establishing the objective 'truth' about anyone's life. But the truth can never be entirely encapsulated by what other people remember. Even if I could have spoken to everyone who had ever known him throughout his life, the blank spaces would still remain, and it is doubtful whether my father would have been able to fill them himself. In the end we remain only partly visible to each other, and perhaps to ourselves as well. The final interpretation of my father's motivations was made up of the parts he had played and the memories he had left behind him. Precisely because these memories were so varied and conflicting, the real truth about his life is even more hypothetical than it is for people with more coherent and integrated personalities.

At different times, and even at the same time, the violent domestic bully could be an idealistic socialist fighting for equality and 'the happiness of all'; the erudite English lecturer could take part in chat shows on children and family life even as his own family sank deeper into gothic disorder; the ferocious father who devastated his first family became the caring stepfather in his second. The generosity and concern for the world's oppressed that infused his politics and teaching co-existed with an awesome capacity for self-destruction.

How is it possible to make an overall judgement of his life from this mass of contradictions, whose only apparent connection is the undeniable fact that they all emanated from the same man? Was his life the noble, heroic drama that Moses Nagamootoo described, or a sad tale of failed promise and self-delusion? Was he really engaged in some weird private atonement for the crimes of the British Empire or was the 'white man's burden' merely another role he adopted? Was all the role-playing itself part of a long fight against depression and incipient madness? Were there even certain times in his life when he was, to all intents and purposes, clinically insane?

The more I try to answer these questions the more I realize that there are no definitive answers, only various possible interpretations and approximations. At times it almost seems possible to establish a thread of rational continuity in his personality and behaviour, and then at other moments the thread becomes snagged, and coherence gives way to the familiar chaos. I often think of his zig-zag trail from Harrogate to Georgetown as a confused revolt against the century in which he found himself. Like his idols Matthew Arnold and D. H. Lawrence, he recoiled in his youth from the crushing uniformity of industrial civilization, with its anonymous urban crowds, its lack of passion and drama, and its flattening-out of individual experience into the same amorphous, indistinguishable material. In his recorded lecture on *Romeo and Juliet* he refers to the Elizabethan era as a 'broader and more generous age than our own'. To some extent he tried to live in that 'broader and more generous' age through the gallery of Shakespearian characters he identified with so strongly and whose speeches he knew by heart.

My father's dramatic role-playing also seems to me to reflect that fragmentation of the personality which is characteristic of the twentieth century – the sense that we carry within us many possible selves and conflicting layers of motivation and that we are responsible for writing the scripts and stories about our own lives. His determination to live his life as if it were a work of fiction reminds me of the Portuguese poet Fernando Pessoa, another lonely, bookish child who would create different poetic characters or 'heteronyms' out of the conflicting forces within his own character, in the process brilliantly challenging the whole concept of individual character and identity. Throughout his short life Pessoa was haunted by the fear of mental illness and his prodigious output was to some extent a sustained rearguard action aimed at holding the divisions within himself together through artistic expression. Borrowing techniques from fiction and the theatre, he created a multitude of poetic voices, with their own separate biographies, styles and ideas, in which the character of 'Fernando Pessoa' was just one more dramatic creation rather than a real person.

This conscious splintering of his own personality into separate fragments on paper allowed Pessoa to blend the conflicting tendencies within himself into a creative whole, without affecting the outwardly placid course of his life. In my father's case the tigers of wrath were always more powerful than the horses of instruction, even if they were not necessarily any wiser, and he was never able to achieve Pessoa's intellectual distance and control. Although aware, like Pessoa, that 'there are multitudes inside us', he preferred to project them outwards, using the world as his stage. At certain moments in his life the actions and emotional responses of 'Bill Carr' became so entangled with those of the fictional characters he read about that he almost became one of them himself. While this compulsive role-playing may have given him the sense of grandeur and intensity that was missing from his everyday life, it was also a form of escapism which took him away from his past but without curing the emotional wounds he had inherited from it.

His preoccupation with the wrongs he had suffered as a child may have been self-indulgent and self-pitying at times, but he clearly was emotionally damaged, and that childhood faultline never healed. On the contrary the masochism and self-destruction of his adult years suggest a deeply unhappy person, whose childhood feelings of rejection and abandonment had been internalized into self-hatred, and whose instinctual rage was as often turned against himself as it was against the outside world. This was a tragedy for a man whose intentions towards the world were mostly benevolent. In his youth he was inspired by Lawrence's maxim, 'To speak for life amid this ruin and destruction,' but it was the ruin and destruction in his own past that eventually overtook him, in spite of the endless attempts to reinvent himself.

In the end his most enduring dramatic creation was probably Bill Carr himself, the Englishman in the tropics. It was an incomplete role that he spent most of his adult life acting out, chopping and changing the script without ever arriving at a final version, but in Guyana and the Caribbean he found a sympathetic audience capable of appreciating some of the transformations. There were times in Guyana when I felt able to appreciate them too. In many ways I even admire him for the way he lived his life after we had gone. Whatever else may be said of him, my father was certainly not ordinary, and if he failed to answer that youthful question of 'how to live' at least he tried to ask it in the first place and was not content to simply jump through the hoops placed by society. At times he did indeed 'walk bravely'. It may be true, as Roxanna Kaiwal suggested, that in a small country like Guyana his talent seemed greater than it actually was. But within that society he gave the best of himself, and he inspired an affection far more genuine than many successful people in big countries ever achieve. I am glad for him, and even proud, that he managed to achieve that.

At the same time I recoil from the wilful waste, destructiveness and self-delusion that were also part of his personality. No matter how much I try to imagine him as other people saw him, my own memories of him can never entirely be erased. 'Bill's life was a tragic life in the heroic sense,' wrote Jean d'Costa, 'a man who blessed others and was accursed to himself.' Perhaps, but he certainly did not bless his own family, and it will never be possible for me to remember him the way she did as 'a beautiful young man'. Whatever he achieved in other areas of his life, as a father to his children he was worse than useless, and his brutality towards his first wife was something that none of us who lived through it will ever forget. I do not believe that my father ever really forgot it either.

All of us have grown up and remade our lives, but the years we shared together in his house are still a part of us, however faded and distant. I am glad I went back to Guyana to find something of the person he became after we left. I have other things to remember about him now, and these new memories will take their place alongside the older ones. In a world which often seems like a permanent, ever-changing present, we need to maintain our links to the past and remember where we came from if our lives are to have any shape or continuity. At a time when I have become a parent myself, it has been a crucial rite of passage for me to see my own father as a human being rather than a pantomime villain, to try and understand both his strengths and his weaknesses, as well as the various pressures, both internal and external, which helped to form his peculiar character.

In that sense I really have killed the father I remembered and discovered him as a man. Perhaps that discovery should have taken place when he was alive, but it never did and it probably never could have done. Yet in some strange way I have come to accept him as a part of myself in a way that I refused, or was afraid to do, for most of my life. And often, as I walk with my daughter through the streets of this rich European city, with its ancient cathedrals, its designer shops and Internet cafés, I find myself thinking of him and the small country on the other side of the world where he lived. One day I will tell her the story of the strange man who was once her grandfather, so that she can know where she came from. It will always be an unfinished story, with many of the pages missing, the story of a father who was blown away from us in a tropical storm like Robinson Crusoe and re-emerged twenty-nine years later as a local hero in a far-off land.

Perhaps more pages will appear in the future, perhaps not. But when I think of him now, I no longer see the mugshot photograph staring at me out of the distant past. Instead I see him, enigmatic, incomprehensible, perhaps mad, staggering down the disused railway track, stick in hand, towards that golden bridge where his mother is waiting to collect him at last. And I would like to think that now, after all this time, the anger is over and there can finally be peace between us. My father the actor, with much love, all burnt. Why it had to be like that no one will ever know, but *'yet the pity of it, Iago! O! Iago, the pity of it'*.

Barcelona, 1997